This publication is designed to provide accurate and authoritative information regarding the subject matter covered. It is sold with the understanding that neither the author nor the publisher is engaged in rendering legal, investment, accounting or other professional services. While the publisher and author have used their best efforts in preparing this book, they make no representations or warranties concerning the accuracy or completeness of the book's contents and expressly disclaim any implied warranties of merchantability or fitness for a particular purpose. Sales representatives or written sales materials may create or extend no warranty. The advice and strategies contained herein may not be suitable for your situation. You should consult with a professional when appropriate. Neither the publisher nor the author shall be liable for any loss of profit or other commercial damages, including but not limited to special, incidental, consequential, personal, or other damages.

Book Cover by Ideogram

Illustrations by Midjourney

1st Edition 2024

Book Description

MAN MADE BEER, GOD MADE WEED

Cannabis/Beer, the Elixir of Life: Unveiling the Nectar for Health

Dive into a rollicking journey of suds and seeds with *"MAN MADE BEER GOD MADE WEED,"* a light hearted insightful exploration of two iconic creations that have shaped human civilization—and perhaps a few late-night decisions. This book uncorks the truth behind mankind's love affair with barley brews and divine greens, blending history, humour, and a spirited debate over what's truly the "nectar of the gods."

With a comedic flair, this book takes you through the ages, from ancient brewers to modern microbreweries, from mystic rituals to medicinal breakthroughs, all while pondering the eternal question: If beer is man-made and weed is God-made, does that make your weekend plans an act of divine inspiration?

Embark on a captivating exploration through the ages with "Man Made Beer, God Made Weed," a groundbreaking narrative that delves into the profound impact of beer and cannabis on human history and health. This enlightening book reveals how these two powerful substances have become revered as elixirs of life and natural nectars for well-being.

Perfect for craft beer connoisseurs, cannabis enthusiasts, and anyone who appreciates a good laugh with their libation. Get ready to laugh, learn, and maybe rethink your Friday night rituals with "MAN MADE BEER GOD MADE WEED"—because sometimes the best answers are brewed, not bought, or blissfully grown from the earth itself. Cheers to a divine read!

Preface

When I started writing "Man Made Beer, God Made Weed," I never imagined how much these two simple pleasures would teach me. What began as an exploration of beer and cannabis turned into a deeper reflection on how these substances influence our lives, cultures, and identities. In a fast-paced world, we often seek relaxation, connection, and enjoyment. "Man Made Beer God Made Weed" celebrates the simple pleasures that can ease our minds and enrich our lives. This book is born from a passion for exploring flavours and cultures and the remarkable ways in which two seemingly different worlds intersect to create joy.

Beer, a product of human ingenuity, has evolved over thousands of years. From ancient brewing techniques in Mesopotamia to the craft beer revolution today, beer has been more than just a drink; it's been a companion in celebrations, a comfort in hard times, and a catalyst for social connection. It is an example of how humans have crafted elements of nature into something uniquely our own. Beer has been brewed and cherished for thousands of years, often regarded as a symbol of camaraderie and celebration, traversing cultures and bringing people together.

On the other hand, cannabis also has deep roots in human history and is known for its soothing properties, spiritual significance, and health benefits. It is a gift from nature with a rich and complex history. For millennia, people have turned to cannabis for everything from medicinal relief to spiritual enlightenment. It has sparked debates, fuelled movements, and, in recent years, begun to reclaim its place in society as a natural alternative for relaxation, wellness, and creativity.

In writing this book, I wanted to explore the intersection of these two worlds in terms of their history, cultural significance, and how they impact our modern lives. How do we navigate the legal and social challenges of beer and weed today? How do they compare in terms of health and wellness? Most importantly, what do they say about us as a society and as individuals?

"Man-Made Beer, God Made Weed" attempts to answer these questions and perhaps ask a few more. It's a book for those who appreciate the craftsmanship of a well-brewed beer and the natural beauty of a well-grown plant. It's for those who believe in the freedom to enjoy life's pleasures responsibly and with an open mind.

This book invites readers to delve into the art and science of beer-making, explore the craftsmanship behind various brews, and unravel the mysteries of cannabis, from horticulture to its myriad uses. It reflects how these two elements of life can coexist as integral parts of our social fabric, enhancing our experiences and weaving connections among friends and family.

As you navigate the pages ahead, I encourage you to keep an open mind and a curious spirit. Whether you're a veteran enthusiast, a curious newcomer, or someone looking to deepen your understanding of these cherished substances, I hope this book inspires you to embrace the moments life offers, find new insights, spark conversations, and maybe even reconsider your perspectives on beer and cannabis. More than anything, I hope this book encourages you to embrace the diversity of experiences that these two substances offer—to understand them, to respect them, and, if you choose, to enjoy them in your own way.

Each chapter will engage you with stories, insights, and considerations that illustrate the significance of these cultural touchstones. Practical knowledge is intertwined with anecdotes reflecting the joy of sharing a drink or conversation while enjoying nature's offerings.

With heartfelt gratitude, I dedicate this exploration to my sons, Adi and Ayush, my nephews Amartya and Anindya, and their friends, who encourage a relaxed, open-minded approach to life. Their enthusiasm for life's simple pleasures inspired this journey, and their passion for exploring new ideas brought this book to life. They remind me daily of the beauty of simple joys and meaningful connections.

As societies evolve, so does our appreciation of these substances, giving rise to a dynamic landscape where tradition meets modern cultural shifts. Thank you for joining me on this exploration. Whether you're a seasoned beer enthusiast, a curious cannabis connoisseur, or simply someone interested in the cultural significance of these two staples, I hope you find this book as enlightening and enjoyable to read as it was to write.

Let's raise a glass—and maybe a joint—to the journey ahead. Cheers!

- FABIAN CHOW

Foreword

"Welcome to "Man Made Beer God Made Weed"—an exploration of the interconnected realms of beer and cannabis. This book delves into the rich heritage of both, examining their significance in human culture and the ways in which they have influenced societies from ancient times to the present. As we immerse ourselves in the contents of this publication, let us acknowledge the complexities of life's demands and the universal desire to seek respite, whether through the friendliness of beer or the contemplative embrace of cannabis.

Beer, a symbol of friendliness and craftsmanship, has historically been a unifying force, fostering camaraderie and jubilation across diverse cultures. Its evolution spans centuries and continents, embodying human innovation and symbolising conviviality.

Conversely, cannabis, a natural gift, has been both revered and misconstrued throughout history. Its multifaceted applications, from healing to spiritual rituals, have entrenched it deeply in human civilisation. Yet, cannabis also embodies contemporary discourses on wellness, autonomy, and the pursuit of leisure and inspiration.

Within the pages of this book, readers will encounter narratives, factual insights, and contemplations on the multifaceted roles of beer and cannabis in shaping societies. There is an examination of their similarities, differences, and potential trajectories in the ever-changing modern world. Additionally, this publication celebrates the contributions of individuals who have shared their knowledge, experiences, and ardour for these two iconic elements of human culture.

For centuries, beer and cannabis have fostered communal bonds, creativity, and much-needed relaxation. This book endeavours to explore their intrinsic value, complexities, and the pleasures they impart. Whether one is a genuine enthusiast of brews and cultivars or is intrigued by the intersections of these realms, this publication offers insights for a broad audience.

This book extends its appeal to individuals who appreciate the art of beer, embrace the tranquil effects of cannabis, or seek to comprehend the interplay between these influences in our world. It caters to traditionalists, innovators, experts, and casual enthusiasts and is particularly relevant to those who value open-mindedness and a tranquil disposition.

Ultimately, if we are to savour life's experiences, let us do so with camaraderie and ease.

Welcome to this enriching venture!

Here's to your journey ahead!"

Sherry Pinto
Leicester, UK

"Where beer brings laughter, cannabis brings peace; together, they offer a complete celebration of life."

– Unknown

MAN MADE BEER
GOD MADE WEED

DEDICATION

This book is dedicated to my terrific sons, Adi and Ayush, my cool nephews Marty and Anindya, and all their amazing friends. You guys are the real champions of the beer and weed culture. Your energy, laughter, and adventurous spirit have inspired me to explore the importance of balance, the simple joys in life, and the value of embracing them.

Your passion and insight have ignited this journey into beer and weed, reminding me of the joy of unwinding with friends and family to relax and chill out. Here's to all of you for lighting the way, and I hope you all enjoy this book as much as I've enjoyed writing it! Cheers!

"Hemp is of first necessity to the wealth and protection of the country."

–Thomas Jefferson

TABLE OF CONTENTS

Introduction 17

The History and Culture of Beer 26

The Science of Brewing 34

Beer in Modern Society 44

The Origins of Cannabis 53

The Biology and Chemistry of Cannabis, Including Cannabinoids and Terpenes 65

Cannabis in Modern Society 77

The Intersection of Beer and Weed 88

Legal and Social Challenges 100

The Future of Beer and Weed 106

Industrial Uses of Cannabis/Hemp 119

My Final Thoughts 144

Conclusion 152

RESOURCES 165

Introduction

The Timeless Debate

It was a warm summer evening, and the air was filled with the sounds of laughter and clinking glasses, sizzling off the barbeque stand roasting meat and freshly mown grass as I found my way around the lively backyard barbecue, where friends old and new were gathered around a roaring fire pit. Among them were Bob and John, my two lifelong friends who, despite their many similarities, were passionately divided on one topic - beer versus weed. I called out greetings to the people I knew as I made a beeline for Bob and John towards the back of the lawn.

Bob, a professional lawyer and craft beer enthusiast, stood by the cooler, pulling out a selection of his favourite brews. "There's nothing like the artistry that goes into making a great beer," he declared, pouring a pale ale into a frosty glass. "The complexity of flavours, the craftsmanship—beer is a testament to human ingenuity."

John, an IT geek and a cannabis connoisseur, leaned back in his chair as he held a joint loosely between his fingers. He took a slow drag and gave a crooked smirk as he exhaled a cloud of fragrant smoke. "Sure, Bob, beer is great," he replied with a grin at me, "but nothing beats the natural, earthy experience of weed. It's a gift from nature, pure and simple. No chemicals, no additives—just pure relaxation and creativity."

Their debate drew the attention of the group around the fire pit, sparking a spirited discussion. Bob told us about his recent visit to a renowned brewery in Belgium, where he learned about centuries-old brewing techniques passed down through the ages from generation to generation. He recounted the intricate process of selecting the finest hops and barley, the meticulous brewing, and the patient ageing that resulted in a perfect pint that he learnt about. "Every sip of beer is a journey through the ages," Bob said, his eyes sparkling and lit up with passion.

John, in turn, countered with his own experience, recalling his travels to a cannabis farm in Humboldt County, California. He spoke of the organic farming methods, the respect for the land and its bounteous gifts by the locals, and the tradition of using cannabis for medicinal and spiritual purposes. "When you sit in a circle and participate in the ritual of filling and lighting up a pipe/chillum," John said, "you're connecting with an ancient tradition and practice that's been healing and inspiring people for thousands of years."

As the conversation ebbed and flowed through the evening, it became clear that this was not just a question of preference but a reflection of more profound cultural, historical, and social influences. The friendly banter between Bob and John and all of us around the fire that evening highlighted the unique appeal of beer and weed, each with its rich tapestry of stories and traditions.

This book, "Man Made Beer - God Made Weed," was inspired that evening and delves into the rich tapestry of history, culture, and personal experiences that surround these two substances. My goal is to explore their significance, unravel their myths, and understand their impact on our lives and society. Through stories, insights, and practical advice, I aim to provide a comprehensive look at how beer and weed have shaped the human experience and to place before you, dear readers, the bare facts to let you decide for yourselves what is what.

In the following pages, we will journey through time and across cultures. We will explore the ancient origins of beer and cannabis, understanding how they have been used, celebrated, and sometimes vilified. We will study the science behind brewing beer and cannabis cultivation and the traditions surrounding their uses and research, uncovering the art and innovation that have driven these practices forward.

We will also look at the modern-day implications of beer and weed. How do they fit into our social fabric today, what are the legal and economic challenges they face, and how do they compare in terms of health and wellness? We will bring these questions to life through personal anecdotes and real-life stories, offering a nuanced perspective that goes well beyond the surface we know.

The Debate - Natural vs Man-Made

At the heart of this exploration is the debate between things natural and those made by man. Beer, a product of human ingenuity, represents the heights of culinary and scientific achievement. It is a testament to our ability to transform the raw ingredients around us into something more. Weed, on the other hand, is a gift from nature, celebrated for its simplicity and its profound effects on the mind and body. This dichotomy raises essential questions about our relationship with nature, technology, tradition, and innovation.

I remember my first encounter with this debate vividly. During a visit to a small, family-owned brewery nestled in the Dutch countryside, I encountered Johann, the brewer, a passionate artisan; the spoke of his craft with reverence, describing the meticulous process of brewing beer as a form of art. Just a week later, I found myself in a different setting, a cannabis farm in a remote native mountain village in Nevada. There, the native cultivator shared his stories of ancient traditions and the healing properties of cannabis, passed down through his generations. Both experiences left a profound impact on me, highlighting the unique yet complementary roles of beer and weed, which have woven themselves into the fabric of countless cultures worldwide, each bearing its unique significance and playing diverse roles across societies in our lives.

Beer in Culture

Beer has been a staple in many civilisations since ancient times. One of the earliest known recipes in Mesopotamia is for beer, highlighting its importance in daily life and religious ceremonies. The Sumerians even had a Goddess of beer, Ninkasi, to whom they sang hymns praising the brewing process.

Beer was a crucial part of the economy and a dietary staple in ancient Egypt. Workers who built the pyramids were often paid in beer, which was considered a nutritious and refreshing beverage essential for their arduous labour. The Egyptians believed that beer was a gift from the gods, providing sustenance and pleasure.

In Europe, beer became a central part of monastic life during the Middle Ages. Monks in monasteries brewed beer not only for their own consumption but also to fund their charitable activities and maintain their religious communities. The brewing techniques developed by these monks laid the foundation for many modern brewing practices.

Today, beer festivals such as Germany's Oktoberfest celebrate the beverage's cultural importance, bringing together millions of people to enjoy and appreciate different varieties of beer. In countries like Germany, the Czech Republic, and Belgium, beer is a national pride deeply embedded in the people's social and cultural identity.

Weed in Culture

The history of cannabis is deeply entangled within human civilisation, dating back thousands of years and has an equally rich cultural history. Cannabis is often referred to as marijuana, weed, or hemp and has a history that spans thousands of years and touches nearly every corner of the globe. The word “marijuana” refers to parts of or some products derived from the plant ‘*Cannabis Sativa*’ that contain substantial amounts of tetrahydrocannabinol (THC). THC is the substance that is primarily responsible for the psychoactive effects on a person’s mental state. From its earliest known uses to its contemporary roles, cannabis has been a persistent presence in human history, enshrined deep within its traditions, culture, and religious practices, valued for its medicinal properties and practical applications. Some cannabis plants contain very little THC, and under U.S. laws, these plants are considered “industrial hemp” rather than marijuana.

It was considered one of ancient India's five sacred plants used in religious rituals and traditional medicine. The Hindu God Shiva is often associated with cannabis, symbolising its significance in spiritual practices. Bhang, a cannabis-infused drink, is still consumed during Hindu festivals like Holi.

In China, cannabis has been used for thousands of years for its medicinal properties. Ancient Chinese texts describe its use in treating various ailments, highlighting its importance in traditional Chinese medicine. The Taoist monks are also known to have used cannabis in their quest for spiritual enlightenment and immortality.

In the Middle East, cannabis, as recorded in history - played a significant role in Sufi traditions, where it was used to enhance spiritual experiences and facilitate mystical practices. Sufi poets often celebrated the use of cannabis in their writings, associating it with divine inspiration and spiritual ecstasy.

In contemporary Western culture, cannabis has experienced a renaissance, particularly in the context of legalisation and decriminalisation movements. In places like Colorado, California, and Canada, cannabis culture is thriving, with a focus on both recreational use and its therapeutic potential. Cannabis festivals and events have become commonplace, celebrating the plant's versatility and fostering a sense of community among users.

As we embark on this journey together, I invite you to keep an open mind and a curious spirit. "Man Made Beer - God Made Weed" is not just a book about two substances but a celebration of culture, history, and the human experience. Whether you are a beer enthusiast, a cannabis connoisseur, or simply someone interested in understanding more about these fascinating topics, there is something here for you.

So, pour yourself a glass of your favourite brew, or light up and join me as we explore some compelling stories, profound insights, and enduring debates that make beer and weed such integral parts of our world.

"Beer is proof that God loves us and wants us to be happy."

– Benjamin Franklin

The History and Culture of Beer

The Origins of Beer

Beer, one of human history's oldest and most beloved beverages, has a rich and fascinating story that begins in the cradle of civilisation. Imagine ancient Mesopotamia around 4,000 BCE, where the Sumerians are bustling in their cities, creating the earliest known recipe for beer. This wasn't just a drink but a divine gift from the gods, celebrated in hymns dedicated to Ninkasi, the Goddess of beer.

In this ancient setting, picture this: It is a bustling marketplace in ancient Sumeria, with people crowding stalls and the streets of the market, trading barley and other grains, not just for bread but for brewing their cherished beer. After the day's trading, they would head back home, where they would take the grain bartered for their beer, crush the barley, mix it with water, and allow natural fermentation to transform it into a mildly alcoholic beverage in earthen urns. This process, though rudimentary, laid the groundwork for the complex brewing methods we know today. It wasn't just a drink but a staple of their diet, providing essential nutrients and a safer alternative to the often-contaminated water.

As we journey forward in time, we find ourselves in ancient Egypt, where beer became even more integral to daily life. Visualise the labourers working tirelessly on the construction of the great pyramids, receiving rations of beer to sustain them through the gruelling heat and heavy lifting. Beer in Egypt wasn't just a drink; it was considered a nutritious food made from wheat and barley, sometimes flavoured with dates and herbs to enhance its taste and health benefits. It was also deeply embedded in their religious and social practices, used in offerings to the Gods and enjoyed during various celebrations and rituals.

The Romans, known for their preference for wine, initially viewed beer as a barbaric drink. However, as their empire expanded into Northern Europe, they encountered tribes who brewed their own beers. Over time, the Romans began to appreciate and adopt these brewing traditions. As we move into the Middle Ages, we see the rise of monastic brewing. In their serene monasteries, monks perfected the art of brewing, incorporating hops for the first time. This not only improved the flavour but also acted as a natural preservative, revolutionising the quality and longevity of beer. Imagine, too, the monks in their cloisters, meticulously crafting beer that would support their communities and serve as a source of income through charitable sales.

Fast-forward to the Renaissance and beyond, and beer brewing transitioned from monastic seclusion to commercial enterprise. The establishment of brewing guilds and regulations in Europe standardised the brewing process, ensuring consistent quality. The Industrial Revolution further transformed beer production, with mechanisation and mass production making beer more accessible to the masses. This era saw the rise of iconic breweries and the global spread of beer culture, setting the stage for today's diverse and dynamic beer industry.

Cultural Significance

Beer has been more than just a beverage; it has been a vital part of human culture and society across the ages. Each culture has imbued beer with unique significance, reflecting its values, traditions, and social structures.

More than a daily staple, beer was a social and religious cornerstone in ancient Egypt and Mesopotamia. Festivals, rituals, and daily life revolved around beer. It was considered a divine gift in Mesopotamia, integral to their ceremonies and offerings. In Egypt, beer was a dietary necessity and a means of connecting with the gods. The workers who built the pyramids were sustained by beer, and its production was a revered craft.

In medieval Europe, beer was central to communal life. With water often unsafe to drink, beer became the go-to beverage for all ages. Imagine the bustling medieval taverns filled with people sharing stories, celebrating, and finding solace in a pint of ale. The monks, brewing in their monasteries, viewed beer as both a sustenance and a spiritual duty. They developed brewing techniques that have influenced modern brewing practices, emphasising purity, quality, and community support.

The cultural significance of beer continued to evolve with time. In Germany, beer became a symbol of national pride and identity. The Bavarian Purity Law of 1516, known as the Reinheitsgebot, set strict standards for brewing, allowing only water, barley, and hops. This law ensured the quality of German beer and became a cultural touchstone, celebrated annually at Oktoberfest. This world-famous festival, held in Munich, brings millions together to celebrate Bavarian culture, beer, and camaraderie.

Belgium, with its rich brewing heritage, offers another fascinating cultural perspective. Belgian beers are known for their variety and complexity, each with its own unique story and flavour profile. The tradition of brewing in Belgium dates back to the Middle Ages, with monasteries and small family-run breweries at the forefront. Today, Belgian beer culture is recognised globally, and in 2016, UNESCO designated it as an Intangible Cultural Heritage of Humanity. Imagine walking through a Belgian city with its quaint breweries and lively beer cafes, each offering a taste of history and tradition.

In the United States, the craft beer revolution has redefined beer culture. Starting in the late 20th century, small, independent breweries began experimenting with new flavours, styles, and brewing techniques. This movement emphasised creativity, quality, and local production, inspiring a new generation of beer enthusiasts. Today, the U.S. is home to thousands of craft breweries, each contributing to the vibrant and diverse landscape of American beer

.

Personal Experience

My journey into the beer world deepened during a memorable trip to Belgium, a country renowned for its rich brewing tradition. One of the highlights of my trip was a visit to the Westvleteren Brewery, operated by Trappist monks at Saint Sixtus' Abbey. This brewery is often hailed as the producer of some of the best beers in the world, such as the Westvleteren 12, Rochefort, Westmalle, Orval, Chinmay, and Achel. It is known for its limited production and exceptional quality.

The journey to the brewery was an adventure in itself. Nestled in the picturesque countryside of West Flanders, the abbey exudes a sense of tranquillity and history. As I approached, the air was filled with the warm, inviting scent of brewing beer—a blend of malted barley and hops that felt like a comforting embrace.

The monks, dedicated to a life of contemplation and prayer, welcomed visitors with genuine hospitality. They explained their brewing process, which has remained essentially unchanged for centuries. Their approach was striking in its simplicity and purity. They used only the finest ingredients and brewed in small batches, ensuring that each bottle was a testament to their dedication and craftsmanship.
Tasting Westvleteren's beer was a revelation. The complex layers of flavour, the perfect balance between sweetness and bitterness, and the smooth, velvety texture were unlike anything I had ever experienced. It was clear why these beers were so highly revered.

What struck me most was the profound sense of history and tradition that permeated every aspect of the brewery. The monks were not just brewing beer but preserving a centuries-old legacy, a craft passed down through generations. This experience deepened my appreciation for beer's cultural and historical significance, highlighting its unique role in human civilisation.

As I sipped my beer in the abbey's quiet courtyard, I reflected on beer's journey through time. From ancient Sumerian brewers to medieval monks and modern craft brewers, beer has been a constant companion to humanity. It has evolved and adapted but has always retained its essence as a symbol of community, creativity, and celebration.

"There is no such thing as a bad beer. It's that some taste better than others."

– Billy Carter

The Science of Brewing

The Brewing Process

Brewing beer is a fascinating blend of science and art, a meticulous process that transforms simple ingredients into a rich, complex beverage. Imagine standing in a bustling brewery, the air filled with the warm, earthy aroma of malted barley and the sharp floral scent of hops. Here, in this dynamic environment, the magic of brewing unfolds.

The process begins with malting, where barley grains are soaked in water, triggering germination. This process awakens enzymes within the grains, converting their starches into fermentable sugars. After a few days, the grains are dried in a kiln, a step that halts germination and develops the malt's flavour. The degree of drying—or roasting—can produce a range of flavours, from light and sweet to dark and robust, setting the foundation for the beer's taste profile; for instance, lightly roasted malts yield pale ales, while darker roasts create rich stouts.

Next comes mashing, where the malted barley is milled into a coarse powder called grist. This grist is mixed with hot water in a large vessel, creating a thick porridge-like mixture. The heat activates the enzymes, breaking down the starches into sugars. The result is a sweet, sugary liquid known as wort, which is carefully separated from the spent grains in a process called lautering. The grains are rinsed with hot water to extract every bit of fermentable sugar, ensuring a rich and flavourful wort.

The wort is then brought to a boil, a critical stage where hops are added. These small, cone-shaped flowers contribute bitterness, flavour, and aroma to the beer, balancing the sweetness of the malt. The timing of adding hops during the boil is crucial—early additions lend bitterness, while later additions enhance flavour and aroma, crafting a complex and well-rounded beer.

After boiling, the hot wort is rapidly cooled and transferred to a fermentation vessel. Here, yeast is added, and the fundamental transformation begins. In the wort, a microscopic organism, yeast consumes the sugars, producing carbon dioxide and alcohol in a process known as fermentation. This stage can last from a few days to several weeks, depending on the type of beer. The yeast works its magic during fermentation, creating a variety of flavours and aromas that define the beer's character. Once fermentation is complete, the beer enters the conditioning phase. This can take place in the fermentation vessel or bottles and kegs. Conditioning allows the flavours to mature and any remaining yeast to settle, resulting in a more transparent and refined beer. This stage can last from a few weeks to several months, with the beer developing greater depth and complexity over time.

Finally, the beer is ready for packaging. It can be bottled, canned, or kegged, each method preserving the beer's freshness and flavour. Some beers undergo natural carbonation through bottle conditioning, where a small amount of sugar is added before sealing, allowing the yeast to produce carbon dioxide and create a lively, effervescent drink.

Innovations in Brewing

The brewing industry has been evolving continuously, driven by innovation and technological advancements that have transformed how beer is produced and enjoyed. Technological advancements have revolutionised modern breweries, where high-tech equipment ensures precision and consistency. One of the most significant breakthroughs was the introduction of refrigeration in the late 19th century. This has permitted brewers to control temperatures during fermentation more precisely, leading to consistent, high-quality beer. Refrigeration also enabled the production of lagers, which require more excellent fermentation conditions, expanding the diversity of beer styles available to consumers. Today, automated mash tuns and fermentation tank systems streamline operations, while sophisticated filtration methods help brewers create more precise, stable beers.

Sustainability has also become a significant focus, with breweries adopting eco-friendly practices to reduce their environmental footprint. Many are implementing water recycling systems, investing in energy-efficient brewing technologies, and finding ways to repurpose spent grains, such as using them for animal feed or compost. Another pivotal innovation was pasteurisation, a process named after Louis Pasteur. Pasteurisation has helped extend the shelf life of beer by heating it to eliminate any remaining yeast and bacteria, making it more stable for distribution. This was a game-changer for breweries, allowing them to reach broader markets with their products.

Modern brewing also benefits from advanced microbial control techniques. Cleanliness and sanitation are paramount, with breweries employing sophisticated equipment to prevent contamination and ensure product consistency. Advances in brewing science have deepened our understanding of yeast genetics, fermentation kinetics, and flavour chemistry. Selective breeding and genetic engineering have produced new yeast strains and hop varieties, expanding the flavour possibilities of beer. Techniques like dry hopping and barrel ageing offer brewers innovative ways to introduce complex flavours, enhancing the beer-drinking experience.

The advent of automation and technology has further revolutionised brewing. Computer-controlled systems monitor and adjust temperatures, pressures, and timings, ensuring precision and efficiency. This technology allows breweries to scale up production while maintaining the artisanal quality that beer enthusiasts cherish.

In recent decades, the craft brewing movement has brought innovation back to the forefront of the industry. Small, independent brewers began experimenting with new ingredients, brewing techniques, and styles, pushing the boundaries of traditional brewing. The craft brewing movement has played a crucial role in revitalising the beer industry. Craft brewers, renowned for their creativity and willingness to experiment, have pushed the boundaries of traditional brewing. Collaborations between breweries and the use of unconventional ingredients such as fruits, spices, and herbs have led to a renaissance in beer diversity and creativity, with craft breweries producing a wide array of unique and flavourful beers or unique beer styles that captivate and delight consumers.

This focus on microbial control has led to the production of safer, higher-quality beer.

Practical Insights for the home brewer

Understanding the process and the different beer styles is essential for those inspired to try their hand at brewing. Here are some practical tips to ensure a successful start. To simplify the process, start with a basic recipe and a homebrew kit. Many homebrew shops offer kits that include all the necessary ingredients and equipment, making it easy to get started.

Sanitation is crucial in brewing. Cleanliness cannot be overstated — ensure all your equipment is thoroughly sanitised to avoid contamination. To prevent contamination, every piece of equipment must be thoroughly cleaned and sanitised before and after use. Even a small number of unwanted bacteria or wild yeast can spoil a batch of beer, so maintaining a clean brewing environment is essential. Controlling fermentation temperature is another critical factor and is very crucial, as each yeast strain has a preferred temperature range that influences the beer's flavour and aroma. The temperature at which fermentation occurs can significantly affect the taste of your beer. Investing in a temperature control system, such as a fermentation chamber or a temperature-controlled water bath, can help you achieve consistent and desirable results.

Keeping detailed records of the ingredients, measurements, and the brewing process helps identify what works well and what doesn't, guiding your future batches. Documenting the ingredients, process, and results can help you troubleshoot issues and replicate successful batches. This record-keeping can also serve as a valuable reference as you continue to refine your brewing skills. Allow your beer to ferment and condition fully before enjoying it, as rushing the process can lead to subpar results. As you gain experience, you can experiment with different malts, hops, and yeast strains, creating your own unique recipes.

Understanding different beer styles can also enhance your brewing experience. Ales, lagers, stouts, and IPAs each have distinct characteristics and brewing requirements. There are also hybrids and speciality beers that incorporate characteristics of both ales and lagers or feature unconventional ingredients. Ales, fermented at warmer temperatures with top-fermenting yeast, include styles like Pale Ale, IPA, Stout, and Porter, often with robust, fruity, or spicy flavours. Lagers, brewed with bottom-fermenting yeast at cooler temperatures, produce clean, crisp beers like

Pilsner, Bock, and Oktoberfest. Kölsch, a hybrid beer, and Belgian Lambics, brewed with wild yeast and bacteria, offer unique tasting experiences. Seasonal and limited-edition beers, such as winter warmers or summer ales, provide an ever-changing landscape of flavours to explore.

Familiarising yourself with these styles can help you tailor your brewing process and ingredient selection to produce the best possible beer. Home brewing is a rewarding hobby that allows you to explore your creativity and enjoy the fruits of your labour. By diving into the science and art of brewing, appreciating the innovations that have shaped the industry, and exploring practical insights for home brewing, you can truly appreciate the craftsmanship behind every pint. Whether you're a seasoned brewer or a curious beginner, understanding the intricate process of brewing deepens your connection to this ancient and beloved beverage.

Beer pairing with food can elevate your dining experience. Matching light beers like Pilsners with seafood or rich stouts with chocolate desserts brings out the best in beer and the food. The proper glassware also matters—a tulip glass perfectly captures the aroma of a Belgian ale, while a pint glass is ideal for an IPA. Serving temperature is another critical factor; ales are typically enjoyed slightly warmer than lagers to experience their flavour profile fully.

Brewing beer is a time-consuming process, and patience is crucial. Rushing the process will lead to disappointing results. Allowing the beer to ferment and condition fully ensures that the flavours develop correctly, resulting in a more enjoyable and satisfying brew. The science of brewing is an intricate and fascinating blend of tradition and innovation. From the essential ingredients to the detailed brewing process and from historical techniques to modern advances, brewing stands as a testimony to human ingenuity and passion. Whether you're just starting or have been brewing for years, the world of beer offers endless opportunities for discovery and enjoyment. So, raise a glass and toast to the journey of brewing — an art and science as timeless as civilisation itself.

"Beer, if drunk in moderation, promotes health and longevity."

– Thomas Jefferson

Beer in Modern Society

The Role of Beer in Modern Social Settings and Celebrations

With its rich history and broad appeal, Beer has cemented its place as a cornerstone of social gatherings worldwide. It is more than just a beverage; it is a social lubricant, a cultural icon, and a bridge that brings people together. Picture a backyard barbecue on a warm summer evening. Friends and family gather around, the grill sizzling with burgers and hot dogs and ice-cold beers clinking together in toasts. From casual get-togethers at local pubs to grand celebrations such as Oktoberfest, this beverage is the beloved of many, often the catalyst for bringing people together, fostering connections, and creating lasting memories. It is present at sporting events, where fans bond over a shared love for their team, raising their pints in unison after a thrilling goal. It is at weddings where toasts are made to the happy couple, and the bubbles in the beer symbolise the effervescent joy of the occasion. It is a staple at music festivals, where it adds to the communal experience of enjoying live performances under the open sky. This scene, repeated countless times across the world, showcases beer's role in modern social settings and celebrations.

In many cultures worldwide, beer is a social lubricant, breaking down barriers and encouraging conversation. Think about the last time you attended a backyard barbecue, a sporting event, or even a simple dinner party. Chances are, beer was present, flowing freely as friends and family caught up on life, celebrated milestones, or simply enjoyed each other's company. Beer's versatility and wide range of styles make it suitable for various occasions, from light lagers at a summer picnic to robust stouts by the fireplace in winter.

Moreover, beer is often at the heart of many cultural and traditional celebrations. A classic example is Germany's Oktoberfest, Munich's most significant annual beer fest. For two weeks, millions of people from around the globe gather to enjoy traditional Bavarian music, food, and, of course, beer. The atmosphere is electric, filled with songs, laughter, and steins clinking. This festival exemplifies how beer can foster community and shared joy, uniting people from different backgrounds. One memorable event that illustrates beer's social impact involves a friend's annual Oktoberfest party. Every year, he transforms his backyard into a miniature Bavarian village, complete with traditional decorations, bratwurst, and various beers. Guests arrive in lederhosen and dirndls, ready to enjoy the festivities. The highlight of the evening is always the beer tasting, where everyone samples different brews, discussing their favourites and discovering new tastes. This event, rooted in the tradition of Germany's famous beer festival, showcases how beer can create a sense of community and shared enjoyment.

Another example is the rising popularity of craft beer festivals, which have become a staple in many cities worldwide. These events celebrate the creativity and uniqueness of craft brewers, offering attendees the opportunity to taste a variety of beers, meet the brewers, and learn about the brewing process. These festivals promote local breweries and create a vibrant community space where novices and enthusiasts can bond over their shared love of beer.

The Economic Significance of the Beer Industry

Beer is essential to any country's economy, as its importance extends beyond its social role. It is a multi-billion-dollar enterprise encompassing brewing, distribution, retail, and hospitality. It provides millions of jobs worldwide, from farmers who grow barley and hops to bartenders who serve the final product. It significantly contributes to the global economy, supporting millions of people. From small craft breweries to large multinational corporations, the production and sale of beer generate significant revenue and stimulate economic activity.

In recent years, the craft beer movement has significantly reshaped the industry. Small and independent breweries have proliferated, bringing with them innovation, diversity, and a resurgence of local pride. Craft breweries rely on local suppliers for ingredients, creating a chain reaction that benefits local farmers, manufacturers, and other small businesses. Consider the local craft brewery. It's not just a place where beer is made; it's a hub of economic activity, contributing to the local economy's vitality. This local focus supports regional economies, promotes sustainable practices, and strengthens community ties.

Large-scale breweries, on the other hand, also have a significant economic impact. They contribute to the economy through mass production, extensive distribution networks, and important marketing efforts. They create thousands of jobs directly and indirectly, from factory workers to marketing professionals, and boost related industries like trucking and packaging. These companies also invest heavily in research and development, leading to technological advancements and improvements in efficiency within the industry. Major beer companies invest in extensive marketing campaigns, sponsor events, and support sports teams, all contributing to the economy. Their reach is global, distributing beer to countless markets and influencing economic activity on a vast scale.

A visit to a renowned brewery, such as the Guinness Storehouse in Dublin, highlights the economic impact of beer. The brewery tour educates visitors about the brewing process and showcases the brand's global reach and economic significance. Terminating the tour with a pint of Guinness in the Gravity Bar, guests enjoy a panoramic view of Dublin. This experience underscores how beer tourism has become a significant economic driver, attracting visitors from around the world and boosting local economies.

Beer has a notable impact on tourism, which includes brewery tours, beer festivals, and pub crawls. These activities attract visitors, generate revenue, and promote cultural exchange. Cities like Brussels, Portland, and Prague are renowned for their beer culture and draw enthusiasts from around the world eager to experience their rich brewing heritage.

Let me share a personal story that captures the essence of beer's role in fostering social bonds. A couple of years ago, my friends and I planned a trip to Belgium to explore the famous Trappist breweries and immerse ourselves in the country's rich beer culture. Our journey took us to the picturesque town of Westvleteren, home to one of the world's most acclaimed Trappist breweries.

On a sunny afternoon, we cycled through rolling hills and quaint villages, finally arriving at St. Sixtus' Abbey. The abbey exuded an aura of serenity and tradition as we settled into its café, eager to taste the revered Westvleteren 12. As we sipped the deep, complex beer, we began to truly appreciate and marvel at the craftsmanship that went into every sip.

That evening, we met fellow beer enthusiasts from different parts of the world. Strangers quickly became friends as we bonded over our shared appreciation for good beer. Language barriers dissolved, and our diverse backgrounds only enriched our discussions. By the night's end, we had created connections that extended far beyond that moment, all thanks to the communal magic of beer.

Another memorable occasion was a local beer festival held in our town. The festival featured dozens of local craft breweries, each showcasing its unique creations. It was a celebration of creativity and community, with live music, food trucks, and plenty of beer. I volunteered with friends to help organise the event, which allowed us to meet countless passionate brewers and excited attendees.

One highlight of the festival was the "homebrew competition," where amateur brewers could enter their best creations. I was particularly moved by a contestant who shared the story behind his brew—he had crafted the beer in honour of his father, who had taught him how to brew. When he won the competition, Oscar's words of appreciation for his father and his art were incredibly emotional and uplifting, exemplifying the deep personal connections and cherished memories that beer can foster.

These stories highlight how beer acts as a catalyst for social interaction, breaking down barriers and fostering a sense of camaraderie. Whether it is a wedding, a block party, or a simple gathering with friends, beer brings people together, creating memorable moments of joy, fun and connection with its unique qualities.

In modern society, beer's influence is multifaceted and profound, extending beyond the glass. It is a catalyst for social interaction, a key player in economic development, and a source of personal joy and community bonding. A cultural touchstone, an economic powerhouse, and a social connector, as we raise our glasses, we celebrate not just the beverage itself but the rich tapestry of experiences, relationships, and communities that it helps to weave. Its impact resonates through our social fabric and economic structures, making it much more than just a beverage but a beloved and integral part of our cultural heritage.

The Natural Wonder of Weed

"When you smoke the herb, it reveals you to yourself."

– Bob Marley

The Origins of Cannabis

The history of cannabis is deeply entwined with human civilisation, dating back thousands of years. Often referred to as marijuana, weed, or hemp, Cannabis has a history that spans thousands of years and touches nearly every corner of the globe. From its earliest known uses to its contemporary roles, cannabis has been a persistent presence in human history, valued for its medicinal properties, psychoactive effects, and practical applications. To understand its journey, we must travel back in time to ancient civilisations, where cannabis was revered for its versatile properties.

Cannabis is known to have originated in Central Asia. It spread quickly, adapting to various climates and cultures in different parts of the world. Archaeological evidence suggests that the use of cannabis dates back to at least 10,000 years ago, with traces found in ancient Chinese and Japanese cultures. The earliest documented uses of cannabis come from an ancient Chinese text, the "Shennong Bencaojing" (The Classic of Herbal Medicine). In ancient China, around 2737 BCE, known as the Father of Chinese Medicine, Emperor Shen Nung, documented the medicinal benefits of cannabis in treating ailments such as gout, rheumatism, and malaria. The Chinese referred to cannabis as "ma," and it played a crucial role in their traditional medicine for millennia. This marks one of the earliest recorded uses of cannabis for therapeutic purposes.

In ancient India, the Atharva Veda, one of the four sacred Hindu texts, describes cannabis as one of the five sacred plants and credits it with both medicinal and psychoactive properties. Known as "bhang," cannabis was used in religious rituals and was considered a sacred plant, believed to be a gift from the gods. The Hindu God Shiva was often associated with cannabis (bhang), which was consumed during religious rituals to attain spiritual enlightenment.
The historical journey of cannabis continues through the ancient civilisations of Egypt, Greece, and Rome. Egyptian texts from around 2000 BCE reference the use of cannabis for treating inflammation and glaucoma. The Greeks and Romans utilised it for its analgesic and anaesthetic properties, often applying cannabis topically for wounds and sores. These early applications highlight the medicinal value placed on cannabis long before modern science confirmed its efficacy. As trade routes expanded, so did the spread of cannabis, which also made its way to the Middle East and Africa. It travelled through the Middle East, reaching the Islamic world, where scholars and physicians like Avicenna praised its medicinal properties. In medieval Europe, cannabis was used

for a variety of purposes, including rope, textiles, and medicinal remedies, further cementing its place in human history.

A nomadic tribe from Central Asia, the Scythians, were known to use cannabis both ceremonially and recreationally. Greek historian Herodotus wrote about the Scythians using cannabis seeds in steam baths to achieve a state of euphoria. By the time of the early Islamic societies, cannabis, particularly in the form of hashish, had become popular for its intoxicating effects despite ongoing debates among scholars about its permissibility. In Africa, cannabis was introduced by Arab traders around the 8th century. It was incorporated into traditional medicine and also used in various social and spiritual contexts. The plant thrived in the continent's climate, and its usage spread rapidly.
Europe encountered cannabis through multiple routes. The ancient Greeks and Romans used hemp (non-psychoactive cannabis) for making ropes and textiles. However, the psychoactive properties of cannabis became more widely recognised in Europe during the Middle Ages and the Renaissance, often in the context of apothecary practices.

By the 16th century, Spanish colonists brought cannabis to the Americas, where it was cultivated primarily for its fibre. The psychoactive use of cannabis began to take hold in the United States in the early 20th century, with immigrants from Mexico introducing recreational use. Despite its widespread historical acceptance, cannabis faced legal and social challenges throughout the 20th century, culminating in widespread prohibition.

However, the late 20th and early 21st centuries saw a resurgence in the recognition of cannabis's medicinal benefits and a gradual shift towards decriminalisation and legalisation in various parts of the world. This contemporary renaissance is driven by scientific research, changing social attitudes, and successful advocacy for cannabis reform.

Cultural and Spiritual Significance

Throughout history, in various cultures and traditions, Cannabis has played a significant role, not only for its medicinal properties but also for its recreational and spiritual uses. Its versatile nature has allowed it to cross cultural boundaries and find a place in a wide range of human activities. In India, as mentioned, cannabis was integral to religious practices. The plant is used to prepare bhang, a traditional drink consumed during festivals like Holi, which symbolises the victory of good over evil every time and the arrival of spring. Hindu sadhus (holy men) use cannabis to aid meditation and religious enlightenment, believing that the plant is a gift from Lord Shiva.

Valued for its medicinal and industrial applications in ancient China, cannabis was derived from the cannabis plant. Hemp was used to produce textiles, paper, and ropes. The cultural significance of cannabis in China extended to its role in traditional Chinese medicine, where it was a staple remedy for numerous ailments.

Moving westward, in the Middle East, cannabis found its place in Sufi practices. The Sufis, a mystical Islamic sect, used cannabis to enhance spiritual experiences and attain a state of divine ecstasy. The plant's psychoactive properties were believed to aid in meditation and deepen the connection with the divine.

In more recent history, the Rastafarian movement in Jamaica embraced cannabis as a sacrament, calling it "Ganja." Rastafarians, like the Indians, believe that cannabis is a gift from God, meant to elevate the mind and spirit. It is regarded as a sacrament that aids spiritual growth and provides a closer connection to the divine. It plays a central role in their religious ceremonies, music, and social gatherings, symbolising peace, love, and unity. Widespread use of cannabis is also found among indigenous groups in the Americas and Africa, where it is used in rituals and ceremonies to promote healing and spiritual well-being.

Medicinal Use

Cannabis has been used as a medicine for thousands of years and has been an integral part of traditional remedies in China. Hildegard of Bingen, a renowned medieval nun and herbalist, praised cannabis for its medicinal properties in her works. In India, Ayurvedic medicine continues to incorporate cannabis to treat a wide range of conditions, such as indigestion, fever, and pain.
Identifying cannabinoids like THC (tetrahydrocannabinol) and CBD (cannabidiol) as active compounds with various therapeutic applications in traditional medication and uses has been validated by modern science. Today, medical cannabis is prescribed for managing chronic pain, epilepsy, multiple sclerosis, and chemotherapy-induced nausea, among other conditions. The ongoing research continues to uncover new potential benefits, fuelling a growing acceptance in mainstream medicine.

Recreational Use

The recreational use of cannabis has been documented since ancient times. In India, bhang is consumed during the festival of Holi, while in ancient Greece and Rome, it was enjoyed at social gatherings. The Middle Eastern practice of smoking hashish spread westward to Europe and southward into Africa, where it became ingrained in social customs.

In the modern era, cannabis gained popularity in the United States and Europe during the 1960s and 1970s counterculture movements, symbolising peace, love, and rebellion against established norms. Today, with the tide of legalisation spreading globally, recreational cannabis has become increasingly accepted, leading to a burgeoning industry with a wide variety of products designed to suit different preferences and lifestyles.

Discovering the Cultural Significance of Cannabis

A couple of years ago, I had the opportunity to visit the beautiful Himalayan region of Himachal Pradesh in India. Known for its stunning landscapes and tranquil mountain villages, this area is also famous for its centuries-old tradition of cannabis cultivation and use.

I arrived in the small village of Malana, where a highly regarded strain of cannabis, often dubbed the "Malana Cream", is produced. Nestled high in the mountains, Malana feels like a world unto itself, with its ancient customs and unique culture. The villagers claim descent from Alexander the Great's soldiers, and their dialect, rituals, and social structure stand as a testament to a rich and isolated heritage.

My journey to Malana coincided with their annual festival, a celebration that encapsulates the village's relationship with cannabis. The village was bustling with activity, and the air was filled with the distinctive scent of cannabis. Families gathered to celebrate, friends reunited, and an unmistakable sense of community and tradition was in the air.

During the festival, I was invited to observe an ancient traditional ceremony passed down from generation to generation. The village elders gathered in the central square, where cannabis plants were offered as a tribute to their local deity, Jamlu Devta. The plants were ritually blessed and then distributed among the villagers. As the sun set behind the mountains, a communal chillum (a traditional smoking pipe) was passed around, and the atmosphere became one of deep relaxation and connection.

It was here that I met Raj, a local farmer who grew cannabis as part of the village's traditional economy. Sitting on his porch, overlooking the terraced fields, he shared stories of how cannabis had always been interwoven with their way of life. The spoke of how it was used for medicinal purposes, as a spiritual aid, and even in daily rituals. Raj's pride in his heritage and respect for the plant was palpable.

This experience highlighted the importance of preserving traditional knowledge and practices and deepened my appreciation for the cultural and spiritual significance of cannabis. The people of Malana view cannabis not merely as a crop but as an integral part of their cultural identity and spiritual practice.
Last year, I had the opportunity to travel to Morocco, a country known for its rich history and diverse culture. While there, I visited the Rif Mountains, a region famous for its cannabis cultivation. This journey was an eye-opening experience that further enhanced my knowledge and appreciation for the cultural significance of cannabis.

In the small village of Ketama, I met with local farmers who had been cultivating cannabis for generations. They welcomed me with open arms and shared stories of how cannabis had been a part of their lives for centuries. The plant was not only a source of livelihood for them but also a cultural cornerstone, similar to the people of Malana. It was

used in traditional medicine, culinary practices, and even in social rituals.
During my stay with them, I joined the villagers for a traditional meal one evening. The highlight of the evening was a dish called "majoun," a sweet treat made with cannabis. As we shared the meal, our conversation flowed back and forth seamlessly, breaking down cultural barriers and creating a sense of camaraderie. The experience illustrated how cannabis, much like beer, has the power to bring people together, fostering connections and understanding.

This journey to Morocco and earlier to Malana underscores the profound cultural significance of cannabis. It is more than just a plant; it symbolises tradition, community, and heritage. The stories and experiences of the people I met in these two countries, separated by thousands of miles, resonate deeply, highlighting the enduring relationship between cannabis and human culture through the centuries.

Cannabis has an illustrious history and a multifaceted role in human society. From its ancient origins in Central Asia to its diverse applications across medicine, recreation, and spirituality, cannabis has proven to be a plant of remarkable versatility and significance. Every culture that embraced cannabis has added a layer to its rich tapestry, weaving stories of healing, enlightenment, and community.

As we continue to explore and understand cannabis, we must appreciate its historical context and cultural importance, recognising it as more than just a plant but as a symbol of our shared human experience. Whether in historic rituals in India, the bustling markets of ancient China, or the modern dispensaries of California, cannabis remains a natural wonder with a profound legacy that continues to shape lives and societies.

"Hemp is the most versatile and beneficial crop known to humankind."

– Jack Herer

The Biology and Chemistry of Cannabis, Including Cannabinoids and Terpenes

Cannabis is a plant of remarkable complexity that has intrigued scientists for centuries. To truly appreciate this plant and its effects, it is essential to understand its biology and the intricate chemistry that defines its characteristics, as that is essential towards appreciating its wide range of effects and uses.

The Cannabis Plant

As part of the Cannabaceae family with three primary species: Cannabis sativa, Cannabis indica, and Cannabis ruderalis, Cannabis is a genus of flowering plants. Each species has unique traits in terms of growth patterns, cannabinoid profiles, and physical appearance. Cannabis plants are dioecious, meaning they have distinct male and female plants. The female plants produce the resinous flowers sought after for their high concentrations of cannabinoids and terpenes, while male plants generate pollen to fertilise the females, resulting in seed production. Its unique properties are due to the rich array of chemical compounds it produces, most notably cannabinoids and terpenes.

In Cannabis, cannabinoids are the active chemical compounds that interact with the body's endocannabinoid system, contributing to its psychoactive and therapeutic effects. Over 100 different cannabinoids have been identified, with THC (tetrahydrocannabinol) and CBD (cannabidiol) being the most well-known and extensively studied. Other significant cannabinoids include CBG (cannabigerol), CBC (cannabichromene), and CBN (cannabinol), each with its own unique effects and potential health benefits, which researchers are currently exploring.

The psychoactive component of cannabis primarily responsible for the "high" associated with its use is THC (Tetrahydrocannabinol). It binds to CB1 receptors in the brain, affecting areas involved in memory, pleasure, and time perception. Besides its psychoactive properties, medicinal benefits for pain relief, appetite stimulation, and muscle relaxation are also a property of THC. THC is responsible for the plant's psychoactive effects, giving users the "high" associated with marijuana. It interacts with the endocannabinoid system in the human body, specifically binding to CB1 receptors in the brain. This interaction influences mood, perception, and behaviour, leading to the characteristic euphoria or relaxation.

CBD (Cannabidiol) - Unlike THC, CBD is non-psychoactive and doesn't produce a high. It is known for its anti-inflammatory, analgesic, anti-anxiety, and anti-seizure properties. It interacts more subtly with the endocannabinoid system, differently than THC, primarily affecting CB2 receptors throughout the immune system. It has been discovered to have a wide range of therapeutic applications.

Another component in cannabis responsible for the plant's distinctive aroma and flavour is Terpenes. It plays an essential role as the combination of cannabinoids and terpenes, known as the entourage effect, work synergistically to enhance the overall impact of cannabis, creating an effect that goes beyond the properties of individual compounds. Common terpenes include – Myrcene, which is known for its earthy and musky scent and has a soothing and anti-inflammatory properties. Limonene, with a citrusy aroma, elevates mood and relieves stress. Linalool exhibits a floral fragrance and has calming and anxiety-reducing effects. Pinene is an anti-inflammatory and bronchodilator with a sharp, pine-like smell, potentially improving respiratory function. Spicy and peppery, Caryophyllene's aroma and unique ability to interact with the CB2 receptors directly offer anti-inflammatory effects.

The Medical Benefits and Current Research on Cannabis

The medical potential of cannabis dates back thousands of years; it is vast and continues to be a subject of extensive research. Cannabis has historically been used for its medicinal properties, and it is only in recent decades that scientific research has begun to validate and expand on traditional knowledge. Today, cannabis is recognised for its therapeutic benefits in treating a variety of conditions.

One of the most well-documented uses of cannabis is in pain management. Both THC and CBD have been shown to alleviate chronic pain, making cannabis a valuable option for patients suffering from conditions such as arthritis, multiple sclerosis, and fibromyalgia. Cannabis works by modulating pain signals in the brain and reducing inflammation, providing relief without the psychoactive implications of opioids. Cannabis is also gaining recognition for its effectiveness in treating disorders in the nervous system. CBD shows promise in reducing the severity of seizures and their frequency in patients with epilepsy, especially in cases that show resistance to conventional treatments. The FDA-approved drug Epidiolex, which contains purified CBD, has been a breakthrough for many families dealing with severe forms of epilepsy.

Moreover, cannabis has potential in the field of mental health. It has been used to alleviate symptoms of anxiety, depression, and PTSD. While THC can sometimes exacerbate anxiety, CBD is known for its calming effects and can help reduce stress and improve mood. Research is ongoing to understand better the optimal strains and dosages for treating mental health conditions. Cannabis is also being explored for its role in cancer care, as it can help in the management of symptoms such as nausea and loss of appetite caused by chemotherapy. There is plenty of preliminary evidence suggesting that cannabinoids may have anti-cancer properties, although more research is needed to understand this potential fully.

Widespread prescription of Cannabis based or as a content in medicines is currently in practice to manage some of the chronic issues. Management of chronic pain is one of the most well-established medical uses of cannabis. Both THC and CBD are known to relieve pain by interacting with pathways in the brain and immune system that regulate pain and inflammation. Conditions such as arthritis, multiple sclerosis, and fibromyalgia often benefit from cannabis-based treatments.

Epilepsy and Seizure Disorders, CBD has gained considerable attention for its efficacy in reducing seizures, particularly in patients with treatment-resistant epilepsy. The FDA-approved drug Epidiolex is derived from CBD and is used for the treatment of Dravet syndrome and Lennox-Gastaut syndrome, which are rare forms of epilepsy.

Anxiety and Depression - cannabis, particularly CBD, shows promise in reducing symptoms of anxiety and depression. By modulating the endocannabinoid system and influencing serotonin receptors, CBD can produce calming and mood-enhancing effects without the psychoactive implications of THC.

PTSD (Post-Traumatic Stress Disorder) - cannabis is increasingly used to help in the management of PTSD symptoms, including anxiety, flashbacks, and insomnia. THC and CBD can work together to promote relaxation, reduce nightmares, and improve sleep quality.

Cancer Treatment - while cannabis is not a cure for cancer, it can alleviate several symptoms, such as nausea and vomiting associated with cancer, its treatment and loss of appetite. Towards a potential breakthrough in finding a cure, THC and CBD have shown potential in inhibiting the growth of specific cancer cells in preliminary studies, and more research is needed to understand these effects fully.

Neurodegenerative Diseases - cannabinoids exhibit neuroprotective properties that may benefit conditions like Alzheimer's disease, Parkinson's disease, and Amyotrophic Lateral Sclerosis (ALS). They can help reduce inflammation, protect against neural damage, and improve motor symptoms.

Other Conditions - beyond these sleep disorders, inflammatory bowel disease (IBD), migraines, and even addiction to other substances are being researched for potential treatment by cannabis.

Understanding Different Strains and Their Effects

The variety of cannabis strains available and their effects can be overwhelming, but understanding their classifications and characteristics can help in choosing the right strain for your needs. Cannabis strains are generally categorised into three main types: Sativa, Indica, and Hybrid.

Sativa strains are typically uplifting and energising, making them suitable for daytime use. They are known for their cerebral effects, enhancing creativity, mood and focus. Sativas often have higher THC levels and lower CBD content, contributing to their stimulating properties. Sativa plants are taller with thinner leaves and take longer to mature. Popular Sativa strains include Sour Diesel, Jack Herer, and Green Crack. A popular Sativa strain, Sour Diesel, provides an energising and uplifting experience, often leading to increased creativity and focus. It's commonly used for stress and depression relief.

Indica strains, on the other hand, are known for their relaxing and soothing effects. They are often used in the evening or before bed to help with sleep and relaxation. Indicas tend to have higher CBD levels, which contribute to their calming effects and are beneficial for pain relief, insomnia, and anxiety. Indica plants are usually shorter and bushier and have broader leaves. Some well-known Indica strains are Northern Lights, Granddaddy Purple, and Blueberry. A classic Indica strain, Northern Lights offers deep relaxation and pain relief, making it ideal for evening use and managing symptoms of insomnia.

Hybrid strains combine Sativa and Indica, offering a balance of effects. Hybrids can be Sativa-dominant, Indica-dominant, or balanced. They are designed to incorporate the desirable traits of both parent strains, providing customised effects vastly different from each other depending on the benefits sought by the user. Popular hybrid strains include Blue Dream, Girl Scout Cookies, and Pineapple Express. Blue Dream, a well-known hybrid strain, is known for its balanced effects. It offers a gentle combination of relaxation and mental stimulation, making it popular for both novice and experienced users.

On the other hand, delivering a potent mix of euphoria and relaxation is the Girl Scout Cookies (GSC). It is effective for pain relief and stress management and often produces a well-balanced effect suitable for various uses.

Tips for Choosing and Using Strains—When choosing a strain, the desired effects and any medical conditions being treated are essential factors to consider. For instance, someone seeking pain relief and relaxation might opt for an Indica strain, while someone looking to enhance creativity and focus might prefer a Sativa. Additionally, the terpene profile can influence the overall experience, so paying attention to the aroma and flavour can also guide strain selection.

Go Slow Start Low - If you're new to cannabis, begin with a low dose, especially when trying out a new strain. Gradually increase the dose till you reach the desired effect.

Consider the Cannabinoid and Terpene Profile - Looking beyond THC and CBD content, Terpenes play a significant role in a strain's overall effects. For example, a strain high in myrcene may have more sedative properties, while a limonene-dominant strain may be more uplifting.

Know Your Goals - Different strains serve different purposes. Are you seeking pain relief, anxiety reduction, or a boost in creativity? Use your goals to guide your strain selection.

Consult a Knowledgeable Source - Dispensaries typically have educated staff (often called budtenders) who can help guide your choices based on their expertise and your needs.

The science of cannabis is a rich, fascinating, and rapidly evolving field. It is driven by the intricate interplay of its biological components, offering insights into the plant's biology, chemistry, and medical potential. A growing body of research into the biology and chemistry of the plant (cannabinoids and terpenes and practical insights into strain selection) supporting its therapeutic potential and medical benefits will enhance your appreciation and effective use of cannabis.

As the stigma surrounding cannabis continues to diminish and research expands, the future holds exciting possibilities for discovering even more about this remarkable plant. Whether used for medical purposes, recreational enjoyment, or spiritual enhancement, cannabis remains a natural wonder, bridging ancient traditions with modern science and providing a versatile tool for both healing and joy

"The illegality of cannabis is outrageous, an impediment to full utilisation of a drug which helps produce the serenity and insight, sensitivity, and fellowship so desperately needed in this increasingly mad and dangerous world."

– Carl Sagan

Cannabis in Modern Society

Social Impact and Role of Cannabis in Modern Social Settings and its Legalization Movement

Cannabis has undergone a remarkable transformation in modern society, shifting from a taboo subject to a widely accepted aspect of contemporary life. It has become a significant cultural and social phenomenon in modern society. This shift is mainly due to changing attitudes and the legalisation movement that has swept across various regions, fundamentally altering the social landscape. It has gained acceptance and is a part of everyday conversations, social gatherings, and even wellness routines. In the past, cannabis was often stigmatised and associated with counterculture movements and illicit activities. However, as scientific research began to uncover its potential benefits and they started getting published, public perception began to shift. Today, cannabis is embraced by many as a legitimate option for relaxation, socialisation, and therapeutic use. This change is evident in the growing number of social settings where cannabis is accepted, from casual gatherings to organised events.

Modern Social Settings

The most significant aspect of cannabis acceptance in modern social settings is the rise of cannabis lounges and cafes, which provide a regulated and safe environment for people to consume cannabis socially, much like bars do for alcohol. A variety of cannabis products, including edibles, beverages, and smokables, catering to diverse preferences can be ordered and consumed here. These venues foster a sense of community, where individuals can connect, learn, share experiences, and enjoy cannabis responsibly in a communal atmosphere.

Cannabis also plays a role in more private gatherings. Whether it's a dinner party, a movie night, or a chill evening with friends, sharing a joint or some edibles has become a social ritual akin to sharing a bottle of wine. This integration into the social fabric is driven by its capacity to enhance mood, stimulate conversation, and deepen connections among users. It is usual for Cannabis to be openly discussed on platforms such as social media and mainstream media. Celebrities, influencers, and public figures advocating for cannabis use have contributed towards reducing stigma and fostering a more accepting view of this fantastic plant.

The legalisation movement has been a driving force behind this social acceptance. Countries and states that have legalised cannabis for recreational use have seen a surge in cannabis-related events, from music festivals to educational workshops. These events not only celebrate cannabis culture but also promote responsible use and educate the public on cannabis and the risks or benefits associated with its use.

Legalisation Movement - Advocates have campaigned relentlessly through the 20th and early 21st centuries for decriminalisation and legalisation of cannabis, arguing for its medicinal benefits, economic potential, and the social injustices of prohibition. This has been the cornerstone for the re-emergence of cannabis in modern society.

Several countries, such as Canada and Uruguay, have fully legalised cannabis for both medical and recreational use, setting precedents and creating regulatory frameworks that others look to. In the United States, an increasing number of states have legalised cannabis for recreational use, with many more allowing medical cannabis.

Legalisation has spurred widespread transparency in national conversation around cannabis policy, public health, and criminal justice reform. It has led to significant changes in public perception and acceptance, with many viewings' cannabis use as a standard and cool practice. The movement continues to gain momentum, promising further expansion of legality and social acceptance in the future.

The Economic Significance of the Cannabis Industry

The economic impact of the cannabis industry is profound and multifaceted, spanning job creation, tax revenue, and secondary market opportunities. Transitioning from an illicit market to a legalised and regulated industry has unlocked significant economic potential, benefiting various stakeholders. Today, there is an open, lucrative market that spans cultivation, production, distribution, and retail. This burgeoning industry has created numerous job opportunities and generated significant tax revenue for governments.

Cannabis is now legal In states like Colorado and California, where this industry has substantially contributed to the economy. Cannabis businesses, from small-scale growers to large dispensaries, have flourished, revitalising communities and driving economic growth. Jobs in various sectors, including agriculture, manufacturing, retail, and marketing, are available, and there is a massive spurt in the development of ancillary businesses, such as packaging, security, and technology solutions.

Job Creation - The cannabis sector has become a significant employment driver, offering diverse job opportunities from cultivation and processing to retail and ancillary businesses. In cannabis-legalised states, it is common to see job postings for budtenders, growers, extraction technicians, compliance officers, and marketing professionals, among others. This job creation is not limited to direct employment only. Secondary markets, including packaging, security, and technology services, are thriving, generating additional employment opportunities and supporting diverse sectors.

Tax Revenue - The tax revenue generated from cannabis sales is another critical economic benefit. Governments have used and are utilising this revenue to fund public services, including education, healthcare, and infrastructure projects. In somc cases, the additional funds have helped address budget deficits and support community programs.

The vast potential for innovation and research has seen advancements in this industry's cultivation techniques, product development, and medical applications. Companies are investing in research to explore new uses for cannabis, from pharmaceuticals to sustainable materials, further expanding the plant's economic potential. The considerable tax revenue generated from cannabis sales is also encouraging other states and countries to consider legalisation to boost their economies and fund public initiatives.

Business Opportunities - The shift from a black-market economy to a regulated, legitimate industry has opened the door for transparent business practices and quality standards. The cannabis industry has become an attractive investment opportunity, with entrepreneurs launching a variety of cannabis-related businesses, from dispensaries to wellness products and tech startups specialising in cannabis cultivation and distribution technologies. Moreover, this industry supports and promotes small businesses and craft growers, encouraging innovation and local economic development.

The stock market has seen the emergence of cannabis-focused companies, offering investors new avenues for portfolio diversification as venture capitalists and private equity firms have surged in investment.

A Memorable Event Centred Around Cannabis

A few summers ago, I attended a cannabis-themed music festival in the heart of Colorado, one of the pioneering states in cannabis legalisation in the US. The festival, known as "Canna-Fest," was a retreat designed to promote wellness and community. It combined the relaxing effects of cannabis with activities such as yoga, meditation, and nature hikes in a vibrant celebration of cannabis culture, drawing people from all walks of life.

Upon arrival, I was struck by the serene setting — nestled in a beautiful valley, the retreat centre offered stunning views, clean mountain air, and a sense of tranquillity that was perfect for unwinding. Participants were of diverse backgrounds, all united by a shared appreciation for the benefits of cannabis. On entering the festival grounds, I was assailed with the fragrant aroma of cannabis, mingling with the sounds of live music and laughter. Food trucks lined the perimeter, offering a variety of cannabis-infused treats, from gourmet edibles to refreshing CBD beverages. The atmosphere was electric, charged with a sense of freedom and camaraderie.

As I wandered through the festival, I met a group of friends who had travelled from different parts of the country to reunite and celebrate their shared love for cannabis. They invited me to join their circle, and we spent the afternoon enjoying the music, sharing stories, and sampling various cannabis products. The festival featured educational workshops, where experts discussed topics like responsible consumption, the benefits of CBD, and the future of cannabis legislation.

One memorable moment was when we attended a "cannabis pairing" session, where a knowledgeable guide introduced us to different strains of cannabis and explained how they complemented various foods and activities. We learned about the nuances of terpenes and cannabinoids, gaining a deeper appreciation for the plant's complexity.

The festival transformed into a dazzling display of lights and sounds as the sun set. The evening began with the group gathering around a communal fire pit. As darkness descended, we passed around a beautifully crafted hookah filled with a mild cannabis blend. The atmosphere was warm and welcoming, with people mingling freely and conversing seamlessly. Stories of healing, creativity, connection, laughter, and friendly debates filled the air as cannabis helped break down social barriers and fostered a sense of unity, illustrating the profound role cannabis plays in promoting relationships and enhancing well-being.

After the communal smoke, we moved to an open-air pavilion for a guided meditation session. The gentle guidance of the instructor, combined with the calming effects of cannabis, created a sublime sense of relaxation and mindfulness. It felt as if time slowed down, allowing each of us to be fully present and connected with ourselves and each other. One experience that a woman named Sarah shared, wherein she narrated how she was using cannabis to manage her chronic pain from an old injury, struck a deep chord in me. She spoke about how discovering cannabis had been life-changing, allowing her to reduce her dependence on prescription painkillers and improve her quality of life. Her story was echoed by others dealing with various health issues, highlighting this plant's diverse therapeutic potential.

The evening progressed with a delicious, cannabis-infused dinner prepared by a local chef. Each dish was thoughtfully crafted to enhance the dining experience without overpowering the senses. As we enjoyed our meal, the conversation turned introspective, with participants sharing their personal journeys with cannabis and its impact on their lives.

This festival was a testament to how cannabis unites people, creating a sense of community and shared purpose. It highlighted the evolving role of cannabis in modern society, where it is not only accepted but celebrated for its ability to enrich social experiences and promote relaxation.

The legalisation movement has paved the way for greater acceptance and integration of cannabis into everyday life. Cannabis's role in modern society is dynamic and multifaceted, impacting social norms, economic landscapes, and personal lives. As it continues to be integrated into our daily lives, its ability to connect, heal, and inspire remains evident, and it has firmly established itself in modern society, transforming social norms and making significant economic contributions. Whether through social gatherings, economic opportunities, or personal experiences, cannabis continues to shape and enhance our contemporary world

"The biggest killer on the planet is stress, and I still think the best medicine is and always has been cannabis."

– Willie Nelson

The Intersection of Beer and Weed

Cultural Comparisons: The Roles of Beer and Weed Across Societies

Beer and weed have been integral parts of human culture, intertwined within the fabric of society in different regions, each playing a unique role therein around the world. While both substances have ancient origins, their cultural significance varies significantly across various regions and historical periods. They have served different purposes and held different places in the cultural landscape.

Beer has been a staple of human civilisation and social life in many cultures for millennia. Ancient civilisations like the Sumerians and Egyptians brewed beer, which was not only a dietary staple but also a significant part of their religious and social rituals. Considered a gift from the gods, beer was used in offerings and consumed during sacred ceremonies, underscoring the drink's dual role in both secular and sacred realms. As civilisations evolved, so did beer's role, becoming a central feature of social gatherings, feasts, and celebrations. In medieval Europe, monasteries became centres of brewing excellence, producing beer that was both a source of nourishment and a means of generating income. It was often considered safer to drink beer than water, and it became a daily staple for people of all ages. Today, beer is synonymous with social gatherings, celebrations, and communal experiences worldwide.

In modern times, beer culture has flourished globally. In Germany, beer is more than just a drink—it is a national treasure and a social institution. Beer gardens and festivals like Oktoberfest celebrate the country's long-standing brewing traditions and showcase the communal aspect of beer culture. Sharing a stein of beer in a beer garden under the chestnut trees is an experience deeply rooted in German social life, embodying a sense of camaraderie and community.

In the United States, craft beer has sparked a renaissance, with microbreweries and brewpubs creating unique and innovative brews that draw enthusiasts from all walks of life. Craft breweries have become community hubs where beer enthusiasts gather for tastings, tours, and social events. These spaces foster a sense of belonging and shared passion, turning the simple act of drinking beer into a communal experience. Similarly, Belgium treats beer almost as a way of life, with a diverse range of styles that reflect the country's regions and heritage. Trappist beers, brewed by monks within monastic communities, are revered for their quality and craftsmanship. Belgium's beer culture is a blend of tradition, innovation, and social camaraderie, where each beer tells a story of the land and the people who crafted it.

Weed, or cannabis, has a similarly ancient history but has experienced a more tumultuous journey through cultural acceptance. It has had a checkered and varied role across different cultures and eras, often entwined with spiritual, medicinal, and recreational use. In ancient China and India, cannabis was used for medicinal and spiritual purposes. It has been an integral part of Ayurvedic medicine and is believed to have healing properties. Cannabis was also used in religious rituals and ceremonies, particularly in Hinduism, where it was associated with the Hindu God 'Lord Shiva'.

As cannabis spread across the globe, it became intertwined with various cultural practices. It was used in Sufi rituals in the Middle East to enhance spiritual experiences. In Africa, cannabis was used by different tribes for medicinal and ceremonial purposes. In Jamaica, cannabis, known as "ganja," is an essential element of Rastafarian culture. It is used as a sacrament to facilitate religious and spiritual practices, fostering a sense of peace, enlightenment, and communal bond. Reggae music, popularised by artists like Bob Marley, has been significant in spreading this cultural association worldwide, symbolising cannabis's spiritual and cultural importance. However, with the advent of modern drug policies in the 20th century, cannabis faced severe stigmatisation and legal challenges, particularly in the Western world. The counterculture movement of the 1960s in the United States, notably, witnessed cannabis as a symbol of rebellion, freedom, and peace. While cannabis use faced significant stigma and legal challenges, it also became associated with creativity, art, and music during this era.

Today, cannabis is experiencing a cultural renaissance similar to beer. The legalisation movement has led to widespread acceptance and integration of cannabis into modern life, making it a mainstream phenomenon. Countries and states that have legalised cannabis for recreational use have seen the emergence of cannabis lounges, with cannabis dispensaries offering a variety of products catering to different needs, cannabis festivals, and tourism. Cannabis culture is now celebrated openly, with events like the Cannabis Cup in Amsterdam and 4/20 celebrations in the United States drawing large crowds.

Interestingly, there are places where beer and cannabis cultures converge. In Amsterdam, for example, the iconic "coffeeshops" offer an environment where patrons can enjoy cannabis in a social setting, often alongside a good beer. These spaces highlight a harmonious blend of both cultures, promoting relaxation, social interaction, and enjoyment, showing that these two substances can coexist and enhance social experiences in complementary ways.

Health Comparisons – Impacts and Benefits of Beer and Cannabis

The health impacts of beer and cannabis are subjects of ongoing research and debate, with each substance having its own set of benefits and risks, often dependent on the mode and moderation of use. When consumed in moderation, beer has been linked to certain health benefits. Studies suggest that the risk of cardiovascular diseases can be reduced by moderate beer consumption due to the presence of antioxidants like polyphenols. Beer also contains dietary silicon, which is beneficial for bone health, as silicon is involved in forming and maintaining bones, potentially reducing the risk of osteoporosis; it is a source of essential nutrients such as vitamins B2 and B3 and minerals like magnesium and potassium. There is enough evidence suggesting beer reduces the risk of developing kidney stones. However, excessive consumption of beer poses significant health risks, including liver disease, obesity, and an increased risk of certain cancers. Alcohol dependence and addiction are serious issues associated with heavy drinking. However, excessive beer consumption carries significant health risks. Liver diseases can develop due to chronic heavy drinking and lead to fatty liver, hepatitis, and cirrhosis. The potential for alcohol dependence and addiction is a severe issue that can result in a myriad of social and health problems. While moderate consumption may be beneficial, the risk of hypertension, stroke, and heart disease increases due to heavy drinking. Beer is also calorically dense, and overconsumption can contribute to weight gain and obesity, compounding other health issues.

Cannabis, on the other hand, is often touted for its medicinal properties but comes with its set of risks, mainly when overused or misused. Cannabinoids like THC and CBD are known to provide relief from chronic pain, inflammation, and conditions such as arthritis, fibromyalgia, anxiety and depression. Cannabis is also used to alleviate neurological disorders symptoms such as multiple sclerosis and epilepsy (even those resistant to conventional treatments), leading to FDA-approved medications like Epidiolex. Cannabinoids possess anti-inflammatory properties, which can help manage conditions like Crohn's disease and multiple sclerosis. Cannabis also exhibits neuroprotective effects that may benefit neurodegenerative diseases such as Parkinson's and Alzheimer's.

Unlike alcohol, cannabis is not physically addictive, and its overdose potential is meagre. However, high doses of THC can exacerbate anxiety, paranoia, and, in some cases, psychotic symptoms, particularly in individuals predisposed to mental health disorders. Long-term, heavy use of cannabis, especially starting at a young age, can affect cognitive function, memory, and attention span. Excessive use can lead to dependency and mental health issues such as anxiety and depression. Smoking cannabis also carries respiratory risks, similar to smoking tobacco, although vaporising and edibles are alternatives that mitigate this risk.

Comparing the two, cannabis is generally considered to have a better safety profile than alcohol. While both substances have potential benefits when used responsibly, they also carry risks that must be managed. The choice between beer and cannabis is a personal preference and individual health considerations.

Personal Reflections On Similarities And Differences On My Experiences With Beer and Cannabis

Throughout my life, my experiences with both beer and cannabis have offered unique insights and memories, each enriching my world in distinct ways.

My journey with beer began in college, a rite of passage into adulthood, marked by social gatherings, sporting events, and the camaraderie of sharing a cold one with friends. Beer became a way to relax after a long week of classes, a social glue that brought people together in communal enjoyment. The clinking of bottles, the shared laughter, and the sense of belonging that came with these gatherings showed me how beer could enhance social bonds and create lasting memories.

On the other hand, my first experience with cannabis was markedly different from beer, and my journey with cannabis began in a much more subdued setting. A close friend introduced me to cannabis during a quiet evening at his home. The process was ritualistic; he carefully ground the cannabis, rolled it into a joint, and we shared it while discussing life, dreams, and everything in between. The experience was introspective and enlightening, providing a different kind of relaxation and connection. The laughter was more resounding, the conversations more profound, and there was a noticeable shift from the outward boisterousness often associated with beer to a more mellow, reflective state. Cannabis became associated with creativity, deep conversations, and a sense of calm that was different from the social buzz of beer, offering a new dimension to social experiences, one where the focus was on deeper connections and personal insights.

Travelling to Germany for Oktoberfest was a dream come true for a beer enthusiast like me. The festival was a spectacular explosion of culture, tradition, and community. Thousands of people from around the world gathered to celebrate, sing, and enjoy beer. I was struck by how ingrained beer was in the local culture, not just as a beverage but as a symbol of hospitality and celebration. The communal tables, the lively music, and the shared steins created an atmosphere of unparalleled joy and unity.

On the other hand, my trip to Amsterdam revealed a whole new side of cannabis culture. Visiting a well-known coffee shop, I experienced the laid-back environment where people from various backgrounds enjoyed cannabis openly without stigma. The atmosphere was relaxed and socially engaging but in a different, more subdued way compared to the lively beer halls of Oktoberfest. The coffee shop experience highlighted how cannabis could foster a sense of community and relaxation, starkly contrasting the energetic beer festivals.

Moderation has always been vital in my approach to both beer and cannabis. I appreciate a well-crafted beer for its flavours, its craftsmanship, and the social experiences it fosters. However, I am conscious of the need to manage my consumption to avoid the health risks associated with excessive drinking. Beer remains a central part of social life, a way to connect with others and enjoy the shared experiences that come with it. On the other hand, CBD has become a part of my wellness routine. I've found that it helps with anxiety and aids in relaxation without the hangover associated with alcohol. Using cannabis mindfully has opened the door to exploring its many health benefits, from improving sleep to managing minor aches and pains. It has provided a way to unwind and enhance my well-being, complementing beer's social and joyful aspects.

Reflecting on my experiences, the similarities and differences between beer and cannabis become apparent. Both have the power to bring people together, enhance social experiences, and offer therapeutic benefits. Each has its own set of risks and rewards, and understanding these can help guide responsible and enjoyable use. Whether it's the communal bonding over a pint of beer or the introspective relaxation brought by cannabis, both substances have enriched my life in different ways, leaving an indelible mark on my personal journey in life. Each has a rich history and a significant place in modern society, influencing how we socialise, celebrate, and heal.

"Why is marijuana against the law? It grows naturally upon our planet. Doesn't the idea of making nature against the law seem to you a bit... unnatural?"

– Bill Hicks

Legal and Social Challenges

Legal Landscape - The Challenges and Regulatory Differences Between Beer and Cannabis

The legal landscape for beer and cannabis is a labyrinthine web of regulations that vary significantly across jurisdictions shaped by historical, cultural, and political factors. While beer has long been a legally accepted part of many societies, cannabis has faced significant legal challenges and disparities in its acceptance. Understanding these regulatory differences and challenges is crucial for appreciating the unique legal status and societal perceptions of these substances.

Beer - The legal history of beer is rooted in centuries-old traditions and regulations, with beer production, sale, and consumption being subject to legal regulation for centuries to ensure quality, safety, and tax revenue. The oldest recorded beer regulation is the Bavarian Purity Law of 1516. This stated that beer could only be made from barley, hops, and water. This law aimed to protect consumers from substandard products and has influenced brewing standards globally. Most countries have established legal drinking ages, licensing requirements for production and sale, and regulations regarding advertising and consumption. For instance, in the United States, the Federal Alcohol Administration Act governs the production and distribution of alcoholic beverages, including beer. States have their own regulations, often reflecting local values and concerns. Legal drinking ages vary globally, with many countries setting the age at 18 or 21.

Despite its widespread acceptance, beer has faced legal challenges, too. In the United States, the legal journey of beer has been very tumultuous. The early 20th century saw the enactment of Prohibition (1920-1933), which banned the production, sale, and consumption of alcoholic beverages—this period had a profound impact on the beer industry, fuelling organised crime, which resulted in a rise of underground illegal brewing/production, distribution and speakeasies. The decision to prohibit it and its negative results eventually led to its repeal, highlighting the difficulties of enforcing such bans. The 21st Amendment in 1933 marked a significant shift, allowing for the resurgence of the beer industry and establishing regulatory frameworks to govern its production and sale.

The craft beer movement, while celebrated, also faces its own set of regulatory hurdles, from complex licensing processes to compliance with strict health and safety standards. Today, the legal landscape for beer in the U.S. is governed by a combination of federal, state, and local laws, navigating the dynamic landscape of health regulations, advertising restrictions, and taxes. The production, distribution, and labelling of beer at the federal level is regulated by the Alcohol, Tobacco Tax and Trade (ATT) Bureau. At the same time, states have their own specific regulations regarding age restrictions, licensing, and sales practices. Despite these regulations, beer enjoys widespread acceptance and is readily available in most regions, reflecting its deeply ingrained cultural status.

Cannabis: The legal status of cannabis is far more complex and contentious, and it has faced a more tumultuous legal journey historically. Cannabis has been utilised for medicinal, spiritual, and recreational purposes across various cultures, dating back thousands of years. Still, the past century saw a global shift towards criminalisation of its production and use, driven by political, racial, and economic factors. In the United States, the Marihuana Tax Act of 1937 effectively banned cannabis's use and sale by imposing heavy taxes and restrictions on its sale and use, thereby setting the stage for decades of stringent laws and heavy penalties.

The global prohibition of cannabis was further solidified by the 1961 United Nations Sole Convention on Narcotic Drugs. In this convention cannabis was classified as a Schedule I substance, indicating it had a high potential for abuse with no accepted medical usage. This classification influenced national drug policies worldwide, leading to harsh penalties for cannabis possession, cultivation, and distribution and had been a significant barrier to research and reform.

However, the past few decades (the late 20th and early 21st centuries) have seen significant changes in attitudes and laws regarding cannabis. The legalisation movement gained momentum with the recognition of cannabis's medicinal benefits and the growing public support for its decriminalisation. Several countries, such as Canada and Uruguay, have fully legalised cannabis for both medical and recreational use. In the United States, a growing number of states have legalised medical cannabis, recreational cannabis, or both, while numerous U.S. states have enacted laws permitting medical and/or recreational cannabis. Despite advancements made, cannabis remains illegal at the federal level in the US, creating a patchwork of regulations that can be confusing and contradictory. This legal ambiguity poses significant challenges for individuals and businesses, particularly in fields like banking, taxation, and interstate commerce. This ongoing conflict between state and federal laws highlights the complexities and uncertainties surrounding cannabis legalisation.

"Beer quenches the thirst, while cannabis soothes the mind; both unite in moments of shared joy."

– Unknown

The Future of Beer and Weed

Emerging Trends and Innovations in the Beer and Cannabis Industries - The beer industry continuously evolves. It continues to thrive, driven by innovation, consumer preferences, demand for diversity, quality and advancements in brewing technology. A few key trends and innovations which are shaping the beer landscape as we look towards the future are:-

Craft Beer Renaissance: One of the most significant developments is the craft beer renaissance. The craft beer movement, which began in the late 20th century, shows no signs of slowing down. Breweries are experimenting with unique ingredients, pushing the boundaries of traditional brewing and flavour profiles as they proliferate. They offer unique and diverse beer styles catering to a wide range of tastes. From sour ales aged in wine barrels to beers brewed with exotic fruits, spices, and herbs, the creativity within the craft beer community is limitless. These small, independent breweries focus on quality, creativity, and local ingredients, fostering a strong sense of community and authenticity.

Sustainability Initiatives: Environmental consciousness is influencing brewing practices. A significant trend in the beer industry is its shift towards sustainability and environmental responsibility. As environmental consciousness grows, breweries are being forced to adopt practices which are sustainable to reduce their ecological footprint. Innovations include water conservation, energy-efficient brewing processes, repurposing spent grains for animal feed or compost, and using renewable energy sources. Breweries are also exploring eco-friendly packaging options, such as biodegradable cans and bottles, to minimise environmental impact.

Low and No-Alcohol Beers: As health consciousness grows, so does the trend towards low and non-alcoholic beers. These beverages offer the complexity and flavour of traditional beer without the intoxicating effects. Advances in brewing technology have made it possible to produce non-alcoholic beers that rival their alcoholic counterparts in taste.

Technological Advancements:
Technological advancements are also revolutionising the brewing process. Automation and precision brewing systems allow for greater consistency and efficiency, enabling brewers to

experiment with new ingredients and techniques. Advanced fermentation control and digital supply chain management optimise efficiency and consistency. Data analytics and artificial intelligence are also utilised to optimise brewing operations and enhance product quality, helping them more precisely predict and tailor flavour profiles. These technological innovations are aiding breweries in producing better beer while reducing waste and improving sustainability.

Health-conscious consumers are also driving changes in the beer industry. With growing focus on health and wellness breweries are developing beers that cater to health-conscious consumers. Low-alcohol and non-alcoholic beers are gaining popularity, offering flavourful alternatives without intoxication. In addition, Functional beers infused with ingredients like probiotics, vitamins, and adaptogens are also emerging, promoting wellness and enjoyment. These health-conscious brews are helping to redefine beer as a part of a balanced and healthy lifestyle.

Cannabis-Infused Beers: Cannabidiol (CBD) and tetrahydrocannabinol (THC)-infused beers are merging the worlds of beer and cannabis. A unique experience is provided by these products blending the effects of cannabis with beer. As cannabis legalisation spreads, cannabis-infused beverages are set to become a significant market segment.

Cannabis - Trends and Innovations

The cannabis industry is also equally dynamic, experiencing rapid growth and transformation, driven by legalisation and medical research, with significant innovations transforming how cannabis is grown, processed, and consumed, along with changing societal attitudes. The industry is becoming highly regulated and standardised as more countries and states legalise cannabis for medical and recreational use. This trend is promoting safety, quality, and consumer trust while also paving the way for broader acceptance and normalisation of cannabis use.

Advanced Cultivation Techniques—Indoor cultivation technology advances rapidly, allowing for precise control over growing conditions. Genetic research is also crucial in developing strains with specific cannabinoid and terpene profiles using vertical farming, hydroponics, and aeroponics techniques, which maximize space and resource efficiency.

Product Diversification - The variety of cannabis products available to consumers has expanded beyond traditional flowers and edibles to include tinctures, topicals, capsules, and innovative delivery methods such as vape pens, transdermal patches, concentrates, and beverages. Customisable experiences, such as tailored cannabinoid profiles and precise dosing, are becoming more accessible, allowing users to find the perfect product for their needs. This product diversity is helping to make cannabis more approachable and user-friendly for a broader audience, as they can provide options to cater to different preferences and medical needs.

Cannabis Wellness Products - The intersection of cannabis and wellness is a burgeoning trend. Current research in the field of medical benefits of cannabis is uncovering new therapeutic applications, such as CBD-infused skincare, bath bombs, and wellness drinks. These are gaining popularity as innovations in extraction techniques and cannabinoid formulations lead to effective and targeted treatments for ailments such as chronic pain, epilepsy, and anxiety. The development of pharmaceutical-grade cannabis products is bridging the gap between traditional medicine and their ability to induce relaxation, lower stress, and promote overall well-being, thus providing alternative therapies as well as offering new options for patients seeking relief.

Microdosing: Microdosing involves consuming tiny amounts of THC to achieve subtle effects without intoxication. This practice is appealing to users seeking the therapeutic benefits of cannabis, such as enhanced creativity and focus, without the high. Microdosed edibles and tinctures are also becoming increasingly available.

Cannabis Tourism: Regions where cannabis is legal are experiencing a boom in cannabis tourism. Tourists are flocking to these destinations for cannabis-friendly experiences, including dispensary tours, cannabis-infused dining, and wellness retreats. This trend is creating new opportunities for the hospitality and tourism industries.

Potential Future Cultural Shifts Regarding Beer and Cannabis - As both industries evolve, so do the cultural perceptions and societal roles of beer and cannabis. Beer has long been a staple in many cultures, associated with social gatherings, celebrations, and leisure. However, cultural perceptions of beer are continually evolving, influenced by health trends, generational preferences, and societal changes. As awareness of the health impacts of alcohol consumption grows, there is a cultural shift towards moderation and responsible drinking. This trend is reflected in the rise of low-alcohol and non-alcoholic beers, as well as the promotion of mindful drinking practices. The beer industry is adapting to these changes by offering healthier alternatives and promoting responsible consumption.

Inclusivity and representation are also becoming more important in the beer industry. Efforts to address the historical underrepresentation of women, people of colour, and LGBTQ+ individuals are gaining momentum. Breweries are championing diversity and inclusion through initiatives, collaborations, and marketing campaigns, reflecting the broader societal push for equality and representation. These efforts are helping in creating a more inclusive and welcoming beer culture for everyone.

Modern consumers seek diverse and unique flavour experiences, driving breweries to experiment with new ingredients and brewing techniques. The cultural appreciation for craft beer fosters a deeper connection between consumers and brewers, emphasising the artistry and craftsmanship behind each brew. This shift towards diverse flavours and experiences is helping to elevate beer as a sophisticated and enjoyable beverage.

Evolving Perceptions, Normalization and Acceptance is a potential cultural shift we are likely to witness as regards cannabis in the coming years, as the stigma surrounding it is diminishing, much like the acceptance that beer gained post-prohibition. Cannabis is undergoing a significant cultural transformation, moving from a stigmatised substance to a widely accepted and celebrated plant. This shift is driven by changing laws, increased education, and evolving societal attitudes. As cannabis legalisation expands, with increased education and awareness of cannabis's benefits, it is becoming normalised and getting integrated into daily life and mainstream culture. We may soon see cannabis' use in normalised social settings, similar to how having a beer at a social gathering is currently accepted.

This shift is reflected in the proliferation of cannabis-friendly events, social clubs, and consumption lounges. The portrayal of cannabis in media and entertainment is also evolving, moving away from negative stereotypes and towards more accurate and positive representations.

While cannabis has historically been associated with younger generations, there is growing acceptance and use among older adults. This intergenerational acceptance is driven by increased education about the medical benefits of cannabis and the desire for alternative treatments for age-related conditions. The cannabis industry is responding by developing products and marketing strategies that cater to older consumers. This trend is helping to normalise the use of cannabis across all age groups.

Holistic Health and Wellness - Both beer and cannabis are finding their place within the holistic health and wellness movement. Craft beers with low ABV (Alcohol by Volume) and health benefits, such as antioxidant properties, resonate with health-conscious consumers. Meanwhile, cannabis, particularly CBD products, is being embraced for its inherent qualities in lowering stress, improving sleep, and managing pain and is being adopted as a part of a holistic wellness lifestyle worldwide. Consumers are using cannabis to enhance their physical and mental well-being, incorporating it into practices such as yoga, meditation, and fitness. This trend is fostering a cultural acceptance of cannabis as a tool for self-care and personal growth. This alignment with wellness trends is likely to grow, reshaping the industry's role in enhancing quality of life while helping to change perceptions and reduce the stigma attached to its use.

Social and Legal Harmonisation—As cannabis legalisation progresses globally, regulations between beer and cannabis will be harmonised. Legal frameworks will evolve to treat both substances similarly, with standardised production, sale, and consumption regulations. This would likely include coordinated public health campaigns promoting responsible use and highlighting potential risks.

Cultural Celebrations and Integration - Cannabis may become more integrated into cultural celebrations and traditions, much like beer festivals. We might see the emergence of cannabis-themed events akin to Oktoberfest, where communities gather to celebrate cannabis culture. Additionally, we could witness the blending of beer and cannabis cultures at events that feature both substances in a controlled and enjoyable environment.

Empowering Informed Choices - As we look towards the future of beer and cannabis, it is essential to encourage and foster informed, responsible perceptions and choices. The evolving landscapes of these industries offer opportunities for personal growth, community connection, and cultural enrichment. Both substances provide unique benefits and experiences but also carry potential risks. The key is to understand and appreciate each within moderation, education, and personal responsibility. By embracing innovation, sustainability, and inclusivity, we can foster a deeper appreciation for beer and cannabis and their roles in our lives. Beer and cannabis have the power to bring people together, enhance social experiences, and contribute to individual well-being. Whether you enjoy a craft beer at the local brewery or use cannabis for medicinal purposes, the emphasis should be on quality, mindfulness, and respect for oneself and others.

Education is a powerful tool for fostering informed choices; hence, educating ourselves and others about the benefits and risks of beer and cannabis is vital. By keeping up-to-date with the latest research, trends, and regulations, we, as consumers, can make decisions and align them with our values and health goals. Public awareness campaigns, educational initiatives such as community workshops, and advertisements can help dispel myths and reduce stigma, promoting a more nuanced understanding of beer and cannabis. Also, by fostering informed choices, we can enjoy these substances responsibly, ensuring that they continue to enrich our lives in positive ways.

Responsible consumption is the key towards enjoying the benefits of beer and cannabis while minimising their potential risks. This involves understanding personal limits, choosing quality products, and being mindful of the context and setting of their use. Beer and cannabis can bring people together, fostering a sense of community and connection. Whether through a shared pint at a local brewery or a cannabis-infused yoga class, these substances are able to enhance social interactions and create memorable experiences. Hence, we can promote moderation and mindfulness by using this trait of these substances. We can also build inclusive and supportive communities while strengthening bonds by celebrating the communal aspects of beer and cannabis to create a culture that values and respects the experiences that beer and cannabis offer.

Finally, it is essential to inspire personal reflection on our perceptions and use of beer and cannabis. The future of beer and cannabis is bright, filled with innovation, cultural shifts, and growth opportunities. With education and critically examining our attitudes and behaviours, we can make choices that align with our values and goals. As we navigate this evolving landscape, let us embrace informed and responsible decisions, celebrate diversity and inclusion, and foster a deeper connection with these ancient and transformative substances. By doing so, we can create a more vibrant, educated, and connected world where beer and cannabis are valued for their unique contributions to our lives and cultures, and this reflective practice may lead to a better appreciation for the cultural, social, and personal significance of these substances.

As you journey through life beyond this book, I encourage you to reflect on your perceptions and use of beer and cannabis. Consider the historical, cultural, and personal stories shared here, and think about how these narratives can shape your understanding. Whether you're a seasoned beer enthusiast, a curious cannabis consumer, or someone new to both - approaching these substances with an open mind and a thoughtful perspective can lead to a more fulfilling and responsible experience.

Informed choices pave the way for a future where beer and cannabis coexist harmoniously within our societies. Let's celebrate their diversity, embrace their potential, and cultivate a culture of informed and respectful use. Cheers to the future of beer and cannabis –where tradition and innovation, education and enjoyment, responsibility and relaxation go hand in hand.

Industrial Uses of Cannabis/Hemp

Cannabis, particularly its non-psychoactive variety known as hemp, has been used industrially for thousands of years. Today, hemp and cannabis applications are experiencing a renaissance as innovations and trends drive their integration into numerous industries. This chapter will explore the multifaceted uses of hemp and cannabis in garments, medicines, and wellness, highlighting the latest trends and their expanding influence on these sectors.

Hemp in Garments

Hemp has long been valued for its robust, versatile fibres, making it an excellent textile material. The resurgence of interest in sustainable fashion and eco-friendly materials has brought hemp back into the spotlight, showcasing its numerous benefits over conventional fibres.

Hemp is celebrated for its minimal environmental impact. Unlike cotton, which requires extensive water usage and chemical inputs, hemp thrives with significantly less water and without the need for harmful pesticides or fertilisers. Its deep roots improve soil health by replenishing nutrients, reducing the need for crop rotation, and helping to prevent erosion.

The fibres of the hemp plant produce exceptionally strong and durable textiles. Clothes made from hemp withstand wear and tear better than many other fabrics, yet they also become softer with each wash, proving comfortable for everyday wear. The combination of durability and comfort makes hemp an ideal clothing choice, from casual to workwear.

One notable trend in hemp fashion is its growing presence in high-quality, stylish designs aimed at the eco-conscious consumer. Major fashion brands are incorporating hemp into their collections, while numerous startups are dedicated entirely to hemp fashion. Technological advancements in textile processing have enabled the production of finer, more versatile hemp fabrics suitable for a wide array of clothing styles.

A particularly vivid example of hemp's versatility is its entry into luxury and high-fashion markets. On a visit to a high-end boutique in Paris, I encountered a beautifully crafted hemp-silk blend dress. The designer explained that this blend not only maintained the strength and durability of hemp but also added a luxurious sheen and softness that appealed to upscale consumers. This integration of hemp into luxury fashion underscores how environmentally friendly materials can still exude elegance and sophistication.

Moreover, hemp is making substantial inroads into activewear and outdoor gear markets. Its natural breathability and durability make it a perfect fit for athletic wear and hiking gear. Brands now craft hemp-based athletic wear, hiking attire, and even sneakers. On a recent trek through the Rockies, I wore a hemp-fabric hiking shirt that was both comfortable and resilient, standing up to the rugged terrain and varying weather conditions. This experience highlighted hemp's potential in creating functional, sustainable products for active and adventurous lifestyles.

Circular fashion models are another progressive trend. Some forward-thinking brands are adopting these principles, where hemp-made garments are designed to be recycled or composted at the end of their lifecycle. This innovative approach reduces waste and enhances the sustainability of hemp-based clothing, creating a more environmentally friendly fashion industry.

Hemp and Cannabis in Medicine

Cannabis, particularly cannabinoids like THC and CBD, has received widespread attention for its therapeutic potential. Hemp, high in CBD and low in THC, provides accessible and legally compliant sources for cannabinoid-based treatments, playing a vital role in the medical field.

CBD is being researched extensively for its medicinal properties, offering benefits without THC's psychoactive effects. Approved in various forms, CBD is used for the treatment of ailments such as epilepsy, chronic pain, anxiety, and multiple sclerosis. Its anti-inflammatory, analgesic, and anticonvulsant properties make it a versatile treatment option for numerous medical conditions.

Hemp is now an essential source of cannabinoid medicines, providing a legal and accessible route for producing CBD-based treatments. These medicines come in multiple forms, including tinctures, capsules, topical creams, and edibles. Anecdotes abound of individuals finding profound relief from these treatments. For instance, a friend's father, who had struggled with chronic arthritis pain for years, found significant relief using a CBD lotion. He could engage in daily activities without the debilitating pain that previously limited his mobility. This story and many others like it exemplify the real-world benefits of hemp-derived medicines.

The latest trends in hemp and cannabis medicine include sophisticated cannabinoid formulations designed to target specific medical conditions. Pharmaceutical companies are developing products that combine multiple cannabinoids and terpenes to enhance therapeutic effects through the entourage effect—a phenomenon where these compounds work synergistically for more significant benefits.

Personalised medicine is another exciting trend. Advances in genetic testing and personalised healthcare are allowing for tailored cannabinoid therapies based on an individual's genetic makeup and specific needs. On a visit to a cannabis clinic in California, I met a patient named Jenna, who had undergone genetic testing and received a customised CBD formulation to manage her anxiety. She reported feeling more balanced and in control than ever before, showcasing the potential of personalised cannabinoid therapy.

The market for over-the-counter CBD products, like pain relief creams and wellness supplements, continues to grow. These products bridge the gap between traditional medicine and wellness, providing accessible options for everyday health concerns. CBD-infused products offer natural relief from muscle soreness to stress and appeal to a broad audience.

Additionally, CBD's use in veterinary medicine is rapidly expanding. With products designed to help pets manage anxiety, pain, and inflammation, pet owners are turning to CBD as a natural remedy vis-s-vis conventional medication. My neighbour's anxious dog, Max, became noticeably calmer and happier after being given CBD treats. This transformation highlighted how cannabis's therapeutic potential extends beyond humans to our furry companions.

Hemp and Cannabis in Wellness

The wellness industry has enthusiastically embraced hemp and cannabis, viewing them as natural supplements that can enhance overall health and well-being. From skincare to dietary supplements, hemp and cannabis offer a wide range of benefits.

Rich in fatty acids, vitamins, and antioxidants, hemp seed oil is gaining popularity in skincare products. It is known for its moisturising properties, ability to balance oily skin, and potential to reduce inflammation and redness. On a visit to a wellness spa, I experienced a hemp-infused facial that left my skin feeling nourished and revitalised. The aesthetician explained to me how hemp oil's vitamins and minerals rejuvenate the skin, providing both hydration and healing.

The incorporation of CBD and other cannabinoids into wellness products has surged. Consumers seek out these products for their potential benefits, including stress relief, improved sleep, and enhanced recovery from physical activity. CBD-infused creams and balms are being marketed for soothing muscle aches and joint pain, offering a natural alternative to traditional and conventional pain-relieving medications.

An exciting trend in wellness is the rise of CBD-infused beauty and skincare products. The beauty industry is booming with CBD-infused creams, serums, masks, and balms. These products are marketed for their potential to soothe inflammation, reduce acne, and provide intense hydration. During a tour of a leading cosmetics company, I learned how they incorporate CBD into their formulations to enhance the therapeutic properties of their skincare lines. The attention to detail and dedication to quality in producing these items reflect a significant commitment to integrating cannabis into mainstream wellness.

Functional beverages are another area where CBD is making waves. The rise of CBD-infused teas, sodas, and energy drinks highlights the trend towards incorporating wellness into daily routines. These functional beverages promise to deliver health benefits alongside refreshments, catering to the growing interest in holistic health. I recently tried a CBD-infused sparkling water that promised relaxation without drowsiness, perfect for a midafternoon break. It tasted refreshing and helped alleviate my stress, illustrating the everyday appeal of such products.

The market for CBD edibles and dietary supplements continues to expand. Gummies, chocolates, capsules, and tinctures are popular formats that people incorporate into their daily health regimen. Providing a convenient and tasty product to be procured to consume CBD and support overall well-being, these products are gaining popularity. A friend told me how a daily CBD gummy helped her manage stress and improved her sleep quality, becoming an integral part of her wellness routine.

Holistic wellness retreats incorporating hemp and cannabis into their programs are also gaining popularity. These retreats offer activities like yoga, meditation, and spa treatments, all enhanced by the calming and therapeutic effects of cannabis. Attending a cannabis wellness retreat in Colorado, I experienced how integrating cannabis into a holistic wellness program can create a serene and rejuvenating environment. Participants reported feeling more balanced and connected, both physically and mentally, showcasing the profound impact of holistic cannabis practices.

The industrial uses of cannabis and hemp are vast and continually evolving. In garments, hemp offers sustainability and durability, aligning perfectly with modern environmental concerns and fashion innovation. In medicine, the therapeutic potential of cannabinoids from hemp is opening new horizons for treatment, leading to more personalised and accessible healthcare options. Within the wellness industry, hemp and cannabis are being embraced for their natural benefits, fostering a holistic approach to health that resonates with contemporary consumers.

As society moves forward, the integration of hemp and cannabis into various sectors will likely continue to grow, driven by ongoing research, regulatory changes, and shifting consumer preferences. Their potential to provide eco-friendly solutions, innovative medical treatments, and comprehensive wellness products positions hemp and cannabis as pivotal players in shaping a healthier and more sustainable future.

This chapter highlights how deeply interconnected our lives have become with these plants, not only as sources of leisure and medicine but also as crucial components of industry and innovation. The future of cannabis and hemp is undoubtedly bright, promising continued advancements and an ever-expanding role in enhancing our quality of life.

As you, dear reader, consider the evolving roles of hemp and cannabis, let this chapter inspire you to explore and embrace the many ways these remarkable plants can contribute to a more sustainable, healthy, and balanced life. Whether through the clothing you wear, the medicines you trust, or the wellness practices you adopt, hemp and cannabis offer a wealth of possibilities that reflect our growing understanding and appreciation of nature's gifts.

Latest and Future Trends

Cannabis has long been intertwined with human civilisation, serving various purposes ranging from medicinal to industrial uses, particularly its versatile variety known as hemp, which has been a cornerstone in the production of different commercial and industrial products. Hemp — a non-psychoactive variety of Cannabis sativa—is well-regarded for its versatility and sustainability. From rope and textiles to food, paper, bioplastics, insulation, and biofuel, the applications of hemp are vast and continually expanding. Historically, hemp fibre has been used to make textiles that are 100% hemp. However, it is often mixed with other fibres, such as flax, cotton, silk, virgin and recycled polyester, to produce woven fabrics for apparel and furnishings. The more wooden inner fibres of the hemp plant are utilised in industrial applications like mulch, animal bedding, and litter.

Hemp oil has diverse applications, from manufacturing oil-based paints to acting as a moisturising agent in creams, used for cooking, and even incorporated into plastics. Interestingly, hemp seeds have a history of use in bird feed mixes. A survey in 2003 revealed that over 95% of hemp seed marketed in Europe was used for animal and bird feed.

Today, as environmental consciousness and technological advancements drive innovation, the industrial applications of hemp are experiencing a significant revival. This chapter delves into the latest trends in the industrial use of cannabis and hemp and projects future trends that could shape the industry.

Industrial Uses of Cannabis/Hemp

As we explore this wonderful gift of GOD to humanity, going ahead into the future, we can visualise that cannabis and hemp, with their myriad industrial applications and remarkable sustainability, present exciting possibilities. From textiles to building materials, biofuels to environmental remediation, hemp's versatility and eco-friendly properties are paving the way for innovative solutions to modern challenges.

Embracing these innovations will help us promote ecological health and integrate sustainable practices into everyday life. As we progress in our exploration of unlocking the potential of cannabis and hemp, we move towards a future where these remarkable plants will play a central role in fostering a more sustainable and resilient world.

Hemp in Construction - Building Materials and Sustainability

Hemp's potential as a building material is making waves in the construction industry due to its eco-friendly properties and versatility. One of the most prominent uses is in creating hempcrete, a bio-composite material made by mixing the wooden core of the hemp plant (hemp hurds) with lime. These products, which are hemp-based, offer solutions to several issues facing current building standards, thanks to properties like being lightweight, thermally insulating, breathability, mould and pest resistant, which are ideal for green, sustainable projects. One of the most common applications of hemp-lime in construction is using hemp-hurd and lime mix while wet to cast it around a timber frame with temporary shuttering. Once the blend solidifies, it forms a firm mass that can be plastered with lime plaster. This method showcases

hemp's versatility and emphasises its contribution to sustainable building practices.
During a co-heating test conducted at the National Non-Food Crops Centre (NNFCC) on the Renewable Housing project at the Building Research Establishment (BRE) in the UK, hemp was found to be a more sustainable construction material compared to most traditional methods used today. Its practical use in construction can reduce energy consumption costs and minimise the creation of secondary pollutants. A classic example is 'Hempcrete', which is making waves in the construction industry as it is an attractive alternative to traditional building materials due to the abovementioned properties.

The University of Bath is researching using hemp-lime panel systems for construction. Funded by the European Union, this research tests panel design for their use in high-quality construction, considering factors like on-site assembly, humidity and moisture penetration, temperature changes, daily performance, and energy-saving documentation. This project, focusing on the British, French, and Spanish markets, aims to perfect protocols of use, application, manufacturing, data gathering, market certification, as well as warranty and insurance.

Food and Nutrition

Hemp seeds are incredibly versatile. They can be eaten raw, ground as hemp meal, sprouted, or converted into dried sprout powder, making them a versatile ingredient in the culinary world. These seeds can also be turned into a slurry for baking or beverages such as hemp milk and herbal teas. Cold-pressed hemp oil from the seeds is renowned for its high content of unsaturated fatty acids.
The Department of Food, Environment and Rural Affairs in the UK categorises hemp as a non-food crop. Hemp seeds can be imported with proper licenses and documented proof of less than 0.3% THC concentration for sowing or for sale as a food ingredient. In contrast, the United States has embraced hemp in food products legally, with hemp items typically being sold in health food stores or through mail orders since 2000.

Hemp seeds are nutritional powerhouses. A 100-gram portion of hulled hemp seeds provides 2,451 kilojoules (586 kilocalories) of food energy and includes 5% water, 5% carbohydrates, 49% total fat, and 31% protein. These seeds are notable for their high protein content, offering 64% of the Daily Value (DV) of protein per 100-gram serving. The proteins primarily found in hemp seeds are edestin (83% of the total protein content), albumin (13%), and ß-conglycinin (up to 5%). These highly digestible proteins make hemp seed protein comparable to other protein-rich foods like meat, milk, eggs, and soy.

Interestingly, hemp seeds also provide a rich source of dietary fibre, B vitamins, and essential nutritional minerals such as manganese, phosphorus, magnesium, zinc, and iron. About 73% of the energy in hemp seeds comes from fats and essential fatty acids, predominantly polyunsaturated fatty acids, linoleic, oleic, and alpha-linolenic acids, making hemp seeds a valuable addition to a balanced diet.

Hemp Plastics/Paper

The global movement to reduce plastic waste is helping hemp-based plastics emerge as a sustainable solution. Hemp bioplastics are biodegradable, require less energy to produce than traditional plastics, and do not involve harmful chemicals. Industries ranging from automotive to packaging are exploring hemp-based plastics to reduce their environmental footprint.

Paper, manufactured from the fibrous stalks of the hemp plant, is an eco-friendly alternative to wood-based paper. Hemp yields significantly more pulp per acre than trees and grows much faster, making it a sustainable raw material source for paper production. The shift towards hemp paper is gradually gaining momentum, particularly in speciality paper markets and artisanal products.

Biofuel and Environmental Remediation

The potential of hemp extends into the energy sector, where biofuels such as biodiesel and ethanol are derived from its seeds and stalks. Biodiesel, sometimes called "hempoline," can be produced from hemp oil, while ethanol can be made by fermenting the whole plant. I remember reading about Rudolf Diesel, who invented the diesel engine intending to power it with different fuels, including vegetable and seed oils. Hemp was among those early choices, illustrating its pioneering role in sustainable energy.

Its high cellulose content and fast growth rate make it a viable candidate for biofuel production. Additionally, hemp is showing promise in environmental remediation. Known as phytoremediation, this process uses hemp to clear impurities from wastewater and contaminated soils. For instance, hemp has been employed to clean contaminants at the Chornobyl nuclear disaster site, demonstrating its capability to clear radioisotopes and other toxins from the environment. Its rapid and dense growth also makes hemp an effective crop for weed control, potentially reducing the use of herbicides and benefiting organic farming practices. While still in the early stages of commercial viability, research is ongoing to optimise the process and make hemp biofuels a more sustainable energy source.

Automotive Applications

The automotive industry is exploring hemp composites to manufacture lighter, more fuel-efficient vehicles. Together with other materials, hemp fibres can create solid yet lightweight components, reducing the vehicle's overall weight and improving fuel efficiency. Companies like BMW have already started incorporating hemp into the interior panelling of their cars.

Fabrics, Fiber and Textile Industry

Historically, Hemp fibre has been a stalwart, used extensively for making items ranging from rope to fabrics and industrial materials. Historically, hemp was also used to make sail canvas—an interesting trivia being that the word "canvas" is derived from "cannabis." Today, the texture of pure hemp is comparable to linen. Thanks to its versatility, it is now utilised in various consumer goods, including clothing, shoes, accessories, dog collars, and even homewares, as hemp fabrics are known for their strength, durability, and breathability and are gaining popularity due to their minimal environmental impact compared to conventional fibres like cotton, polyester or rayon.

Occasionally, hemp is mixed with other sustainable fibres like lyocell, further enhancing its appeal in fashion-related industries. I once visited a sustainable fashion expo where a designer showcased a beautiful collection of hemp-linen blend garments. The clothes were stylish and comfortable and represented a significant step towards more sustainable fashion choices. Today, hemp has gained significant applications in clothing, home textiles, and industrial fabrics.

Sustainable Packaging

Hemp-based packaging solutions are on the rise as companies seek sustainable alternatives to traditional materials. Hemp's strength and biodegradability make it an excellent choice for creating durable, eco-friendly packaging. Innovations in this space include hemp-based cartons, bags, and pouches, which are gaining traction in the food and consumer goods industries.

Industrial Hemp Cultivation

The cultivation of industrial hemp is seeing significant innovation with the introduction of new cultivars tailored for specific industrial applications. Advances in breeding techniques are producing hemp strains with optimised fibre content, resin production, and growth cycles, improving yield and quality. Integrating advanced technologies like AI, IoT, and blockchain could further revolutionise hemp farming and production. AI can assist in optimising growing conditions, IoT devices can monitor the crop's health in real-time, and blockchain can ensure transparency and traceability throughout the supply chain. As concerns about soil health and contamination grow, hemp could play a critical role as the leading tool in rehabilitating polluted lands and contributing towards environmental sustainability.

Biodegradable Products

In addition to hemp plastics, therc is a push towards creating a range of hemp-based biodegradable products. From disposable cutlery and straws to agricultural mulch films, hemp-based biodegradables address the environmental concerns of single-use plastics.

Integration of Technology

Integrating advanced technologies like AI, IoT, and blockchain could revolutionise hemp farming and production. AI can optimise growing conditions, IoT devices can monitor crop health in real time, and blockchain can ensure transparency and tracking of the materials throughout their progress in the supply chain.

Hemp and Nanotechnology

An exciting area is the exploration of hemp in nanotechnology, as research into the use of hemp in nanotechnology is poised to unlock new applications. Hemp-based nanomaterials could be used in high-performance materials for electronics, medical devices, and energy storage solutions, offering superior properties over traditional materials and aiding in creating a future where hemp-derived components form the backbone of high-tech innovations, marrying sustainability with cutting-edge technology.

Expansion of Hemp Biofuels

Further, as the demand for renewable energy sources intensifies, the production of hemp biofuels is likely to expand and gain prominence. With continued research and investment, hemp could become a mainstream source of biodiesel and ethanol, helping reduce our reliance on fossil fuels. Hemp's phytoremediation properties also point towards its future role in environmental restoration.

Hemp in Environmental Remediation

Hemp's phytoremediation properties, which allow it to cleanse soil of heavy metals and toxins, are being explored for environmental clean-up projects. As environmental restoration becomes increasingly essential, hemp could be crucial in rehabilitating contaminated lands.

Commercialisation of Hemp-Based Construction Materials

Greater commercialisation of hemp-based construction materials is expected as market acceptance grows. Developing hempcrete and other hemp-based composites for mainstream construction could lead to more sustainable building practices and broader adoption of green building technologies.

Hemp in Energy Storage

Innovative research explores using hemp fibres for energy storage systems, such as batteries and supercapacitors. Hemp-derived Materials may offer better performance and sustainability than current energy storage solutions, paving the way for greener energy technologies.

During a sustainable construction expo visit, I met with a small startup showcasing hempcrete blocks. The founder, an architect passionate about eco-friendly materials, shared how hempcrete's insulating properties had transformed a renovation project. "The client's energy bills dropped significantly, and the house remained cool in the summer and warm in the winter. Hempcrete not only offered a sustainable solution but also added immense value to the property," he explained.

In another instance, a renowned automotive company invited me to tour their innovation lab, where hemp composites were being tested for vehicle interiors. Seeing hemp integrated into sleek, modern car designs was eye-opening. The lead engineer explained, "Hemp reduces the weight of vehicle parts, which improves fuel efficiency without compromising strength. It's part of our commitment to developing greener vehicles."

Similarly, during a hemp innovation summit, I had the opportunity to meet a researcher working on hemp biofuels. She passionately described how hemp's high cellulose content made it a promising candidate for sustainable energy. "The goal is to create a commercially viable hemp biofuel that can compete with traditional fossil fuels in efficiency and cost," she said. "Hemp biofuel has the potential to reduce our carbon footprint significantly."

At a fashion show dedicated to sustainable clothing, I encountered a designer who had created an entire line from hemp fabric. The garments were not only stylish and comfortable but also carried the story of sustainability. "Each piece represents a step towards a greener future," the designer noted. "Using hemp allows us to reduce environmental impact while offering high-quality clothing."

Summarisation

The journey of these remarkable plants from ancient uses to modern innovations reflects their enduring relevance and potential to address contemporary challenges. Embracing hemp and cannabis in industrial applications paves the way for a future that marries sustainability with technological advancement. The industrial uses of cannabis and hemp are vast, varied, and continuously evolving. As we embrace these innovations and trends as they unfold, it is clear that the renaissance of the hemp and cannabis industries is not just a fleeting phenomenon but a sustainable transformation with far-reaching impacts and implications.

Looking to the future, the integration of advanced technologies, the expansion of renewable energy applications, and the commercialisation of hemp-based products will likely shape the industrial landscape as environmental concerns, technological advancements, and consumer preferences drive innovation. Hemp's role in environmental remediation and energy storage points to a greener, more sustainable future, with hemp standing out as a versatile and sustainable resource in varied fields like construction, textiles, biodegradable products and biofuels, showcasing hemp's potential, which is being unlocked in unprecedented ways.

"In a world of constant change, beer and weed remain timeless companions."

– Unknown

My Final Thoughts

Legal Challenges

Beer and cannabis, both widely popular, face distinct legal and economic landscapes that shape their production, distribution, and consumption.

Beer has long enjoyed legal status in most parts of the world, with strict regulations governing its production and sale. Breweries, distributors, and retailers must obtain expensive and difficult-to-acquire licenses in many countries. For instance, in the United States, each state has its own laws regulating the sale and distribution of beer, which can complicate operations for brewers trying to expand their market. Age restrictions are firmly in place, typically requiring consumers to be 18 or 21 years old. These restrictions are enforced through rigorous identification checks and penalties for non-compliance. Furthermore, beer advertising is closely regulated to avoid targeting underage consumers, with specific guidelines on where and how it can be marketed.

Cannabis, on the other hand, faces a more complex legal environment. While some countries and states have legalised its use for medical and recreational purposes, it remains illegal at the federal level in many places. This legal discrepancy creates significant challenges. In the United States, for example, while some states have legalised cannabis, it remains federally illegal, leading to a conflict that affects banking, taxation, and interstate commerce. Cannabis businesses must navigate a labyrinth of licensing requirements and compliance standards, including security measures and product testing, which add to operational costs and complexity. This fragmented legal status also impacts investment and financial transactions, as traditional banking services are often inaccessible to cannabis businesses.

Economic Challenges

The economic challenges faced by the beer and cannabis industries are equally distinct.

Beer markets are highly competitive, with large corporations dominating the industry. This makes it difficult for small craft breweries to compete and gain market share. Beer is also subject to various federal, state, and local taxes, which can significantly impact pricing and profitability. Additionally, the beer industry relies on agricultural products like barley and hops, subject to price fluctuations and supply chain disruptions. For example, climate change has affected hop yields in key producing regions, increasing brewers' costs.

Cannabis faces significant economic hurdles due to its legal status. One of the biggest challenges is the need for access to traditional banking services, forcing businesses to operate on a cash basis, which is risky and cumbersome. The high compliance costs with rigorous regulatory standards, such as mandatory product testing and security measures, further strain financial resources. Additionally, the cannabis industry struggles to attract investment due to legal uncertainties, impacting its ability to raise capital and grow. Despite these challenges, the cannabis industry has shown remarkable resilience and growth potential, driven by increasing legalisation and consumer acceptance.

Social Acceptance

Beer and cannabis both play significant roles in contemporary society, but they do so in different ways and with varying implications.

Beer is deeply ingrained in many cultures worldwide. It is associated with socialising, celebrations, and rituals. From Oktoberfest in Germany to casual pub gatherings, beer is a social lubricant that helps break the ice and facilitate conversation. Its presence in mainstream media, through advertising and popular culture, contributes to its normalisation and acceptance. For instance, beer commercials during major sports events like the Super Bowl are a staple in American culture.

Cannabis, while historically stigmatised, is experiencing a shift in perception, particularly as more places legalise its use. What was once viewed primarily as an illicit drug is now being recognised for its medicinal benefits and potential for responsible recreational use. This changing perception is reflected in the growing number of cannabis-friendly social events and communities, such as cannabis clubs and festivals. Moreover, the legalisation movement is often linked to broader social justice issues, including the disproportionate impact of drug laws on marginalised communities, leading to advocacy and reform efforts aimed at rectifying past injustices.

Social Behaviour and Interaction

Beer plays a pivotal role in social bonding and communal activities. It is a staple at sporting events, barbecues, and parties, where it helps create a convivial atmosphere. Rituals and traditions, such as toasting and beer festivals, further highlight its role in social interaction. For example, the tradition of sharing a round of beers can strengthen friendships and build camaraderie.

Cannabis also facilitates social interactions, particularly within communities with a common interest in its use. Cannabis clubs and events provide spaces for people to connect and share experiences, fostering community and belonging. Despite increasing acceptance, cannabis use can still carry a stigma, affecting how openly individuals discuss and use it in social settings. However, as legalisation spreads and perceptions shift, cannabis is becoming more integrated into social activities, similar to how beer has been for centuries.

Health and Wellness

The health implications of beer and cannabis are complex and multifaceted, with both substances offering potential benefits and risks.

Beer has been studied for its potential health benefits when consumed in moderation. Some research suggests that moderate beer consumption due to its silicon content can reduce the risk of cardiovascular disease and improve bone density. Additionally, beer contains vitamins and minerals such as B vitamins, potassium, and magnesium, contributing to its nutritional value. However, these benefits must be weighed against the presence of alcohol, which can negate positive effects if consumed excessively.

Cannabis is renowned for its medicinal properties. It is used to treat various medical conditions, including chronic pain, epilepsy, multiple sclerosis, and nausea associated with chemotherapy. Cannabinoids like CBD lack the psychoactive effects of THC and are noted for their therapeutic benefits and has shown promise in the treatment of anxiety, depression, and PTSD, although its effects can vary widely among individuals.

Health Risks

Beer consumption, especially in excess, can lead to a range of health issues. These include liver disease, cardiovascular problems, and addiction. Alcohol impairs judgment and coordination, increasing the risk of accidents and injuries. Additionally, beer is high in calories and can lead to weight gain other related health problems such as diabetes and obesity.

Cannabis also carries health risks, particularly when smoked, as it can negatively affect respiratory health, similar to tobacco. However, alternative consumption methods like edibles and vaporisers can mitigate this risk. While cannabis can benefit mental health, it can also exacerbate conditions such as anxiety and schizophrenia in susceptible individuals. The risk of dependency, though generally considered lower than with alcohol, is still present.

Modern-Day Implications

The ongoing legalisation and changing social acceptance of cannabis, alongside the established role of beer, highlight a dynamic interplay of cultural, economic, and health-related factors. Both substances have their place in modern society, but their integration and impact vary significantly. Understanding these nuances gives a more informed perspective on the roles beer and cannabis play in shaping social behaviours, health outcomes, and economic trends. Embracing an informed perspective enables responsible use and a deeper appreciation of their contributions to our lives. Individuals can make more informed and accountable choices by approaching these substances with an open mind and a balanced understanding of their benefits and risks.

"Give me a woman who loves beer, and I will conquer the world."

– Kaiser Wilhelm

"Herb is the healing of a nation; alcohol is the destruction."

– Bob Marley

Conclusion

Embracing Diversity

Throughout this "Man Made Beer - God Made Weed" journey, we've delved into the fascinating histories, cultures, and contemporary landscapes of beer and cannabis. We've explored their origins, tracing beer back to ancient civilisations of Mesopotamia and Egypt and tracked cannabis to its uses in ancient China and India. It is crucial to reflect on the multifaceted roles beer and cannabis play in our lives as we dig into their rich histories, significant cultural impacts, and evolving societal perceptions, as both these substances have profound roots in various cultures, playing pivotal roles in social, medicinal, and spiritual contexts.

We began our journey by exploring beer's ancient origins, its scientific brewing process, and its profound social significance. We traced beer's historical journey from the rudimentary brews of ancient civilisations to the sophisticated craft beers of today. The brewing process revealed itself as a meticulous blend of art and science, an alchemy that transforms simple ingredients into a beverage celebrated across the globe. We also examined beer's role in various cultural settings—from the social glue that binds friendships during casual get-togethers to the centrepiece of grand festivals like Oktoberfest.

Equally compelling is the story of cannabis, a plant that has been intertwined with human culture for thousands of years. Our exploration uncovered cannabis's origins, its biological and chemical properties, and its wide-ranging medicinal uses. Cannabis's role in different cultures, from ancient rituals in India to its modern use in wellness and recreation, highlighted its versatility and enduring significance. The evolution of cannabis from a legal and societal outcast to a widely accepted and celebrated substance underscores the dynamic nature of cultural attitudes and legal frameworks.

In the chapters on modern society, we discussed how beer and cannabis have evolved to fit into today's social settings. Beer remains a central part of celebrations and gatherings, while cannabis is increasingly accepted and integrated into social events, especially in regions where it has been legalised. We've examined the economic impact of both industries, highlighting their substantial contributions to local and global economies. The craft beer revolution has invigorated the beer market, bringing innovation and variety, while the cannabis industry continues to grow, driven by legalisation and medical advancements.

The chapters on science provided insights into the brewing and cultivation processes and the health implications of both substances. We learned about the complexities of brewing beer, from fermentation to flavouring, and the intricate biology of cannabis, including cannabinoids and terpenes. Medical research on cannabis has opened up new possibilities for treatment, while innovations in brewing have led to more sustainable and health-conscious beer options.

In comparing beer and cannabis, we highlighted their unique cultural roles, health benefits, and challenges. Both substances have faced legal and social hurdles, but their growing acceptance signals a shift in societal attitudes. Personal anecdotes and reflections brought these themes to life, showing how beer and cannabis can foster connections, enhance experiences, and contribute to well-being.
Moving to the modern era, we compared the cultural and health impacts of beer and cannabis, reflecting on personal stories that brought these substances to life. Both beer and cannabis have faced legal and social challenges, navigating complex landscapes of regulation and stigma. Yet, they've shown remarkable resilience and adaptability, continually

reinventing themselves in response to changing societal norms and consumer demands.

The future of beer and cannabis looks promising, with trends pointing towards sustainability, innovation, and a greater emphasis on health and wellness. As legalisation continues to spread and societal perceptions evolve, both industries are poised to grow and diversify, offering new and exciting possibilities for consumers.

Understanding and respecting the diverse roles of beer and cannabis in society is crucial. Both substances have shaped and have been shaped in turn by cultural, social, and economic forces. With its centuries-old tradition, Beer has evolved from a staple of ancient civilisations to a symbol of camaraderie and celebration. Beer and cannabis, though distinct in their characteristics and uses, share common threads that weave through the tapestry of human history. Cannabis, once shrouded in stigma, is now being recognised for its medicinal properties and potential to enhance well-being. These are more than mere substances; they are cultural artefacts reflecting our collective journey, creative spirit, and quest for connection and wellness.

The diversity of experiences with beer and cannabis reflects their multifaceted nature. Understanding the diverse roles of beer and cannabis in society encourages us to appreciate their contributions beyond their immediate effects. They are not just beverages or plants; they are cultural artefacts, social catalysts, and, for many, sources of personal enjoyment and relief. With its rich traditions and communal essence, beer and cannabis, with its therapeutic potential and spiritual significance, offer unique ways to enrich our lives. They remind us of the importance of tradition, the power of innovation, and the value of shared experiences.

This diversity underscores the importance of an open-minded approach. By appreciating the historical significance and contemporary relevance of beer and cannabis, we can foster a more inclusive and understanding society. The rich traditions associated with beer are a testament to its deep-rooted place in human society. From ancient Sumerian brews to the modern craft beer movement, beer has continually evolved, mirroring our societal changes. It symbolises celebration and social bonding, a drink that brings people together across cultures and generations. Think of the grand halls of Oktoberfest in Munich, the cosy pubs of Ireland, or the new wave of craft breweries popping up in urban centres worldwide. Each sip of beer carries the essence of centuries of brewing expertise, cultural nuances, and a sense of community that transcends borders.

Cannabis, on the other hand, has walked a more turbulent path. From being revered in ancient rituals to being demonised by 20th-century propaganda, cannabis has always been intertwined with human history. The resurgence of cannabis in modern times, driven by both medical discoveries and changing social attitudes, showcases its resilience and versatility. Traditional ceremonies in India, where bhang is consumed during Holi, illustrate its longstanding cultural significance, while contemporary wellness trends highlight its therapeutic potential. This plant, capable of fostering spiritual enlightenment and physical healing, underscores the interconnectedness of the world's cultures and the evolving perceptions of natural remedies.

Respecting these substances involves recognising their benefits and acknowledging their risks. Advocacy for responsible use, promotion of informed choices, and support for continued research and education are pivotal. This journey of understanding and respect is what ultimately allows us to integrate beer and cannabis into our lives in ways that are both enjoyable and mindful, fostering positive experiences and connections.

As we conclude this journey and exploration, I call you all to action and encourage you, dear reader, to approach the topic of beer and cannabis with an open mind and a curious heart. Recognise the rich histories and cultures that have shaped their use and consider how these substances can fit into a modern context responsibly and respectfully. Challenge preconceived notions and stereotypes and explore the rich history and cultural significance of these substances. Whether you are a seasoned enthusiast, a consumer, a producer, an interested observer, or a novice, there's always more to learn, understand and discover.

Visualise the broader implications of beer and cannabis beyond their immediate consumption. Each glass of beer, each puff of cannabis, carries with it a history, a tradition, and often a story of resilience and innovation. Please think of the countless brewers meticulously refining their craft, ensuring each batch maintains a perfect balance of flavours. Picture the growers and scientists working tirelessly to unlock the medicinal secrets of cannabis, driven by a desire to improve lives. These efforts reflect the passion and dedication embedded in the fabric of these industries.

Our society is at a pivotal point. The public discourse surrounding beer and cannabis is more open and dynamic than ever before. This presents a unique opportunity to reshape narratives and push for policies that promote education, safety, and accessibility. Embrace the diversity of experiences and perspectives surrounding beer and cannabis. Engage in community discussions/conversations, attend events, and explore new products with curiosity and respect. Advocate for sensible regulations and support measures to reduce harm and increase understanding.

Beyond advocacy, consider how you can contribute to a culture of informed and respectful use in your daily life and how your perceptions and choices can influence others. Share your knowledge and experiences with others, highlighting both the joys and responsibilities of consumption. Challenge misconceptions and advocate for responsible use. Whether it's explaining the complex flavours of a craft beer to a friend or discussing the therapeutic benefits of CBD with a family member, your voice can make a difference. In doing so, you will contribute to a culture of informed and mindful consumption, where beer and cannabis are appreciated for their unique contributions to our lives and help to build a community that values education, inclusivity, and sustainability.

In understanding beer and cannabis, we also learn about ourselves and our societies. We uncover stories of human ingenuity, resilience, and the inherent quest for connection and meaning. These stories remind us that beer and cannabis are more than just consumer products; they are reflections of our humanity. Embrace the diversity of beer and cannabis, and let this exploration inspire you to continue your journey. Savour the communal joy of sharing a well-crafted beer or the therapeutic calm of a thoughtfully chosen cannabis strain. Celebrate the moments these substances enhance, whether simple gatherings with friends, personal moments of relaxation, or cultural festivals that unite communities.

Support local businesses that emphasise quality and community. Visit local breweries and dispensaries, and take the time to appreciate the craftsmanship and passion that go into creating quality products. These establishments often serve as community hubs, fostering connections and providing a space for learning and sharing. In embracing the diversity of beer and cannabis, we recognise their potential to bring joy, healing, and connection. Let us move forward with a commitment to understanding, respecting, and responsible enjoyment, ensuring that the rich legacy of these substances continues to thrive for generations to come.

As you progress, may you find joy in your journey and personal exploration of beer and cannabis. May your experiences be filled with discovery, connection, and fulfilment as the journey of beer and cannabis is ongoing, shaped by innovation, cultural shifts, and evolving legal landscapes. Stay informed about the latest developments, support sustainable practices, and celebrate the creativity and passion of those in the beer and cannabis industries. Together, we can create a future where beer and cannabis are accepted and celebrated for their positive societal impacts.

Reflecting on both industries' legal and social challenges reveals broader issues of regulation, stigma, and societal norms. The path to legalisation and acceptance has been fraught with obstacles, yet the progress made is a testament to changing perceptions and the power of advocacy. Let the lessons learned, and the stories discovered to guide you toward a more informed and respectful appreciation of beer and cannabis. As these substances continue to evolve alongside society, we, too, must grow in our understanding and approach, ensuring that the future of beer and cannabis is one of celebration, health, and community. Cheers to the rich history, the vibrant present, and the promising future of beer and cannabis – a future built on knowledge, respect, and a shared appreciation for the wonders of these remarkable substances. Remember the stories shared in this book, the cultural threads that connect us, and the ongoing evolution of both industries. This evolution reminds us that societal change is possible and that informed, compassionate dialogue is essential for development and progress

NOTES

RESOURCES

Books

1. "How to Brew" by John J. Palmer

2. "The Complete Joy of Homebrewing" by Charlie Papazian - Offers insights into the brewing process and the cultural significance of beer.

3. "Brewmaster's Bible: Gold Standard for Home Brewers" by Stephen Snyder - Provides a detailed guide on brewing beer and understanding its history

4. "Tasting Beer: An Insider's Guide to the World's Greatest Drink" by Randy Mosher - Explores the sensory experience of beer and its role in culture and society.

5. "Beer School: Bottling Success at the Brooklyn Brewery" by Steve Hindy and Tom Potter - Details the economic impact and business side of brewing.

6. Bamforth, Charles W. "Beer: Tap into the Art and Science of Brewing." Oxford University Press, 2009.

7. Mosher, Randy. "Tasting Beer, 2nd Edition: An Insider's Guide to the World's Greatest Drink." Storey Publishing, 2017.

8. Smith, Gregg, and Lucy Saunders. "Beer: A History of Suds and Civilization from Mesopotamia to Microbreweries." Avon Books, 1995.

9. Russo, Ethan B. "Cannabis and Cannabinoids: Pharmacology, Toxicology, and Therapeutic Potential." Routledge, 2020.

10. Holland, Julie. "The Pot Book: A Complete Guide to Cannabis." Park Street Press, 2010.

11. Clarke, Robert Connell, and Mark D. Merlin. "Cannabis: Evolution and Ethnobotany." University of California Press, 2013.

12. Brown, Ken Albala. "Alcohol in Popular Culture: An Encyclopaedia." ABC-CLIO, 2010.

13. Timmen, Chris. "Beer and Weed: The Pursuit of Hoppiness." Quik Publishing, 2021.

14. "The Oxford Companion to Beer" by Garrett Oliver.

15. "Brewmaster's Art: The History and Craft of Beer" by Charles Bamforth.

16. "Cannabis: Evolution and Ethnobotany" by Robert Clarke and Mark Merlin

17. "Smoke Signals: A Social History of Marijuana – Medical, Recreational and Scientific" by Martin A. Lee

18. "Drugs and Drug Policy: What Everyone Needs to Know" by Mark A.R. Kleiman, Jonathan P. Caulkins, and Angela Hawken

19. "The Politics of Marijuana: A New Paradigm" by Timothy McGettigan and Earl Smith

20. Cook, Philip J. "Paying the Tab: The Economics of Alcohol." Princeton University Press, 2007.

21. Caulkins, Jonathan P., et al. "Marijuana Legalization: What Everyone Needs to Know." Oxford University Press, 2016.

22. Musto, David F. "The American Disease: Origins of Narcotic Control." Oxford University Press, 1999.

23. Keller, Mark. "Alcohol and Society." Cambridge University Press, 1979.

24. Booth, Martin. "Cannabis: A History." St. Martin's Griffin, 2005.

25. McFarland, Ben. "World's Best Beers: One Thousand Artisan Brews from Around the Globe." Sterling Publishing, 2009.

Academic Articles and Journals

26. Articles from journals like the "Journal of the Institute of Brewing.

Journal of the Institute of Brewing. (2022). *Journal of the Institute of Brewing.*

https://doi.org/10.1002/(issn)2050-0416

27. Research papers on brewing science are available on platforms like Google Scholar.

Journal of the Institute of Brewing. (2022). *Journal of the Institute of Brewing.*

https://doi.org/10.1002/(issn)2050-0416

28. "Journal of the Institute of Brewing" – Contains peer-reviewed articles on the science and economics of brewing.

Reglitz, K., Féchir, M., Mall, V., Voigt, J., & Steinhaus, M. (2022). The impact of caramel and roasted wheat malts on aroma compounds in top-fermented wheat beer. *Journal of the Institute of Brewing*, *128*(4), 138–149.

https://doi.org/10.1002/jib.701

29. "Beer and Society: How Beer Contributes to Culture and Society" by Brewers of Europe – A report detailing the social and cultural impact of beer.

European Union - the brewers of Europe. (2023, December 21). The Brewers of Europe.

https://brewersofeurope.eu/eu-beer-trends/european-union/

30. McGovern, Patrick E., et al. "Fermented beverages of pre- and proto-historic China." Proceedings of the National Academy of Sciences 101.51 (2004): 17593–17598.

McGovern, P. E., Zhang, J., Tang, J., Zhang, Z., Hall, G. R., Moreau, R. A., Nuñez, A., Butrym,

E. D., Richards, M. P., Wang, C., Cheng, G., Zhao, Z., & Wang, C. (2004). Fermented beverages of pre- and proto-historic China. *Proceedings of the National Academy of Sciences*, *101*(51), 17593–17598.

https://doi.org/10.1073/pnas.0407921102

31. Bamforth, Charles W. "Beer, health, and nutrition." WIRES Cognitive Science 5.5 (2004): 529–538.

Beer: Health and Nutrition: Bamforth, Charles W.: 9780632064465: Amazon.com: Books. (n.d.).

https://www.amazon.com/Beer-Nutrition-Charles-W-Bamforth/dp/0632064463

32. Brown, C. (2004). "The Historical Use of Beer as a Medicine." Journal of Nutritional Health & Food Engineering, 1(3).

Krupp, A. (2020, April 3). *Could this popular, bitter drink have healing powers?* Healthline.

https://www.healthline.com/health/food-nutrition/medicinal-beers

33. Mechoulam, Raphael, and Linda A. Parker. "The endocannabinoid system and the brain." Annual Review of Psychology, 64 (2013): 21–47.

Mechoulam, R., & Parker, L. A. (2013). The endocannabinoid system and the brain. *Annual Review of Psychology*, *64*(1), 21–47.

https://doi.org/10.1146/annurev-psych-113011-143739

34. Devinsky, Orrin, et al. "Trial of cannabidiol for drug-resistant seizures in the Dravet syndrome." New England Journal of Medicine 378.20 (2017): 1938–1947.

Devinsky, O., Cross, J. H., Laux, L., Marsh, E., Miller, I., Nabbout, R., Scheffer, I. E., Thiele, E. A., & Wright, S. (2017). Trial of cannabidiol for Drug-Resistant seizures in the Dravet Syndrome. *New England Journal of Medicine*, *376*(21), 2011–2020.

https://doi.org/10.1056/nejmoa1611618

35. Borgelt, Laura M., et al. "The pharmacologic and clinical effects of medical cannabis." Pharmacotherapy: The Journal of Human

Pharmacology and Drug Therapy 33.2 (2013): 195–209.

Borgelt, L. M., Franson, K. L., Nussbaum, A. M., & Wang, G. S. (2013). The pharmacologic and clinical effects of medical cannabis. *Pharmacotherapy the Journal of Human Pharmacology and Drug Therapy*, *33*(2), 195–209.

https://doi.org/10.1002/phar.1187

36. "Beer in America: The Early Years—1587-1840: Beer's Role in the Settling of America and the Birth of a Nation" by Gregg Smith

The Early Years-1587-1840: Beer's Role in the Settling of America and the Birth of a Nation Book Online at Low Prices in India | Beer in America: The Early Years-1587-1840: Beer's Role in the Settling of America and the Birth of a Nation Reviews & Ratings - Amazon.in. (n.d.).

https://www.amazon.in/Beer-America-Beers-Settling-Nation/dp/0937381659

37. Journal of Cannabis Research - "The Health Effects of Cannabis and Cannabinoids".

The health effects of cannabis and cannabinoids. (2017). In *National Academies Press eBooks*.

https://doi.org/10.17226/24625

38. "Cannabis The Current State of Evidence and Recommendations for Research" by the National Academies of Sciences, Engineering, and Medicine

The health effects of cannabis and cannabinoids. (2017). In *National Academies Press eBooks*.

https://doi.org/10.17226/24625

39. Harvard Law Review articles on cannabis and alcohol legislation - "Social and Legal Issues of Marijuana: Recent Developments and Trends" by various authors in law journals.

Carliner, H., Brown, Q. L., Sarvet, A. L., & Hasin, D. S. (2017). Cannabis use, attitudes, and legal status in the U.S.: A review. *Preventive Medicine*, *104*, 13–23.

https://doi.org/10.1016/j.ypmed.2017.07.008

40. Room, Robin, et al. "Alcohol in Developing Societies: A Public Health Approach." World Health Organization, 2002.

Alcohol, D. a. a. B. (2002, October 18). *Summary: Alcohol in Developing Societies: A Public Health approach.*

https://www.who.int/publications/i/item/alcohol-in-developing-societies-a-public-health-approach

41. Pacula, Rosalie Liccardo, et al. "State Medical Marijuana Laws: Understanding the Laws and their Limitations." Journal of Public Health Policy, 27.4 (2002): 413-439.

State medical marijuana laws: understanding the laws and their limitations. (2002). PubMed.

https://pubmed.ncbi.nlm.nih.gov/12532682/

42. Room, Robin. "Stigma, Social Inequality and Alcohol and Drug Use. Drug and Alcohol Review", 24.2 (2005): 143-155.

Room, R. (2005). Stigma, social inequality and alcohol and drug use. *Drug and Alcohol Review, 24*(2), 143–155.

https://doi.org/10.1080/09595230500102434

43. Hughes, Trevor L., et al. "The Influence of Social Stigma on Alcohol Use Among Sexual Minority Women." Substance Use & Misuse, 45.10 (2010): 1619-1628.

Hughes, T. L., Veldhuis, C. B., Drabble, L. A., & Wilsnack, S. C. (2020). Research on alcohol and other drug (AOD) use among sexual minority women: A global scoping review. *PLoS ONE*, *15*(3), e0229869.

https://doi.org/10.1371/journal.pone.0229869

Brewing Associations, Blogs and Websites

44. The Brewers Association - (www.brewersassociation.org) - Provides extensive resources on the brewing industry, its economic impact, and trends.

Brewers Association. (2024, August 5). *Brewers Association | Promoting independent craft brewers*.

https://www.brewersassociation.org/

45. American Homebrewers Association - (www.homebrewersassociation.org) - Offers guides, recipes, and articles on homebrewing and the cultural aspects of beer.

American Homebrewers Association. (2024, August 5). *The Community for Homebrewers | Homebrewers Association*.

https://www.homebrewersassociation.org/

46. BeerAdvocate - (www.beeradvocate.com) - Contains reviews, articles, and forums discussing various aspects of beer and brewing.

BeerAdvocate. (n.d.). BeerAdvocate.

https://www.beeradvocate.com/

47. Homebrew Talk (www.homebrewtalk.com)

Homebrew Talk - Beer, Wine, Mead, & Cider Brewing Discussion Forum. (2024, June 13). Homebrew Talk - Beer, Wine, Mead, & Cider Brewing Discussion Forum.

https://www.homebrewtalk.com/

48. The Mad Fermentationist (www.themadfermentationist.com)

The Mad Fermentationist - Homebrewing blog. (n.d.).

https://www.themadfermentationist.com/

Web Articles

49. "The History of Beer" on History.com - A comprehensive overview of the origins and evolution of beer.

Andrews, E., & Andrews, E. (2023, March 28). *Who invented beer?* HISTORY.

https://www.history.com/news/who-invented-beer

50. "How Bccr Changcd thc World" on Smithsonian Magazine - Discusses the historical and cultural significance of beer.

a) Daley, J. (2019, February 1). Oldest evidence of British beer found in Highway Dig. *Smithsonian Magazine*.

https://www.smithsonianmag.com/smart-news/oldest-evidence-british-beer-found-highway-dig-180971403/

b) Magazine, S. (n.d.). *Smithsonian Magazine: Explore History, Science, Arts & Culture*. Smithsonian Magazine.

https://www.smithsonianmag.com/

51. "The Economic Impact of the Beer Industry" on Statista - Provides statistical data on the economic contributions of the beer industry.

Statista. (n.d.). *Beer - Worldwide | Statista market forecast*.

https://www.statista.com/outlook/cmo/alcoholic-drinks/beer/worldwide

WEBSITES

52. National Institute on Drug Abuse (NIDA): Provides a comprehensive overview of the effects of cannabis.

National Institute on Drug Abuse. (2024, April 5). National Institute on Drug Abuse.

https://nida.nih.gov/publications/research-reports/marijuana/what-are-marijuanas-effects

53. NORML: Provides information on cannabis laws, advocacy, and research.

Norml. (2024, July 15). *NORML submits public comments to DEA calling for the removal of cannabis from Schedule I.* NORML.

https://norml.org/

54. Project CBD: Offers research and resources on the therapeutic use of CBD and other cannabinoids.

Noel. (2024, March 15). *Project CBD | Everything you need to know about CBD*. Project CBD.

https://projectcbd.org/

55. Leafly: Provides news and research on both cannabis and its cultural impacts.

Leafly. (2024, August 5). *The latest cannabis news today | Leafly*.

https://www.leafly.com/news

56. PubMed: A database of scientific studies, including those on the health effects of beer and cannabis.

MacCallum, C. A., & Russo, E. B. (2018). Practical considerations in medical cannabis administration and dosing. *European Journal of Internal Medicine*, *49*, 12–19.

https://doi.org/10.1016/j.ejim.2018.01.004

57. Alcohol and Tobacco Tax and Trade Bureau (www.ttb.gov)

TTB: Alcohol and Tobacco Tax and Trade Bureau. (2024, August 1).

https://www.ttb.gov/

58. Marijuana Policy Project (www.mpp.org)

Project, M. P. (n.d.). *Chicago Committee to implement Illinois's medical marijuana program*. MPP.

https://blog.mpp.org/medical-marijuana/chicago-committee-to-implement-illinoiss-medical-marijuana-program/

59. American Medical Association (ama-assn.org)

Policy Finder | AMA. (n.d.).

https://policysearch.ama-assn.org/policyfinder/search/Cannabis%20and%20healthcare/relevant/1/

60. Centers for Disease Control and Prevention (cdc.gov)

About CBD. (2024, February 15). Cannabis and Public Health.

https://www.cdc.gov/cannabis/about/about-cbd.html

61. Pew Research Center reports on public opinion regarding cannabis legalization (pewresearch.org)

Blazina, C. (2024, April 14). Americans overwhelmingly say marijuana should be legal for medical or recreational use. *Pew Research Center*.

https://www.pewresearch.org/short-reads/2022/11/22/americans-overwhelmingly-say-marijuana-should-be-legal-for-medical-or-recreational-use/

Personal Insights (Documentaries and Interviews)

62. "The Business of Being High." Documentary series exploring the legal cannabis industry and the lives of people involved in it.

Wwd. (2024, July 22). 10 Must-See Weed and Psychedelics Documentaries » Winnipeg Weed Delivery. *Winnipeg Weed Delivery*.

https://winnipegweeddelivery.shop/weed-and-psychedelics-documentaries

63. "Crafting a Nation." Documentary featuring stories of craft brewers around the United States.

Crafting A Nation (2013) 6.4 | Documentary, news. (2013, May 13). IMDb.

https://www.imdb.com/title/tt2576452/

64. *History of cannabis*. (n.d.). The University of Sydney.

https://www.sydney.edu.au/lambert/medicinal-cannabis/history-of-cannabis.html#:~:text=Hindu%20legend%20holds%20that%20Shiva,the%20gods%20such%20as%20Shiva.

65. *Cannabis and Lord Shiva - Google Search*. (n.d.).

https://www.google.com/search?q=Cannabis+and+Lord+Shiva&sca_esv=0859001573093002&rlz=1C5MACD_enIN1035IN1037&sxsrf=ADLYWIJHfHArcXw_z2_sXQxeGEEJ9jWYWQ%3A1721374109705&ei=nRWaZtvbKvar4-EP-KKx2Q8&ved=0ahUKEwibntaiyrKHAxX21TgGHXhRLPsQ4dUDCA8&uact=5&oq=Cannabis+and+Lord+Shiva&gs_lp=Egxnd3Mtd2l6LXNlcnAiF0Nhbm5hYmlzIGFuZCBMb3JkIFNoaXZhSOBiUABY4F1wA3gBkAEAmAHRAqABziGqAQgwLjI0LjEuMbgBA8gBAPgBAZgCEKAChhbCAgoQIxiABBgnGIoFwgITEC4YgAQYxwEYJxiKBRiOBRivAcICBBAjGCfCAgsQLhiABBiRAhiKBcICCxAAGIAEGJECGIoFwgIIEAAYgAQYsQPCAhEQLhiABBixAxjRAxiDARjHAcICCxAAGIAEGLEDGIMBwgIKEAAYgAQYQxiKBcICFhAuGIAEGLEDGNEDGEMYgwEYxwEYigXCAg4QABiABBixAxiDARiKBcICChAuGIAEGEMYigXCAgUQABiABMICDhAAGIAEGJECGLEDGIoFwgIIEC4YgAQYsQPCAgsQLhiABBixAxiDAcICDhAuGIAEGLEDGIMBGNQCwgIaEC4YgAQYsQMYgwEYlwUY3AQY3gQY3wTYAQHCAgUQLhiABMICBxAAGIAEGArCAg0QABiABBixAxhDGIoFwgIQEC4YgAQYsQMYQxjUAhiKBcICDRAAGIAEGLEDGEYY-QHCAicQABiABBixAxhGGPkBGJcFGIwFGN0EGEYY-QEY9AMY9QMY9gPYAQLCAgoQABiABBgUGIcCwgIGEAAYFhgewgIIEAAYgAQYogSYAwC6BgYIARABGBS6BgYIAhABGBOSBwgwLjE0LjEuMaAHh78B&sclient=gws-wi

66. *Cannabis (Marijuana) and cannabinoids: What you need to know*. (n.d.). NCCIH.

https://www.nccih.nih.gov/health/cannabis-marijuana-and-cannabinoids-what-you-need-to-know

67. *Malana village in Himachal is famous for what purpose - Google Search*. (n.d.). https://www.google.com/search?q=malana+village+in+himachal+is+famous+for+what+purpose&sca_esv=0859001573093002&rlz=1C5MACD_enIN1035IN1037&sxsrf=ADLYWIJyxrMGwukMMRYpRpKu7Vbutz_oaw%3A1721373920554&ei=4BSaZtfGIa2J4-EPnP2AgAc&oq=malana+village+in+himachal+is+famous+for+&gs_lp=Egxnd3Mtd2l6LXNlcnAiKW1hbGFuYSB2aWxsYWdlIGluIGhpbWFjaGFsIGlzIGZhbW91cyBmb3IgKgIIATIFECEYoAEyBRAhGKABMgUQIRigAUiTWVDHB1ifTXABeAGQAQCYAdgBoAGnGaoBBjAuMTcuMrgBAcgBAPgBAZgCFKACvhrCAgoQABiwAxjWBBhHwgIHEC4YgAQYDcICBxAAGIAEGA3CAgsQABiABBiGAxiKBcICCBAAGIAEGKIEwgIWEC4YgAQYDRiXBRjcBBjeBBjgBNgBAcICCBAAGAcYCBgewgILEC4YgAQYkQIYigXCAgYQABgIGB7CAhoQLhiABBiRAhiKBRiXBRjcBBjeBBjgBNgBAcICBhAAGBYYHsICBRAhGJ8FwgIHECEYoAEYCpgDAIgGAZAGB7oGBggBEAEYFJIHBjEuMTcuMqAHmWU&sclient=gws-wiz-serp

68. Martínez, A. (2023, October 16). *Ketama, the cradle of the best hash in the world*. Pevgrow.com.

https://pevgrow.com/blog/en/ketama-the-cradle-of-the-best-hash-in-the-world/

69. *medical use of cannabinoids - Google Search*. (n.d.).

https://www.google.com/search?q=medical+use+of+cannabinoids&rlz=1C5MACD_enIN1035IN1037&oq=Medical+use+of+Cananboids&gs_lcrp=EgZjaHJvbWUqCQgBEAAYDRiABDIGCAAQRRg5MgkIARAAGA0YgAQyCQgCEAAYDRiABDIICAMQABgNGB4yDQgEEAAYhgMYgAQYigUyDQgFEAAYhgMYgAQYigUyDQgGEAAYhgMYgAQYigUyDQgHEAAYhgMYgAQYigUyCggIEAAYgAQYogTSAQkxNzc0NWowajSoAgCwAgA&sourceid=chrome&ie=UTF-8

70. *marijuana discovery - Google Search*. (n.d.).

https://www.google.com/search?q=marijuana+discovery&sca_esv=0859001573093002&rlz=1C5MACD_enIN1035IN1037&sxsrf=ADLYWIIWGTfYznCNWrR6K7p-4DbkxnCYRA%3A1721373957275&ei=BRWaZsC-ELuP4-EPl_yfmAs&oq=first+discovery+of+marijuana+in+the+world&gs_lp=Egxnd3Mtd2l6LXNlcnAiKWZpcnN0IGRpc2NvdmVyeSBvZiBtYXJpanVhbmEgaW4gdGhlIHdvcmxkKgIIADIIEAAYgAQYogQyCBAAGKIEGIkFMggQABiABBiiBDIIEAAYgAQYogQyCBAAGIAEGKIESKnAAVAAWIGhAXABeAGQAQCYAZsCoAHINaoBBjAuNDAuMrgBAcgBAPgBAZgCJqAC0zGoAhTCAgoQIxiABBgnGIoFwgIKEC4YgAQYJxiKBcICCxAAGIAEGJECGIoFwgILEC4YgAQYkQIYigXCAhEQLhiABBixAxjRAxiDARjHAcICDhAuGIAEGLEDGIMBGIoFwgIIEAAYgAQYsQPCAgcQLhgnGOoCwgIHECMYJxjqAsICFBAAGIAEGOMEGLQCGOkEGOoC2AEBwgIWEAAYAxi0AhjlAhjqAhiMAxiPAdgBAsICBBAjGCfCAgoQABiABBhDGIoFwgIQEC4YgAQY0QMYQxjHARiKBcICCxAAGIAEGLEDGIMBwgIWEC4YgAQYQxjHARiYBRiKBRiaBRivAcICFhAuGIAEGEMYxwEYmAUYmQUYigUYrwHCAhAQLhiABBhDGMcBGIoFGK8BwgINEAAYgAQYsQMYQxiKBcICEBAAGIAEGLEDGEMYyQMYigXCAhoQLhiABBiRAhiKBRiXBRjcBBjeBBjgBNgBA8ICBRAAGIAEwgILEC4YgAQYsQMYgwHCAg0QLhiABBjRAxjHARgKwgIIEC4YgAQYsQPCAgsQABiABBixAxiKBcICGhAuG

71. Grotenhermen, F., & Müller-Vahl, K. (2016). Medicinal uses of marijuana and cannabinoids. *Critical Reviews in Plant Sciences*, *35*(5–6), 378–405.

https://doi.org/10.1080/07352689.2016.1265360

72. Medical marijuana: benefits and side effects. (2024, January 9). WebMD.

https://www.webmd.com/a-to-z-guides/medical-marijuana-faq

73. *Cannabis (Marijuana) and cannabinoids: What you need to know.* (n.d.-b). NCCIH.

https://www.nccih.nih.gov/health/cannabis-marijuana-and-cannabinoids-what-you-need-to-know

74. The textile applications of hemp | ALLIANCE. (n.d.).

https://allianceflaxlinenhemp.eu/en/textile-applications-hemp

75. The industrial uses of hemp | ALLIANCE. (n.d.).

https://allianceflaxlinenhemp.eu/en/industrial-uses-hemp

76. *A, S. (2024, June 28). The Future of Industrial hemp: Key trends shaping the market landscape.*

https://www.linkedin.com/pulse/future-industrial-hemp-key-trends-shaping-market-landscape-shweta-a-cbeve/

77. Rajput, S. (2024, March 29). The Hemp seed Revolution: Top 7 trends shaping the market. Verified Market Reports® | Get Market Analysis and Research Reports.

https://www.verifiedmarketreports.com/blog/the-hemp-seed-revolution-top-7-trends-shaping-the-market/

78. *4 stunning books on beer worthy of a look.* (n.d.).

https://www.startribune.com/4-stunning-books-on-beer-worthy-of-a-look/564564052/.

79. *Lautering explained.* (n.d.).

https://makebeereasy.com/lautering/.

80. *Catalysts*. (n.d.).

https://www.thecatalystsgroup.com/blog/the-vital-role-of-yeast-in-the-microbrewery-industry-a-symphony-of-fermentation-and-flavor.

www.ingramcontent.com/pod-product-compliance
Lightning Source LLC
Chambersburg PA
CBHW062138160726
48282CB00027B/860

मुंशी प्रेमचन्द का मूल नाम धनपतराय श्रीवास्तव था। प्रेमचन्द का जन्म 31 जुलाई सन् 1880 को बनारस से चार मील दूर लमही गाँव में हुआ था। उनका जीवन गरीबी में ही पला। उनका पहला विवाह 15 साल की आयु में उनके पिता ने उनसे बड़ी उम्र की लड़की से करा दिया। विवाह के एक साल बाद पिताजी का देहान्त हो गया। अचानक उनके सिर पर पूरे घर का बोझ आ गया। प्रेमचन्द की आर्थिक विपत्तियों का अनुमान इस घटना से लगाया जा सकता है कि पैसे के अभाव में उन्हे अपना कोट बेचना पड़ा और पुस्तकें बेचनीं पड़ीं।

सन् 1905 मे उनकी पहली पत्नी पारिवारिक कटुताओं के कारण घर छोड़कर मायके चली गई, फिर वह कभी नहीं आई। सन् 1905 में उन्होनें शिवरानी देवी से दूसरी शादी कर ली। शिवरानी देवी एक बाल-विधवा थीं और इनके प्रति वो सदा स्नेह के पात्र रहे थे। यह कहा जा सकता है कि दूसरी शादी के पश्चात उनके जीवन में परिस्थितियां कुछ बदलीं और आर्थिक तंगी कम हुई। उनके लेखन में सजगता आई।

तेरह वर्ष की उम्र से ही उन्होंने लिखना आरंभ कर दिया था। शुरू में उन्होंने कुछ नाटक लिखे फिर बाद में उर्दू में उपन्यास लिखना आरंभ किया। इस तरह उनका साहित्यिक सफ़र शुरू हुआ जो मरते दम तक साथ था। उनके लेखन में ग्रामीण भारत का चरित्र उजागर होता था। वो हमेशा सामाजिक कुरीतियों के बारे में लिखते थे, जिसमें जाति-प्रथा, गरीबों एवं दलितों का शोषण एवं नारियों के विषय में बहुत कुछ होता था।

उपन्यास के क्षेत्र में उनके योगदान को देखकर बंगाल के विख्यात उपन्यासकार शरतचंद्र चट्टोपाध्याय ने उनको उपन्यास सम्राट कहकर संबोधित किया था। उनका लेखन हिन्दी साहित्य की एक ऐसी विरासत है जिसके बिना हिन्दी के विकास का अध्ययन अधूरा रहेगा। प्रेमचन्द एक संवेदनशील लेखक, सचेत नागरिक, कुशल वक्ता तथा सुधी संपादक थे। उनके कुछ प्रसिद्ध उपन्यास हैंः गोदान, ग़बन, रंगभूमि, कर्मभूमि, प्रेमाश्रम, निर्मला तथा कुछ प्रमुख कहानियाँ नमक का दारोगा, प्रेम पचीसी, मंत्र, पूस की रात, सद्गति, कफ़न आदि हैं।

सन् 1936 में प्रेमचन्द बीमार रहने लगे। आर्थिक कष्टों तथा इलाज ठीक से न कराए जाने के कारण 8 अक्टूबर सन् 1936 को उनका देहान्त हो गया।

1

यों तो बाबू उदयभानुलाल के परिवार में बीसों ही प्राणी थे, कोई ममेरा भाई था, कोई फुफेरा, कोई भांजा था, कोई भतीजा, लेकिन यहां हमें उनसे कोई प्रयोजन नहीं, वह अच्छे वकील थे, लक्ष्मी प्रसन्न थीं और कुटुम्ब के दरिद्र प्राणियों को आश्रय देना उनका कर्त्तव्य ही था। हमारा सम्बन्ध तो केवल उनकी दोनों कन्याओं से है, जिनमें बड़ी का नाम निर्मला और छोटी का कृष्णा था। अभी कल दोनों साथ-साथ गुड़िया खेलती थीं।

निर्मला का पन्द्रहवां साल था, कृष्णा का दसवां, फिर भी उनके स्वभाव में कोई विशेष अन्तर न था। दोनों चंचल, खिलाड़िन और सैर-तमाशे पर जान देती थीं। दोनों गुड़िया का धूमधाम से ब्याह करती थीं, सदा काम से जी चुराती थीं। मां पुकारती रहती थी, पर दोनों कोठे पर छिपी बैठी रहती थीं कि न जाने किस काम के लिए बुलाती हैं। दोनों अपने भाइयों से लड़ती थीं, नौकरों को डांटती थीं और बाजे की आवाज सुनते ही द्वार पर आकर खड़ी हो जाती थीं, पर आज एकाएक एक ऐसी बात हो गई है, जिसने बड़ी को बड़ी और छोटी को छोटी बना दिया है। कृष्णा यही है, पर निर्मला बड़ी गम्भीर, एकान्तप्रिय और लज्जाशील हो गई है।

इधर महीनों से बाबू उदयभानुलाल निर्मला के विवाह की बातचीत कर रहे थे। आज उनकी मेहनत ठिकाने लगी है। बाबू भालचन्द्र सिन्हा के ज्येष्ठ पुत्र भुवनमोहन सिन्हा से बात पक्की हो गई है। वर के पिता ने कह दिया है कि आपकी खुशी हो तो दहेज दें, या न दें, मुझे इसकी परवाह नहीं; हां, बारात में जो लोग जाएं उनका आदर-सत्कार अच्छी

तरह होना चहिए, जिससे मेरी और आपकी जग-हंसाई न हो। बाबू उदयभानुलाल थे तो वकील, पर संचय करना न जानते थे। दहेज उनके सामने कठिन समस्या थी। इसलिए जब वर के पिता ने स्वयं कह दिया कि मुझे दहेज की परवाह नहीं, तो मानों उन्हें आंखें मिल गई। डरते थे, न जाने किस-किस के सामने हाथ फैलाना पड़े, दो-तीन महाजनों को ठीक कर रखा था। उनका अनुमान था कि हाथ रोकने पर भी बीस हजार से कम खर्च न होंगे। यह आश्वासन पाकर वे खुशी के मारे फूले न समाये।

इसकी सूचना ने अज्ञान बलिका को मुंह ढांप कर एक कोने में बिठा रखा है। उसके हृदय में एक विचित्र शंका समा गई है, रोम-रोम में एक अज्ञात भय का संचार हो गया है, न जाने क्या होगा। उसके मन में वे उमंगें नहीं हैं, जो युवतियों की आंखों में तिरछी चितवन बनकर, ओंठों पर मधुर हास्य बनकर और अंगों में आलस्य बनकर प्रकट होती है। नहीं, वहां अभिलाषाएं नहीं हैं, वहां केवल शंकाएं, चिन्ताएं और भीरू कल्पनाएं हैं। यौवन का अभी तक पूर्ण प्रकाश नहीं हुआ है।

कृष्णा कुछ-कुछ जानती है, कुछ-कुछ नहीं जानती। जानती है, बहन को अच्छे-अच्छे गहने मिलेंगे, द्वार पर बाजे बजेंगे, मेहमान आयेंगे, नाच होगा—यह जानकर प्रसन्न है और यह भी जानती है कि बहन सबके गले मिलकर रोयेगी, यहां से रो-धोकर विदा हो जाएगी, मैं अकेली रह जाऊंगी—यह जानकर दुःखी है, पर यह नहीं जानती कि यह किसलिए हो रहा है, माताजी और पिताजी क्यों बहन को इस घर से निकालने को इतने उत्सुक हो रहे हैं। बहन ने तो किसी को कुछ नहीं कहा, किसी से लड़ाई नहीं की, क्या इसी तरह एक दिन मुझे भी ये लोग निकाल देंगे? मैं भी इसी तरह कोने में बैठकर रोऊंगी और किसी को मुझ पर दया न आयेगी? इसलिए वह भयभीत भी है।

संध्या का समय था, निर्मला छत पर जाकर अकेली बैठी आकाश की ओर तृषित नेत्रों से ताक रही थी। ऐसा मन होता था कि पंख होते, तो वह उड़ जाती और इन सारे झंझटों से छूट जाती। इस समय बहुधा दोनों बहनें कहीं सैर करने जाया करती थीं। बग्घी खाली न होती, तो

बगीचे में ही टहला करतीं, इसलिए कृष्णा उसे खोजती फिरती थी, जब कहीं न पाया, तो छत पर आई और उसे देखते ही हंसकर बोली–तुम यहां आकर छिपी बैठी हो और मैं तुम्हें ढूंढती फिरती हूं। चलो, बग्घी तैयार करा आयी हूं।

निर्मला ने उदासीन भाव से कहा–तू जा, मैं न जाऊंगी।

कृष्णा–नहीं मेरी अच्छी दीदी, आज जरूर चलो। देखो, कैसी ठण्डी-ठण्डी हवा चल रही है।

निर्मला–मेरा मन नहीं चाहता, तू चली जा।

कृष्णा की आंखें डबडबा आई। कांपती हुई आवाज से बोली–आज तुम क्यों नहीं चलतीं? मुझसे क्यों नहीं बोलतीं क्यों इधर-उधर छिपी-छिपी फिरती हो? मेरा जी अकेले बैठे-बैठे घबड़ाता है। तुम न चलोगी, तो मैं भी न जाऊंगी। यहीं तुम्हारे साथ बैठी रहूंगी।

निर्मला–और जब मैं चली जाऊंगी तब क्या करेगी? तब किसके साथ खेलेगी और किसके साथ घूमने जाएगी, बता?

कृष्णा–मैं भी तुम्हारे साथ चलूंगी। अकेले मुझसे यहां न रहा जाएगा।

निर्मला मुस्कराकर बोली–तुझे अम्मा न जाने देंगी।

कृष्णा–तो मैं भी तुम्हें न जाने दूंगी। तुम अम्मा से कह क्यों नहीं देती कि मैं न जाउंगी।

निर्मला–कह तो रही हूं, कोई सुनता है!

कृष्णा तो क्या यह तुम्हारा घर नहीं है?

निर्मला–नहीं, मेरा घर होता, तो कोई क्यों जबर्दस्ती निकाल देता?

कृष्णा–इसी तरह किसी दिन मैं भी निकाल दी जाऊंगी?

निर्मला–और नहीं तो क्या तू बैठी रहेगी! हम लड़कियां हैं, हमारा घर कहीं नहीं होता।

कृष्णा–चन्दर भी निकाल दिया जाएगा?

निर्मला–चन्दर तो लड़का है, उसे कौन निकालेगा?

कृष्णा–तो लड़कियां बहुत खराब होती होंगी?

निर्मला–खराब न होतीं, तो घर से भगाई क्यों जाती?

कृष्णा–चन्दर इतना बदमाश है, उसे कोई नहीं भगाता। हम-तुम तो कोई बदमाशी भी नहीं करतीं।

एकाएक चन्दर धम-धम करता हुआ छत पर आ पहुंचा और निर्मला को देखकर बोला–अच्छा आप यहां बैठी हैं। ओहो! अब तो बाजे बजेंगे, दीदी दुल्हन बनेंगी, पालकी पर चढ़ेंगी, ओहो! ओहो!

चन्दर का पूरा नाम चन्द्रभानु सिन्हा था। निर्मला से तीन साल छोटा और कृष्णा से दो साल बड़ा।

निर्मला–चन्दर, मुझे चिढ़ाओगे तो अभी जाकर अम्मा से कह दूंगी।

चन्दर–तो चिढ़ती क्यों हो तुम भी बाजे सुनना। ओ हो-हो! अब आप दुल्हन बनेंगी। क्यों किशनी, तू बाजे सुनेगी न वैसे बाजे तूने कभी न सुने होंगे।

कृष्णा–क्या बैण्ड से भी अच्छे होंगे?

चन्दर–हां-हां, बैण्ड से भी अच्छे, हजार गुने अच्छे, लाख गुने अच्छे। तुम जानो क्या एक बैण्ड सुन लिया, तो समझने लगीं कि उससे अच्छे बाजे नहीं होते। बाजे बजानेवाले लाल-लाल वर्दियां और काली-काली टोपियां पहने होंगे। ऐसे खबूसूरत मालूम होंगे कि तुमसे क्या कहूं! आतिशबाजियां भी होंगी, हवाइयां आसमान में उड़ जाएंगी और वहां तारों में लगेंगी तो लाल, पीले, हरे, नीले तारे टूट-टूटकर गिरेंगे। बड़ा बजा आयेगा।

कृष्णा–और क्या-क्या होगा चन्दर, बता दे मेरे भैया?

चन्दर–मेरे साथ घूमने चल, तो रास्ते में सारी बातें बता दूं। ऐसे-ऐसे तमाशे होंगे कि देखकर तेरी आंखें खुल जाएंगी। हवा में उड़ती हुई परियां होंगी, सचमुच की परियां।

कृष्णा–अच्छा चलो, लेकिन न बताओगे, तो मारूंगी।

चन्दर और कृष्णा चले गए, पर निर्मला अकेली बैठी रह गई। कृष्णा के चले जाने से इस समय उसे बड़ा क्षोभ हुआ। कृष्णा, जिसे वह प्राणों से भी अधिक प्यार करती थी, आज इतनी निष्ठुर हो गई। अकेली छोड़कर चली गई। बात कोई न थी, लेकिन दुःखी हृदय दुखती हुई आंख है, जिसमें हवा से भी पीड़ा होती है। निर्मला बड़ी देर तक

बैठी रोती रही। भाई-बहन, माता-पिता, सभी इसी भांति मुझे भूल जाएंगे, सबकी आंखें फिर जाएंगी, फिर शायद इन्हें देखने को भी तरस जाऊं।

बाग में फूल खिले हुए थे। मीठी-मीठी सुगन्ध आ रही थी। चैत की शीतल मन्द समीर चल रही थी। आकाश में तारे छिटके हुए थे।

निर्मला इन्हीं शोकमय विचारों में पड़ी-पड़ी सो गई और आंख लगते ही उसका मन स्वप्न-देश में, विचरने लगा। क्या देखती है कि सामने एक नदी लहरें मार रही है और वह नदी के किनारे नाव की बाट देख रही है। सन्ध्या का समय है। अंधेरा किसी भयंकर जन्तु की भांति बढ़ता चला आता है। वह घोर चिन्ता में पड़ी हुई है कि कैसे यह नदी पार होगी, कैसे पहुंचूंगी! रो रही है कि कहीं रात न हो जाए, नहीं तो मैं अकेली यहां कैसे रहूंगी।

एकाएक उसे एक सुन्दर नौका घाट की ओर आती दिखाई देती है। वह खुशी से उछल पड़ती है और ज्यों ही नाव घाट पर आती है, वह उस पर चढ़ने के लिए बढ़ती है, लेकिन जब नाव के पटरे पर पैर रखना चाहती है, उसका मल्लाह बोल उठता है–तेरे लिए यहां जगह नहीं है!

वह मल्लाह की खुशामद करती है, उसके पैरों पड़ती है, रोती है, लेकिन वह यह कहे जाता है, तेरे लिए यहां जगह नहीं है। एक क्षण में नाव खुल जाती है। वह चिल्ला-चिल्लाकर रोने लगती है। नदी के निर्जन तट पर रात भर कैसे रहेगी, यह सोच वह नदी में कूद कर उस नाव को पकड़ना चाहती है कि इतने में कहीं से आवाज आती है–ठहरो, ठहरो, नदी गहरी है, डूब जाओगी। वह नाव तुम्हारे लिए नहीं है, मैं आता हूं, मेरी नाव में बैठ जाओ। मैं उस पार पहुंचा दूंगा।

वह भयभीत होकर इधर-उधर देखती है कि यह आवाज कहां से आई? थोड़ी देर के बाद एक छोटी-सी डोंगी आती दिखाई देती है। उसमें न पाल है, न पतवार और न मस्तूल। पेंदा फटा हुआ है, तख्ते टूटे हुए, नाव में पानी भरा हुआ है और एक आदमी उसमें से पानी उलीच रहा है। वह उससे कहती है, यह तो टूटी हुई है, यह कैसे पार लगेगी?

मल्लाह कहता है–तुम्हारे लिए यही भेजी गई है, आकर बैठ जाओ! वह एक क्षण सोचती है–इसमें बैठूं या न बैठूं? अन्त में वह

निश्चय करती है—बैठ जाऊं। यहां अकेली पड़ी रहने से नाव में बैठ जाना फिर भी अच्छा है। किसी भयंकर जन्तु के पेट में जाने से तो यही अच्छा है कि नदी में डूब जाऊं। कौन जाने, नाव पार पहुंच ही जाए। यह सोचकर वह प्राणों को मुट्ठी में लिए हुए नाव पर बैठ जाती है।

कुछ देर तक नाव डगमगाती हुई चलती है, लेकिन प्रतिक्षण उसमें पानी भरता जाता है। वह भी मल्लाह के साथ दोनों हाथों से पानी उलीचने लगती है। यहां तक कि उनके हाथ थक जाते हैं, पर पानी बढ़ता ही चला जाता है, आखिर नाव चक्कर खाने लगती है, मालूम होती है—अब डूबी, अब डूबी। तब वह किसी अदृश्य सहारे के लिए दोनों हाथ फैलाती है, नाव नीचे जाती है और उसके पैर उखड़ जाते हैं।

वह जोर से चिल्लाई और चिल्लाते ही उसकी आंखें खुल गई। देखा, तो माता सामने खड़ी उसका कन्धा पकड़कर हिला रही थी।

बाबू उदयभानुलाल का मकान बाजार बना हुआ है। बरामदे में सुनार के हथौड़े और कमरे में दर्जी की सुईयां चल रही हैं। सामने नीम के नीचे बढ़ई चारपाइयां बना रहा है। खपरैल में हलवाई के लिए भट्ठा खोदा गया है। मेहमानों के लिए अलग एक मकान ठीक किया गया है। यह प्रबन्ध किया जा रहा है कि हरेक मेहमान के लिए एक-एक चारपाई, एक-एक कुर्सी और एक-एक मेज हो। हर तीन मेहमानों के लिए एक-एक कहार रखने की तजवीज हो रही है। अभी बारात आने में एक महीने की देर है, लेकिन तैयारियां अभी से हो रही हैं। बारातियों का ऐसा सत्कार किया जाए कि किसी को जबान हिलाने का मौका न मिले। वे लोग भी याद करें कि किसी के यहां बारात में गये थे। पूरा मकान बर्तनों से भरा हुआ है। चाय के सेट हैं, नाश्ते की तश्तरियां, थाल, लोटे, गिलास।

जो लोग नित्य खाट पर पड़े हुक्का पीते रहते थे, बड़ी तत्परता से काम में लगे हुए हैं। अपनी उपयोगिता सिद्ध करने का ऐसा अच्छा अवसर उन्हें फिर बहुत दिनों के बाद मिलेगा। जहां एक आदमी को

जाना होता है, पांच दौड़ते हैं। काम कम होता है, हुल्लड़ अधिक। जरा-जरा सी बात पर घण्टों तर्क-वितर्क होता है और अन्त में वकील साहब को आकर निर्णय करना पड़ता है। एक कहता है, यह घी खराब है, दूसरा कहता है, इससे अच्छा बाजार में मिल जाए तो टांग की राह से निकल जाऊं। तीसरा कहता है, इसमें तो हीक आती है। चौथा कहता है, तुम्हारी नाक ही सड़ गई है, तुम क्या जानो घी किसे कहते हैं। जब से यहां आये हो, घी मिलने लगा है, नहीं तो घी के दर्शन भी न होते थे! इस पर तकरार बढ़ जाती है और वकील साहब को झगड़ा चुकाना पड़ता है।

रात के नौ बजे थे। उदयभानुलाल अन्दर बैठे हुए खर्च का तखमीना लगा रहे थे। वह प्रायः रोज ही तखमीना लगाते थे पर रोज ही उसमें कुछ-न-कुछ परिवर्तन और परिवर्धन करना पड़ता था। सामने कल्याणी भौंहे सिकोड़े हुए खड़ी थी। बाबू साहब ने बड़ी देर के बाद सिर उठाया और बोले–दस हजार से कम नहीं होता, बल्कि शायद और बढ़ जाए।

कल्याणी–दस दिन में पांच से दस हजार हुए। एक महीने में तो शायद एक लाख की नौबत आ जाए।

उदयभानुलाल–क्या करूं, जग हंसाई भी तो अच्छी नहीं लगती। कोई शिकायत हुई तो लोग कहेंगे, नाम बड़े दर्शन थोड़े। फिर जब वह मुझसे दहेज एक पाई नहीं लेते तो मेरा भी कर्तव्य है कि मेहमानों के आदर-सत्कार में कोई बात उठा न रखूं।

कल्याणी–जब रो ब्रह्मा ने सृष्टि रची, तब से आज तक कभी बारातियों को कोई प्रसन्न नहीं रख सकता। उन्हें दोष निकालने और निन्दा करने का कोई-न-कोई अवसर मिल ही जाता है। जिसे अपने घर सूखी रोटियां भी मयस्सर नहीं वह भी बारात में जाकर तानाशाह बन बैठता है। तेल खुशबूदार नहीं, साबुन टके सेर का जाने कहां से बटोर लाये, कहार बात नहीं सुनते, लालटेनें धुआं देती हैं, कुर्सियों में खटमल है, चारपाइयां ढीली हैं, जनवासे की जगह हवादार नहीं। ऐसी-ऐसी हजारों शिकायतें होती रहती हैं। उन्हें आप कहां तक रोकियेगा? अगर यह मौका न मिला, तो और कोई ऐब निकाल लिये

जाएंगे। भई, यह तेल तो रंडियों के लगाने लायक है, हमें तो सादा तेल चाहिए। जनाब ने यह साबुन नहीं भेजा है, अपनी अमीरी की शान दिखाई है, मानो हमने साबुन देखा ही नहीं। ये कहार नहीं यमदूत हैं, जब देखिये सिर पर सवार! लालटेनें ऐसी भेजी हैं कि आंखें चमकने लगती हैं, अगर दस-पांच दिन इस रोशनी में बैठना पड़े तो आंखें फूट जाएं। जनवासा क्या है, अभागे का भाग्य है, जिस पर चारों तरफ से झोंके आते रहते हैं। मैं तो फिर यही कहूंगी कि बारातियों के नखरों का विचार ही छोड़ दो।

उदयभानुलाल–तो आखिर तुम मुझे क्या करने को कहती हो?

कल्याणी–कह तो रही हूं, पक्का इरादा कर लो कि मैं पांच हजार से अधिक न खर्च करूंगा। घर में तो टका है नहीं, कर्ज ही का भरोसा ठहरा, तो इतना कर्ज क्यों लें कि जिन्दगी में अदा न हो। आखिर मेरे और बच्चे भी तो हैं, उनके लिए भी तो कुछ चाहिए।

उदयभानुलाल–तो आज मैं मरा जाता हूं?

कल्याणी–जीने-मरने का हाल कोई नहीं जानता।

उदयभानुलाल–तो तुम बैठी यही मनाया करती हो?

कल्याणी–इसमें बिगड़ने की तो कोई बात नहीं। मरना एक दिन सभी को है। कोई यहां अमर होकर थोड़े ही आया है। आंखें बन्द कर लेने से तो होनेवाली बात न टलेगी। रोज आंखों देखती हूं, बाप का देहान्त हो जाता है, उसके बच्चे गली-गली ठोकरें खाते फिरते हैं। आदमी ऐसा काम ही क्यों करे?

उदयभानुलाल ने जलकर कहा–तो अब समझ लूं कि मेरे मरने के दिन निकट आ गये, यही तुम्हारी भविष्यवाणी है! सुहाग से स्त्रियों का जी ऊबते नहीं सुना था, आज यह नई बात मालूम हुई। रंडापे में भी कोई सुख होगा ही!

कल्याणी–तुमसे दुनिया की कोई भी बात कही जाती है, तो जहर उगलने लगते हो। इसलिए न कि जानते हो, इसे कहीं टिकना नहीं है, मेरी ही रोटियों पर पड़ी हुई है या और कुछ! जहां कोई बात कही, बस सिर हो गये, मानों मैं घर की लौंडी हूं, मेरा केवल रोटी और कपड़े

का नाता है। जितना ही मैं दबती हूं, तुम और भी दबाते हो। मुफ्तखोर माल उड़ायें, कोई मुंह न खोले, शराब-कबाब में रूपये लुटें, कोई जबान न हिलाये। ये सारे कांटे मेरे बच्चों ही के लिए तो बोये जा रहे है।

उदयभानु लाल–तो मैं क्या तुम्हारा गुलाम हूं?

कल्याणी–तो क्या मैं तुम्हारी लौंडी हूं?

उदयभानुलाल–ऐसे मर्द और होंगे, जो औरतों के इशारों पर नाचते हैं।

कल्याणी–तो ऐसी स्त्रियों भी होंगी, जो मर्दों की जूतियां सहा करती हैं।

उदयभानुलाल–मैं कमाकर लाता हूं जैसे चाहूं खर्च कर सकता हूं। किसी को बोलने का अधिकार नहीं।

कल्याणी–तो आप अपना घर संभलिये! ऐसे घर को मेरा दूर ही से सलाम है, जहां मेरी कोई पूछ नहीं घर में तुम्हारा जितना अधिकार है, उतना ही मेरा भी। इससे जौ भर भी कम नहीं। अगर तुम अपने मन के राजा हो, तो मैं भी अपने मन की रानी हूं। तुम्हारा घर तुम्हें मुबारक रहे, मेरे लिए पेट की रोटियों की कमी नहीं है। तुम्हारे बच्चे हैं, मारो या जिलाओ। न आंखों से देखूंगी, न पीड़ा होगी। आंखें फूटीं, पीर गई!

उदयभानुलाल–क्या तुम समझती हो कि तुम न संभालेगी तो मेरा घर ही न संभलेगा? मैं अकेले ऐसे-ऐसे दस घर संभाल सकता हूं।

कल्याणी–कौन? अगर 'आज के महीने दिन मिट्टी में न मिल जाए, तो कहना कोई कहती थी!

यह कहते–कहते कल्याणी का चेहरा तमतमा उठा, वह झमककर उठी और कमरे के द्वार की ओर चली। वकील साहब मुकदमें में तो खूब मीन-मेख निकालते थे, लेकिन स्त्रियों के स्वभाव का उन्हें कुछ यों ही-सा ज्ञान था। यही एक ऐसी विद्या है, जिसमें आदमी बूढ़ा होने पर भी कोरा रह जाता है। अगर वे अब भी नरम पड़ जाते और कल्याणी का हाथ पकड़कर बिठा लेते, तो शायद वह रूक जाती, लेकिन आपसे यह तो हो न सका, उल्टे चलते-चलते एक और चरका दिया।

बोले–मैके का घमण्ड होगा?

कल्याणी ने द्वार पर रूक कर पति की ओर लाल-लाल नेत्रों से देखा और बिफरकर बोली–मैके वाले मेरे तकदीर के साथी नहीं है और न मैं इतनी नीच हूं कि उनकी रोटियों पर जा पड़ूं।

उदयभानुलाल–तब कहां जा रही हो?

कल्याणी–तुम यह पूछने वाले कौन होते हो? ईश्वर की सृष्टि में असंख्य प्राणियों के लिए जगह है, क्या मेरे ही लिए जगह नहीं है?

यह कहकर कल्याणी कमरे के बाहर निकल गई। आंगन में आकर उसने एक बार आकाश की ओर देखा, मानो तारागण को साक्षी दे रही है कि मैं इस घर में कितनी निर्दयता से निकाली जा रही हूं। रात के ग्यारह बज गये थे। घर में सन्नाटा छा गया था, दोनों बेटों की चारपाई उसी के कमरे में रहती थी। वह अपने कमरे में आई, देखा चन्द्रभानु सोया है, सबसे छोटा सूर्यभानु चारपाई पर उठ बैठा है। माता को देखते ही वह बोला–तुम तहां दई तीं अम्मां?

कल्याणी दूर ही से खड़े-खड़े बोली–कहीं तो नहीं बेटा, तुम्हारे बाबूजी के पास गई थी।

सूर्यभानु–तुम तली दई, मुधे अतेले दर लदता था। तुम क्यों तली दई तीं, बताओ?

यह कहकर बच्चे ने गोद में चढ़ने के लिए दोनों हाथ फैला दिये।

कल्याणी अब अपने को न रोक सकी। मातृ-स्नेह के सुधा-प्रवाह से उसका संतप्त हृदय परिप्लावित हो गया। हृदय के कोमल पौधे, जो क्रोध के ताप से मुरझा गये थे, फिर हरे हो गये। आंखें सजल हो गई। उसने बच्चे को गोद में उठा लिया और छाती से लगाकर बोली–तुमने पुकार क्यों न लिया, बेटा?

सूर्यभानु–पुतालता तो ता, तुम थुनती न तीं, बताओ अब तो कबी न दाओगी।

कल्याणी–नहीं भैया, अब नहीं जाऊंगी।

यह कहकर कल्याणी सूर्यभानु को लेकर चारपाई पर लेटी। मां के हृदय से लिपटते ही बालक निःशंक होकर सो गया, कल्याणी के मन में संकल्प-विकल्प होने लगे, पति की बातें याद आतीं तो मन होता–घर

को तिलांजलि देकर चली जाऊं, लेकिन बच्चों का मुंह देखती, तो वासल्य से चित्त गद्गद हो जाता। बच्चों को किस पर छोड़कर जाऊं? मेरे इन लालों को कौन पालेगा, ये किसके होकर रहेंगे? कौन प्रातःकाल इन्हें दूध और हलवा खिलायेगा, कौन इनकी नींद सोयेगा, इनकी नींद जागेगा? बेचारे कौड़ी के तीन हो जाएंगे। नहीं प्यारों, मैं तुम्हें छोड़कर नहीं जाऊंगी। तुम्हारे लिए सब कुछ सह लूंगी। निरादर-अपमान, जली-कटी, खोटी-खरी, घुड़की-झिड़की सब तुम्हारे लिए सहूंगी।

कल्याणी तो बच्चे को लेकर लेटी, पर बाबू साहब को नींद न आई उन्हें चोट करनेवाली बातें बड़ी मुश्किल से भूलती थी। उफ, यह मिजाज! मानों मैं ही इनकी स्त्री हूं। बात मुंह से निकालनी मुश्किल है। अब मैं इनका गुलाम होकर रहूं। घर में अकेली यह रहें और बाकी जितने अपने बेगाने हैं, सब निकाल दिये जाएं। जला करती हैं। मनाती हैं कि यह किसी तरह मरें, तो मैं अकेली आराम करूं। दिल की बात मुंह से निकल ही आती है, चाहे कोई कितना ही छिपाये। कई दिन से देख रहा हूं ऐसी ही जली-कटी सुनाया करती हैं। मैके का घमण्ड होगा, लेकिन वहां कोई भी न पूछेगा, अभी सब आवभगत करते हैं। जब जाकर सिर पड़ जाएंगी तो आटे-दाल का भाव मालूम हो जाएगा। रोती हुई आएंगी। वाह रे घमण्ड! सोचती हैं–मैं ही यह गृहस्थी चलाती हूं। अभी चार दिन को कहीं चला जाऊं, तो मालूम हो जाएगा, सारी शेखी किरकिरी हो जाएगी। एक बार इनका घमण्ड तोड़ ही दूं। जरा वैधव्य का मजा भी चखा दूं। न जाने इनकी हिम्मत कैसे पड़ती है कि मुझे यों कोसने लगती हैं। मालूम होता है, प्रेम इन्हें छू नहीं गया या समझती हैं, यह घर से इतना चिमटा हुआ है कि इसे चाहे जितना कोसूं, टलने का नाम न लेगा। यही बात है, पर यहां संसार से चिमटनेवाले जीव नहीं हैं! जहन्नुम में जाए यह घर, जहां ऐसे प्राणियों से पाला पड़े। घर है या नरक? आदमी बाहर से थका-मांदा आता है, तो उसे घर में आराम मिलता है। यहां आराम के बदले कोसने सुनने पड़ते हैं। मेरी मृत्यु के लिए व्रत रखे जाते हैं। यह है पचीस वर्ष के दाम्पत्य जीवन का अन्त! बस, चल ही दूं। जब देख लूंगा इनका सारा घमण्ड धूल में मिल गया

और मिजाज ठण्डा हो गया, तो लौट आऊंगा। चार-पांच दिन काफी होंगे। लो, तुम भी याद करोगी किसी से पाला पड़ा था।

यही सोचते हुए बाबू साहब उठे, रेशमी चादर गले में डाली, कुछ रूपये लिये, अपना कार्ड निकालकर दूसरे कुर्ते की जेब में रखा, छड़ी उठाई और चुपके से बाहर निकले। सब नौकर नींद में मस्त थे। कुत्ता आहट पाकर चौंक पड़ा और उनके साथ हो लिया, पर यह कौन जानता था कि यह सारी लीला विधि के हाथों रची जा रही है। जीवन-रंगशाला का वह निर्दय सूत्रधार किसी अगम गुप्त स्थान पर बैठा हुआ अपनी जटिल क्रूर क्रीड़ा दिखा रहा है। यह कौन जानता था कि नकल असल होने जा रही है, अभिनय सत्य का रूप ग्रहण करने वाला है।

निशा ने इन्दु को परास्त करके अपना साम्राज्य स्थापित कर लिया था। उसकी पैशाचिक सेना ने प्रकृति पर आतंक जमा रखा था। सद्वृत्तियां मुंह छिपाये पड़ी थीं और कुवृत्तियां विजय-गर्व से इठलाती फिरती थीं। वन में वन्यजन्तु शिकार की खोज में विचार रहे थे और नगरों में नर-पिशाच गलियों में मंडराते फिरते थे।

बाबू उदयभानुलाल लपके हुए गंगा की ओर चले जा रहे थे। उन्होंने अपना कुर्ता घाट के किनारे रखकर पांच दिन के लिए मिर्जापुर चले जाने का निश्चय किया था। उनके कपड़े देखकर लोगों को डूब जाने का विश्वास हो जाएगा, कार्ड कुर्ते की जेब में था। पता लगाने में कोई दिक्कत न हो सकती थी। दम-के-दम में सारे शहर में खबर मशहूर हो जाएगी। आठ बजते-बजते तो मेरे द्वार पर सारा शहर जमा हो जाएगा, तब देखूं, देवी जी क्या करती हैं?

यही सोचते हुए बाबू साहब गलियों में चले जा रहे थे, सहसा उन्हें अपने पीछे किसी दूसरे आदमी के आने की आहट मिली, समझे कोई होगा। आगे बढ़े, लेकिन जिस गली में वह मुड़ते उसी तरफ यह आदमी भी मुड़ता था। तब बाबू साहब को आशंका हुई कि यह आदमी मेरा पीछा कर रहा है। ऐसा आभास हुआ कि इसकी नीयत साफ नहीं है। उन्होंने तुरन्त जेबी लालटेन निकाली और उसके प्रकाश में उस आदमी को देखा। एक बलिष्ठ मनुष्य कन्धे पर लाठी रखे चला आता

था। बाबू साहब उसे देखते ही चौंक पड़े। यह शहर का छंटा हुआ बदमाश था। तीन साल पहले उस पर डाके का अभियोग चला था। उदयभानु ने उस मुकदमे में सरकार की ओर से पैरवी की थी और इस बदमाश को तीन साल की सजा दिलाई थी। तभी से वह इनके खून का प्यासा हो रहा था। कल ही वह छूटकर आया था। आज दैवात् साहब अकेले रात को दिखाई दिये, तो उसने सोचा यह इनसे दांव चुकाने का अच्छा मौका है। ऐसा मौका शायद ही फिर कभी मिले। तुरन्त पीछे हो लिया और वार करने की घात ही में था कि बाबू साहब ने जेबी लालटेन जलाई। बदमाश जरा ठिठककर बोला—क्यों बाबूजी पहचानते हो? मैं हूं मतई।

बाबू साहब ने डपटकर कहा—तुम मेरे पीछे-पीछे क्यों आ रहे हो?

मतई—क्यों, किसी को रास्ता चलने की मनाही है? यह गली तुम्हारे बाप की है?

बाबू साहब जवानी में कुश्ती लड़े थे, अब भी हृष्ट-पुष्ट आदमी थे। दिल के भी कच्चे न थे। छड़ी संभालकर बोले—अभी शायद मन नहीं भरा। अबकी सात साल को जाओगे।

मतई—मैं सात साल को जाऊंगा या चौदह साल को, पर तुम्हें जिंदा न छोड़ूंगा। हां, अगर तुम मेरे पैरों पर गिरकर कसम खाओ कि अब किसी को सजा न कराऊंगा, तो छोड़ दूं। बोलो मंजूर है?

उदयभानुलाल—तेरी शामत तो नहीं आई?

मतई शामत मेरी नहीं आई, तुम्हारी आई है। बोलो खाते हो कसम—एक!

उदयभानुलाल—तुम हटते हो कि मैं पुलिसमैन को बुलाऊं।

मतई—दो!

उदयभानुलाल—(गरजकर) हट जा बदमाश, सामने से!

मतई—तीन!

मुंह से 'तीन' शब्द निकालते ही बाबू साहब के सिर पर लाठी का ऐसा तुला हाथ पड़ा कि वह अचेत होकर जमीन पर गिर पड़े। मुंह से केवल इतना ही निकला—हाय! मार डाला!

मतई ने समीप आकर देखा, तो सिर फट गया था और खून की धार निकल रही थी। नाड़ी का कहीं पता न था। समझ गया कि काम तमाम हो गया। उसने कलाई से सोने की घड़ी खोल ली, कुर्ते से सोने के बटन निकाल लिये, उंगली से अंगूठी उतारी और अपनी राह चला गया, मानो कुछ हुआ ही नहीं। हां, इतनी दया की कि लाश रास्ते से घसीटकर किनारे डाल दी। हाय, बेचारे क्या सोचकर चले थे, क्या हो गया! जीवन, तुमसे ज्यादा असार भी दुनिया में कोई वस्तु है? क्या वह उस दीपक की भांति ही क्षणभंगुर नहीं है, जो हवा के एक झोंके से बुझ जाता है! पानी के एक बुलबुले को देखते हो, लेकिन उसे टूटते भी कुछ देर लगती है, जीवन में उतना सार भी नहीं। सांस का भरोसा ही क्या और इसी नश्वरता पर हम अभिलाषाओं के कितने विशाल भवन बनाते हैं! नहीं जानते, नीचे जानेवाली सांस ऊपर आयेगी या नहीं, पर सोचते इतनी दूर की हैं, मानो हम अमर हैं।

2

विधवा का विलाप और अनाथों का रोना सुनाकर हम पाठकों का दिल न दुखायेंगे। जिसके ऊपर पड़ती है, वह रोता है, विलाप करता है, पछाड़ें खाता है। यह कोई नयी बात नहीं। हां, अगर आप चाहें तो कल्याणी की उस घोर मानसिक यातना का अनुमान कर सकते हैं, जो उसे इस विचार से हो रही थी कि मैं ही अपने प्राणाधार की घातिका हूं। वे वाक्य जो क्रोध के आवेश में उसके असंयत मुख से निकले थे, अब उसके हृदय को बाणों की भांति छेद रहे थे।

अगर पति ने उसकी गोद में कराह-कराहकर प्राण-त्याग दिए होते, तो उसे संतोष होता कि मैंने उनके प्रति अपने कर्तव्य का पालन किया। शोकाकुल हृदय को इससे ज्यादा सान्त्वना और किसी बात से नहीं होती। उसे इस विचार से कितना संतोष होता कि मेरे स्वामी मुझसे प्रसन्न गये, अन्तिम समय तक उनके हृदय में मेरा प्रेम बना रहा। कल्याणी को यह संतोष न था। वह सोचती थी–हा! मेरी पचीस बरस की तपस्या निष्फल हो गई। मैं अन्त समय अपने प्राणपति के प्रेम से वंचित हो गयी। अगर मैंने उन्हें ऐसे कठोर शब्द न कहे होते, तो वह कदापि रात को घर से न जाते। न जाने उनके मन में क्या-क्या विचार आये हों? उनके मनोभावों की कल्पना करके और अपने अपराध को बढ़ा-बढ़ाकर वह आठों पहर कुढ़ती रहती थी। जिन बच्चों पर वह प्राण देती थी, अब उनकी सूरत से चिढ़ती। इन्हीं के कारण मुझे अपने स्वामी से रार मोल लेनी पड़ी। यही मेरे शत्रु हैं।

जहां आठों पहर कचहरी-सी लगी रहती थी, वहां अब खाक उड़ती है। वह मेला ही उठ गया। जब खिलानेवाला ही न रहा, तो खानेवाले

कैसे पड़े रहते। धीरे-धीरे एक महीने के अन्दर सभी भांजे-भतीजे बिदा हो गये। जिनका दावा था कि हम पानी की जगह खून बहानेवालों में हैं, वे ऐसा सरपट भागे कि पीछे फिरकर भी न देखा। दुनिया ही दूसरी हो गयी। जिन बच्चों को देखकर प्यार करने को जी चाहता था उनके चेहरे पर अब मक्खियां भिनभिनाती थीं। न जाने वह कांति कहां चली गई?

शोक का आवेग कम हुआ, तो निर्मला के विवाह की समस्या उपस्थित हुई। कुछ लोगों की सलाह हुई कि विवाह इस साल रोक दिया जाए, लेकिन कल्याणी ने कहा–इतनी तैयारियों के बाद विवाह को रोक देने से सब किया-धरा मिट्टी में मिल जाएगा और दूसरे साल फिर यही तैयारियां करनी पड़ेंगी, जिसकी कोई आशा नहीं। विवाह कर ही देना अच्छा है। कुछ लेना-देना तो है ही नहीं। बारातियों के सेवा-सत्कार का काफी सामान हो चुका है, विलम्ब करने में हानि-ही-हानि है। अतएव महाशय भालचन्द्र को शोक-सूचना के साथ यह सन्देश भी भेज दिया गया।

कल्याणी ने अपने पत्र में लिखा–

> इस अनाथिनी पर दया कीजिए और डूबती हुई नाव को पार लगाइये। स्वामीजी के मन में बड़ी-बड़ी कामनाएं थीं, किंतु ईश्वर को कुछ और ही मंजूर था। अब मेरी लाज आपके हाथ है। कन्या आपकी हो चुकी। मैं लोगों के सेवा-सत्कार करने को अपना सौभाग्य समझती हूं, लेकिन यदि इसमें कुछ कमी हो, कुछ त्रुटि पड़े, तो मेरी दशा का विचार करके क्षमा कीजियेगा। मुझे विश्वास है कि आप इस अनाथिनी की निन्दा न होने देंगे, आदि।

कल्याणी ने यह पत्र डाक से न भेजा, बल्कि पुरोहित से कहा–आपको कष्ट तो होगा, पर आप स्वयं जाकर यह पत्र दीजिए और मेरी ओर से बहुत विनय के साथ कहियेगा कि जितने कम आदमी आयें, उतना ही अच्छा। यहां कोई प्रबन्ध करनेवाला नहीं है।

पुरोहित मोटेराम यह सन्देश लेकर तीसरे दिन लखनऊ जा पहुँचे।

संध्या का समय था। बाबू भालचन्द्र दीवानखाने के सामने आरामकुर्सी पर नंग-धड़ंग लेटे हुए हुक्का पी रहे थे। बहुत ही स्थूल, ऊंचे कद के आदमी थे। ऐसा मालूम होता था कि काला देव है या कोई हब्शी अफ्रीका से पकड़कर आया है। सिर से पैर तक एक ही रंग था–काला। चेहरा इतना स्याह था कि मालूम न होता था कि माथे का अंत कहां है सिर का आरम्भ कहां। बस, कोयले की एक सजीव मूर्ति थी। आपको गर्मी बहुत सताती थी। दो आदमी खड़े पंखा झल रहे थे, उस पर भी पसीने का तार बंधा हुआ था।

आप आबकारी के विभाग में एक ऊंचे ओहदे पर थे। पांच सौ रूपये वेतन मिलता था। ठेकेदारों से खूब रिश्वत लेते थे। ठेकेदार शराब के नाम पानी बेचें, चौबीसों घंटे दुकान खुली रखें, आपको केवल खुश रखना काफी था। सारा कानून आपकी खुशी थी। इतनी भयंकर मूर्ति थी कि चांदनी रात में लोग उन्हें देख कर सहसा चौंक पड़ते थे–बालक और स्त्रियां ही नहीं, पुरूष तक सहम जाते थे। चांदनी रात इसलिए कहा गया कि अंधेरी रात में तो उन्हें कोई देख ही न सकता था–श्यामलता अन्धकार में विलीन हो जाती थी। केवल आंखों का रंग लाल था। जैसे पक्का मुसलमान पांच बार नमाज पढ़ता है, वैसे ही आप भी पांच बार शराब पीते थे, मुफ्त की शराब तो काजी को हलाल है, फिर आप तो शराब के अफसर ही थे, जितनी चाहें पियें, कोई हाथ पकड़ने वाला न था। जब प्यास लगती शराब पी लेते। जैसे कुछ रंगों में परस्पर सहानुभूति है, उसी तरह कुछ रंगों में परस्पर विरोध है। लालिमा के संयोग से कालिमा और भी भयंकर हो जाती है।

बाबू साहब ने पंडितजी को देखते ही कुर्सी से उठकर कहा–अक्खाह! आप हैं? आइए-आइए। धन्य भाग! अरे कोई है। कहां चले गये सब-के-सब, झगड़ू, गुरदीन, छकौड़ी, भवानी, रामगुलाम कोई है घर में? क्या सब-के-सब मर गये! चलो रामगुलाम, भवानी, छकौड़ी, गुरदीन, झगड़ू। कोई नहीं बोलता, सब मर गये! दर्जन-भर आदमी हैं, पर मौके पर एक की भी सूरत नहीं नजर आती, न जाने सब कहां गायब हो जाते हैं। कोई आपके वास्ते कुर्सी लाओ।

बाबू साहब ने ये पांचों नाम कई बार दुहराये, लेकिन यह न हुआ कि पंखा झलनेवाले दोनों आदमियों में से किसी को कुर्सी लाने को भेज देते। तीन-चार मिनट के बाद एक काना आदमी खांसता हुआ आकर बोला–सरकार, ईतना की नौकरी हमार कीन न होई ! कहां तक उधार-बाढ़ी लै-लै खाई मांगत–मांगत थेथर होय गयेन।

भालचन्द्र–बको मत, जाकर कुर्सी लाओ। जब कोई काम करने को कहा गया, तो रोने लगता है। कहिए पडितजी, वहां सब कुशल है?

मोटेराम–क्या कुशल कहूं बाबूजी, अब कुशल कहां? सारा घर मिट्टी में मिल गया।

इतने में कहार ने एक टूटा हुआ चीड़ का सन्दूक लाकर रख दिया और बोला–कुर्सी-मेज हमारे उठाये नाहीं उठत है।

पंडितजी शर्माते हुए डरते-डरते उस पर बैठे कि कहीं टूट न जाए और कल्याणी का पत्र बाबू साहब के हाथ में रख दिया।

भालचन्द्र–अब और कैसे मिट्टी में मिलेगा? इससे बड़ी और कौन विपत्ति पड़ेगी? बाबू उदयभानुलाल से मेरी पुरानी दोस्ती थी। आदमी नहीं, हीरा था! क्या दिल था, क्या हिम्मत थी, (आंखें पोंछकर) मेरा तो जैसे दाहिना हाथ ही कट गया। विश्वास मानिए, जबसे यह खबर सुनी है, आंखों में अंधेरा-सा छा गया है। खाने बैठता हूं, तो कौर मुंह में नहीं जाता। उनकी सूरत आंखों के सामने खड़ी रहती है। मुंह जूठा करके उठ जाता हूं। किसी काम में दिल नहीं लगता। भाई के मरने का रंज भी इससे कम ही होता है। आदमी नहीं, हीरा था!

मोटेराम–सरकार, नगर में अब ऐसा कोई रईस नहीं रहा।

भालचन्द्र–मैं खूब जानता हूं, पंडितजी, आप मुझसे क्या कहते हैं। ऐसा आदमी लाख-दो-लाख में एक होता है। जितना मैं उनको जानता था, उतना दूसरा नहीं जान सकता। दो-ही-तीन बार की मुलाकात में उनका भक्त हो गया और मरते दम तक रहूंगा। आप समधिन साहब से कह दीजिएगा, मुझे दिली रंज है।

मोटेराम–आपसे ऐसी ही आशा थी! आप-जैसे सज्जनों के दर्शन दुर्लभ हैं। नहीं तो आज क़ौन बिना दहेज के पुत्र का विवाह करता है।

भालचन्द्र–महाराज, दहेज की बातचीत ऐसे सत्यवादी पुरूषों से नहीं की जाती। उनसे सम्बन्ध हो जाना ही लाख रूपये के बराबर है। मैं इसी को अपना अहोभाग्य समझता हूं। हा! कितनी उदार आत्मा थी। रूपये को तो उन्होंने कुछ समझा ही नहीं, तिनके के बराबर भी परवाह नहीं की। बुरा रिवाज है, बेहद बुरा! मेरा बस चले, तो दहेज लेनेवालों और दहेज देनेवालों दोनों ही को गोली मार दूं, हां साहब, साफ गोली मार दूं, फिर चाहे फांसी ही क्यों न हो जाए! पूछो, आप लड़के का विवाह करते हैं कि उसे बेचते हैं? अगर आपको लड़के के शादी में दिल खोलकर खर्च करने का अरमान है, तो शौक के खर्च कीजिए, लेकिन जो कुछ कीजिए, अपने बल पर। यह क्या कि कन्या के पिता का गला रेतिए। नीचता है, घोर नीचता! मेरा बस चले, तो इन पाजियों को गोली मार दूं।

मोटेराम–धन्य हो सरकार! भगवान् ने आपको बड़ी बुद्धि दी है। यह धर्म का प्रताप है। मालकिन की इच्छा है कि विवाह का मुहूर्त वही रहे और तो उन्होंने सारी बातें पत्र में लिख दी हैं। बस, अब आप ही उबारें तो हम उबर सकते हैं। इस तरह तो बारात में जितने सज्जन आयेंगे, उनकी सेवा-सत्कार हम करेंगे ही, लेकिन परिस्थिति अब बहुत बदल गयी है सरकार, कोई करने-धरनेवाला नहीं है। बस ऐसी बात कीजिए कि वकील साहब के नाम पर बट्टा न लगे।

भालचन्द्र एक मिनट तक आंखें बन्द किये बैठे रहे, फिर एक लम्बी सांस खींच कर बोले–ईश्वर को मंजूर ही न था कि वह लक्ष्मी मेरे घर आती, नहीं तो क्या यह वज्र गिरता? सारे मनसूबे खाक में मिल गये। फूला न समाता था कि वह शुभ-अवसर निकट आ रहा है, पर क्या जानता था कि ईश्वर के दरबार में कुछ और षड्यन्त्र रचा जा रहा है। मरनेवाले की याद ही रूलाने के लिए काफी है। उसे देखकर तो जख्म और भी हरा जो जाएगा। उस दशा में न जाने क्या कर बैठूं। इसे गुण समझिए, चाहे दोष कि जिससे एक बार मेरी घनिष्ठता हो गयी, फिर उसकी याद चित्त से नहीं उतरती। अभी तो खैर इतना ही है कि उनकी सूरत आंखों के सामने नाचती रहती है, लेकिन यदि वह कन्या घर में

आ गयी, तब मेरा जिन्दा रहना कठिन हो जाएगा। सच मानिए, रोते-रोते मेरी आंखें फूट जाएंगी। जानता हूं, रोना-धोना व्यर्थ है। जो मर गया वह लौटकर नहीं आ सकता। सब्र करने के सिवाय और कोई उपाय नहीं है, लेकिन दिल से मजबूर हूं। उस अनाथ बालिका को देखकर मेरा कलेजा फट जाएगा।

मोटेराम–ऐसा न कहिए सरकार! वकील साहब नहीं तो क्या, आप तो हैं। अब आप ही उसके पिता-तुल्य हैं। वह अब वकील साहब की कन्या नहीं, आपकी कन्या है। आपके हृदय के भाव तो कोई जानता नहीं, लोग समझेंगे, वकील साहब का देहान्त हो जाने के कारण आप अपने वचन से फिर गये। इसमें आपकी बदनामी है। चित्त को समझाइए और हंसी-खुशी कन्या का पाणिग्रहण करा लीजिए। हाथी मरे तो नौ लाख का। लाख विपत्ति पड़ी है, लेकिन मालकिन आप लोगों की सेवा-सत्कार करने में कोई बात न उठा रखेंगी।

बाबू साहब समझ गये कि पंडित मोटेराम कोरे पोथी के ही पंडित नहीं, वरन व्यवहार-नीति में भी चतुर हैं। बोले–पंडितजी, हलफ से कहता हूं, मुझे उस लड़की से जितना प्रेम है, उतना अपनी लड़की से भी नहीं है, लेकिन जब ईश्वर को मंजूर नहीं है, तो मेरा क्या बस है? वह मृत्यु एक प्रकार की अमंगल सूचना है, जो विधाता की ओर से हमें मिली है। यह किसी आनेवाली मुसीबत की आकाशवाणी है विधाता स्पष्ट रीति से कह रहा है कि यह विवाह मंगलमय न होगा। ऐसी दशा में आप ही सोचिये, यह संयोग कहां तक उचित है। आप तो विद्वान आदमी हैं। सोचिए, जिस काम का आरम्भ ही अमंगल से हो, उसका अंत मंगलमय हो सकता है? नहीं, जानबूझकर मक्खी नहीं निगली जाती। समधिन साहब को समझाकर कह दीजिएगा, मैं उनकी आज्ञापालन करने को तैयार हूं, लेकिन इसका परिणाम अच्छा न होगा। स्वार्थ के वश में होकर मैं अपने परम मित्र की सन्तान के साथ यह अन्याय नहीं कर सकता।

इस तर्क ने पडितजी को निरुत्तर कर दिया। वादी ने यह तीर छोड़ा था, जिसकी उनके पास कोई काट न थी। शत्रु ने उन्हीं के हथियार से उन पर वार किया था और वह उसका प्रतिकार न कर

सकते थे। वह अभी कोई जवाब सोच ही रहे थे, कि बाबू साहब ने फिर नौकरों को पुकारना शुरू किया–अरे, तुम सब फिर गायब हो गये–झगड़ू, छकौड़ी, भवानी, गुरूदीन, रामगुलाम! एक भी नहीं बोलता, सब-के-सब मर गये। पंडितजी के वास्ते पानी-वानी की फिक्र है? ना जाने इन सबों को कोई कहां तक समझये। अक्ल छू तक नहीं गयी। देख रहे हैं कि एक महाशय दूर से थके-मांदे चले आ रहे हैं, पर किसी को जरा भी परवाह नहीं। लाओ, पानी-वानी रखो। पडितजी, आपके लिए शर्बत बनवाऊं या फलाहारी मिठाई मंगवा दूं।

मोटेरामजी मिठाइयों के विषय में किसी तरह का बन्धन न स्वीकार करते थे। उनका सिद्धान्त था कि घृत से सभी वस्तुएं पवित्र हो जाती हैं। रसगुल्ले और बेसन के लड्डू उन्हें बहुत प्रिय थे, पर शर्बत से उन्हें रुचि न थी। पानी से पेट भरना उनके नियम के विरूद्ध था।

सकुचाते हुए बोले–शर्बत पीने की तो मुझे आदत नहीं, मिठाई खा लूंगा।

भालचन्द्र–फलाहारी न?

मोटेराम–इसका मुझे कोई विचार नहीं।

भालचन्द्र–है तो यही बात। छूत-छात सब ढकोसला है। मैं स्वयं नहीं मानता। अरे, अभी तक कोई नहीं आया? छकौड़ी, भवानी, गुरुदीन, रामगुलाम, कोई तो बोले!

अबकी भी वही बूढ़ा कहार खांसता हुआ आकर खड़ा हो गया और बोला–सरकार, मोर तलब दै दीन जाए। ऐसी नौकरी मोसे न होई। कहां ले दौरी, दौरत-दौरत गोड़ पिराय लागत है।

भालचन्द्र–काम कुछ करो या न करो, पर तलब पहिले चहिए! दिन भर पड़े-पड़े खांसा करो, तलब तो तुम्हारी चढ़ रही है। जाकर बाजार से एक आने की ताजी मिठाई ला। दौड़ता हुआ जा।

कहार को यह हुक्म देकर बाबू साहब घर में गये और स्त्री से बोले–वहां से एक पंडितजी आये हैं। यह खत लाये हैं, जरा पढ़ो तो।

पत्नी जी का नाम रंगीलीबाई था। गोरे रंग की प्रसन्न-मुख महिला थीं। रूप और यौवन उनसे विदा हो रहे थे, पर किसी प्रेमी मित्र

की भांति मचल-मचल कर तीस साल तक जिसके गले से लगे रहे, उसे छोड़ते न बनता था।

रंगीलीबाई बैठी पान लगा रही थीं। बोली—कह दिया न कि हमें वहां ब्याह करना मंजूर नहीं।

भालचन्द्र—हां, कह तो दिया, पर मारे संकोच के मुंह से शब्द न निकलता था। झूठ-मूठ का हीला करना पड़ा।

रंगीलीबाई—साफ बात करने में संकोच क्या? हमारी इच्छा है, नहीं करते। किसी का कुछ लिया तो नहीं है? जब दूसरी जगह दस हजार नगद मिल रहे हैं, तो वहां क्यों न करूं? उनकी लड़की कोई सोने की थोड़े ही है। वकील साहब जीते होते तो शरमाते-शरमाते पन्द्रह-बीस हजार दे मरते। अब वहां क्या रखा है?

भालचन्द्र—एक दफा जबान देकर मुकर जाना अच्छी बात नहीं। कोई मुख से कुछ न कहे, पर बदनामी हुए बिना नहीं रहती। मगर तुम्हारी जिद से मजबूर हूं।

रंगीलीबाई ने पान खाकर खत खोला और पढ़ने लगीं। हिन्दी का अभ्यास बाबू साहब को तो बिल्कुल न था और यद्यपि रंगीलीबाई भी शायद ही कभी किताब पढ़ती हों, पर खत-वत पढ़ लेती थीं। पहली ही पांति पढ़कर उनकी आंखें सजल हो गयीं और पत्र समाप्त किया तो उनकी आंखों से आंसू बह रहे थे। एक-एक शब्द करुणा के रस में डूबा हुआ था। एक-एक अक्षर से दीनता टपक रही थी।

3

रंगीलीबाई की कठोरता पत्थर की नहीं, लाख की थी, जो एक ही आंच से पिघल जाती है। कल्याणी के करूणोत्पादक शब्दों ने उनके स्वार्थ-मंडित हृदय को पिघला दिया। रूंधे हुए कंठ से बोली—अभी ब्राह्मण बैठा है न?

भालचन्द्र पत्नी के आंसुओं को देख-देखकर सूखे जाते थे। अपने ऊपर झल्ला रहे थे कि नाहक मैंने यह खत इसे दिखाया। इसकी जरूरत क्या थी? इतनी बड़ी भूल उनसे कभी न हुई थी। संदिग्ध भाव से बोले—शायद बैठा हो, मैंने तो जाने को कह दिया था।

रंगीली ने खिड़की से झांककर देखा। पंडित मोटेराम जी बगुले की तरह ध्यान लगाये बाजार के रास्ते की ओर ताक रहे थे। लालसा में व्यग्र होकर कभी यह पहलू बदलते, कभी वह पहलू। 'एक आने की मिठाई' ने तो आशा की कमर ही तोड़ दी थी, उसमें भी यह विलम्ब, दारूण दशा थी।

उन्हें बैठे देखकर रंगीलीबाई बोली—है-है अभी है, जाकर कह दो, हम विवाह करेंगे, जरूर करेंगे। बेचारी बड़ी मुसीबत में है।

भालचन्द्र—तुम भी कभी-कभी बच्चों की-सी बातें करने लगती हो, अभी उससे कह आया हूं कि मुझे विवाह करना मंजूर नहीं। एक लम्बी-चौड़ी भूमिका बांधनी पड़ी। अब जाकर यह संदेश कहूंगा, तो वह अपने दिल में क्या कहेगा, जरा सोचो तो? यह शादी-विवाह का मामला है। लड़कों का खेल नहीं कि अभी एक बात तय की, अभी पलट गये। भले आदमी की बात न हुई, दिल्लगी हुई।

रंगीलीबाई—अच्छा, तुम अपने मुंह से न कहो, उस ब्राह्मण को मेरे पास भेज दो। मैं इस तरह समझा दूंगी कि तुम्हारी बात भी रह जाये और मेरी भी। इसमें तो तुम्हें कोई आपत्ति नहीं है।

भालचन्द्र–तुम अपने सिवा सारी दुनिया को नादान समझती हो। तुम कहो या मैं कहूं, बात एक ही है। जो बात तय हो गयी, वह हो गई, अब मैं उसे फिर नहीं उठाना चाहता। तुम्हीं तो बार-बार कहती थीं कि मैं वहां न करूंगी। तुम्हारे ही कारण मुझे अपनी बात खोनी पड़ी। अब तुम फिर रंग बदलती हो। यह तो मेरी छाती पर मूंग दलना है। आखिर तुम्हें कुछ तो मेरे मान-अपमान का विचार करना चाहिए।

रंगीलीबाई–तो मुझे क्या मालूम था कि विधवा की दशा इतनी हीन हो गयी है? तुम्हीं ने तो कहा था कि उसने पति की सारी सम्पत्ति छिपा रखी है और अपनी गरीबी का ढोंग रचकर काम निकालना चाहती है। एक ही छंटी हुई औरत है। तुमने जो कहा, वह मैंने मान लिया। भलाई करके बुराई करने में तो लज्जा और संकोच है। बुराई करके भलाई करने मे कोई संकोच नहीं। अगर तुम 'हां' कर आये होते और मैं 'नहीं' करने को कहती, तो तुम्हारा संकोच उचित था। 'नहीं' करने के बाद 'हां' करने में तो अपना बड़प्पन है।

भालचन्द्र–तुम्हें बड़प्पन मालूम होता हो, मुझे तो लुच्चापन ही मालूम होता है। फिर तुमने यह कैसे मान लिया कि मैंने वकीलाइन के विषय में जो बात कही थी, वह झूठी थी! क्या वह पत्र देखकर? तुम जैसी खुद सरल हो, वैसे ही दूसरे को भी सरल समझती हो।

रंगीलीबाई–इस पत्र में बनावट नहीं मालूम होती। बनावट की बात दिल में चुभती नहीं। उसमें बनावट की गन्ध अवश्य रहती है।

भालचन्द्र–बनावट की बात तो ऐसी चुभती है कि सच्ची बात उसके सामने बिल्कुल फीकी मालूम होती है। यह किस्से-कहानियां लिखने वाले जिनकी किताबें पढ़-पढ़कर तुम घण्टों रोती हो, क्या सच्ची बातें लिखते है? सरासर झूठ का तुमार बांधते हैं। यह भी एक कला है।

रंगीलीबाई–क्यों जी, तुम मुझसे भी उड़ते हो! दाई से पेट छिपाते हो? मैं तुम्हारी बातें मान जाती हूं, तो तुम समझते हो, इसे चकमा दिया। मगर मैं तुम्हारी एक-एक नस पहचानती हूं। तुम अपना ऐब मेरे सिर मढ़कर खुद बेदाग बचना चाहते हो। बोलो, कुछ झूठ कहती हूं, जब वकील साहब जीते थे, जो तुमने सोचा था कि ठहराव

की जरूरत ही क्या है, वे खुद ही जितना उचित समझेंगे देंगे, बल्कि बिना ठहराव के और भी ज्यादा मिलने की आशा होगी। अब वकील साहब का देहान्त हो गया, तो तरह-तरह के हीले-हवाले करने लगे। यह भलमनसी नहीं, छोटापन है, इसका इलजाम भी तुम्हारे सिर है। मैं अब शादी-ब्याह के नगीच न जाऊंगी। तुम्हारी जैसी इच्छा हो, करो। ढोंगी आदमियों से मुझे चिढ़ है। जो बात करो, सफाई से करो, बुरा हो या अच्छा। 'हाथी के दांत खाने के और दिखाने के और' वाली नीति पर चलना तुम्हें शोभा नहीं देता। बोलो, अब भी वहां शादी करते हो या नहीं?

भालचन्द्र–जब मैं बेईमान, दगाबाज और झूठा ठहरा, तो मुझसे पूछना ही क्या! मगर खूब पहचानती हो आदमियों को! क्या कहना है, तुम्हारी इस सूझ-बूझ की, बलैया ले लें!

रंगीलीबाई–हो बड़े हयादार, अब भी नहीं शरमाते। ईमान से कहो, मैंने बात ताड़ ली कि नहीं?

भालचन्द्र–अजी जाओ, वह दूसरी औरतें होती हैं जो मर्दों को पहचानती हैं। अब तक मैं यही समझता था कि औरतों की दृष्टि बड़ी सूक्ष्म होती है, पर आज यह विश्वास उठ गया और महात्माओं ने औरतों के विषय में जो तत्व की बाते कही है, उनको मानना पड़ा।

रंगीलीबाई–जरा आईने में अपनी सूरत तो देख आओं, तुम्हें मेरी कसम है। जरा देख लो, कितना झेंपे हुए हो।

भालचन्द्र–सच कहना, कितना झेंपा हुआ हूं?

रंगीलीबाई–उतना ही, जितना कोई भलामानस चोर चोरी खुल जाने पर झेंपता है।

भालचन्द्र–खैर, मैं झेंपा ही सही, पर शादी वहां न होगी।

रंगीलीबाई–मेरी बला से, जहां चाहो करो। क्यों, भुवन से एक बार क्यों नहीं पूछ लेते?

भालचन्द्र–अच्छी बात है, उसी पर फैसला रहा।

रंगीलीबाई–जरा भी इशारा न करना!

भालचन्द्र–अजी, मैं उसकी तरफ ताकूंगा भी नहीं।

संयोग से ठीक इसी वक्त भुवनमोहन भी आ पहुंचा। ऐसे सुन्दर, सुडौल, बलिष्ठ युवक कालेजों में बहुत कम देखने में आते हैं। बिल्कुल मां को पड़ा था, वही गोरा-चिट्टा रंग, वही पतले-पतले गुलाब की पत्ती के-से ओंठ, वही चौड़ा, माथा, वही बड़ी-बड़ी आंखें, डील-डौल बाप का-सा था। ऊंचा कोट, ब्रीचेज, टाई, बूट, हैट उस पर खूब खिल रहे थे। हाथ में एक हाकी-स्टिक थी। चाल में जवानी का गरूर था, आंखों में आमत्मगौरव।

रंगीलीबाई ने कहा—आज बड़ी देर लगाई तुमने? यह देखो, तुम्हारी ससुराल से यह खत आया है। तुम्हारी सास ने लिखा है। साफ-साफ बतला दो, अभी सबेरा है। तुम्हें वहां शादी करना मंजूर है या नहीं?

भुवन—शादी करनी तो चाहिए अम्मां, पर मैं करूंगा नहीं।

रंगीलीबाई—क्यों?

भुवन—कहीं ऐसी जगह शादी करवाइये कि खूब रूपये मिलें। और न सही एक लाख का तो डौल हो। वहां अब क्या रखा है? वकील साहब रहे ही नहीं, बुढ़िया के पास अब क्या होगा?

रंगीलीबाई—तुम्हें ऐसी बातें मुंह से निकालते शर्म नहीं आती?

भुवन—इसमें शर्म की कौन-सी बात है? रूपये किसे काटते हैं? लाख रूपये तो लाख जन्म में भी न जमा कर पाऊंगा। इस साल पास भी हो गया, तो कम-से-कम पांच साल तक रूपये की सूरत नजर न आयेगी। फिर सौ-दो-सौ रूपये महीने कमाने लगूंगा। पांच-छः तक पहुंचते-पहुंचते उम्र के तीन भाग बीत जायेंगे। रूपये जमा करने की नौबत ही न आयेगी। दुनिया का कुछ मजा न उठा सकूंगा। किसी धनी की लड़की से शादी हो जाती, तो चैन से कटती। मैं ज्यादा नहीं चाहता, बस एक लाख नगद हो या फिर कोई ऐसी जायदादवाली बेवा मिले, जिसके एक ही लड़की हो।

रंगीलीबाई—चाहे औरत कैसी ही मिले।

भुवन—धन सारे ऐबों को छिपा देगा। मुझे वह गालियां भी सुनाये, तो भी चूं न करूं। दुधारू गाय की लात किसे बुरी मालूम होती है?

बाबू साहब ने प्रशंसा-सूचक भाव से कहा—हमें उन लोगों के साथ सहानुभति है और दुःख है कि ईश्वर ने उन्हें विपत्ति में डाला,

लेकिन बुद्धि से काम लेकर ही कोई निश्चय करना चहिए। हम कितने ही फटे-हाल हो जायें, फिर भी अच्छी-खासी बारात हो जायेगी। वहां भोजन का भी ठिकाना नहीं। सिवा इसके कि लोग हंसें और कोई नतीजा न निकलेगा।

रंगीलीबाई–तुम बाप-पूत दोनों एक ही थैली के चट्टे-बट्टे हो। दोनों उस गरीब लड़की के गले पर छुरी फेरना चाहते हो।

भुवन–जो गरीब है, उसे गरीबों ही के यहां सम्बन्ध करना चहिए। अपनी हैसियत से बढ़कर...।

रंगीलीबाई–चुप भी रह, आया है वहां से हैसियत लेकर। तुम कहां के धन्ना-सेठ हो? कोई आदमी द्वार पर आ जाये, तो एक लोटे पानी को तरस जाये। बड़े हैसियतवाले बने हो!

यह कहकर रंगीलीबाई वहां से उठकर रसोई का प्रबन्ध करने चली गयी।

भुवनमोहन मुस्कराता हुआ अपने कमरे में चला गया और बाबू साहब मूछों पर ताव देते हुए बाहर आये कि मोटेराम को अन्तिम निश्चय सुना दें। पर उनका कहीं पता न था।

मोटेरामजी कुछ देर तक तो कहार की राह देखते रहे, जब उसके आने में बहुत देर हुई, तो उनसे बैठा न गया। सोचा यहां बैठे-बैठे काम न चलेगा, कुछ उद्योग करना चाहिए। भाग्य के भरोसे यहां अड़ी किये बैठे रहें, तो भूखों मर जायेंगे। यहां तुम्हारी दाल नहीं गलने की। चुपके से लकड़ी उठायी और जिधर वह कहार गया था, उसी तरफ चले। बाजार थोड़ी ही दूर पर था, एक क्षण में जा पहुंचे। देखा, तो बुड्ढा एक हलवाई की दूकान पर बैठा चिलम पी रहा था। उसे देखते ही आपने बड़ी बेतकल्लुफी से कहा–अभी कुछ तैयार नहीं है क्या महरा? सरकार वहां बैठे बिगड़ रहे हैं कि जाकर सो गया या ताड़ी पीने लगा। मैंने कहा–'सरकार यह बात नहीं, बुढ्डा आदमी है, आते ही आते तो आयेगा।' बड़े विचित्र जीव हैं। न जाने इनके यहां कैसे नौकर टिकते हैं।

कहार–मुझे छोड़कर आज तक दूसरा कोई टिका नहीं, और न टिकेगा। साल-भर से तलब नहीं मिली। किसी को तलब नहीं देते।

जहां किसी ने तलब मांगी और लगे डांटने। बेचारा नौकरी छोड़कर भाग जाता है। वे दोनों आदमी, जो पंखा झल रहे थे, सरकारी नौकर हैं। सरकार से दो अर्दली मिले हैं न! इसी से पड़े हुए हैं। मैं भी सोचता हूं, जैसा तेरा ताना-बाना वैसे मेरी भरनी! दस साल कट गये हैं, साल दो साल और इसी तरह कट जायेंगे।

मोटेराम–तो तुम्हीं अकेले हो? नाम तो कई कहारों का लेते है।

कहार–वह सब इन दो-तीन महीनों के अन्दर आये और छोड़-छोड़ कर चले गये। यह अपना रोब जमाने को अभी तक उनका नाम जपा करते हैं। कहीं नौकरी दिलाइएगा, तो मैं भी चलूं?

मोटेराम–अजी, बहुत नौकरी है। कहार तो आजकल ढूंढे नहीं मिलते। तुम तो पुराने आदमी हो, तुम्हारे लिए नौकरी की क्या कमी है। यहां कोई ताजी चीज है? मुझसे कहने लगे, खिचड़ी बनाइएगा या बाटी लगाइएगा? मैंने कह दिया–सरकार, बुढ्डा आदमी है, रात को उसे मेरा भोजन बनाने में कष्ट होगा, मैं कुछ बाजार ही से खा लूंगा। इसकी आप चिन्ता न करें। बोले, अच्छी बात है, कहार आपको दुकान पर मिलेगा। बोलो साहजी, कुछ तर माल तैयार है? लड्डू तो ताजे मालूम होते हैं। तौल दो एक सेर भर, आ जाऊं वहीं ऊपर न?

यह कहकर मोटेरामजी हलवाई की दूकान पर जा बैठे और तर माल चखने लगे। खूब छककर खाया। ढाई-तीन सेर चट कर गये। खाते जाते थे और हलवाई की तारीफ करते जाते थे–शाहजी, तुम्हारी दुकान का जैसा नाम सुना था, वैसा ही माल भी पाया। बनारसवाले ऐसे रसगुल्ले नहीं बना पाते, कलाकन्द अच्छी बनाते हैं, पर तुम्हारी उनसे बुरी नहीं, माल डालने से अच्छी चीज नहीं बन जाती, विद्या चहिए।

हलवाई–कुछ और लीजिए महाराज! थोड़ी-सी रबड़ी मेरी तरफ से लीजिए।

मोटेराम–इच्छा तो नहीं है, लेकिन दे दो पाव-भर।

हलवाई–पाव-भर क्या लीजिएगा? चीज अच्छी है, आध सेर तो लीजिए।

खूब इच्छापूर्ण भोजन करके पंडितजी ने थोड़ी देर तक बाजार की सैर की और नौ बजते-बजते मकान पर आये। यहां सन्नाटा-सा छाया हुआ था। एक लालटेन जल रही थी। आपने चबूतरे पर बिस्तर जमाया और सो गये।

सबेरे अपने नियमानुसार कोई आठ बजे उठे, तो देखा कि बाबूसाहब टहल रहे हैं। इन्हें जगा देखकर वह पालागन कर बोले–महाराज, आप रात कहां चले गये? मैं बड़ी रात तक आपकी राह देखता रहा। भोजन का सब सामान बड़ी देर तक रखा रहा। जब आप न आये, तो रखवा दिया गया। आपने कुछ भोजन किया था या नहीं?

मोटेराम–हलवाई की दूकान में कुछ खा आया था।

भालचन्द्र–अजी पूरी-मिठाई में वह आनन्द कहां, जो बाटी और दाल में है। दस-बारह आने खर्च हो गये होंगे, फिर भी पेट न भरा होगा, आप मेरे मेहमान हैं, जितने पैसे लगे हों ले लीजिएगा।

मोटेराम–आप ही के हलवाई की दूकान पर खाया था, वह जो नुक्कड़ पर बैठता है।

भालचन्द्र–कितने पैसे देने पड़े?

मोटेराम–आपके हिसाब में लिखा दिये हैं।

भालचन्द्र–जितनी मिठाइयां ली हों, मुझे बता दीजिए, नहीं तो पीछे से बेईमानी करने लगेगा। एक ही ठग है।

मोटेराम–कोई ढाई सेर मिठाई थी और आधा सेर रबड़ी।

बाबू साहब ने विस्फरित नेत्रों से पंडितजी को देखा, मानो कोई अचम्भे की बात सुनी हो। तीन सेर तो कभी यहां महीने भर का टोटल भी न होता था और यह महाशय एक ही बार में कोई चार रूपये का माल उड़ा गये। अगर एक आध दिन और रह गये, तो बधिया बैठ जायेगी। पेट है या शैतान की कब्र? तीन सेर! कुछ ठिकाना है! उद्विग्न दशा में दौड़े हुए अन्दर गये और रंगीलीबाई से बोले–कुछ सुनती हो, यह महाशय कल तीन सेर मिठाई उड़ा गये। तीन सेर पक्की तौल!

रंगीलीबाई ने विस्मित होकर कहा–अजी नहीं, तीन सेर भला क्या खा जायेगा! आदमी है या बैल?

भालचन्द्र–तीन सेर तो अपने मुंह से कह रहा है। चार सेर से कम न होगा, पक्की तौल!

रंगीलीबाई–पेट में सनीचर है क्या?

भालचन्द्र–आज और रह गया तो छः सेर पर हाथ फेरेगा।

रंगीलीबाई–तो आज रहे ही क्यों, खत का जवाब जो देना हो, देकर विदा करो। अगर रहे तो साफ कह देना कि हमारे यहां मिठाई मुफ्त नहीं आती। खिचड़ी बनाना हो, बनावे, नहीं तो अपनी राह ले। जिन्हें ऐसे पेटुओं को खिलाने से मुक्ति मिलती हो, वे खिलायें हमें ऐसी मुक्ति न चाहिये! मगर पंडित विदा होने को तैयार बैठे थे, इसलिए बाबूसाहब को कौशल से काम लेने की जरूरत न पड़ी। पूछा–क्या तैयारी कर दी महाराज?

मोटेराम–हां सरकार, अब चलूंगा। नौ बजे की गाड़ी मिलेगी न?

भालचन्द्र–भला आज तो और रहिए।

यह कहते–कहते बाबूजी को भय हुआ कि कहीं यह महाराज सचमुच न रह जायें, इसलिये वाक्य को यों पूरा किया–हां, वहां भी लोग आपका इन्तजार कर रहे होंगे।

मोटेराम–एक-दो दिन की तो कोई बात न थी और विचार भी यही था कि त्रिवेणी का स्नान करूंगा, पर बुरा न मानिए तो कहूं, आप लोगों में ब्राह्मणों के प्रति लेशमात्र भी श्रद्धा नहीं है। हमारे जजमान हैं, जो हमारा मुंह जोहते रहते हैं कि पंडितजी कोई आज्ञा दें, तो उसका पालन करें। हम उनके द्वार पहुंच जाते हैं, तो वे अपना धन्य भाग्य समझते हैं और सारा घर, छोटे से बड़े तक हमारी सेवा-सत्कार में मग्न हो जाते हैं। जहां अपना आदर नहीं, वहां एक क्षण भी ठहरना असह्य है। जहां ब्राह्मण का आदर नहीं, वहां कल्याण नहीं हो सकता।

भालचन्द्र–महाराज, हमसे तो ऐसा अपराध नहीं हुआ।

मोटेराम–अपराध नहीं हुआ! और अपराध कहते किसे हैं? अभी आप ही ने घर में जाकर कहा कि यह महाशय तीन सेर मिठाई चट कर गये, पक्की तौल। आपने अभी खानेवाले देखे कहां? एक बार खिलाइये तो आंखें खुल जायें। ऐसे-ऐसे महान पुरूष पड़े हैं, जो पसेरी भर मिठाई खा

जायें और डकार तक न लें। एक-एक मिठाई खाने के लिए हमारी चिरौरी की जाती है, रूपये दिये जाते हैं। हम भिक्षुक ब्राह्मण नहीं हैं, जो आपके द्वार पर पड़े रहें। आपका नाम सुनकर आये थे, यह न जानते थे कि यहां मेरे भोजन के भी लाले पड़ेंगे। जाइये, भगवान् आपका कल्याण करें!

बाबू साहब ऐसा झेंपे कि मुंह से बात न निकली। जिन्दगी भर में उन पर कभी ऐसी फटकार न पड़ी थी। बहुत बातें बनायीं–आपकी चर्चा न थी, एक दूसरे ही महाशय की बात थी, लेकिन पंडितजी का क्रोध शान्त न हुआ। वह सब कुछ सह सकते थे, पर अपने पेट की निन्दा न सह सकते थे। औरतों को रूप की निन्दा जितनी अप्रिय लगती है, उससे कहीं अधिक अप्रिय पुरूषों को अपने पेट की निन्दा लगती है। बाबू साहब मनाते तो थे, पर धड़का भी समाया हुआ था कि यह टिक न जायें। उनकी कृपणता का परदा खुल गया था, अब इसमें सन्देह न था। उस पर्दे को ढांकना जरूरी था। अपनी कृपणता को छिपाने के लिए उन्होंने कोई बात उठा न रखी पर होनेवाली बात होकर रही। पछता रहे थे कि कहां से घर में इसकी बात कहने गया और कहा भी तो उच्च स्वर में। यह दुष्ट भी कान लगाये सुनता रहा, किन्तु अब पछताने से क्या हो सकता था? न जाने किस मनहूस की सूरत देखी थी कि यह विपत्ति गले पड़ी। अगर इस वक्त यहां से रूष्ट होकर चला गया, तो वहां जाकर बदनाम करेगा और मेरा सारा कौशल खुल जायेगा। अब तो इसका मुंह बन्द कर देना ही पड़ेगा।

यह सोच–विचार करते हुए वह घर गें जाकर रंगीलीबाई से बोले– इस दुष्ट ने हमारी-तुम्हारी बातें सुन ली। रूठकर चला जा रहा है।

रंगीलीबाई–जब तुम जानते थे कि द्वार पर खड़ा है, तो धीरे से क्यों न बोले?

भालचन्द्र–विपत्ति आती है तो अकेले नहीं आती। यह क्या जानता था कि वह द्वार पर कान लगाये खड़ा है।

रंगीलीबाई–न जाने किसका मुंह देखा था?

भालचन्द्र–वही दुष्ट सामने लेटा हुआ था। जानता तो उधर ताकता ही नहीं। अब तो इसे कुछ दे-दिलाकर राजी करना पड़ेगा।

रंगीलीबाई—ऊंह, जाने भी दो। जब तुम्हें वहां विवाह ही नहीं करना है, तो क्या परवाह है? जो चाहे समझे, जो चाहे कहे।

भालचन्द्र—यों जान न बचेगी। लाओ दस रूपये विदाई के बहाने दे दूं। ईश्वर फिर इस मनहूस की सूरत न दिखाये। रंगीलीबाई ने बहुत पछताते-पछताते दस रुपये निकाले और बाबू साहब ने उन्हें ले जाकर पंडितजी के चरणों पर रख दिया। पंडितजी ने दिल में कहा—धत्तेरे मक्खीचूस की! ऐसा रगड़ा कि याद करोगे। तुम समझते होगे कि दस रुपये देकर इसे उल्लू बना लूंगा। इस फेर में न रहना। यहां तुम्हारी नस-नस पहचानते हैं। रुपये जेब में रख लिये और आशीर्वाद देकर अपनी राह ली।

बाबू साहब बड़ी देकर तक खड़े सोच रहे थे—मालूम नहीं, अब भी मुझे कृपण ही समझ रहा है या परदा ढंक गया। कहीं ये रुपये भी तो पानी में नहीं गिर पड़े।

4

कल्याणी के सामने अब एक विषम समस्या आ खड़ी हुई। पति के देहान्त के बाद उसे अपनी दुरावस्था का यह पहला और बहुत ही कड़वा अनुभव हुआ। दरिद्र विधवा के लिए इससे बड़ी और क्या विपत्ति हो सकती है कि जवान बेटी सिर पर सवार हो? लड़के नंगे पांव पढ़ने जा सकते हैं, चौका-बर्तन भी अपने हाथ से किया जा सकता है, रूखा-सूखा खाकर निर्वाह किया जा सकता है, झोपड़े में दिन काटे जा सकते हैं, लेकिन युवती कन्या घर में नहीं बैठाई जा सकती।

कल्याणी को भालचन्द्र पर ऐसा क्रोध आता था कि स्वयं जाकर उसके मुंह में कालिख लगाऊं, सिर के बाल नोच लूं, कहूं कि तू अपनी बात से फिर गया, तू अपने बाप का बेटा नहीं।

पंडित मोटेराम ने उनकी कपट-लीला का नग्न वृत्तान्त सुना दिया था। वह इसी क्रोध में भरी बैठी थी कि कृष्णा खेलती हुई आयी और बोली–कै दिन में बारात आयेगी अम्मां? पंडित तो आ गये।

कल्याणी–बारात का सपना देख रही है क्या?

कृष्णा–वही चन्दर तो कह रहा है कि-दो-तीन दिन में बारात आएगी, क्या न आएगी अम्मां?

कल्याणी–एक बार तो कह दिया, सिर क्यों खाती है?

कृष्णा–सबके घर तो बारात आ रही है, हमारे यहां क्यों नहीं आती?

कल्याणी–तेरे यहां जो बारात लाने वाला था, उसके घर में आग लग गई।

कृष्णा–सच, अम्मां! तब तो सारा घर जल गया होगा। कहां रहते होंगे? बहन कहां जाकर रहेगी?

कल्याणी–अरे पगली! तू तो बात ही नहीं समझती। आग नहीं लगी। वह हमारे यहां ब्याह न करेगा।

कृष्णा–यह क्यों अम्मां? पहले तो वहीं ठीक हो गया था न?

कल्याणी–बहुत से रुपये मांगता है। मेरे पास उसे देने को रुपये नहीं हैं।

कृष्णा–क्या बड़े लालची हैं, अम्मां?

कल्याणी–लालची नहीं तो और क्या है। पूरा कसाई निर्दयी, दगाबाज।

कृष्णा–तब तो अम्मां, बहुत अच्छा हुआ कि उसके घर बहन का ब्याह नहीं हुआ। बहन उसके साथ कैसे रहती? यह तो खुश होने की बात है अम्मां, तुम रंज क्यों करती हो?

कल्याणी ने पुत्री को स्नेहमयी दृष्टि से देखा। इनका कथन कितना सत्य है? भोले शब्दों में समस्या का कितना मार्मिक निरूपण है? सचमुच यह तो प्रसन्न होने की बात है कि ऐसे कुपात्रों से सम्बन्ध नहीं हुआ, रंज की कोई बात नहीं। ऐसे कुमानुसों के बीच में बेचारी निर्मला की न जाने क्या गति होती अपने नसीबों को रोती। जरा सा घी दाल में अधिक पड़ जाता, तो सारे घर में शोर मच जाता, जरा खाना ज्यादा पक जाता, तो सास दुनिया सिर पर उठा लेती। लड़का भी ऐसा लोभी है। बड़ी अच्छी बात हुई, नहीं, बेचारी को उम्र भर रोना पड़ता।

कल्याणी यहां से उठी, तो उसका हृदय हल्का हो गया था। लेकिन विवाह तो करना ही था और हो सके तो इसी साल, नहीं तो दूसरे साल फिर नये सिरे से तैयारियां करनी पडेगी। अब अच्छे घर की जरूरत न थी। अच्छे वर की जरूरत न थी। अभागिनी को अच्छा घर-वर कहां मिलता! अब तो किसी भांति सिर का बोझा उतारना था, किसी भांति लड़की को पार लगाना था, उसे कुएं में झोंकना था। वह रूपवती है, गुणशीला है, चतुर है, कुलीन है, तो हुआ करें, दहेज नहीं तो उसके सारे गुण दोष हैं, दहेज हो तो सारे दोष गुण हैं। प्राणी का कोई मूल्य नहीं, केवल दहेज का मूल्य है। कितनी विषम भग्यलीला है!

कल्याणी का दोष कुछ कम न था। अबला और विधवा होना ही उसे दोषों से मुक्त नहीं कर सकता। उसे अपने लड़के अपनी लड़कियों

से कहीं ज्यादा प्यारे थे। लड़के हल के बैल हैं, भूसे खली पर पहला हक उनका है, उनके खाने से जो बचे वह गायों का! मकान था, कुछ नकद था, कई हजार के गहने थे, लेकिन उसे अभी दो लड़कों का पालन-पोषण करना था, उन्हें पढ़ाना-लिखाना था। एक कन्या और भी चार-पांच साल में विवाह करने योग्य हो जायेगी। इसलिए वह कोई बड़ी रकम दहेज में न दे सकती थी, आखिर लड़कों को भी तो कुछ चाहिए। वे क्या समझेंगे कि हमारा भी कोई बाप था।

पंडित मोटेराम को लखनऊ से लौटे पन्द्रह दिन बीत चुके थे। लौटने के बाद दूसरे ही दिन से वह वर की खोज में निकले थे। उन्होंने प्रण किया था कि मैं लखनऊ वालों को दिखा दूंगा कि संसार में तुम्हीं अकेले नहीं हो, तुम्हारे जैसे और भी कितने पड़े हुए हैं। कल्याणी रोज दिन गिना करती थी। आज उसने उन्हें पत्र लिखने का निश्चय किया और कलम-दवात लेकर बैठी ही थी कि पंडित मोटेराम ने पदार्पण किया।

कल्याणी–आइये पंडितजी, मैं तो आपको खत लिखने जा रही थी, कब लौटे?

मोटेराम–लौटा तो प्रातःकाल ही था, पर उसी समय एक सेठ के यहां से निमन्त्रण आ गया। कई दिन से तर माल न मिले थे। मैंने कहा कि लगे हाथ यह भी काम निपटाता चलूं। अभी उधर ही से लौटा आ रहा हूं, कोई पांच सौ ब्राह्मणों की पंगत थी।

कल्याणी कुछ कार्य भी सिद्ध हुआ या रास्ता ही नापना पड़ा।

मोटेराम–कार्य क्यों न सिद्ध होगा? भला, यह भी कोई बात है? पांच जगह बातचीत कर आया हूं। पांचों की नकल लाया हूं। उनमें से आप चाहे जिसे पसन्द करें। यह देखिए इस लड़के का बाप डाक के सीगे में सौ रूपये महीने का नौकर है। लड़का अभी कालेज में पढ़ रहा है। मगर नौकरी का भरोसा है, घर में कोई जायदाद नहीं। लड़का होनहार मालूम होता है। खानदान भी अच्छा है दो हजार में बात तय हो जायेगी। मांगते तो यह तीन हजार हैं।

कल्याणी–लड़के के कोई भाई है?

मोटेराम–नहीं, मगर तीन बहनें हैं और तीनों क्वांरी। माता जीवित है। अच्छा अब दूसरी नकल देखिये। यह लड़का रेल के सीगे में पचास रूपये महीना पाता है। मां-बाप नहीं हैं। बहुत ही रूपवान् सुशील और शरीर से खूब हृष्ट-पुष्ट कसरती जवान है। मगर खानदान अच्छा नहीं, कोई कहता है, मां नाइन थी, कोई कहता है, ठकुराइन थी। बाप किसी रियासत में मुख्तार थे। घर पर थोड़ी सी जमींदारी है, मगर उस पर कई हजार का कर्ज है। वहां कुछ लेना-देना न पड़ेगा। उम्र कोई बीस साल होगी।

कल्याणी–खानदान में दाग न होता, तो मंजूर कर लेती। देखकर तो मक्खी नहीं निगली जाती।

मोटेराम–तीसरी नकल देखिए। एक जमींदार का लड़का है, कोई एक हजार सालाना नफा है। कुछ खेती-बारी भी होती है। लड़का पढ़ा-लिखा तो थोड़ा ही है, कचहरी-अदालत के काम में चतुर है। दुहाजू है, पहली स्त्री को मरे दो साल हुए। उससे कोई संतान नहीं, लेकिन रहन-सहन, मोटा है। पीसना-कूटना घर ही में होता है।

कल्याणी–कुछ दहेज मांगते हैं?

मोटेराम–इसकी कुछ न पूछिए। चार हजार सुनाते हैं। अच्छा यह चौथी नकल देखिये। लड़का वकील है, उम्र कोई पैंतीस साल होगी। तीन-चार सौ की आमदनी है। पहली स्त्री मर चुकी है उससे तीन लड़के भी हैं। अपना घर बनवाया है। कुछ जायदाद भी खरीदी है। यहां भी लेन-देन का झगड़ा नहीं है।

कल्याणी–खानदान कैसा है?

मोटेराम–बहुत ही उत्तम, पुराने रईस हैं। अच्छा, यह पांचवीं नकल देखिये। बाप का छापाखाना है। लड़का पढ़ा तो बी. ए. तक है, पर उसी छापेखाने में काम करता है। उम्र अठारह साल की होगी। घर में प्रेस के सिवाय कोई जायदाद नहीं है, मगर किसी का कर्ज सिर पर नहीं। खानदान न बहुत अच्छा है, न बुरा। लड़का बहुत सुन्दर और सच्चरित्र है। मगर एक हजार से कम में मामला तय न होगा, मांगते तो वह तीन हजार हैं। अब बताइए, आप कौन-सा वर पसन्द करती हैं?

कल्याणी–आपकों सबों में कौन पसन्द है?

मोटेराम–मुझे तो दो वर पसन्द हैं। एक वह जो रेलवई में है और दूसरा जो छापेखाने में काम करता है।

कल्याणी–मगर पहले के तो खानदान में आप दोष बताते हैं?

मोटेराम–हां, यह दोष तो है। छापेखाने वाले को ही रहने दीजिये।

कल्याणी–यहां एक हजार देने को कहां से आयेगा? एक हजार तो आपका अनुमान है, शायद वह और मुंह फैलाये। आप तो इस घर की दशा देख ही रहे हैं, भोजन मिलता जाये, यही गनीमत है। रूपये कहां से आयेंगे? जमींदार साहब चार हजार सुनाते हैं, डाक बाबू भी दो हजार का सवाल करते हैं। इनको जाने दीजिए। बस, वकील साहब ही बच रहे हैं। पैंतीस साल की उम्र भी कोई ज्यादा नहीं। इन्हीं को क्यों न रखिए।

मोटेराम–आप खूब सोच-विचार लें। मैं यों आपकी मर्जी का ताबेदार हूं। जहां कहिएगा वहां जाकर टीका कर आऊंगा। मगर हजार का मुंह न देखिए, छापेखाने वाला लड़का रत्न है। उसके साथ कन्या का जीवन सफल हो जाएगा। जैसी यह रूप और गुण की पूरी है, वैसा ही लड़का भी सुन्दर और सुशील है।

कल्याणी–पसन्द तो मुझे भी यही है महाराज, पर रुपये किसके घर से आयें! कौन देने वाला है! है कोई दानी? खानेवाले खा-पीकर चंपत हुए। अब किसी की भी सूरत नहीं दिखाई देती, बल्कि और मुझसे बुरा मानते हैं कि हमें निकाल दिया। जो बात अपने बस के बाहर है, उसके लिए हाथ ही क्यों फैलाऊं? सन्तान किसको प्यारी नहीं होती? कौन उसे सुखी नहीं देखना चाहता? पर जब अपना काबू भी हो। आप ईश्वर का नाम लेकर वकील साहब को टीका कर आइये। आयु कुछ अधिक है, लेकिन मरना-जीना विधि के हाथ है। पैंतीस साल का आदमी बुढ्डा नहीं कहलाता। अगर लड़की के भाग्य में सुख भोगना बदा है, तो जहां जायेगी सुखी रहेगी, दुःख भोगना है, तो जहां जायेगी दुःख झेलेगी। हमारी निर्मला को बच्चों से प्रेम है। उनके बच्चों को अपना समझेगी। आप शुभ मुहूर्त देखकर टीका कर आयें।

5

निर्मला का विवाह हो गया। ससुराल आ गयी। वकील साहब का नाम था मुंशी तोताराम। सांवले रंग के मोटे-ताजे आदमी थे। उम्र तो अभी चालीस से अधिक न थी, पर वकालत के कठिन परिश्रम ने सिर के बाल पका दिये थे। व्यायाम करने का उन्हें अवकाश न मिलता था। यहां तक कि कभी कहीं घूमने भी न जाते, इसलिए तोंद निकल आई थी। देह के स्थूल होते हुए भी आये दिन कोई-न-कोई शिकायत रहती थी। मंदाग्नि और बवासीर से तो उनका चिरस्थायी सम्बन्ध था। अतएव बहुत फूंक-फूंककर कदम रखते थे। उनके तीन लड़के थे। बड़ा मंसाराम सोहल वर्ष का था, मंझला जियाराम बारह और सियाराम सात वर्ष का। तीनों अंग्रेजी पढ़ते थे। घर में वकील साहब की विधवा बहिन के सिवा और कोई औरत न थी। वही घर की मालकिन थी। उनका नाम था रुक्मिणी और अवस्था पचास के ऊपर थी। ससुराल में कोई न था। स्थायी रीति से यहीं रहती थीं।

तोताराम दम्पति-विज्ञान में कुशल थे। निर्मला को प्रसन्न रखने के लिए उनमें जो स्वाभाविक कमी थी, उसे वह उपहारों से पूरी करना चाहते थे। यद्यपि वह बहुत ही मितव्ययी पुरूष थे, पर निर्मला के लिए कोई-न-कोई तोहफा रोज लाया करते। मौके पर धन की परवाह न करते थे। लड़के के लिए थोड़ा दूध आता था, पर निर्मला के लिए मेवे, मुरब्बे, मिठाइयां–किसी चीज की कमी न थी। अपनी जिन्दगी में कभी सैर-तमाशे देखने न गये थे, पर अब छुट्टियों में निर्मला को सिनेमा, सरकस, थिएटर, दिखाने ले जाते थे। अपने बहुमूल्य समय का थोडा-सा हिस्सा उसके साथ बैंठकर ग्रामोफोन बजाने में व्यतीत किया करते थे।

लेकिन निर्मला को न जाने क्यों तोताराम के पास बैठने और हंसने-बोलने में संकोच होता था। इसका कदाचित् यह कारण था कि अब तक ऐसा ही एक आदमी उसका पिता था, जिसके सामने वह सिर झुकाकर, देह चुराकर निकलती थी, अब उनकी अवस्था का एक आदमी उसका पति था। वह उसे प्रेम की वस्तु नहीं सम्मान की वस्तु समझती थी। उनसे भागती फिरती, उनको देखते ही उसकी प्रफुल्लता पलायन कर जाती थी।

वकील साहब को उनके दम्पत्ति-विज्ञान ने सिखाया था कि युवती के सामने खूब प्रेम की बातें करनी चाहिये। दिल निकालकर रख देना चहिये, यही उसके वशीकरण का मुख्य मंत्र है। इसलिए वकील साहब अपने प्रेम–प्रदर्शन में कोई कसर न रखते थे, लेकिन निर्मला को इन बातों से घृणा होती थी। वही बातें, जिन्हें किसी युवक के मुख से सुनकर उनका हृदय प्रेम से उन्मत्त हो जाता, वकील साहब के मुंह से निकलकर उसके हृदय पर शर के समान आघात करती थीं। उनमें रस न था उल्लास न था, उन्माद न था, हृदय न था, केवल बनावट थी, घोखा था और शुष्क, नीरस शब्दाडम्बर। उसे इत्र और तेल बुरा न लगता, सैर-तमाशे बुरे न लगते, बनाव-सिंगार भी बुरा न लगता था, बुरा लगता था, तो केवल तोताराम के पास बैठना। वह अपना रूप और यौवन उन्हें न दिखाना चाहती थी, क्योंकि वहां देखने वाली आंखें न थीं। वह उन्हें इन रसों का आस्वादन लेने योग्य न समझती थी। कली प्रभात-समीर ही के स्पर्श से खिलती है। दोनों में समान सारस्य है। निर्मला के लिए वह प्रभात समीर कहां था?

पहला महीना गुजरते ही तोताराम ने निर्मला को अपना खजांची बना लिया। कचहरी से आकर दिन-भर की कमाई उसे दे देते। उनका ख्याल था कि निर्मला इन रूपयों को देखकर फूली न समाएगी। निर्मला बड़े शौक से इस पद का काम अंजाम देती। एक-एक पैसे का हिसाब लिखती, अगर कभी रूपये कम मिलते, तो पूछती आज कम क्यों हैं। गृहस्थी के सम्बन्ध में उनसे खूब बातें करती। इन्हीं बातों के लायक वह उनको समझती थी। ज्योंही कोई विनोद की बात उनके मुंह से निकल जाती, उसका मुख मलिन हो जाता था।

निर्मला जब वस्त्राभूषणों से अलंकृत होकर आइने के सामने खड़ी होती और उसमें अपने सौन्दर्य की सुषमापूर्ण आभा देखती, तो उसका हृदय एक सतृष्ण कामना से तड़प उठता था। उस वक्त उसके हृदय में एक ज्वाला-सी उठती। मन में आता इस घर में आग लगा दूं। अपनी माता पर क्रोध आता, पर सबसे अधिक क्रोध बेचारे निरपराध तोताराम पर आता। वह सदैव इस ताप से जला करती। बांका सवार लद्दू-टट्टू पर सवार होना कब पसन्द करेगा, चाहे उसे पैदल ही क्यों न चलना पड़े? निर्मला की दशा उसी बांके सवार की-सी थी। वह उस पर सवार होकर उड़ना चाहती थी, उस उल्लासमयी विद्युत् गति का आनन्द उठाना चाहती थी, टट्टू के हिनहिनाने और कनौतियां खड़ी करने से क्या आशा होती? संभव था कि बच्चों के साथ हंसने-खेलने से वह अपनी दशा को थोड़ी देर के लिए भूल जाती, कुछ मन हरा हो जाता, लेकिन रुक्मिणी देवी लड़कों को उसके पास फटकने तक न देतीं, मानो वह कोई पिशाचिनी है, जो उन्हें निगल जाएगी।

रुक्मिणी देवी का स्वभाव सारे संसार से निराला था, यह पता लगाना कठिन था कि वह किस बात से खुश होती थीं और किस बात से नाराज। एक बार जिस बात से खुश हो जाती थीं, दूसरी बार उसी बात से जल जाती थी। अगर निर्मला अपने कमरे में बैठी रहती, तो कहतीं कि न जाने कहां की मनहूसिन है! अगर वह कोठे पर चढ़ जाती या महरियों से बातें करती, तो छाती पीटने लगतीं—न लाज है, न शरम, निगोड़ी ने हया भून खाई! अब क्या कुछ दिनों में बाजार में नाचेगी!

जब से वकील साहब ने निर्मला के हाथ में रुपये-पैसे देने शुरू किये, रुक्मिणी उसकी आलोचना करने पर आरूढ़ हो गयी। उन्हें मालूम होता था कि अब प्रलय होने में बहुत थोड़ी कसर रह गयी है। लड़कों को बार-बार पैसों की जरूरत पड़ती। जब तक खुद स्वामिनी थीं, उन्हें बहला दिया करती थीं। अब सीधे निर्मला के पास भेज देतीं। निर्मला को लड़कों का चटोरापन अच्छा न लगता था। कभी-कभी पैसे देने से इन्कार कर देती। रुक्मिणी को अपने वाग्बाण सर करने का अवसर मिल जाता—अब तो मालकिन हुई है, लड़के काहे को जियेंगे। बिना मां

के बच्चे को कौन पूछे? रूपयों की मिठाइयां खा जाते थे, अब धेले-धेले को तरसते हैं।

निर्मला अगर चिढ़कर किसी दिन बिना कुछ पूछे-ताछे पैसे दे देती, तो देवीजी उसकी दूसरी ही आलोचना करतीं–इन्हें क्या, लड़के मरे या जियें, इनकी बला से, मां के बिना कौन समझाये कि बेटा, बहुत मिठाइयां मत खाओ। आयी-गयी तो मेरे सिर जाएगी, इन्हें क्या?

यहीं तक होता, तो निर्मला शायद जब्त कर जाती, पर देवीजी तो खुफिया पुलिस के सिपाही की भांति निर्मला का पीछा करती रहती थीं। अगर वह कोठे पर खड़ी है, तो अवश्य ही किसी पर निगाह डाल रही होगी, महरी से बातें करती है, तो अवश्य ही उनकी निन्दा करती होगी। बाजार से कुछ मंगवाती है, तो अवश्य कोई विलास वस्तु होगी। वह बराबर उसके पत्र पढ़ने की चेष्टा किया करती। छिप-छिपकर बातें सुना करती।

निर्मला उनकी दोधारी तलवार से कांपती रहती थी। यहां तक कि उसने एक दिन पति से कहा–आप जरा जीजी को समझा दीजिए, क्यों मेरे पीछे पड़ी रहती हैं?

तोताराम ने तेज होकर कहा–तुम्हें कुछ कहा है, क्या?

'रोज ही कहती हैं। बात मुंह से निकालना मुश्किल है। अगर उन्हें इस बात की जलन हो कि यह मालकिन क्यों बनी हुई है, तो आप उन्हीं को रूपये-पैसे दीजिये, मुझे न चाहिये, वही मालकिन बनी रहें। मैं तो केवल इतना चाहती हूं कि कोई मुझे ताने-मेहने न दिया करे।'

यह कहते–कहते निर्मला की आंखों से आंसू बहने लगे।

तोताराम को अपना प्रेम दिखाने का यह बहुत ही अच्छा मौका मिला। बोले–मैं आज ही उनकी खबर लूंगा। साफ कह दूंगा, मुंह बन्द करके रहना है, तो रहो, नहीं तो अपनी राह लो। इस घर की स्वामिनी वह नहीं है, तुम हो। वह केवल तुम्हारी सहायता के लिए हैं। अगर सहायता करने के बदले तुम्हें दिक करती हैं, तो उनके यहां रहने की जरूरत नहीं। मैंने सोचा था कि विधवा हैं, अनाथ हैं, पाव भर आटा खायेंगी, पड़ी रहेंगी। जब और नौकर-चाकर खा रहे हैं, तो वह तो

अपनी बहिन ही है। लड़कों की देखभाल के लिए एक औरत की जरूरत भी थी, रख लिया, लेकिन इसके यह माने नहीं कि वह तुम्हारे ऊपर शासन करें।

निर्मला ने फिर कहा–लड़कों को सिखा देती हैं कि जाकर मां से पैसे मांगो, कभी कुछ-कभी कुछ। लड़के आकर मेरी जान खाते हैं। घड़ी भर लेटना मुश्किल हो जाता है। डांटती हूं, तो वह आंखें लाल-पीली करके दौड़ती हैं। मुझे समझती हैं कि लड़कों को देखकर जलती है। ईश्वर जानते होंगे कि मैं बच्चों को कितना प्यार करती हूं। आखिर मेरे ही बच्चे तो हैं। मुझे उनसे क्यों जलन होने लगी?

तोताराम क्रोध से कांप उठे। बोले–तुम्हें जो लड़का दिक करे, उसे पीट दिया करो। मैं भी देखता हूं कि लौंडे शरीर हो गये हैं। मंसाराम को तो मैं बोर्डिंग हाउस में भेज दूंगा। बाकी दोनों को तो आज ही ठीक किये देता हूं।

उस वक्त तोताराम कचहरी जा रहे थे, डांट-डपट करने का मौका न था, लेकिन कचहरी से लौटते ही उन्होंने घर में रुक्मिणी से कहा–क्यों बहिन, तुम्हें इस घर में रहना है या नहीं? अगर रहना है, शान्त होकर रहो। यह क्या कि दूसरों का रहना मुश्किल कर दो।

रुक्मिणी समझ गयीं कि बहू ने अपना वार किया, पर वह दबने वाली औरत न थीं। एक तो उम्र में बड़ी तिस पर इसी घर की सेवा में जिन्दगी काट दी थी। किसकी मजाल थी कि उन्हें बेदखल कर दे! उन्हें भाई की इस क्षुद्रता पर आश्चर्य हुआ। बोलीं–तो क्या लौंडी बनाकर रखोगे? लौंडी बनकर रहना है, तो इस घर की लौंडी न बनूंगी। अगर तुम्हारी यह इच्छा हो कि घर में कोई आग लगा दे और मैं खड़ी देखा करूं, किसी को बेराह चलते देखूं, तो चुप साध लूं, जो जिसके मन में आये करे, मैं मिट्टी की देवी बनी रहूं, तो यह मुझसे न होगा। हुआ क्या, जो तुम इतना आपे से बाहर हो रहे हो? निकल गयी सारी बुद्धिमानी, कल की लौंडिया चोटी पकड़कर नचाने लगी? कुछ पूछना न ताछना, बस, उसने तार खींचा और तुम काठ के सिपाही की तरह तलवार निकालकर खड़े हो गये।

तोताराम—सुनता हूं कि तुम हमेशा खुचर निकालती रहती हो, बात-बात पर ताने देती हो। अगर कुछ सीख देनी हो, तो उसे प्यार से, मीठे शब्दों में देनी चाहिये। तानों से सीख मिलने के बदले उल्टा और जी जलने लगता है।

रुक्मिणी—तो तुम्हारी यह मर्जी है कि किसी बात में न बोलूं, यही सही, लेकिन फिर यह न कहना, कि तुम घर में बैठी थीं, क्यों नहीं सलाह दी। जब मेरी बातें जहर लगती हैं, तो मुझे क्या कुत्ते ने काटा है, जो बोलूं? मसल है—'नाटों खेती, बहुरियों घर।' मैं भी देखूं, बहुरिया कैसे घर चलाती है!

इतने में सियाराम और जियाराम स्कूल से आ गये। आते ही आते दोनों बुआजी के पास जाकर खाने को मांगने लगे।

रुक्मिणी ने कहा—जाकर अपनी नयी अम्मां से क्यों नहीं मांगते, मुझे बोलने का हुक्म नहीं है।

तोताराम—अगर तुम लोगों ने उस घर में कदम रखा, तो टांग तोड़ दूंगा। बदमाशी पर कमर बांधी है।

जियाराम जरा शोख था। बोला—उनको तो आप कुछ नहीं कहते, हमीं को धमकाते हैं। कभी पैसे नहीं देतीं।

सियाराम ने इस कथन का अनुमोदन किया—कहती हैं, मुझे दिक करोगे तो कान काट लूंगी। कहती है कि नहीं जिया?

निर्मला अपने कमरे से बोली—मैंने कब कहा था कि तुम्हारे कान काट लूंगी? अभी से झूठ बोलने लगे!

इतना सुनना था कि तोताराम ने सियाराम के दोनों कान पकड़कर उठा लिया। लड़का जोर से चीख मारकर रोने लगा।

रुक्मिणी ने दौड़कर बच्चे को मुंशीजी के हाथ से छुड़ा लिया और बोलीं—बस, रहने भी दो, क्या बच्चे को मार डालोगे? हाय-हाय! कान लाल हो गया। सच कहा है, नयी बीवी पाकर आदमी अन्धा हो जाता है। अभी से यह हाल है, तो इस घर के भगवान ही मालिक हैं।

निर्मला अपनी विजय पर मन-ही-मन प्रसन्न हो रही थी, लेकिन जब मुंशीजी ने बच्चे का कान पकड़कर उठा लिया, तो उससे न रहा गया।

छुड़ाने को दौड़ी, पर रुक्मिणी पहले ही पहुंच गयी थीं। बोलीं–पहले आग लगा दी, अब बुझाने दौड़ी हो। जब अपने लड़के होंगे, तब आंखें खुलेंगी। पराई पीर क्या जानो?

निर्मला–खड़े तो हैं, पूछ लो न, मैंने क्या आग लगा दी? मैंने इतना ही कहा था कि लड़के मुझे पैसों के लिए बार-बार दिक करते हैं, इसके सिवाय जो मेरे मुंह से कुछ निकला हो, तो मेरी आंखें फूट जाएं।

तोताराम–मैं खुद इन लौंडों की शरारत देखा करता हूं, अन्धा थोड़े ही हूं। तीनों जिद्दी और शरीर हो गये हैं। बड़े मियां को तो मैं आज ही होस्टल में भेजता हूं।

रुक्मिणी–अब तक तुम्हें इनकी कोई शरारत न सूझी थी, आज आंखें क्यों इतनी तेज हो गयीं?

तोताराम–तुम्हीं ने इन्हें इतना शोख कर रखा है।

रुक्मिणी–तो मैं ही विष की गांठ हूं। मेरे ही कारण तुम्हारा घर चौपट हो रहा है। लो मैं जाती हूं, तुम्हारे लड़के हैं, मारो चाहे काटो, न बोलूंगी।

यह कहकर वह वहां से चली गयीं।

निर्मला बच्चे को रोते देखकर विह्वल हो उठी। उसने उसे छाती से लगा लिया और गोद में लिए हुए अपने कमरे में लाकर उसे चुमकारने लगी, लेकिन बालक और भी सिसक-सिसक कर रोने लगा। उसका अबोध हृदय इस प्यार में वह मातृ-स्नेह न पाता था, जिससे दैव ने उसे वंचित कर दिया था। यह वात्सल्य न था, केवल दया थी। यह वह वस्तु थी, जिस पर उसका कोई अधिकार न था, जो केवल भिक्षा के रूप में उसे दी जा रही थी। पिता ने पहले भी दो-एक बार मारा था, जब उसकी मां जीवित थी, लेकिन तब उसकी मां उसे छाती से लगाकर रोती न थी। वह अप्रसन्न होकर उससे बोलना छोड़ देती, यहां तक कि वह स्वयं थोड़ी ही देर के बाद कुछ भूलकर फिर माता के पास दौड़ा जाता था।

शरारत के लिए सजा पाना तो उसकी समझ में आता था, लेकिन मार खाने पर चुमकारा जाना उसकी समझ में न आता था।

मातृ-प्रेम में कठोरता होती थी, लेकिन मृदुलता से मिली हुई। इस प्रेम में करूणा थी, पर वह कठोरता न थी, जो आत्मीयता का गुप्त संदेश है। स्वस्थ अंग की परवाह कौन करता है? लेकिन वही अंग जब किसी वेदना से टपकने लगता है, तो उसे ठेस और घक्के से बचाने का यत्न किया जाता है। निर्मला का करूण रोदन बालक को उसके अनाथ होने की सूचना दे रहा था। वह बड़ी देर तक निर्मला की गोद में बैठा रोता रहा और रोते-रोते सो गया। निर्मला ने उसे चारपाई पर सुलाना चाहा, तो बालक ने सुषुप्तावस्था में अपनी दोनों कोमल बाहें उसकी गर्दन में डाल दीं और ऐसा चिपट गया, मानो नीचे कोई गढ़ा हो। शंका और भय से उसका मुख विकृत हो गया।

निर्मला ने फिर बालक को गोद में उठा लिया, चारपाई पर न सुला सकी। इस समय बालक को गोद में लिये हुए उसे वह तुष्टि हो रही थी, जो अब तक कभी न हुई थी, आज पहली बार उसे आत्मवेदना हुई, जिसके बिना आंख नहीं खुलती, अपना कर्त्तव्य-मार्ग नहीं समझता। वह मार्ग अब दिखायी देने लगा।

उस दिन अपने प्रगाढ़ प्रणय का सबल प्रमाण देने के बाद मुंशी तोताराम को आशा हुई थी कि निर्मला के मर्म-स्थल पर मेरा सिक्का जम जाएगा, लेकिन उनकी यह आशा लेशमात्र भी पूरी न हुई बल्कि पहले तो वह कभी-कभी उनसे हंसकर बोला भी करती थी, अब बच्चों ही के लालन-पालन में व्यस्त रहने लगी। जब घर आते, बच्चों को उसके पास बैठे पाते। कभी देखते कि उन्हें ला रही है, कभी कपड़े पहना रही है, कभी कोई खेल, खेला रही है और कभी कोई कहानी कह रही है।

निर्मला का तृषित ह्रदय प्रणय की ओर से निराश होकर इस अवलम्ब ही को गनीमत समझने लगा, बच्चों के साथ हंसने-बोलने में उसकी मातृ-कल्पना तृप्त होती थीं। पति के साथ हंसने-बोलने में उसे जो संकोच, जो अरुचि तथा जो अनिच्छा होती थी, यहां तक कि वह उठकर भाग जाना चाहती, उसके बदले बालकों के सच्चे, सरल स्नेह से चित्त प्रसन्न हो जाता था। पहले मंसाराम उसके पास आते हुए झिझकता था, लेकिन मानसिक विकास में पांच साल छोटा। हॉकी और

फुटबाल ही उसका संसार, उसकी कल्पनाओं का मुक्त-क्षेत्र तथा उसकी कामनाओं का हरा-भरा बाग था। इकहरे बदन का छरहरा, सुन्दर, हंसमुख, लज्जाशील बालक था, जिसका घर से केवल भोजन का नाता था, बाकी सारे दिन न जाने कहां घूमा करता। निर्मला उसके मुंह से खेल की बातें सुनकर थोड़ी देर के लिए अपनी चिन्ताओं को भूल जाती और चाहती थी एक बार फिर वही दिन आ जाते, जब वह गुड़िया खेलती और उसके ब्याह रचाया करती थी और जिसे अभी छोड़े बहुत ही थोड़े दिन गुजरे थे।

मुंशी तोताराम अन्य एकान्त-सेवी मनुष्यों की भांति विषयी जीव थे। कुछ दिनों तो वह निर्मला को सैर-तमाशे दिखाते रहे, लेकिन जब देखा कि इसका कुछ फल नहीं होता, तो फिर एकान्त-सेवन करने लगे।

दिन-भर के कठिन मानसिक परिश्रम के बाद उनका चित्त आमोद-प्रमोद के लिए लालयित हो जाता, लेकिन जब अपनी विनोद-वाटिका में प्रवेश करते और उसके फूलों को मुरझाया, पौधों को सूखा और क्यारियों से धूल उड़ती हुई देखते, तो उनका जी चाहता—क्यों न इस वाटिका को उजाड़ दूं?

निर्मला उनसे क्यों विरक्त रहती है, इसका रहस्य उनकी समझ में न आता था। दम्पति शास्त्र के सारे मन्त्रों की परीक्षा कर चुके, पर मनोरथ पूरा न हुआ। अब क्या करना चाहिये, यह उनकी समझ में न आता था।

एक दिन वह इसी चिंता में बैठे हुए थे कि उनके सहपाठी मित्र नयनसुखराम आकर बैठ गये और सलाम-वलाम के बाद मुस्कराकर बोले—आजकल तो खूब गहरी छनती होगी। नयी बीवी का आलिंगन करके जवानी का मजा आ जाता होगा? बड़े भाग्यवान हो! भई रूठी हुई जवानी को मनाने का इससे अच्छा कोई उपाय नहीं कि नया विवाह हो जाए। यहां तो जिन्दगी बवाल हो रही है। पत्नी जी इस बुरी तरह चिमटी हैं कि किसी तरह पिण्ड ही नहीं छोड़ती। मैं तो दूसरी शादी

की फिक्र में हूं। कहीं डौल हो, तो ठीक-ठाक करा दो। दस्तूरी में एक दिन तुम्हें उसके हाथ के बने हुए पान खिला देंगे।

तोताराम ने गम्भीर भाव से कहा—कहीं ऐसी हिमाकत न कर बैठना, नहीं तो पछताओगे। लौंडियां तो लौंडों से ही खुश रहती हैं। हम तुम अब उस काम के नहीं रहे। सच कहता हूं मैं तो शादी करके पछता रहा हूं, बुरी बला गले पड़ी! सोचा था, दो-चार साल और जिन्दगी का मजा उठा लूं, पर उलटी आंतें गले पड़ीं।

नयनसुख—तुम क्या बातें करते हो। लौंडियों को पंजों में लाना क्या मुश्किल बात है, जरा सैर-तमाशे दिखा दो, उनके रूप-रंग की तारीफ कर दो, बस, रंग जम गया।

तोताराम—यह सब कुछ कर-धर के हार गया।

नयनसुख—अच्छा, कुछ इत्र-तेल, फूल-पत्ते, चाट-वाट का भी मजा चखाया?

तोताराम—अजी, यह सब कर चुका। दम्पत्ति-शास्त्र के सारे मन्त्रों का इम्तहान ले चुका, सब कोरी गप्पे हैं।

नयनसुख—अच्छा, तो अब मेरी एक सलाह मानो, जरा अपनी सूरत बनवा लो। आजकल यहां एक बिजली के डॉक्टर आये हुए हैं, जो बुढ़ापे के सारे निशान मिटा देते हैं। क्या मजाल कि चेहरे पर एक झुर्री या सिर का बाल पका रह जाए। न जाने क्या जादू कर देते हैं कि आदमी का चोला ही बदल जाता है।

तोताराम—फीस क्या लेते हैं?

नयनसुख—फीस तो सुना है, शायद पांच सौ रूपये!

तोताराम—अजी, कोई पाखण्डी होगा, बेवकूफों को लूट रहा होगा। कोई रोगन लगाकर दो-चार दिन के लिए जरा चेहरा चिकना कर देता होगा। इश्तहारी डॉक्टरों पर तो अपना विश्वास ही नहीं। दस-पांच की बात होती, तो कहता, जरा दिल्लगी ही सही। पांच सौ रूपये बड़ी रकम है।

नयनसुख—तुम्हारे लिए पांच सौ रूपये कौन बड़ी बात है। एक महीने की आमदनी है। मेरे पास तो भाई पांच सौ रूपये होते, तो सबसे

पहला काम यही करता। जवानी के एक घण्टे की कीमत पांच सौ रूपये से कहीं ज्यादा है।

तोताराम–अजी, कोई सस्ता नुस्खा बताओ, कोई फकीरी जड़ी-बूटी जो कि बिना हर्र-फिटकरी के रंग चोखा हो जाए। बिजली और रेडियम बड़े आदमियों के लिए रहने दो। उन्हीं को मुबारक हो।

नयन–तो फिर रंगीलेपन का स्वांग रचो। यह ढीला-ढाला कोट फेंकों, तंजेब की चुस्त अचकन हो, चुन्नटदार पाजामा, गले में सोने की जंजीर पड़ी हुई, सिर पर जयपुरी साफा बांधा हुआ, आंखों में सुरमा और बालों में हिना का तेल पड़ा हुआ। तोंद का पिचकना भी जरूरी है। दोहरा कमरबन्द बांधे। जरा तकलीफ तो होगी, पर अचकन सज उठेगी। खिजाब मैं ला दूंगा। सौ-पचास गजलें याद कर लो और मौके-मौके से शेर पढ़ो। बातों में रस भरा हो। ऐसा मालूम हो कि तुम्हें दीन और दुनिया की कोई फिक्र नहीं है, बस, जो कुछ है, प्रियतमा ही है। जवांमर्दी और साहस के काम करने का मौका ढूंढते रहो। रात को झूठ-मूठ शोर करो–चोर-चोर और तलवार लेकर अकेले पिल पड़ो। हां, जरा मौका देख लेना, ऐसा न हो कि सचमुच कोई चोर आ जाए और तुम उसके पीछे दौड़ो, नहीं तो सारी कलई खुल जाएगी और मुफ्त के उल्लू बनोगे। उस वक्त तो जवांमर्दी इसी में है कि दम साधे खड़े रहो, जिससे वह समझे कि तुम्हें खबर ही नहीं हुई, लेकिन ज्योंही चोर भाग खड़ा हो, तुम भी उछलकर बाहर निकलो और तलवार लेकर 'कहां? कहां?' कहते दौड़ो। ज्यादा नहीं, एक महीना मेरी बातों का इम्तहान करके देखें। अगर वह तुम्हारी दम न भरने लगे, तो जो जुर्माना कहो, वह दूं।

तोताराम ने उस वक्त तो यह बातें हंसी में उड़ा दीं, जैसा कि एक व्यवहार कुशल मनुष्य को करना चहिए था, लेकिन इसमें की कुछ बातें उसके मन में बैठ गयी। उनका असर पड़ने में कोई संदेह न था। धीरे-धीरे रंग बदलने लगे, जिसमें लोग खटक न जाएं। पहले बालों से शुरू किया, फिर सुरमे की बारी आयी, यहां तक कि एक-दो महीने में उनका कलेवर ही बदल गया। गजलें याद करने का प्रस्ताव तो हास्यास्पद था, लेकिन वीरता की डींग मारने में कोई हानि न थी।

उस दिन से वह रोज अपनी जवांमर्दी का कोई-न-कोई प्रसंग अवश्य छेड़ देते। निर्मला को सन्देह होने लगा कि कहीं इन्हें उन्माद का रोग तो नहीं हो रहा है। जो आदमी मूंग की दाल और मोटे आटे के दो फुलके खाकर भी नमक सुलेमानी का मुहताज हो, उसके छैलेपन पर उन्माद का सन्देह हो, तो आश्चर्य ही क्या?

निर्मला पर इस पागलपन का और क्या रंग जमता? हां उसे उन पर दया आने लगी। क्रोध और घृणा का भाव जाता रहा। क्रोध और घृणा उन पर होती है, जो अपने होश में हो, पागल आदमी तो दया ही का पात्र है। वह बात-बात में उनकी चुटकियां लेती, उनका मजाक उड़ाती, जैसे लोग पागलों के साथ किया करते हैं। हां, इसका ध्यान रखती थी कि वह समझ न जाएं। वह सोचती, बेचारा अपने पाप का प्रायश्चित कर रहा है।

यह सारा स्वांग केवल इसलिए तो है कि मैं अपना दुःख भूल जाऊं। आखिर अब भाग्य तो बदल सकता नहीं, इस बेचारे को क्यों जलाऊं?

एक दिन रात को नौ बजे तोताराम बांके बने हुए सैर करके लौटे और निर्मला से बोले–आज तीन चोरों से सामना हो गया। जरा शिवपुर की तरफ चला गया था। अंधेरा था ही। ज्योंही रेल की सड़क के पास पहुंचा, तो तीन आदमी तलवार लिए हुए न जाने किधर से निकल पड़े। यकीन मानो, तीनों काले देव थे। मैं बिल्कुल अकेला, पास में सिर्फ यह छड़ी थी। उधर तीनों तलवार बांधे हुए, होश उड़ गये। समझ गया कि जिन्दगी का यहीं तक साथ था, मगर मैंने भी सोचा, मरता ही हूं, तो वीरों की मौत क्यों न मरुं। इतने में एक आदमी ने ललकार कर कहा–रख दे तेरे पास जो कुछ हो और चुपके से चला जा।

मैं छड़ी संभालकर खड़ा हो गया और बोला–मेरे पास तो सिर्फ यह छड़ी है और इसका मूल्य एक आदमी का सिर है।

मेरे मुंह से इतना निकलना था कि तीनों तलवार खींचकर मुझ पर झपट पड़े और मैं उनके वारों को छड़ी पर रोकने लगा। तीनों झल्ला-झल्लाकर वार करते थे, खटाके की आवाज होती थी और मैं बिजली की तरह झपटकर उनके वारों को काट देता था। कोई दस

मिनट तक तीनों ने खूब तलवार के जौहर दिखाये, पर मुझ पर रेफ तक न आयी। मजबूरी यही थी कि मेरे हाथ में तलवार न थी। यदि कहीं तलवार होती, तो एक को जीता न छोड़ता। खैर, कहां तक बयान करुं। उस वक्त मेरे हाथों की सफाई देखने काबिल थी। मुझे खुद आश्चर्य हो रहा था कि यह चपलता मुझमें कहां से आ गयी। जब तीनों ने देखा कि यहां दाल नहीं गलने की, तो तलवार म्यान में रख ली और पीठ ठोककर बोले–जवान, तुम-सा वीर आज तक नहीं देखा। हम तीनों तीन सौ पर भारी गांव-के-गांव ढोल बजाकर लूटते हैं, पर आज तुमने हमें नीचा दिखा दिया। हम तुम्हारा लोहा मान गए। यह कहकर तीनों फिर नजरों से गायब हो गए।

निर्मला ने गम्भीर भाव से मुस्कराकर कहा–इस छड़ी पर तो तलवार के बहुत से निशान बने हुए होंगे?

मुंशीजी इस शंका के लिए तैयार न थे, पर कोई जवाब देना आवश्यक था, बोले–मैं वारों को बराबर खाली कर देता। दो-चार चोटें छड़ी पर पड़ीं भी, तो उचटती हुई, जिनसे कोई निशान नहीं पड़ सकता था।

अभी उनके मुंह से पूरी बात भी न निकली थी कि सहसा रुक्मिणी देवी बदहवास दौड़ती हुई आयीं और हांफते हुए बोलीं–तोता है कि नहीं? मेरे कमरे में सांप निकल आया है। मेरी चारपाई के नीचे बैठा हुआ है। मैं उठकर भागी। मुआ कोई दो गज का होगा। फन निकाले फुफकार रहा है, जरा चलो तो। डंडा लेते चलना।

तोताराम के चेहरे का रंग उड़ गया, मुंह पर हवाइयां छुटने लगीं, मगर मन के भावों को छिपाकर बोले–सांप यहां कहां? तुम्हें धोखा हुआ होगा। कोई रस्सी होगी।

रुक्मिणी–अरे, मैंने अपनी आंखों देखा है। जरा चलकर देख लो न। हैं, हैं...मर्द होकर डरते हो?

मुंशीजी घर से तो निकले, लेकिन बरामदे में फिर ठिठक गये। उनके पांव ही न उठते थे कलेजा धड़-धड़ कर रहा था।

सांप बड़ा क्रोधी जानवर है। कहीं काट ले तो मुफ्त में प्राण से हाथ धोना पड़े। बोले–डरता नहीं हूं। सांप ही तो है, शेर तो नहीं, मगर

सांप पर लाठी नहीं असर करती, जाकर किसी को भेजूं, किसी के घर से भाला लाये।

यह कहकर मुंशीजी लपके हुए बाहर चले गये। मंसाराम बैठा खाना खा रहा था। मुंशीजी तो बाहर चले गये, इधर वह खाना छोड़, अपनी हॉकी का डंडा हाथ में ले, कमरे में घुस ही तो पड़ा और तुरंत चारपाई खींच ली।

सांप मस्त था, भागने के बदले फन निकालकर खड़ा हो गया। मंसाराम ने चटपट चारपाई की चादर उठाकर सांप के ऊपर फेंक दी और ताबड़तोड़ तीन-चार डंडे कसकर जमाये।

सांप चादर के अंदर तड़प कर रह गया। तब उसे डंडे पर उठाये हुए बाहर चला। मुंशीजी कई आदमियों को साथ लिये चले आ रहे थे। मंसाराम को सांप लटकाये आते देखा, तो सहसा उनके मुंह से चीख निकल पड़ी, मगर फिर संभल गये और बोले—मैं तो आ ही रहा था, तुमने क्यों जल्दी की? दे दो, कोई फेंक आए।

यह कहकर बहादुरी के साथ रुक्मिणी के कमरे के द्वार पर जाकर खड़े हो गये और कमरे को खूब देखभाल कर मूंछों पर ताव देते हुए निर्मला के पास जाकर बोले—मैं जब तक आऊं-जाऊं, मंसाराम ने मार डाला। बेसमझ लड़का डंडा लेकर दौड़ पड़ा। सांप हमेशा भाले से मारना चाहिए। यही तो लड़कों में ऐब है। मैंने ऐसे-ऐसे कितने सांप मारे हैं। सांप को खिला-खिलाकर मारता हूं। कितनों ही को मुट्ठी से पकड़कर मसल दिया है।

रुक्मिणी ने कहा—जाओ भी, देख ली तुम्हारी मर्दानगी।

मुंशीजी झेंपकर बोले—अच्छा जाओ, मैं डरपोक ही सही, तुमसे कुछ इनाम तो नहीं मांग रहा हूं। जाकर महाराज से कहो, खाना निकाले।

मुंशीजी तो भोजन करने गये और निर्मला द्वार की चौखट पर खड़ी सोच रही थी—भगवान्। क्या इन्हें सचमुच कोई भीषण रोग हो रहा है? क्या मेरी दशा को और भी दारुण बनाना चाहते हो? मैं इनकी सेवा कर सकती हूं, सम्मान कर सकी हूं, अपना जीवन इनके चरणों पर अर्पण कर सकती हूं, लेकिन वह नहीं कर सकती, जो मेरे किये नहीं

हो सकता। अवस्था का भेद मिटाना मेरे वश की बात नहीं । आखिर यह मुझसे क्या चाहते हैं–समझ् गयी। आह यह बात पहले ही नहीं समझी थी, नहीं तो इनको क्यों इतनी तपस्या करनी पड़ती क्यों इतने स्वांग भरने पड़ते।

उस दिन से निर्मला का रंग-ढंग बदलने लगा। उसने अपने को कर्त्तव्य पर मिटा देने का निश्चय कर दिया। अब तक नैराश्य के संताप में उसने कर्त्तव्य पर ध्यान ही न दिया था उसके हृदय में विप्लव की ज्वाला-सी दहकती रहती थी, जिसकी असह्य वेदना ने उसे संज्ञाहीन-सा कर रखा था। अब उस वेदना का वेग शांत होने लगा।

उसे ज्ञात हुआ कि मेरे लिए जीवन का कोई आंनद नहीं। उसका स्वप्न देखकर क्यों इस जीवन को नष्ट करुं।

संसार में सब-के-सब प्राणी सुख-सेज ही पर तो नहीं सोते। मैं भी उन्हीं अभागों में से हूं। मुझे भी विधाता ने दुख की गठरी ढोने के लिए चुना है। वह बोझ सिर से उतर नहीं सकता। उसे फेंकना भी चाहूं, तो नहीं फेंक सकती। उस कठिन भार से चाहे आंखों में अंधेरा छा जाए, चाहे गर्दन टूटने लगे, चाहे पैर उठाना दुस्तर हो जाए, लेकिन वह गठरी ढोनी ही पड़ेगी ? उम्र भर का कैदी कहां तक रोयेगा? रोये भी तो कौन देखता है? किसे उस पर दया आती है? रोने से काम में हर्ज होने के कारण उसे और यातनाएं ही तो सहनी पड़ती हैं।

दूसरे दिन वकील साहब कचहरी से आये तो देखा–निर्मला की सहास्य मूर्ति अपने कमरे के द्वार पर खड़ी है। वह अनिन्द्य छवि देखकर उनकी आंखें तृप्त हो गयीं। आज बहुत दिनों के बाद उन्हें यह कमल खिला हुआ दिखलाई दिया। कमरे में एक बड़ा-सा आईना दीवार में लटका हुआ था। उस पर एक परदा पड़ा रहता था। आज उसका परदा उठा हुआ था।

वकील साहब ने कमरे में कदम रखा, तो शीशे पर निगाह पड़ी। अपनी सूरत साफ-साफ दिखाई दी। उनके हृदय में चोट-सी लग गयी।

दिन भर के परिश्रम से मुख की कांति मलिन हो गयी थी, भांति-भांति के पौष्टिक पदार्थ खाने पर भी गालों की झुर्रियां साफ दिखाई दे रही थीं। तोंद कसी होने पर भी किसी मुंहजोर घोड़े की भांति बाहर निकली हुई थी।

आईने के ही सामने किन्तू दूसरी ओर ताकती हुई निर्मला भी खड़ी हुई थी। दोनों सूरतों में कितना अंतर था।

एक रत्न जटित विशाल भवन, दूसरा टूटा-फूटा खंडहर। वह उस आईने की ओर न देख सके। अपनी यह हीनावस्था उनके लिए असह्य थी। वह आईने के सामने से हट गये, उन्हें अपनी ही सूरत से घृणा होने लगी। फिर इस रूपवती कामिनी का उनसे घृणा करना कोई आश्चर्य की बात न थी। निर्मला की ओर ताकने का भी उन्हें साहस न हुआ। उसकी यह अनुपम छवि उनके हृदय का शूल बन गयी।

निर्मला ने कहा–आज इतनी देर कहां लगायी? दिन भर राह देखते-देखते आंखे फूट जाती हैं।

तोताराम ने खिड़की की ओर ताकते हुए जवाब दिया–मुकदमों के मारे दम मारने की छुट्टी नहीं मिलती। अभी एक मुकदमा और था, लेकिन मैं सिरदर्द का बहाना करके भाग खड़ा हुआ।

निर्मला–तो क्यों इतने मुकदमे लेते हो? काम उतना ही करना चाहिए जितना आराम से हो सके। प्राण देकर थोड़े ही काम किया जाता है। मत लिया करो, बहुत मुकदमे। मुझे रुपयों का लालच नहीं। तुम आराम से रहोगे, तो रुपये बहुत मिलेंगे।

तोताराम–भई, आती हुई लक्ष्मी भी तो नहीं ठुकराई जाती।

निर्मला–लक्ष्मी अगर रक्त और मांस की भेंट लेकर आती है, तो उसका न आना ही अच्छा। मैं धन की भूखी नहीं हूं।

इस वक्त मंसाराम भी स्कूल से लौटा। धूप में चलने के कारण मुख पर पसीने की बूंदे आयी हुई थीं, गोरे मुखड़े पर खून की लाली दौड़ रही थी, आंखों से ज्योति-सी निकलती मालूम होती थी। द्वार पर खड़ा होकर बोला–अम्मां जी, लाइए, कुछ खाने को निकालिए, जरा खेलने जाना है।

निर्मला जाकर गिलास में पानी लाई और एक तश्तरी में कुछ मेवे रखकर मंसाराम को दिए। मंसाराम जब खाकर चलने लगा, तो निर्मला ने पूछा–कब तक आओगे?

मंसाराम–कह नहीं सकता, गोरों के साथ हॉकी का मैच है। बैरक यहां से बहुत दूर है।

निर्मला–भई, जल्द आना। खाना ठण्डा हो जाएगा, तो कहोगे मुझे भूख नहीं है।

मंसाराम ने निर्मला की ओर सरल स्नेह भाव से देखकर कहा–मुझे देर हो जाए तो समझ लीजिएगा, वहीं खा रहा हूं। मेरे लिए बैठने की जरुरत नहीं।

वह चला गया, तो निर्मला बोली–पहले तो घर में आते ही न थे, मुझसे बोलते शर्माते थे। किसी चीज की जरुरत होती, तो बाहर से ही मंगवा भेजते। जब से मैंनें बुलाकर कहा, तब से आने लगे हैं।

तोताराम ने कुछ चिढ़कर कहा–यह तुम्हारे पास खाने-पीने की चीजें मांगने क्यों आता है? दीदी से क्यों नही कहता?

निर्मला ने यह बात प्रशंसा पाने के लोभ से कही थी। वह यह दिखाना चाहती थी कि मैं तुम्हारे लड़कों को कितना चाहती हूं। यह कोई बनावटी प्रेम न था। उसे लड़कों से सचमुच स्नेह था। उसके चरित्र में अभी तक बाल-भाव ही प्रधान था, उसमें वही उत्सुकता, वही चंचलता, वही विनोदप्रियता विद्यमान थी और बालकों के साथ उसकी ये बालवृत्तियां प्रस्फुटित होती थीं।

पत्नी-सुलभ ईर्ष्या अभी तक उसके मन में उदय नहीं हुई थी, लेकिन पति के प्रसन्न होने के बदले नाक-भौं सिकोड़ने का आशय न समझकर बोली–मैं क्या जानूं, उनसे क्यों नहीं मांगते? मेरे पास आते हैं, तो दुत्कार नहीं देती। अगर ऐसा करुं, तो यही होगा कि यह लड़कों को देखकर जलती है।

मुंशीजी ने इसका कुछ जवाब न दिया, लेकिन आज उन्होंने मुवक्किलों से बातें नहीं कीं, सीधे मंसाराम के पास गये और उसका इम्तहान लेने लगे।

यह जीवन में पहला ही अवसर था कि इन्होंने मंसाराम या किसी लड़के की शिक्षोन्नति के विषय में इतनी दिलचस्पी दिखायी हो। उन्हें अपने काम से सिर उठाने की फुरसत ही न मिलती थी। उन्हें इन विषयों को पढ़े हुए चालीस वर्ष के लगभग हो गये थे। तब से उनकी ओर आंख तक न उठायी थी। वह कानूनी पुस्तकों और पत्रों के सिवा और कुछ पढ़ते ही न थे। इसका समय ही न मिलता, पर आज उन्हीं विषयों में मंसाराम की परीक्षा लेने लगे।

मंसाराम जहीन था और इसके साथ ही मेहनती भी था। खेल में भी टीम का कैप्टन होने पर भी वह क्लास में प्रथम रहता था। जिस पाठ को एक बार देख लेता, पत्थर की लकीर हो जाती थी।

मुंशीजी को उतावली में ऐसे मार्मिक प्रश्न तो सूझे नहीं, जिनके उत्तर देने में चतुर लड़के को भी कुछ सोचना पड़ता और ऊपरी प्रश्नों को मंसाराम से चुटकियों में उड़ा दिया। कोई सिपाही अपने शत्रु पर वार खाली जाते देखकर जैसे झल्ला-झल्लाकर और भी तेजी से वार करता है, उसी भांति मंसाराम के जवाबों को सुन-सुनकर वकील साहब भी झल्लाते थे। वह कोई ऐसा प्रश्न करना चाहते थे, जिसका जवाब मंसाराम से न बन पड़े। देखना चाहते थे कि इसका कमजोर पहलू कहां है। यह देखकर अब उन्हें संतोष न हो सकता था कि वह क्या करता है। वह यह देखना चाहते थे कि यह क्या नहीं कर सकता। कोई अभ्यस्त परीक्षक मंसाराम की कमजोरियों को आसानी से दिखा देता, पर वकील साहब अपनी आधी शताब्दी की भूली हुई शिक्षा के आधार पर इतने सफल कैसे होते? अंत में उन्हें अपना गुस्सा उतारने के लिए कोई बहाना न मिला तो बोले—मैं देखता हूं, तुम सारे दिन इधर-उधर मटरगश्ती किया करते हो, मैं तुम्हारे चरित्र को तुम्हारी बुद्धि से बढ़कर समझता हूं और तुम्हारा यों आवारा घूमना मुझे कभी गवारा नहीं हो सकता।

मंसाराम ने निर्भीकता से कहा—मैं शाम को एक घण्टा खेलने के लिए जाने के सिवा दिन भर कहीं नहीं जाता। आप अम्मां या बुआजी से पूछ लें। मुझे खुद इस तरह घूमना पसंद नहीं। हां, खेलने के

लिए हेड मास्टर साहब आग्रह करके बुलाते हैं, तो मजबूरन जाना पड़ता है। अगर आपको मेरा खेलने जाना पसंद नहीं है, तो कल से न जाऊंगा।

मुंशीजी ने देखा कि बातें दूसरी ही रुख पर जा रही हैं, तो तीव्र स्वर में बोले–मुझे इस बात का इतमीनान क्योंकर हो कि खेलने के सिवा कहीं नहीं घूमने जाते? मैं बराबर शिकायतें सुनता हूं।

मंसाराम ने उत्तेजित होकर कहा–किन महाशय ने आपसे यह शिकायत की है, जरा मैं भी तो सुनूं?

वकील–कोई हो, इससे तुमसे कोई मतलब नहीं। तुम्हें इतना विश्वास होना चाहिए कि मैं झूठा आक्षेप नहीं करता।

मंसाराम–अगर मेरे सामने कोई आकर कह दे कि मैंने इन्हें कहीं घूमते देखा है, तो मुंह न दिखाऊं।

वकील–किसी को ऐसी क्या गरज पड़ी है कि तुम्हारी मुंह पर तुम्हारी शिकायत करे और तुमसे बैर मोल ले? तुम अपने दो-चार साथियों को लेकर उसके घर की खपरैल फोड़ते फिरो। मुझसे इस किस्म की शिकायत एक आदमी ने नहीं, कई आदमियों ने की है और कोई वजह नहीं है कि मैं अपने दोस्तों की बात पर विश्वास न करूं। मैं चाहता हूं कि तुम स्कूल ही में रहा करो।

मंसाराम ने मुंह गिराकर कहा–मुझे वहां रहने में कोई आपत्ति नहीं है, जब से कहिये, चला जाऊं।

वकील–तुमने मुंह क्यों लटका लिया? क्या वहां रहना अच्छा नहीं लगता? ऐसा मालूम होता है, मानों वहां जाने के भय से तुम्हारी नानी मरी जा रही है। आखिर बात क्या है, वहां तुम्हें क्या तकलीफ होगी?

मंसाराम छात्रालय में रहने के लिए उत्सुक नहीं था, लेकिन जब मुंशीजी ने यही बात कह दी और इसका कारण पूछा, तो वह अपनी झेंप मिटाने के लिए प्रसन्नचित्त होकर बोला–मुंह क्यों लटकाऊं? मेरे लिए जैसे घर, वैसे बोर्डिंग हाउस। तकलीफ भी कोई नहीं, और हो भी तो उसे सह सकता हूं। मैं कल से चला जाऊंगा। हां अगर जगह न खाली हुई तो मजबूरी है।

मुंशीजी वकील थे। समझ गये कि यह लौंडा कोई ऐसा बहाना ढूंढ रहा है, जिसमें मुझे वहां जाना भी न पड़े और कोई इल्जाम भी सिर पर न आये। बोले–सब लड़कों के लिए जगह है, तुम्हारे ही लिये जगह न होगी?

मंसाराम–कितने ही लड़कों को जगह नहीं मिली और वे बाहर किराये के मकानों में पड़े हुए हैं। अभी बोर्डिंग हाउस में एक लड़के का नाम कट गया था, तो पचास अर्जियां उस जगह के लिए आयी थीं।

वकील साहब ने ज्यादा तर्क-वितर्क करना उचित नहीं समझा। मंसाराम को कल तैयार रहने की आज्ञा देकर अपनी बग्घी तैयार करायी और सैर करने चल गये। इधर कुछ दिनों से वह शाम को प्रायः सैर करने चले जाया करते थे। किसी अनुभवी प्राणी ने बतलाया था कि दीर्घ जीवन के लिए इससे बढ़कर कोई मंत्र नहीं है। उनके जाने के बाद मंसाराम आकर रुक्मिणी से बोला बुआजी, बाबूजी ने मुझे कल से स्कूल में रहने को कहा है।

रुक्मिणी ने विस्मित होकर पूछा–क्यों?

मंसाराम–मैं क्या जानू? कहने लगे कि तुम यहां आवारों की तरह इधर-उधर फिरा करते हो।

रुक्मिणी–तूने कहा नहीं कि मैं कहीं नहीं जाता।

मंसाराम–कहा क्यों नहीं, मगर वह जब मानें तब न!

रुक्मिणी–तुम्हारी नयी अम्मा जी की कृपा होगी और क्या?

मंसाराम–नहीं, बुआजी, मुझे उन पर संदेह नहीं है, वह बेचारी भूल से कभी कुछ नहीं कहतीं। कोई चीज़ मांगने जाता हूं, तो तुरन्त उठाकर दे देती हैं।

रुक्मिणी–तू यह त्रिया-चरित्र क्या जाने, यह उन्हीं की लगाई हुई आग है। देख, मैं जाकर पूछती हूं।

रुक्मिणी झल्लाई हुई निर्मला के पास जा पहुंची। उसे आड़े हाथों लेने का, कांटों में घसीटने का, तानों से छेदने का, रुलाने का सुअवसर वह हाथ से न जाने देती थी। निर्मला उनका आदर करती थी, उनसे दबती थी, उनकी बातों का जवाब तक न देती थी। वह चाहती थी कि

वह सिखावन की बातें कहें, जहां मैं भूलूं वहां सुधारें, सब कामों की देख-रेख करती रहें, पर रुक्मिणी उससे तनी ही रहती थी।

निर्मला चारपाई से उठकर बोली—आइए दीदी, बैठिए।

रुक्मिणी ने खड़े-खड़े कहा—मैं पूछती हूं क्या तुम सबको घर से निकालकर अकेले ही रहना चाहती हो?

निर्मला ने कातर भाव से कहा—क्या हुआ दीदी जी? मैंने तो किसी से कुछ नहीं कहा।

रुक्मिणी—मंसाराम को घर से निकाले देती हो, तिस पर कहती हो, मैंने तो किसी से कुछ नहीं कहा। क्या तुमसे इतना भी देखा नहीं जाता?

निर्मला—दीदी जी, तुम्हारे चरणों को छूकर कहती हूं, मुझे कुछ नहीं मालूम। मेरी आंखे फूट जाएं, अगर उसके विषय में मुंह तक खोला हो।

रुक्मिणी—क्यों व्यर्थ कसमें खाती हो। अब तक तोताराम कभी लड़के से नहीं बोलते थे। एक हफ्ते के लिए मंसाराम ननिहाल चला गया था, तो इतने घबराए कि खुद जाकर लिवा लाए। अब इसी मंसाराम को घर से निकालकर स्कूल में रखे देते हैं। अगर लड़के का बाल भी बांका हुआ, तो तुम जानोगी। वह कभी बाहर नहीं रहा, उसे न खाने की सुध रहती है, न पहनने की—जहां बैठता, वहीं सो जाता है। कहने को तो जवान हो गया, पर स्वभाव बालकों-सा है। स्कूल में उसकी मरन हो जाएगी। वहां किसे फिक्र है कि इसने खाया या नहीं, कहां कपड़े उतारे, कहां सो रहा है। जब घर में कोई पूछने वाला नहीं, तो बाहर कौन पूछेगा मैंने तुम्हें चेता दिया, आगे तुम जानो, तुम्हारा काम जाने।

यह कहकर रुक्मिणी वहां से चली गयी।

6

वकील साहब सैर करके लौटे, तो निर्मला ने तुरंत यह विषय छेड़ दिया—मंसाराम से वह आजकल थोड़ी अंग्रेजी पढ़ती थी। उसके चले जाने पर फिर उसके पढ़ने का हरज न होगा? दूसरा कौन पढ़ायेगा? वकील साहब को अब तक यह बात न मालूम थी। निर्मला ने सोचा था कि जब कुछ अभ्यास हो जाएगा, तो वकील साहब को एक दिन अंग्रेजी में बातें करके चकित कर दूंगी। कुछ थोड़ा-सा ज्ञान तो उसे अपने भाइयों से ही हो गया था। अब वह नियमित रूप से पढ़ रही थी।

यह जानकर वकील साहब की छाती पर सांप-सा लोट गया, त्योरियां बदलकर बोले—वह कब से पढ़ा रहा है, तुम्हें। मुझसे तुमने कभी नही कहा।

निर्मला ने उनका यह रूप केवल एक बार देखा था, जब उन्होने सियाराम को मारते-मारते बेदम कर दिया था। वही रूप और भी विकराल बनकर आज उसे फिर दिखाई दिया।

सहमती हुई बोली—उनके पढ़ने में तो इससे कोई हरज नहीं होता, मैं उसी वक्त उनसे पढ़ती हूं जब उन्हें फुरसत रहती है। पूछ लेती हूं कि तुम्हारा हरज होता हो, तो जाओ। बहुधा जब वह खेलने जाने लगते हैं, तो दस मिनट के लिए रोक लेती हूं। मैं खुद चाहती हूं कि उनका नुकसान न हो।

बात कुछ न थी, मगर वकील साहब हताश से होकर चारपाई पर गिर पड़े और माथे पर हाथ रखकर चिंता में मग्न हो गये। उन्होंने जितना समझा था, बात उससे कहीं अधिक बढ़ गयी थी। उन्हें अपने ऊपर क्रोध आया कि मैंने पहले ही क्यों न इस लौंडे को बाहर रखने

का प्रबंध किया। आजकल जो यह महारानी इतनी खुश दिखाई देती हैं, इसका रहस्य अब समझ में आया। पहले कभी कमरा इतना सजा-सजाया न रहता था, बनाव-चुनाव भी न करती थीं, पर अब देखता हूं कायापलट-सी हो गयी है। जी में तो आया कि इसी वक्त चलकर मंसाराम को निकाल दें, लेकिन प्रौढ़ बुद्धि ने समझाया कि इस अवसर पर क्रोध की जरूरत नहीं। कहीं इसने भांप लिया, तो गजब ही हो जाएगा। हां, जरा इसके मनोभावों को टटोलना चाहिए।

वकील साहब गंभीरता से बोले–यह तो मैं जानता हूं कि तुम्हें दो-चार मिनट पढ़ाने से उसका हरज नहीं होता, लेकिन आवारा लड़का है, अपना काम न करने का उसे एक बहाना तो मिल जाता है। कल अगर फेल हो गया, तो साफ कह देगा–मैं तो दिन भर पढ़ाता रहता था। मैं तुम्हारे लिए कोई मिस नौकर रख दूंगा। कुछ ज्यादा खर्च न होगा। तुमने मुझसे पहले कहा ही नहीं। यह तुम्हें भला क्या पढ़ाता होगा, दो-चार शब्द बताकर भाग जाता होगा। इस तरह तो तुम्हें कुछ भी न आयेगा।

निर्मला ने तुरन्त इस आक्षेप का खण्डन किया–नहीं, यह बात तो नहीं। वह मुझे दिल लगा कर पढ़ाते हैं और उनकी शैली भी कुछ ऐसी है कि पढ़ने में मन लगता है। आप एक दिन जरा उनका समझाना देखिए। मैं तो समझती हूं कि मिस इतने ध्यान से न पढ़ायेगी।

मुंशीजी अपनी प्रश्न-कुशलता पर मूंछों पर ताव देते हुए बोले–दिन में एक ही बार पढ़ाता है या कई बार?

निर्मला अब भी इन प्रश्नों का आशय न समझी। बोली–पहले तो शाम ही को पढ़ा देते थे, अब कई दिनों से एक बार आकर लिखना भी देख लेते हैं। वह तो कहते हैं कि मैं अपने क्लास में सबसे अच्छा हूं। अभी परीक्षा में इन्हीं को प्रथम स्थान मिला था, फिर आप कैसे समझते हैं कि उनका पढ़ने में जी नहीं लगता? मैं इसलिए और भी कहती हूं कि दीदी समझेंगी, इसी ने यह आग लगाई है। मुफ्त में मुझे ताने सुनने पड़ेंगे। अभी जरा ही देर हुई, धमकाकर गयी हैं।

मुंशीजी ने दिल में कहा–खूब समझता हूं। तुम कल की छोकरी होकर मुझे चराने चलीं। दीदी का सहारा लेकर अपना मतलब पूरा

करना चाहती हैं। बोले—मैं नहीं समझता, बोर्डिंग का नाम सुनकर क्यों लौंडे की नानी मरती है। और लड़के खुश होते हैं कि अब अपने दोस्तों में रहेंगे, यह उल्टे रो रहा है। अभी कुछ दिन पहले तक यह दिल लगाकर पढ़ता था, यह उसी मेहनत का नतीजा है कि अपने क्लास में सबसे अच्छा है, लेकिन इधर कुछ दिनों से इसे सैर-सपाटे का चस्का पड़ चला है। अगर अभी से रोकथाम न की गयी, तो पीछे करते-धरते न बन पड़ेगा। तुम्हारे लिए मैं एक मिस रख दूंगा।

दूसरे दिन मुंशीजी प्रातःकाल कपड़े—लत्ते पहनकर बाहर निकले। दीवानखाने में कई मुवक्किल बैठे हुए थे। इनमें एक राजा साहब भी थे, जिनसे मुंशीजी को कई हजार सालाना मेहनताना मिलता था, मगर मुंशीजी उन्हें वहीं बैठे छोड़ दस मिनट में आने का वादा करके बग्घी पर बैठकर स्कूल के हेडमास्टर के यहां जा पहुँचे। हेडमास्टर साहब बड़े सज्जन पुरुष थे। वकील साहब का बहुत आदर—सत्कार किया, पर उनके यहा एक लड़के की भी जगह खाली न थी। सभी कमरे भरे हुए थे। इंस्पेक्टर साहब की कड़ी ताकीद थी कि मुफस्सिल के लड़कों को जगह देकर तब शहर के लड़कों को दिया जाए। इसीलिए यदि कोई जगह खाली भी हुई, तो भी मंसाराम को जगह न मिल सकेगी, क्योंकि कितने ही बाहरी लड़कों के प्रार्थना—पत्र रखे हुए थे।

मुंशीजी वकील थे, रात दिन ऐसे प्राणियों से साबिका रहता था, जो लोभवश असंभव को भी संभव, असाध्य को भी साध्य बना सकते हैं। समझे शायद कुछ दे-दिलाकर काम निकल जाए, दफ्तर क्लर्क से ढंग की कुछ बातचीत करनी चाहिए, पर उसने हंसकर कहा—मुंशीजी यह कचहरी नहीं, स्कूल है, हैडमास्टर साहब के कानों में इसकी भनक भी पड़ गयी, तो जामे से बाहर हो जाएंगे और मंसाराम को खड़े-खड़े निकाल देंगे। संभव है, अफसरों से शिकायत कर दें। बेचारे मुंशीजी अपना-सा मुंह लेकर रह गये। दस बजते-बजते झुंझलाये हुए घर लौटे। मंसाराम उसी वक्त घर से स्कूल जाने को निकला मुंशीजी ने कठोर नेत्रों से उसे देखा, मानो वह उनका शत्रु हो और घर में चले गये।

इसके बाद दस-बारह दिनों तक वकील साहब का यही नियम रहा कि कभी सुबह कभी शाम, किसी-न-किसी स्कूल के हेडमास्टर से मिलते और मंसाराम को बोर्डिंग हाउस में दाखिल करने की चेष्टा करते, पर किसी स्कूल में जगह न थी। सभी जगहों से कोरा जवाब मिल गया।

अब दो ही उपाय थे—या तो मंसाराम को अलग किराये के मकान में रख दिया जाए या किसी दूसरे स्कूल में भर्ती करा दिया जाए। ये दोनों बातें आसान थीं। मुफस्सिल के स्कूलों में जगह अक्सर खाली रहती थी, लेकिन अब मुंशीजी का शंकित हृदय कुछ शांत हो गया था।

उस दिन से उन्होंने मंसाराम को कभी घर में जाते न देखा। यहां तक कि अब वह खेलने भी न जाता था। स्कूल जाने के पहले और आने के बाद, बराबर अपने कमरे में बैठा रहता। गर्मी के दिन थे, खुले हुए मैदान में भी देह से पसीने की धारें निकलती थीं, लेकिन मंसाराम अपने कमरे से बाहर न निकलता। उसका आत्माभिमान आवारापन के आक्षेप से मुक्त होने के लिए विकल हो रहा था। वह अपने आचरण से इस कलंक को मिटा देना चाहता था।

एक दिन मुंशीजी बैठे भोजन कर रहे थे, कि मंसाराम भी नहाकर खाने आया, मुंशीजी ने इधर उसे महीनों से नंगे बदन न देखा था। आज उस पर निगाह पड़ी, तो होश उड़ गये। हड्डियों का ढांचा सामने खड़ा था। मुख पर अब भी ब्रह्मचर्य का तेज था, पर देह घुलकर कांटा हो गयी थी। पूछा—आजकल तुम्हारी तबीयत अच्छी नहीं है, क्या? इतने दुर्बल क्यों हो?

मंसाराम ने धोती ओढ़कर कहा—तबीयत तो बिल्कुल अच्छी है।

मुंशीजी—फिर इतने दुर्बल क्यों हो?

मंसाराम—दुर्बल तो नहीं हूं। मैं इससे ज्यादा मोटा कब था?

मुंशीजी—वाह, आधी देह भी नहीं रही और कहते हो, मैं दुर्बल नहीं हूं? क्यों दीदी, यह ऐसा ही था?

रुक्मिणी आंगन में खड़ी तुलसी को जल चढ़ा रही थी, बोली—दुबला क्यों होगा, अब तो बहुत अच्छी तरह लालन-पालन हो रहा है। मैं गंवारिन थी, लड़कों को खिलाना-पिलाना नहीं जानती थी। खोमचा

खिला-खिलाकर इनकी आदत बिगाड़ देती थी। अब तो एक पढ़ी-लिखी, गृहस्थी के कामों में चतुर औरत पान की तरह फेर रही है न। दुबला हो उसका दुश्मन।

मुंशीजी—दीदी, तुम बड़ा अन्याय करती हो। तुमसे किसने कहा कि लड़कों को बिगाड़ रही हो। जो काम दूसरों के किये न हो सके, वह तुम्हें खुद करने चाहिए। यह नहीं कि घर से कोई नाता न रखो। जो अभी खुद लड़की है, वह लड़कों की देख-रेख क्या करेगी? यह तुम्हारा काम है।

रुक्मिणी—जब तक अपना समझती थी, करती थी। जब तुमने गैर समझ लिया, तो मुझे क्या पड़ी है कि मैं तुम्हारे गले से चिपटूं? पूछो, कै दिन से दूध नहीं पिया? जाके कमरे में देख आओ, नाश्ते के लिए जो मिठाई भेजी गयी थी, वह पड़ी सड़ रही है। मालकिन समझती हैं, मैंने तो खाने का सामान रख दिया, कोई न खाये तो क्या मैं मुंह में डाल दूं? तो भैया, इस तरह वे लड़के पलते होंगे, जिन्होंने कभी लाड़-प्यार का सुख नहीं देखा। तुम्हारे लड़के बराबर पान की तरह फेरे जाते रहे हैं, अब अनाथों की तरह रहकर सुखी नहीं रह सकते। मैं तो बात साफ कहती हूं। बुरा मानकर ही कोई क्या कर लेगा? उस पर सुनती हूं कि लड़के को स्कूल में रखने का प्रबंध कर रहे हो। बेचारे को घर में आने तक की मनाही है। मेरे पास आते भी डरता है, और फिर मेरे पास रखा ही क्या रहता है, जो जाकर खिलाऊंगी।

इतने में मंसाराम दो फुलके खाकर उठ खड़ा हुआ। मुंशीजी ने पूछा—तुम खा चुके? अभी बैठे एक मिनट से ज्यादा नहीं हुआ। तुमने खाया क्या, दो ही फुलके तो लिये थे।

मंसाराम ने सकुचाते हुए कहा—दाल और तरकारी भी तो थी। ज्यादा खा जाता हूं, तो गला जलने लगता है, खट्टी डकारें आने लगतीं हैं।

मुंशीजी भोजन करके उठे तो बहुत चिंतित थे। अगर यों ही दुबला होता गया, तो उसे कोई भंयकर रोग पकड़ लेगा। उन्हें रुक्मिणी पर इस समय बहुत क्रोध आ रहा था। उन्हें यही जलन है कि मैं घर की मालकिन नहीं हूं। यह नहीं समझतीं कि मुझे घर की मालकिन बनने का

क्या अधिकार है? जिसे रुपये का हिसाब तक नहीं अता, वह घर की स्वामिनी कैसे हो सकती है? बनीं तो थीं साल भर तक मालकिन, एक पाई की बचत न होती थी। इस आमदनी में रूपकला दो-ढाई सौ रुपये बचा लेती थी। इनके राज में वही आमदनी खर्च को भी पूरी न पड़ती थी। कोई बात नहीं, लाड़-प्यार ने इन लड़कों को चौपट कर दिया। इतने बड़े-बड़े लड़कों को इसकी क्या जरूरत कि जब कोई खिलाये तो खायें। इन्हें तो खुद अपनी फिक्र करनी चाहिए।

मुंशीजी दिनभर उसी उधेड़-बुन में पड़े रहे। दो-चार मित्रों से भी जिक्र किया। लोगों ने कहा—उसके खेल-कूद में बाधा न डालिए, अभी से उसे कैद न कीजिए, खुली हवा में चरित्र के भ्रष्ट होने की उससे कम संभावना है, जितना बन्द कमरे में। कुसंगत से जरूर बचाइए, मगर यह नहीं कि उसे घर से निकलने ही न दीजिए। युवावस्था में एकान्तवास चरित्र के लिए बहुत ही हानिकारक है।

मुंशीजी को अब अपनी गलती मालूम हुई। घर लौटकर मंसाराम के पास गये। वह अभी स्कूल से आया था और बिना कपड़े उतारे, एक किताब सामने खोलकर, सामने खिड़की की ओर ताक रहा था। उसकी दृष्टि एक भिखारिन पर लगी हुई थी, जो अपने बालक को गोद में लिए भिक्षा मांग रही थी। बालक माता की गोद में बैठा ऐसा प्रसन्न था, मानो वह किसी राजसिंहासन पर बैठा हो।

मंसाराम उस बालक को देखकर रो पड़ा। यह बालक क्या मुझसे अधिक सुखी नहीं है? इस अन्नत विश्व में ऐसी कौन-सी वस्तु है, जिसे वह इस गोद के बदले पाकर प्रसन्न हो? ईश्वर भी ऐसी वस्तु की सृष्टि नहीं कर सकते। ईश्वर ऐसे बालकों को जन्म ही क्यों देते हो, जिनके भाग्य में मातृ-वियोग का दुख भोगना बदा हो? आज मुझ-सा अभागा संसार में और कौन है? किसे मेरे खाने-पीने की, मरने-जीने की सुध है। अगर मैं आज मर भी जाऊं, तो किसके दिल को चोट लगेगी। पिता को अब मुझे रुलाने में मजा आता है, वह मेरी सूरत भी नहीं देखना चाहते, मुझे घर से निकाल देने की तैयारियां हो रही हैं। आह माता। तुम्हारा लाड़ला बेटा आज आवारा कहा जा रहा है। वही पिताजी, जिनके हाथ

में तुमने हम तीनों भाइयों के हाथ पकड़ाये थे, आज मुझे आवारा और बदमाश कह रहे हैं। मैं इस योग्य भी नहीं कि इस घर में रह सकूं। यह सोचते-सोचते मंसाराम अपार वेदना से फूट-फूटकर रोने लगा।

उसी समय तोताराम कमरे में आकर खड़े हो गये। मंसाराम ने चटपट आंसू पोंछ डाले और सिर झुकाकर खड़ा हो गया। मुंशीजी ने शायद यह पहली बार उसके कमरे में कदम रखा था। मंसाराम का दिल धड़धड़ करने लगा कि देखें आज क्या आफत आती है।

मुंशीजी ने उसे रोते देखा, तो एक क्षण के लिए उनका वात्सल्य घोर निद्रा से चौंक पड़ा। घबराकर बोले–क्यों, रोते क्यों हो बेटा! किसी ने कुछ कहा है?

मंसाराम ने बड़ी मुश्किल से उमड़ते हुए आंसुओं को रोककर कहा–जी नहीं, रोता तो नहीं हूं।

मुंशीजी–तुम्हारी अम्मां ने तो कुछ नहीं कहा?

मंसाराम–जी नहीं, वह तो मुझसे बोलती ही नहीं।

मुंशीजी–क्या करुं बेटा, शादी तो इसलिए की थी कि बच्चों को मां मिल जाएगी, लेकिन वह आशा पूरी नहीं हुई, तो क्या बिल्कुल नहीं बोलतीं?

मंसाराम–जी नहीं, इधर महीनों से नहीं बोलीं।

मुंशीजी–विचित्र स्वभाव की औरत है, मालूम ही नहीं होता कि क्या चाहती है? मैं जानता कि उसका ऐसा मिजाज होगा, तो कभी शादी न करता रोज एक–न–एक बात लेकर उठ खड़ी होती है। उसी ने मुझसे कहा था कि यह दिन भर न जाने कहां गायब रहता है। मैं उसके दिल की बात क्या जानता था? समझा, तुम कुसंगत में पड़कर शायद दिनभर घूमा करते हो। कौन ऐसा पिता है, जिसे अपने प्यारे पुत्र को आवारा फिरते देखकर रंज न हो? इसीलिए मैंने तुम्हें बोर्डिंग हाउस में रखने का निश्चय किया था। बस, और कोई बात नहीं थी, बेटा। मैं तुम्हारा खेलना-कूदना बंद नहीं करना चाहता था। तुम्हारी यह दशा देखकर मेरे दिल के टुकड़े हुए जाते हैं। कल मुझे मालूम हुआ मैं भ्रम में था। तुम शौक से खेलो, सुबह-शाम मैदान में निकल जाया करो। ताजी हवा से

तुम्हें लाभ होगा। जिस चीज की जरूरत हो मुझसे कहो, उनसे कहने की जरूरत नहीं। समझ लो कि वह घर में है ही नहीं। तुम्हारी माता छोड़कर चली गयी तो मैं तो हूं।

बालक का सरल निष्कपट हृदय पितृ-प्रेम से पुलकित हो उठा। मालूम हुआ कि साक्षात् भगवान् खड़े हैं। नैराश्य और क्षोभ से विकल होकर उसने मन में अपने पिता को निष्ठुर और न जाने क्या-क्या समझ रखा था। विमाता से उसे कोई गिला न था। अब उसे ज्ञात हुआ कि मैंने अपने देवतुल्य पिता के साथ कितना अन्याय किया है। पितृ-भक्ति की एक तरंग-सी हृदय में उठी, और वह पिता के चरणों पर सिर रखकर रोने लगा।

मुंशीजी करुणा से विह्वल हो गये। जिस पुत्र को क्षण भर आंखों से दूर देखकर उनका हृदय व्यग्र हो उठता था, जिसके शील, बुद्धि और चरित्र का अपने-पराये सभी बखान करते थे, उसी के प्रति उनका हृदय इतना कठोर क्यों हो गया? वह अपने ही प्रिय पुत्र को शत्रु समझने लगे, उसको निर्वासन देने को तैयार हो गये।

निर्मला पुत्र और पिता के बीच में दीवार बनकर खड़ी थी। निर्मला को अपनी ओर खींचने के लिए पीछे हटना पड़ता था, और पिता तथा पुत्र में अंतर बढ़ता जाता था। फलतः आज यह दशा हो गयी है कि अपने अभिन्न पुत्र से उन्हें इतना छल करना पड़ रहा है। आज बहुत सोचने के बाद उन्हें एक एक ऐसी युक्ति सूझी है, जिससे आशा हो रही है कि वह निर्मला को बीच से निकालकर अपने दूसरे बाजू को अपनी तरफ खींच लेंगे। उन्होंने उस युक्ति का आरंभ भी कर दिया है, लेकिन इसमें अभीष्ट सिद्ध होगा या नहीं, इसे कौन जानता है।

जिस दिन से तोताराम ने निर्मला के बहुत मिन्नत-समाजत करने पर भी मंसाराम को बोर्डिंग हाउस में भेजने का निश्चय किया था, उसी दिन से उसने मंसाराम से पढ़ना छोड़ दिया। यहां तक कि बोलती भी न थी। उसे स्वामी की इस अविश्वासपूर्ण तत्परता का कुछ-कुछ आभास हो गया था। ओफ्फोह। इतना शक्की मिजाज। ईश्वर ही इस घर की लाज रखें। इनके मन में ऐसी-ऐसी दुर्भावनाएं भरी हुई हैं। मुझे यह इतनी

गयी-गुजरी समझते हैं। ये बातें सोच-सोचकर वह कई दिन रोती रही। तब उसने सोचना शुरू किया, इन्हें क्यों ऐसा संदेह हो रहा है? मुझ में ऐसी कौन-सी बात है, जो इनकी आंखों में खटकती है। बहुत सोचने पर भी उसे अपने में कोई ऐसी बात नजर न आयी। तो क्या उसका मंसाराम से पढ़ना, उससे हंसना-बोलना ही इनके संदेह का कारण है, तो फिर मैं पढ़ना छोड़ दूंगी, भूलकर भी मंसाराम से न बोलूंगी, उसकी सूरत न देखूंगी।

लेकिन यह तपस्या उसे असाध्य जान पड़ती थी। मंसाराम से हंसने-बोलने में उसकी विलासिनी कल्पना उत्तेजित भी होती थी और तृप्त भी। उसे बातें करते हुए उसे अपार सुख का अनुभव होता था, जिसे वह शब्दों में प्रकट न कर सकती थी। कुवासना की उसके मन में छाया भी न थी। वह स्वप्न में भी मंसाराम से कलुषित प्रेम करने की बात न सोच सकती थी। प्रत्येक प्राणी को अपने हमजोलियों के साथ, हंसने-बोलने की जो एक नैसर्गिक तृष्णा होती है, उसी की तृप्ति का यह एक अज्ञात साधन था। अब वह अतृप्त तृष्णा निर्मला के हृदय में दीपक की भांति जलने लगी। रह-रहकर उसका मन किसी अज्ञात वेदना से विकल हो जाता। खोयी हुई किसी अज्ञात वस्तु की खोज में इधर-उधर घूमती-फिरती, जहां बैठती, वहां बैठी ही रह जाती, किसी काम में जी न लगता। हां, जब मुंशीजी आ जाते, वह अपनी सारी तृष्णाओं को नैराश्य में डुबाकर, उनसे मुस्कराकर इधर-उधर की बातें करने लगती।

कल जब मुंशीजी भोजन करके कचहरी चले गये, तो रुक्मिणी ने निर्मला को खुब तानों से छेदा—जानती तो थी कि यहां बच्चों का पालन-पोषण करना पड़ेगा, तो क्यों घरवालों से नहीं कह दिया कि वहां मेरा विवाह न करो? वहां जाती जहां पुरुष के सिवा और कोई न होता। वही यह बनाव-चुनाव और छवि देखकर खुश होता, अपने भाग्य को सराहता। यहां बुड्ढा आदमी तुम्हारे रंग-रूप, हाव-भाव पर क्या लट्टू होगा? इसने इन्हीं बालकों की सेवा करने के लिए तुमसे विवाह किया है, भोग-विलास के लिए नहीं।

वह बड़ी देर तक घाव पर नमक छिड़कती रही, पर निर्मला ने चूं तक न की। वह अपनी सफाई तो पेश करना चाहती थी, पर न कर सकती थी। अगर कहे कि मैं वही कर रही हूं, जो मेरे स्वामी की इच्छा है तो घर का भण्डा फूटता है। अगर वह अपनी भूल स्वीकार करके उसका सुधार करती है, तो भय है कि उसका न जाने क्या परिणाम हो? वह यों बड़ी स्पष्टवादिनी थी, सत्य कहने में उसे संकोच या भय न होता था, लेकिन इस नाजुक मौके पर उसे चुप्पी साधनी पड़ी। इसके सिवा दूसरा उपाय न था। वह देखती थी मंसाराम बहुत विरक्त और उदास रहता है, यह भी देखती थी कि वह दिन-दिन दुर्बल होता जाता है, लेकिन उसकी वाणी और कर्म दोनों ही पर मोहर लगी हुई थी। चोर के घर चोरी हो जाने से उसकी जो दशा होती है, वही दशा इस समय निर्मला की हो रही थी।

जब कोई बात हमारी आशा के विरुद्ध होती है, तभी दुख होता है। मंसाराम को निर्मला से कभी इस बात की आशा न थी कि वे उसकी शिकायत करेंगी। इसलिए उसे घोर वेदना हो रही थी। वह क्यों मेरी शिकायत करती है? क्या चाहती है? यही न कि वह मेरे पति की कमाई खाता है, इसके पढ़ाने-लिखाने में रुपये खर्च होते हैं, कपड़ा पहनता है। उनकी यही इच्छा होगी कि यह घर में न रहे। मेरे न रहने से उनके रुपये बच जाएंगे। वह मुझसे बहुत प्रसन्नचित्त रहती हैं। कभी मैंने उनके मुंह से कटु शब्द नहीं सुने। क्या यह सब कौशल है? हो सकता है? चिड़िया को जाल में फंसाने के पहले शिकारी दाने बिखेरता है। आह। मैं नहीं जानता था कि दाने के नीचे जाल है, यह मातृ-स्नेह केवल मेरे निर्वासन की भूमिका है।

अच्छा, मेरा यहां रहना क्यों बुरा लगता है? जो उनका पति है, क्या वह मेरा पिता नहीं है? क्या पिता-पुत्र का संबंध स्त्री-पुरुष के संबंध से कुछ कम घनिष्ट है? अगर मुझे उनके संपूर्ण आधिपत्य से ईर्ष्या नहीं होती, वह जो चाहे करें, मैं मुंह नहीं खोल सकता, तो वह मुझे एक अंगुल-भर भूमि भी देना नहीं चाहतीं। आप पक्के महल में रहकर क्यों मुझे वृक्ष की छाया में बैठा नहीं देख सकतीं।

हां, वह समझती होंगी कि वह बड़ा होकर मेरे पति की सम्पत्ति का स्वामी हो जाएगा, इसलिए अभी से निकाल देना अच्छा है। उनको कैसे विश्वास दिलाऊं कि मेरी ओर से यह शंका न करें। उन्हें क्योंकर बताऊं कि मंसाराम विष खाकर प्राण दे देगा, इसके पहले कि उनका अहित करे। उसे चाहे कितनी ही कठिनाइयां सहनी पड़ें वह उनके हृदय का शूल न बनेगा।

यों तो पिताजी ने मुझे जन्म दिया है और अब भी मुझ पर उनका स्नेह कम नहीं है, लेकिन क्या मैं इतना भी नहीं जानता कि जिस दिन पिताजी ने उनसे विवाह किया, उसी दिन उन्होंने हमें अपने हृदय से बाहर निकाल दिया? अब हम अनाथों की भांति यहां पड़े रह सकते हैं, इस घर पर हमारा कोई अधिकार नहीं है। कदाचित् पूर्व संस्कारों के कारण यहां अन्य अनाथों से हमारी दशा कुछ अच्छी है, पर हैं अनाथ ही। हम उसी दिन अनाथ हुए, जिस दिन अम्मां जी परलोक सिधारीं। जो कुछ कसर रह गयी थी, वह इस विवाह ने पूरी कर दी।

मैं तो खुद पहले इनसे विशेष संबंध न रखता था। अगर, उन्हीं दिनों पिताजी से मेरी शिकायत की होती, तो शायद मुझे इतना दुख न होता। मैं तो उस आघात के लिए तैयार बैठा था। संसार में क्या मैं मजदूरी भी नहीं कर सकता? लेकिन बुरे वक्त में इन्होंने चोट की। हिंसक पशु भी आदमी को गाफिल पाकर ही चोट करते हैं। इसीलिए मेरी आवभगत होती थी, खाना खाने के लिए उठने में जरा भी देर हो जाती थी, तो बुलावे पर बुलावे आते थे, जलपान के लिए प्रातः हलुआ बनाया जाता था, बार-बार पूछा जाता था—रुपयों की जरूरत तो नहीं है? इसीलिए वह सौ रुपयों की घड़ी मंगवाई थी।

मगर क्या इन्हें क्या दूसरी शिकायत न सूझी, जो मुझे आवारा कहा? आखिर उन्होंने मेरी क्या आवारगी देखी? यह कह सकती थीं कि इसका मन पढ़ने-लिखने में नहीं लगता, एक-न-एक चीज के लिए नित्य रुपये मांगता रहता है। यही एक बात उन्हें क्यों सूझी? शायद इसीलिए कि यही सबसे कठोर आघात है, जो वह मुझ पर कर सकती हैं। पहली ही बार इन्होंने मुझ पर अग्नि-बाण चला दिया, जिससे कहीं

शरण नहीं। इसीलिए न कि वह पिता की नजरों से गिर जाए? मुझे बोर्डिंग-हाउस में रखने का तो एक बहाना था। उद्देश्य यह था कि इसे दूध की मक्खी की तरह निकाल दिया जाए। दो-चार महीने के बाद खर्च-वर्च देना बंद कर दिया जाए, फिर चाहे मरे या जिये।

अगर मैं जानता कि यह प्रेरणा इनकी ओर से हुई है, तो कहीं जगह न रहने पर भी जगह निकाल लेता। नौकरों की कोठरियों में तो जगह मिल जाती, बरामदे में पड़े रहने के लिए बहुत जगह मिल जाती। खैर, अब सबेरा है। जब स्नेह नहीं रहा, तो केवल पेट भरने के लिए यहां पड़े रहना बेहयाई है, यह अब मेरा घर नहीं। इसी घर में पैदा हुआ हूं, यहीं खेला हूं, पर यह अब मेरा नहीं। पिताजी भी मेरे पिता नहीं हैं। मैं उनका पुत्र हूं, पर वह मेरे पिता नहीं हैं। संसार के सारे नाते स्नेह के नाते हैं। जहां स्नेह नहीं, वहां कुछ नहीं। हाय, अम्मांजी, तुम कहां हो?

यह सोचकर मंसाराम रोने लगा। ज्यों-ज्यों मातृ स्नेह की पूर्व स्मृतियां जागृत होती थीं, उसके आंसू उमड़ते आते थे। वह कई बार अम्मां-अम्मां पुकार उठा, मानो वह खड़ी सुन रही हैं। मातृ-हीनता के दुःख का आज उसे पहली बार अनुभव हुआ। वह आत्माभिमानी था, साहसी था, पर अब तक सुख की गोद में लालन-पालन होने के कारण वह इस समय अपने आप को निराधार समझ रहा था।

रात के दस बज गये थे। मुंशीजी आज कहीं दावत खाने गये हुए थे। दो बार महरी मंसाराम को भोजन करने के लिए बुलाने आ चुकी थी। मंसाराम ने पिछली बार उससे झुंझलाकर कह दिया था-मुझे भूख नहीं है, कुछ न खाऊंगा। बार-बार आकर सिर पर सवार हो जाती है। इसीलिए जब निर्मला ने उसे फिर उसी काम के लिए भेजना चाहा, तो वह न गयी। बोली–बहूजी, वह मेरे बुलाने से न आवेंगे।

निर्मला–आयेंगे क्यों नहीं? जाकर कह दे खाना ठण्डा हुआ जाता है। दो चार कौर खा लें।

महरी–मैं यह सब कह के हार गयी, नहीं आते।

निर्मला–तूने यह कहा था कि वह बैठी हुई हैं।

महरी–नहीं बहूजी, यह तो मैंने नहीं कहा, झूठ क्यों बोलूं।

निर्मला–अच्छा, तो जाकर यह कह देना, वह बैठी तुम्हारी राह देख रही हैं। तुम न खाओगे तो वह रसोई उठाकर सो रहेंगी। मेरी भूंगी, सुन, अबकी और चली जा। (हंसकर) न आवें, तो गोद में उठा लाना।

भूंगी नाक-भौं सिकोड़ते गयी, पर एक ही क्षण में आकर बोली–अरे बहूजी, वह तो रो रहे हैं। किसी ने कुछ कहा है क्या?

निर्मला इस तरह चौंककर उठी और दो-तीन पग आगे चली, मानो किसी माता ने अपने बेटे के कुएं में गिर पड़ने की खबर पायी हो, फिर वह ठिठक गयी और भूंगी से बोली–रो रहे हैं? तूने पूछा नहीं क्यों रो रहे हैं?

भूंगी–नहीं बहूजी, यह तो मैंने नहीं पूछा। झूठ क्यों बोलूं?

वह रो रहे हैं। इस निस्तब्ध रात्रि में अकेले बैठै हुए वह रो रहे हैं। माता की याद आयी होगी? कैसे जाकर उन्हें समझाऊं? हाय, कैसे समझाऊं? यहां तो छींकते नाक कटती है। ईश्वर, तुम साक्षी हो अगर मैंने उन्हें भूल से भी कुछ कहा हो, तो वह मेरे आगे आये। मैं क्या करुं? वह दिल में समझते होंगे कि इसी ने पिताजी से मेरी शिकायत की होगी। कैसे विश्वास दिलाऊं कि मैंने कभी तुम्हारे विरुद्ध एक शब्द भी मुंह से नहीं निकाला? अगर मैं ऐसे देवकुमार के-से चरित्र रखने वाले युवक का बुरा चेतूं, तो मुझसे बढ़कर राक्षसी संसार में न होगी।

निर्मला देखती थी कि मंसाराम का स्वास्थ्य दिन-दिन बिगड़ता जाता है, वह दिन-दिन दुर्बल होता जाता है, उसके मुख की निर्मल कांति दिन-दिन मलिन होती जाती है, उसका सहास बदन संकुचित होता जाता है। इसका कारण भी उससे छिपा न था, पर वह इस विषय में अपने स्वामी से कुछ न कह सकती थी। यह सब देख-देखकर उसका हृदय विदीर्ण होता रहता था, पर उसकी जबान न खुल सकती थी। वह कभी-कभी मन में झुंझलाती कि मंसाराम क्यों जरा–सी बात पर इतना क्षोभ करता है? क्या इनके आवारा कहने से वह आवारा हो गया? मेरी

और बात है, एक जरा-सा शक मेरा सर्वनाश कर सकता है, पर उसे ऐसी बातों की इतनी क्या परवाह?

उसके जी में प्रबल इच्छा हुई कि चलकर उन्हें चुप कराऊं और लाकर खाना खिला दूं। बेचारे रात-भर भूखे पड़े रहेंगे। हाय। मैं इस उपद्रव की जड़ हूं। मेरे आने के पहले इस घर में शांति का राज्य था। पिता बालकों पर जान देता था, बालक पिता को प्यार करते थे। मेरे आते ही सारी बाधाएं आ खड़ी हुईं। इनका अंत क्या होगा? भगवान् ही जाने। भगवान् मुझे मौत भी नहीं देते। बेचारा अकेले भूखों पड़ा है। उस वक्त भी मुंह जूठा करके उठ गया था। और उसका आहार ही क्या है, जितना वह खाता है, उतना तो साल-दो-साल के बच्चे खा जाते हैं।

निर्मला चली। पति की इच्छा के विरुद्ध चली। जो नाते में उसका पुत्र होता था, उसी को मनाने जाते उसका ह्रदय कांप रहा था। उसने पहले रुक्मिणी के कमरे की ओर देखा, वह भोजन करके बेखबर सो रही थीं, फिर बाहर कमरे की ओर गयी। वहां सन्नाटा था। मुंशीजी अभी न आये थे। यह सब देख-भालकर वह मंसाराम के कमरे के सामने जा पहुंची। कमरा खुला हुआ था, मंसाराम एक पुस्तक सामने रखे मेज पर सिर झुकाये बैठा हुआ था, मानो शोक और चिन्ता की सजीव मूर्ति हो। निर्मला ने पुकारना चाहा पर उसके कंठ से आवाज़ न निकली। सहसा मंसाराम ने सिर उठाकर द्वार की ओर देखा। निर्मला को देखकर अंधेरे में पहचान न सका। चौंककर बोला—कौन?

निर्मला ने कांपते हुए स्वर में कहा—मैं तो हूं। भोजन करने क्यों नहीं चल रहे हो? कितनी रात गयी।

मंसाराम ने मुंह फेरकर कहा—मुझे भूख नहीं है।

निर्मला—यह तो मैं तीन बार भूंगी से सुन चुकी हूं।

मंसाराम—तो चौथी बार मेरे मुंह से सुन लीजिए।

निर्मला—शाम को भी तो कुछ नहीं खाया था, भूख क्यों नहीं लगी?

मंसाराम ने व्यंग्य की हंसी हंसकर कहा—बहुत भूख लगेगी, तो आयेगा कहां से?

यह कहते-कहते मंसाराम ने कमरे का द्वार बंद करना चाहा, लेकिन निर्मला किवाड़ों को हटाकर कमरे में चली आयी और मंसाराम का हाथ पकड़ सजल नेत्रों से विनय-मधुर स्वर में बोली–मेरे कहने से चलकर थोड़ा-सा खा लो। तुम न खाओगे, तो मैं भी जाकर सो रहूंगी। दो ही कौर खा लेना। क्या मुझे रात-भर भूखों मारना चाहते हो?

मंसाराम सोच में पड़ गया। अभी भोजन नहीं किया, मेरे ही इंतजार में बैठी रहीं। यह स्नेह, वात्सल्य और विनय की देवी हैं या ईर्ष्या और अमंगल की मायाविनी मूर्ति? उसे अपनी माता का स्मरण हो आया। जब वह रुठ जाता था, तो वे भी इसी तरह मनाने आ करती थीं और जब तक वह न जाता था, वहां से न उठती थीं। वह इस विनय को अस्वीकार न कर सका। बोला–मेरे लिए आपको इतना कष्ट हुआ, इसका मुझे खेद है। मैं जानता कि आप मेरे इंतजार में भूखी बैठी हैं, तो तभी खा आया होता।

निर्मला ने तिरस्कार भाव से कहा–यह तुम कैसे समझ सकते थे कि तुम भूखे रहोगे और मैं खाकर सो रहूंगी? क्या विमाता का नाता होने से ही मैं ऐसी स्वार्थिनी हो जाऊंगी?

सहसा मर्दाने कमरे में मुंशीजी के खांसने की आवाज आयी। ऐसा मालूम हुआ कि वह मंसाराम के कमरे की ओर आ रहे हैं। निर्मला के चेहरे का रंग उड़ गया। वह तुरंत कमरे से निकल गयी और भीतर जाने का मौका न पाकर कठोर स्वर में बोली–मैं लौंडी नहीं हूं कि इतनी रात तक किसी के लिए रसोई के द्वार पर बैठी रहूं। जिसे न खाना हो, वह पहले ही कह दिया करे।

मुंशीजी ने निर्मला को वहां खड़े देखा। यह अनर्थ! यह यहां क्या करने आ गयी? बोले–यहां क्या कर रही हो?

निर्मला ने कर्कश स्वर में कहा–कर क्या रही हूं, अपने भाग्य को रो रही हूं। बस, सारी बुराइयों की जड़ मैं ही हूं। कोई इधर रुठा है, कोई उधर मुंह फुलाये खड़ा है। किस-किस को मनाऊं और कहां तक मनाऊं।

मुंशीजी कुछ चकित होकर बोले–बात क्या है?

निर्मला–भोजन करने नहीं जाते और क्या बात है? दस दफे महरी को भेजी, आखिर आप दौड़ी आयी। इन्हें तो इतना कह देना आसान है, मुझे भूख नहीं है, यहां तो घर भर की लौंडी हूं, सारी दुनिया मुंह में कालिख पोतने को तैयार। किसी को भूख न हो, पर कहने वालों को यह कहने से कौन रोकेगा कि पिशाचिनी किसी को खाना नहीं देती।

मुंशीजी ने मंसाराम से कहा–खाना क्यों नहीं खा लेते जी? जानते हो क्या वक्त है?

मंसाराम स्तम्भित–सा खड़ा था। उसके सामने एक ऐसा रहस्य हो रहा था, जिसका मर्म वह कुछ भी न समझ सकता था। जिन नेत्रों में एक क्षण पहले विनय के आंसू भरे हुए थे, उनमें अकस्मात् ईर्ष्या की ज्वाला कहां से आ गयी? जिन अधरों से एक क्षण पहले सुधा-वृष्टि हो रही थी, उनमें से विष प्रवाह क्यों होने लगा? उसी अर्ध चेतना की दशा में बोला–मुझे भूख नहीं है।

मुंशीजी ने घुड़ककर कहा–क्यों भूख नहीं है? भूख नहीं थी, तो शाम को क्यों न कहला दिया? तुम्हारी भूख के इंतजार में कौन सारी रात बैठा रहे? तुममें पहले तो यह आदत न थी। रुठना कब से सीख लिया? जाकर खा लो।

मंसाराम–जी नहीं, मुझे जरा भी भूख नहीं है।

तोताराम ने दांत पीसकर कहा–अच्छी बात है, जब भूख लगे तब खाना। यह कहते हुए वह अंदर चले गये।

निर्मला भी उनके पीछे ही चली गयी। मुंशीजी तो लेटने चले गये, उसने जाकर रसोई उठा दी और कुल्लाकर, पान खा मुस्कराती हुई आ पहुंची। मुंशीजी ने पूछा–खाना खा लिया न?

निर्मला–क्या करती, किसी के लिए अन्न-जल छोड़ दूंगी?

मुंशीजी–इसे न जाने क्या हो गया है, कुछ समझ में नहीं आता? दिन-दिन घुलता चला जाता है, दिन भर उसी कमरे में पड़ा रहता है।

निर्मला कुछ न बोली। वह चिंता के अपार सागर में डुबकियां खा रही थी। मंसाराम ने मेरे भाव-परिवर्तन को देखकर दिल में क्या-क्या समझा होगा? क्या उसके मन में यह प्रश्न उठा होगा कि पिताजी

को देखते ही इसकी त्योरियां क्यों बदल गयीं? इसका कारण भी क्या उसकी समझ में आ गया होगा? बेचारा खाने आ रहा था, तब तक यह महाशय न जाने कहां से फट पड़े? इस रहस्य को उसे कैसे समझाऊं समझाना संभव भी है? मैं किस विपत्ति में फंस गयी?

सवेरे वह उठकर घर के काम-धंधे में लगी। सहसा नौ बजे भूंगी ने आकर कहा—मंसा बाबू तो अपने कागज-पत्तर सब इक्के पर लाद रहे हैं।

निर्मला ने हकबकाकर कहा—इक्के पर लाद रहे हैं! कहां जाते हैं?

भूंगी—मैंने पूछा तो बोले, अब स्कूल में ही रहूंगा।

मंसाराम प्रातःकाल उठकर अपने स्कूल के हेडमास्टर साहब के पास गया था और अपने रहने का प्रबंध कर आया था। हेडमास्टर साहब ने पहले तो कहा—यहां जगह नहीं है, तुमसे पहले के कितने ही लड़कों के प्रार्थना—पत्र पड़े हुए हैं, लेकिन जब मंसाराम ने कहा—मुझे जगह न मिलेगी, तो कदाचित् मेरा पढ़ना न हो सके और मैं इम्तहान में शरीक न हो सकूं तो हेडमास्टर साहब को हार माननी पड़ी।

मंसाराम के प्रथम श्रेणी में पास होने की आशा थी। अध्यापकों को विश्वास था कि वह उस शाला की कीर्ति को उज्जवल करेगा। हेडमास्टर साहब ऐसे लड़कों को कैसे छोड़ सकते थे? उन्होने अपने दफ्तर का कमरा खाली करा दिया। इसीलिए मंसाराम वहां से आते ही अपना सामान इक्के पर लादने लगा।

मुंशीजी ने कहा—अभी ऐसी क्या जल्दी है? दो-चार दिन में चले जाना। मैं चाहता हूं, तुम्हारे लिए कोई अच्छा सा रसोइया ठीक कर दूं।

मंसाराम—वहां का रसोइया बहुत अच्छा भोजन पकाता है।

मुंशीजी—अपने स्वास्थ्य का ध्यान रखना। ऐसा न हो कि पढ़ने के पीछे स्वास्थ्य खो बैठो।

मंसाराम—वहां नौ बजे के बाद कोई पढ़ने नहीं पाता और सबको नियम के साथ खेलना पड़ता है।

मुंशीजी—बिस्तर क्यों छोड़े देते हो? सोओगे किस पर?

मंसाराम—कंबल लिए जाता हूं। बिस्तर की जरुरत नहीं।

मुंशीजी–कहार जब तक तुम्हारा सामान रख रहा है, जाकर कुछ खा लो। रात भी तो कुछ नहीं खाया था।

मंसाराम–वहीं खा लूंगा। रसोइये से भोजन बनाने को कह आया हूं यहां खाने लगूंगा तो देर होगी।

घर में जियाराम और सियाराम भी भाई के साथ जाने के जिद कर रहे थे निर्मला उन दोनों को बहला रही थी–बेटा, वहां छोटे नहीं रहते, सब काम अपने ही हाथ से करना पड़ता है।

एकाएक रुक्मिणी ने आकर कहा–तुम्हारा वज्र का हृदय है, महारानी। लड़के ने रात भी कुछ नहीं खाया, इस वक्त भी बिना खाय-पीये चला जा रहा है और तुम लड़कों को लिए बातें कर रही हो? उसको तुम जानती नहीं हो। यह समझ लो कि वह स्कूल नहीं जा रहा है, बनवास ले रहा है, लौटकर फिर न आयेगा। यह उन लड़कों में नहीं है, जो खेल में मार भूल जाते हैं। बात उसके दिल पर पत्थर की लकीर हो जाती है।

निर्मला ने कातर स्वर में कहा–क्या करुं, दीदीजी? वह किसी की सुनते ही नहीं। आप जरा जाकर बुला लें। आपके बुलाने से आ जाएंगे।

रुक्मिणी हाथ हिलाते हुए गंभीरता से बोली–आखिर हुआ क्या, जिस पर भागा जाता है? घर से उसका जी कभी उचाट न होता था। उसे तो अपने घर के सिवा और कहीं अच्छा ही न लगता था। तुम्हीं ने उसे कुछ कहा होगा, या उसकी कुछ शिकायत की होगी। क्यों अपने लिए कांटे बो रही हो? रानी, घर को मिट्टी में मिलाकर चैन से न बैठने पाओगी।

निर्मला ने रोकर कहा–मैंने उन्हें कुछ कहा हो, तो मेरी जबान कट जाए। हां, सौतेली मां होने के कारण बदनाम तो हूं ही। आपके हाथ जोड़ती हूं जरा जाकर उन्हें बुला लाइये।

रुक्मिणी ने तीव्र स्वर में कहा–तुम क्यों नहीं बुला लातीं? क्या छोटी हो जाओगी? अपना होता, तो क्या इसी तरह बैठी रहती?

निर्मला की दशा उस पंखहीन पक्षी की तरह हो रही थी, जो सर्प को अपनी ओर आते देख कर उड़ना चाहता है, पर उड़ नहीं सकता,

उछलता है और गिर पड़ता है, पंख फड़फड़ाकर रह जाता है। उसका हृदय अंदर ही अंदर तड़प रहा था, पर बाहर न जा सकती थी।इतने में दोनों लड़के आकर बोले–भैयाजी चले गये।

निर्मला मूर्तिवत् खड़ी रही, मानो संज्ञाहीन हो गयी हो। चले गये? घर में आये तक नहीं, मुझसे मिले तक नहीं चले गये। मुझसे इतनी घृणा। मैं उनकी कोई न सही, उनकी बुआ तो थीं। उनसे तो मिलने आना चाहिए था? मैं यहां थी न। अंदर कैसे कदम रखते? मैं देख लेती न। इसीलिए चले गये।

7

मंसाराम के जाने से घर सूना हो गया। दोनों छोटे लड़के उसी स्कूल में पढ़ते थे। निर्मला रोज उनसे मंसाराम का हाल पूछती। आशा थी कि छुट्टी के दिन वह आयेगा, लेकिन जब छुट्टी के दिन गुजर गये और वह न आया, तो निर्मला की तबीयत घबराने लगी। उसने उसके लिए मूंग के लड्डू बना रखे थे। सोमवार को प्रातः भूंगी को लड्डू देकर मदरसे भेजा। नौ बजे भूंगी लौट आयी। मंसाराम ने लड्डू ज्यों-के-त्यों लौटा दिये थे।

निर्मला ने पूछा–पहले से कुछ हरे हुए हैं, रे?

भूंगी–हरे-वरे तो नहीं हुए, और सूख गये हैं।

निर्मला–क्या जी अच्छा नहीं है?

भूंगी–यह तो मैंने नहीं पूछा बहूजी, झूठ क्यों बोलूं? हां, वहां का कहार मेरा देवर लगता है। वह कहता था कि तुम्हारे बाबूजी की खुराक कुछ नहीं है। दो फुलकियां खाकर उठ जाते हैं, फिर दिन भर कुछ नहीं खाते। हरदम पढ़ते रहते हैं।

निर्मला–तूने पूछा नहीं, लड्डू क्यों लौटाये देते हो?

भूंगी–बहूजी, झूठ क्यों बोलूं? यह पूछने की तो मुझे सुध ही न रही। हां, यह कहते थे कि अब तू यहां कभी न आना, न मेरे लिए कोई चीज लाना और अपनी बहूजी से कह देना कि मेरे पास कोई चिट्ठी-पत्तरी न भेजें। लड़कों से भी मेरे पास कोई संदेशा न भेजें और एक ऐसी बात कही कि मेरे मुंह से निकल नहीं सकती, फिर रोने लगे।

निर्मला–कौन बात थी कह तो?

भूंगी–क्या कहूं कहते थे मेरे जीने को धिक्कार है? यही कहकर रोने लगे।

निर्मला के मुंह से एक ठंडी सांस निकल गयी। ऐसा मालूम हुआ, मानो कलेजा बैठा जाता है। उसका रोम-रोम आर्तनाद करने लगा। वह वहां बैठी न रह सकी। जाकर बिस्तर पर मुंह ढांपकर लेट रही और फूट–फूटकर रोने लगी। 'वह भी जान गये'। उसके अन्तःकरण में बार–बार यही आवाज़ गूंजने लगी–'वह भी जान गये'। भगवान् अब क्या होगा? जिस संदेह की आग में वह भस्म हो रही थी, अब शतगुणा वेग से धधकने लगी। उसे अपनी कोई चिंता न थी। जीवन में अब सुख की क्या आशा थी, जिसकी उसे लालसा होती? उसने अपने मन को इस विचार से समझाया था कि यह मेरे पूर्व कर्मों का प्रायश्चित है।

कौन प्राणी ऐसा निर्लज्ज होगा, जो इस दशा में बहुत दिन जी सके? कर्त्तव्य की वेदी पर उसने अपना जीवन और उसकी सारी कामनाएं होम कर दी थीं। हृदय रोता रहता था, पर मुख पर हंसी का रंग भरना पड़ता था। जिसका मुंह देखने को जी न चाहता था, उसके सामने हंस-हंसकर बातें करनी पड़ती थीं। जिस देह का स्पर्श उसे सर्प के शीतल स्पर्श के समान लगता था, उससे आलिंगित होकर उसे जितनी घृणा, जितनी मर्मवेदना होती थी, उसे कौन जान सकता है? उस समय उसकी यही इच्छा थी कि धरती फट जाए और मैं उसमें समा जाऊं। लेकिन सारी विडम्बना अब तक अपने ही तक थी। अपनी चिंता उसने छोड़ दी थी, लेकिन वह समस्या अब अत्यंत भयंकर हो गयी थी। वह अपनी आंखों से मंसाराम की आत्मपीड़ा नहीं देख सकती थी।

मंसाराम जैसे मनस्वी, साहसी युवक पर इस आक्षेप का जो असर पड़ सकता था, उसकी कल्पना ही से उसके प्राण कांप उठते थे। अब चाहे उस पर कितने ही संदेह क्यों न हों, चाहे उसे आत्महत्या ही क्यों न करनी पड़े, पर वह चुप नहीं बैठ सकती। मंसाराम की रक्षा करने के लिए वह विकल हो गयी। उसने संकोच और लज्जा की चादर उतारकर फेंक देने का निश्चय कर लिया।

वकील साहब भोजन करके कचहरी जाने के पहले एक बार उससे अवश्य मिल लिया करते थे। उनके आने का समय हो गया था। आ ही रहे होंगे, यह सोचकर निर्मला द्वार पर खड़ी हो गयी और उनका

इंतजार करने लगी लेकिन यह क्या? वह तो बाहर चले जा रहे है। गाड़ी जुतकर आ गयी, यह हुक्म वह यहीं से दिया करते थे। तो क्या आज वह न आयेंगे, बाहर-ही-बाहर चले जाएंगे। नहीं, ऐसा नहीं होने पायेगा। उसने भूंगी से कहा–जाकर बाबूजी को बुला ला। कहना, एक जरुरी काम है, सुन लीजिए।

मुंशीजी जाने को तैयार ही थे। यह संदेशा पाकर अंदर आये, पर कमरे में न आकर दूर से ही पूछा–क्या बात है भाई? जल्दी कह दो, मुझे एक जरुरी काम से जाना है। अभी थोड़ी देर हुई, हेडमास्टर साहब का एक पत्र आया है कि मंसाराम को ज्वर आ गया है, बेहतर हो कि आप घर ही पर उसका इलाज करें। इसलिए उधर ही से होता हुआ कचहरी जाऊंगा। तुम्हें कोई खास बात तो नहीं कहनी है।

निर्मला पर मानो वज्र गिर पड़ा। आंसुओं के आवेग और कंठ-स्वर में घोर संग्राम होने लगा। दोनों पहले निकलने पर तुले हुए थे। दो में से कोई एक कदम भी पीछे हटना नहीं चाहता था। कंठ-स्वर की दुर्बलता और आंसुओं की सबलता देखकर यह निश्चय करना कठिन नहीं था कि एक क्षण यही संग्राम होता रहा तो मैदान किसके हाथ रहेगा। आखिर दोनों साथ-साथ निकले, लेकिन बाहर आते ही बलवान ने निर्बल को दबा लिया। केवल इतना मुंह से निकला–कोई खास बात नहीं थी। आप तो उधर जा ही रहे हैं।

मुंशीजी–मैंने लड़कों से पूछा था, तो वे कहते थे, कल बैठे पढ़ रहे थे, आज न जाने क्या हो गया।

निर्मला ने आवेश से कांपते हुए कहा–यह सब आप कर रहे हैं।

मुंशीजी ने त्योरियां बदलकर कहा–मैं कर रहा हूं? मैं क्या कर रहा हूं?

निर्मला–अपने दिल से पूछिए।

मुंशीजी–मैंने तो यही सोचा था कि यहां उसका पढ़ने में जी नहीं लगता, वहां और लड़कों के साथ खामाख्वाह पढ़ेगा ही। यह तो बुरी बात न थी और मैंने क्या किया?

निर्मला–खूब सोचिए, इसीलिए आपने उन्हें वहां भेजा था? आपके मन में और कोई बात न थी।

मुंशीजी जरा हिचकिचाए और अपनी दुर्बलता को छिपाने के लिए मुस्कराने की चेष्टा करके बोले—और क्या बात हो सकती थी? भला तुम्हीं सोचो।

निर्मला—खैर, यही सही। अब आप कृपा करके उन्हें आज ही लेते आइयेगा, वहां रहने से उनकी बीमारी बढ़ जाने का भय है। यहां दीदीजी जितनी तीमारदारी कर सकती हैं, दूसरा नहीं कर सकता।

एक क्षण के बाद उसने सिर नीचा करके कहा—मेरे कारण न लाना चाहते हों, तो मुझे घर भेज दीजिए। मैं वहां आराम से रहूंगी।

मुंशीजी ने इसका कुछ जवाब न दिया। बाहर चले गये, और एक क्षण में गाड़ी स्कूल की ओर चली।

मन! तेरी गति कितनी विचित्र है, कितनी रहस्य से भरी हुई, कितनी दुर्भेद्य। तू कितनी जल्द रंग बदलता है? इस कला में तू निपुण है। आतिशबाजी की चर्खी को भी रंग बदलते कुछ देरी लगती है, पर तुझे रंग बदलने में उसका लक्षांश समय भी नहीं लगता। जहां अभी वात्सल्य था, वहां फिर संदेह ने आसन जमा लिया।

वह सोचते थे—कहीं उसने बहाना तो नहीं किया है?

मंसाराम दो दिन तक गहरी चिंता में डूबा रहा। बार-बार अपनी माता की याद आती, न खाना अच्छा लगता, न पढ़ने ही में जी लगता। उसकी कायापलट-सी हो गई। दो दिन गुजर गये और छात्रालय में रहते हुए भी उसने वह काम न किया, जो स्कूल के मास्टरों ने घर से कर लाने को दिया था। परिणाम स्वरुप उसे बेंच पर खड़ा रहना पड़ा। जो बात कभी न हुई थी, वह आज हो गई। यह असह्य अपमान भी उसे सहना पड़ा।

तीसरे दिन वह इन्हीं चिंताओं में मग्न हुआ अपने मन को समझा रहा था—क्या संसार में अकेले मेरी ही माता मरी है? विमाताएं तो सभी इसी प्रकार की होती हैं। मेरे साथ कोई नई बात नहीं हो रही है। अब मुझे पुरुषों की भांति द्विगुण परिश्रम से अपना काम करना चाहिए, जैसे माता-पिता राजी रहें, वैसे उन्हें राजी रखना चाहिए। इस साल अगर छात्रवृत्ति मिल गई, तो मुझे घर से कुछ लेने की जरुरत ही न रहेगी।

कितने ही लड़के अपने ही बल पर बड़ी-बड़ी उपाधियां प्राप्त कर लेते हैं। भाग्य के नाम को रोने-कोसने से क्या होगा।

इतने में जियाराम आकर खड़ा हो गया।

मंसाराम ने पूछा–घर का क्या हाल है जिया? नई अम्मांजी तो बहुत प्रसन्न होंगी?

जियाराम–उनके मन का हाल तो मैं नहीं जानता, लेकिन जब से तुम आये हो, उन्होने एक जून भी खाना नहीं खाया। जब देखो, तब रोया करती हैं। जब बाबूजी आते हैं, तब अलबत्ता हंसने लगती हैं। तुम चले आये तो मैंने भी शाम को अपनी किताबें संभाली। यहीं तुम्हारे साथ रहना चाहता था। भूंगी चुड़ैल ने जाकर अम्मांजी से कह दिया। बाबूजी बैठे थे, उनके सामने ही अम्मांजी ने आकर मेरी किताबें छीन लीं और रोकर बोलीं, तुम भी चले जाओगे, तो इस घर में कौन रहेगा? अगर मेरे कारण तुम लोग घर छोड़-छोड़कर भागे जा रहे तो लो, मैं ही कहीं चली जाती हूं। मैं तो झल्लाया हुआ था ही, वहां अब बाबूजी भी न थे, बिगड़कर बोला, आप क्यों कहीं चली जाएंगी? आपका तो घर है, आप आराम से रहिए। गैर तो हमीं लोग हैं, हम न रहेंगे, तब तो आपको आराम-ही-आराम होगा।

मंसाराम–तुमने खूब कहा, बहुत ही अच्छा कहा। इस पर और भी झल्लाई होंगी और जाकर बाबूजी से शिकायत की होगी।

जियाराम–नहीं, यह कुछ नहीं हुआ। बेचारी जमीन पर बैठकर रोने लगीं। मुझे भी करुणा आ गयी। मैं भी रो पड़ा। उन्होने आंचल से मेरे आंसू पोंछे और बोलीं, जिया। मैं ईश्वर को साक्षी देकर कहती हूं कि मैंने तुम्हारे भैया के विषय में तुम्हारे बाबूजी से एक शब्द भी नहीं कहा। मेरे भाग में कलंक लिखा हुआ है, वही भोग रही हूं। फिर और न जाने क्या-क्या कहा, जो मेरी समझ में नहीं आया। कुछ बाबूजी की बात थी।

मंसाराम ने उद्विग्नता से पूछा–बाबूजी के विषय में क्या कहा? कुछ याद है?

जियाराम–बातें तो भई, मुझे याद नहीं आती। मेरी 'मेमोरी' कौन बड़ी तेज है, लेकिन उनकी बातों का मतलब कुछ ऐसा मालूम होता था

कि उन्हें बाबूजी को प्रसन्न रखने के लिए यह स्वांग भरना पड़ रहा है। न जाने धर्म-अधर्म की कैसी बातें करती थीं जो मैं बिल्कुल न समझ सका। मुझे तो अब इसका विश्वास आ गया है कि उनकी इच्छा तुम्हें यहां भेजने की न थी।

मंसाराम–तुम इन चालों का मतलब नहीं समझ सकते। ये बड़ी गहरी चालें हैं।

जियाराम–तुम्हारी समझ में होंगी, मेरी समझ में नहीं हैं।

मंसाराम–जब तुम ज्योमेट्री नहीं समझ सकते, तो इन बातों को क्या समझ सकोगे? उस रात को जब मुझे खाना खाने के लिए बुलाने आयी थीं और उनके आग्रह पर मैं जाने को तैयार भी हो गया था, उस वक्त बाबूजी को देखते ही उन्होने जो कैंडा बदला, वह क्या मैं कभी भी भूल सकता हूं?

जियाराम–यही बात मेरी समझ में नहीं आती। अभी कल ही मैं यहां से गया, तो लगीं तुम्हारा हाल पूछने। मैंने कहा, वह तो कहते थे कि अब कभी इस घर में कदम न रखूंगा। मैंने कुछ झूठ तो कहा नहीं, तुमने मुझसे कहा ही था। इतना सुनना था कि फूट-फूटकर रोने लगीं मैं दिल में बहुत पछताया कि कहां-से-कहां मैंने यह बात कह दी। बार-बार यही कहती थीं, क्या वह मेरे कारण घर छोड़ देंगे? मुझसे इतने नाराज है? चले गये और मुझसे मिले तक नहीं। खाना तैयार था, खाने तक नहीं आये। हाय। मैं क्या बताऊं, किस विपत्ति में हूं। इतने में बाबूजी आ गये। बस तुरन्त आंखें पोंछकर मुस्कुराती हुई उनके पास चली गई। यह बात मेरी समझ में नहीं आती। आज मुझे बड़ी मिन्नत की कि उनको साथ लेते आना। आज मैं तुम्हें खींच ले चलूंगा। दो दिन में वह कितनी दुबली हो गयी हैं, तुम्हें यह देखकर उन पर दया आएगी। तो चलोगे न?

मंसाराम ने कुछ जवाब न दिया। उसके पैर कांप रहे थे। जियाराम तो हाजिरी की घंटी सुनकर भागा, पर वह बेंच पर लेट गया और इतनी लम्बी सांस ली, मानो बहुत देर से उसने सांस ही नहीं ली है। उसके मुख से दुस्सह वेदना में डूबे हुए शब्द निकले–हाय ईश्वर। इस नाम के सिवा उसे अपना जीवन निराधार मालूम होता था। इस एक उच्छवास

में कितना नैराश्य था, कितनी संवेदना, कितनी करुणा, कितनी दीन–प्रार्थना भरी हुई थी, इसका कौन अनुमान कर सकता है। अब सारा रहस्य उसकी समझ में आ रहा था और बार-बार उसका पीड़ित हृदय आर्तनाद कर रहा था–हाय ईश्वर। इतना घोर कलंक।

क्या जीवन में इससे बड़ी विपत्ति की कल्पना की जा सकती है? क्या संसार में इससे घोरतम नीचता की कल्पना हो सकती है? आज तक किसी पिता ने अपने पुत्र पर इतना निर्दय कलंक न लगाया होगा। जिसके चरित्र की सभी प्रशंसा करते थे, जो अन्य युवकों के लिए आदर्श समझा जाता था, जिसने कभी अपवित्र विचारों को अपने पास नहीं फटकने दिया, उसी पर यह घोरतम कलंक। मंसाराम को ऐसा मालूम हुआ, मानों उसका दिल फटा जाता है।

दूसरी घंटी भी बज गई। लड़के अपने-अपने कमरे में गए, पर मंसाराम हथेली पर गाल रखे अनिमेष नेत्रों से भूमि की ओर देख रहा था, मानो उसका सर्वस्व जलमग्न हो गया हो, मानो वह किसी को मुंह न दिखा सकता हो। स्कूल में गैरहाजिरी हो जाएगी, जुर्माना हो जाएगा, इसकी उसे चिंता नहीं, जब उसका सर्वस्व लुट गया, तो अब इन छोटी-छोटी बातों का क्या भय? इतना बड़ा कलंक लगने पर भी अगर जीता रहूं, तो मेरे जीने को धिक्कार है।

उसी शोकातिरेक दशा में वह चिल्ला पड़ा–माताजी। तुम कहां हो? तुम्हारा बेटा, जिस पर तुम प्राण देती थीं, जिसे तुम अपने जीवन का आधार समझती थीं, आज घोर संकट में है। उसी का पिता उसकी गर्दन पर छुरी फेर रहा है। हाय, अम्मांजी तुम कहां हो?

मंसाराम फिर शांतचित्त से सोचने लगा–मुझ पर यह संदेह क्यों हो रहा है? इसका क्या कारण है? मुझमें ऐसी कौन-सी बात उन्होंने देखी, जिससे उन्हें यह संदेह हुआ? वह हमारे पिता हैं, मेरे शत्रु नहीं है, जो अनायास ही मुझ पर यह अपराध लगाने बैठ जाएं। जरुर उन्होनें कोई-न-कोई बात देखी या सुनी है। उनका मुझ पर कितना स्नेह था। मेरे बगैर भोजन न करते थे, वही मेरे शत्रु हो जाएं, यह बात अकारण नहीं हो सकती।

अच्छा, इस संदेह का बीजारोपण किस दिन हुआ? मुझे बोर्डिंग हाउस में ठहराने की बात तो पीछे की है। उस दिन रात को वह मेरे कमरे में आकर मेरी परीक्षा लेने लगे थे, उसी दिन उनकी त्योरियां बदली हुईं थीं। उस दिन ऐसी कौन-सी बात हुई, जो अप्रिय लगी हो। मैं नई अम्मां से कुछ खाने को मांगने गया था। बाबूजी उस समय वहां बैठे थे। हां, अब याद आती है, उसी वक्त उनका चेहरा तमतमा गया था। उसी दिन से नई अम्मां ने मुझसे पढ़ना छोड़ दिया। अगर मैं जानता कि मेरा घर में आना-जाना, अम्मांजी से कुछ कहना-सुनना और उन्हें पढ़ाना-लिखाना पिताजी को बुरा लगता है, तो आज क्यों यह नौबत आती? और नई अम्मां। उन पर क्या बीत रही होगी?

मंसाराम ने अब तक निर्मला की ओर ध्यान नहीं दिया था। निर्मला का ध्यान आते ही उसके रोंये खड़े हो गये। हाय उनका सरल स्नेहशील हृदय यह आघात कैसे सह सकेगा? आह। मैं कितने भ्रम में था। मैं उनके स्नेह को कौशल समझता था। मुझे क्या मालूम था कि उन्हें पिताजी का भ्रम शांत करने के लिए मेरे प्रति इतना कटु व्यवहार करना पड़ता है। आह! मैंने उन पर कितना अन्याय किया है। उनकी दशा तो मुझसे भी खराब हो रही होगी। मैं तो यहां चला आया, मगर वह कहां जाएंगी? जिया कहता था, उन्होंने दो दिन से भोजन नहीं किया। हरदम रोया करती हैं। कैसे जाकर समझाऊं। वह इस अभागे के पीछे क्यों अपने सिर यह विपत्ति ले रही हैं? वह बार-बार मेरा हाल पूछती हैं? क्यों बार-बार मुझे बुलाती हैं? कैसे कह दूं कि माता मुझे तुमसे जरा भी शिकायत नहीं, मेरा दिल तुम्हारी तरफ से साफ है।

वह अब भी बैठी रो रही होंगी। कितना बड़ा अनर्थ है। बाबूजी को यह क्या हो रहा है? क्या इसीलिए विवाह किया था? एक बालिका की हत्या करने के लिए ही उसे लाये थे? इस कोमल पुष्प को मसल डालने के लिए ही तोड़ा था।

उनका उद्धार कैसे होगा। उस निरपराधिनी का मुख कैसे उज्जवल होगा? उन्हें केवल मेरे साथ स्नेह का व्यवहार करने के लिए यह दंड दिया जा रहा है। उनकी सज्जनता का उन्हें यह उपहार मिल रहा है।

मैं उन्हें इस प्रकार निर्दय आघात सहते देखकर बैठा रहूंगा? अपनी मान-रक्षा के लिए न सही, उनकी आत्मरक्षा के लिए इन प्राणों का बलिदान करना पड़ेगा। इसके सिवाय उद्धार का कोई उपाय नहीं। आह। दिल में कैसे-कैसे अरमान थे। वे सब खाक में मिला देने होंगे। एक सती पर संदेह किया जा रहा है और मेरे कारण। मुझे अपनी प्राणों से उनकी रक्षा करनी होगी, यही मेरा कर्त्तव्य है। इसी में सच्ची वीरता है। माता, मैं अपने रक्त से इस कालिमा को धो दूंगा। इसी में मेरा और तुम्हारा दोनों का कल्याण है।

वह दिन भर इन्हीं विचारों मे डूबा रहा। शाम को उसके दोनों भाई आकर घर चलने के लिए आग्रह करने लगे।

सियाराम–चलते क्यों नही? मेरे भैयाजी, चले चलो न।

मंसाराम–मुझे फुरसत नहीं है कि तुम्हारे कहने से चला चलूं।

जियाराम–आखिर कल तो इतवार है ही।

मंसाराम–इतवार को भी काम है।

जियाराम–अच्छा, कल आओगे न?

मंसाराम–नहीं, कल मुझे एक मैच में जाना है।

सियाराम–अम्मांजी मूंग के लड्डू बना रही हैं। न चलोगे तो एक भी न पाओगे। हम तुम मिल के खा जाएंगे, जिया इन्हें न देंगे।

जियाराम–भैया, अगर तुम कल न गये तो शायद अम्मांजी यहीं चली आयें।

मंसाराम–सच। नहीं ऐसा क्यों करेंगी। यहां आयीं, तो बड़ी परेशानी होगी। तुम कह देना, वह कहीं मैच देखने गये हैं।

जियाराम–मैं झूठ क्यों बोलने लगा। मैं कह दूंगा, वह मुंह फुलाये बैठे थे। देख लेना उन्हें साथ लाता हूं कि नहीं।

सियाराम–हम कह देंगे कि आज पढ़ने नहीं गये। पड़े-पड़े सोते रहे।

मंसाराम ने इन दूतों से कल आने का वादा करके गला छुड़ाया। जब दोनों चले गये, तो फिर चिंता में डूबा। रात-भर उसे करवटें बदलते गुजरी। छुट्टी का दिन भी बैठे-बैठे कट गया, उसे दिन भर शंका

होती रहती कि कहीं अम्मांजी सचमुच न चली आयें। किसी गाड़ी की खड़खड़ाहट सुनता, तो उसका कलेजा धकधक करने लगता। कहीं आ तो नहीं गयीं?

छात्रालय में एक छोटा-सा औषधालय था। एक डाक्टर साहब संध्या समय एक घण्टे के लिए आ जाया करते थे। अगर कोई लड़का बीमार होता तो उसे दवा देते। आज वह आये तो मंसाराम कुछ सोचता हुआ उनके पास जाकर खड़ा हो गया। वह मंसाराम को अच्छी तरह जानते थे।

डाक्टर साहब उसे देखकर आश्चर्य से बोले–यह तुम्हारी क्या हालत है जी? तुम तो मानो गले जा रहे हो। कहीं बाजार का का चस्का तो नहीं पड़ गया? आखिर तुम्हें हुआ क्या? जरा यहां तो आओ।

मंसाराम ने मुस्कराकर कहा–मुझे जिन्दगी का रोग है। आपके पास इसकी भी कोई दवा है?

डाक्टर–मैं तुम्हारी परीक्षा करना चाहता हूं। तुम्हारी सूरत ही बदल गयी है, पहचाने भी नहीं जाते।

यह कहकर, उन्होने मंसाराम का हाथ पकड़ लिया और छाती, पीठ, आंखें, जीभ सब बारी-बारी से देखीं। तब चिंतित होकर बोले–वकील साहब से मैं आज ही मिलूंगा। तुम्हें थाइसिस हो रहा है। सारे लक्षण उसी के हैं।

मंसाराम ने बड़ी उत्सुकता से पूछा–कितने दिनों में काम तमाम हो जाएगा, डाक्टर साहब?

डाक्टर–कैसी बात करते हो जी। मैं वकील साहब से मिलकर तुम्हें किसी पहाड़ी जगह भेजने की सलाह दूंगा। ईश्वर ने चाहा, तो बहुत जल्द अच्छे हो जाओगे। बीमारी अभी पहले स्टेज में है।

मंसाराम–तब तो अभी साल दो साल की देर मालूम होती है। मैं तो इतना इंतजार नहीं कर सकता। सुनिए, मुझे थायसिस-वायसिस कुछ नहीं है, न कोई दूसरी शिकायत ही है, आप बाबूजी को नाहक तरद्दुद में न डालिएगा। इस वक्त मेरे सिर में दर्द है, कोई दवा दीजिए। कोई ऐसी दवा हो, जिससे नींद भी आ जाए। मुझे दो रात से नींद नहीं आती।

डॉक्टर ने जहरीली दवाइयों की आलमारी खोली और शीशी से थोड़ी सी दवा निकालकर मंसाराम को दी। मंसाराम ने पूछा—यह तो कोई जहर है भला इसे कोई पी ले तो मर जाए?

डॉक्टर—नहीं, मर तो नहीं जाए, पर सिर में चक्कर जरूर आ जाए।

मंसाराम—कोई ऐसी दवा भी इसमें है, जिसे पीते ही प्राण निकल जाएं?

डॉक्टर—ऐसी एक-दो नहीं कितनी ही दवाएं हैं। यह जो शीशी देख रहे हो, इसकी एक बूंद भी पेट में चली जाए, तो जान न बचे। आनन-फानन में मौत हो जाए।

मंसाराम—क्यों डॉक्टर साहब, जो लोग जहर खा लेते हैं, उन्हें बड़ी तकलीफ होती होगी?

डॉक्टर—सभी जहरों में तकलीफ नहीं होती। बाज तो ऐसे हैं कि पीते ही आदमी ठंडा हो जाता है। यह शीशी इसी किस्म की है, इसे पीते ही आदमी बेहोश हो जाता है, फिर उसे होश नहीं आता।

मंसाराम ने सोचा—तब तो प्राण देना बहुत आसान है, फिर क्यों लोग इतना डरते हैं? यह शीशी कैसे मिलेगी? अगर दवा का नाम पूछकर शहर के किसी दवा-फरोश से लेना चाहूं, तो वह कभी न देगा। ऊंह, इसे मिलने में कोई दिक्कत नहीं। यह तो मालूम हो गया कि प्राणों का अन्त बड़ी आसानी से किया जा सकता है। मंसाराम इतना प्रसन्न हुआ, मानो कोई इनाम पा गया हो। उसके दिल पर से बोझ-सा हट गया। चिंता की मेघ-राशि जो सिर पर मंडरा रही थी, छिन्न-भिन्न हो गयी। महीनों बाद आज उसे मन में एक स्फूर्ति का अनुभव हुआ।

लड़के थियेटर देखने जा रहे थे, निरीक्षक से आज्ञा ले ली थी। मंसाराम भी उनके साथ थियेटर देखने चला गया। ऐसा खुश था, मानो उससे ज्यादा सुखी जीव संसार में कोई नहीं है। थियेटर में नकल देखकर तो वह हंसते-हंसते लोट गया। बार-बार तालियां बजाने और 'वन्स मोर' की हांक लगाने में पहला नम्बर उसी का था। गाना सुनकर वह मस्त हो जाता था, और 'ओहो हो' करके चिल्ला उठता था। दर्शकों की निगाहें बार-बार उसकी तरफ उठ जाती थीं। थियेटर के

पात्र भी उसी की ओर ताकते थे और यह जानने को उत्सुक थे कि कौन महाशय इतने रसिक और भावुक हैं। उसके मित्रों को उसकी उच्छृंखलता पर आश्चर्य हो रहा था। वह बहुत ही शांतचित्त, गम्भीर स्वभाव का युवक था। आज वह क्यों इतना हास्यशील हो गया है, क्यों उसके विनोद का पारावार नहीं है।

दो बजे रात को थियेटर से लौटने पर भी उसका हास्योन्माद कम नहीं हुआ। उसने एक लड़के की चारपाई उलट दी, कई लड़कों के कमरे के द्वार बाहर से बंद कर दिये और उन्हें भीतर से खट-खट करते सुनकर हंसता रहा। यहां तक कि छात्रालय के अध्यक्ष महोदय की नींद भी शोरगुल सुनकर खुल गयी और उन्होंने मंसाराम की शरारत पर खेद प्रकट किया। कौन जानता है कि उसके अन्तःस्थल में कितनी भीषण क्रांति हो रही है? संदेह के निर्दय आघात ने उसकी लज्जा और आत्मसम्मान को कुचल डाला है। उसे अपमान और तिरस्कार का लेशमात्र भी भय नहीं है। यह विनोद नहीं, उसकी आत्मा का करुण विलाप है। जब और सब लड़के सो गये, तो वह भी चारपाई पर लेटा, लेकिन उसे नींद नहीं आयी। एक क्षण के बाद वह बैठा और अपनी सारी पुस्तकें बांधकर संदूक में रख दीं। जब मरना ही है, तो पढ़कर क्या होगा? जिस जीवन में ऐसी-ऐसी बाधाएं हैं, ऐसी-ऐसी यातनाएं हैं, उससे मृत्यु कहीं अच्छी।

यह सोचते-सोचते तड़का हो गया। तीन रात से वह एक क्षण भी न सोया था। इस वक्त वह उठा तो उसके पैर थर-थर कांप रहे थे और सिर में चक्कर सा आ रहा था। आंखें जल रही थीं और शरीर के सारे अंग शिथिल हो रहे थे। दिन चढ़ता जाता था और और उसमें इतनी शक्ति भी न थी कि उठकर मुंह हाथ धो डाले। एकाएक उसने भूंगी को रूमाल में कुछ लिए हुए एक कहार के साथ आते देखा। उसका कलेजा सन्न रह गया। हाय! ईश्वर वे आ गयीं। अब क्या होगा? भूंगी अकेले नहीं आयी होगी? बग्घी जरूर बाहर खड़ी होगी? कहां तो उससे उठा नहीं जाता था, कहां भूंगी को देखते ही दौड़ा और घबराई हुई आवाज में बोला—अम्मांजी भी आयी हैं, क्या रे?

जब मालूम हुआ कि अम्मांजी नहीं आयी, तब उसका चित्त शांत हुआ।

भूंगी ने कहा–भैया। तुम कल गये नही, बहूजी तुम्हारी राह देखती रह गयीं। उनसे क्यों रुठे हो भैया? कहती हैं, मैंने उनकी कुछ भी शिकायत नहीं की है। मुझसे आज रोकर कहने लगीं–उनके पास यह मिठाई लेती जा और कहना, मेरे कारण क्यों घर छोड़ दिया है? कहां रख दूं यह थाली?

मंसाराम ने रुखाई से कहा–यह थाली अपने सिर पर पटक दे चुड़ैल। वहां से चली है मिठाई लेकर। खबरदार, जो फिर कभी इधर आयी। सौगात लेकर चली है। जाकर कह देना, मुझे उनकी मिठाई नहीं चाहिए। जाकर कह देना, तुम्हारा घर है तुम रहो, वहां वे बड़े आराम से हैं। खूब खाते और मौज करते हैं। सुनती है, बाबूजी के मुंह पर कहना, समझ गयी? मुझे किसी का डर नहीं है, और जो करना चाहें, कर डालें, जिससे दिल में कोई अरमान न रह जाए। कहें तो इलाहाबाद, लखनऊ, कलकत्ता चला जाऊं। मेरे लिए जैसे बनारस वैसे दूसरा शहर। यहां क्या रखा है?

भूंगी–भैया, मिठाई रख लो, नहीं रो-रोकर मर जाएंगी। सच मानो रो-रोकर मर जाएंगी।

मंसाराम ने आंसुओं के उठते हुए वेग को दबाकर कहा–मर जाएंगी, मेरी बला से। कौन मुझे बड़ा सुख दे दिया है, जिसके लिए पछताऊं। मेरा तो उन्होंने सर्वनाश कर दिया। कह देना, मेरे पास कोई संदेशा न भेजें, कुछ जरूरत नहीं।

भूंगी–भैया, तुम तो कहते हो यहां खूब खाता हूं और मौज करता हूं, मगर देह तो आधी भी न रही। जैसे आये थे, उससे आधे भी न रहे।

मंसाराम–यह तेरी आंखों का फेर है। देखना, दो-चार दिन में मुटाकर कोल्हू हो जाता हूं कि नहीं। उनसे यह भी कह देना कि रोना-धोना बंद करें। जो मैंने सुना कि रोती हैं और खाना नहीं खातीं, मुझसे बुरा कोई नहीं होगा। मुझे घर से निकाला है, तो आप चैन से रहें। चली हैं, प्रेम दिखाने। मैं ऐसे त्रिया-चरित्र बहुत पढ़े बैठा हूं।

भूंगी चली गयी। मंसाराम को उससे बातें करते ही कुछ ठण्ड मालूम होने लगी थी। यह अभिनय करने के लिए उसे अपने मनोभावों को जितना दबाना पड़ा था, वह उसके लिए असाध्य था। उसका आत्म-सम्मान उसे इस कुटिल व्यवहार का जल्द-से-जल्द अंत कर देने के लिए बाध्य कर रहा था, पर इसका परिणाम क्या होगा? निर्मला क्या यह आघात सह सकेगी? अब तक वह मृत्यु की कल्पना करते समय किसी अन्य प्राणी का विचार न करता था, पर आज एकाएक ज्ञान हुआ कि मेरे जीवन के साथ एक और प्राणी का जीवन-सूत्र भी बंधा हुआ है।

निर्मला यह समझेगी कि मेरी निष्ठुरता ही ने इनकी जान ली। यह समझकर उसका कोमल हृदय फट न जाएगा? उसका जीवन तो अब भी संकट में है। संदेह के कठोर पंजे में फंसी हुई अबला क्या अपने को हत्यारिणी समझकर बहुत दिन जीवित रह सकती है?

मंसाराम ने चारपाई पर लेटकर लिहाफ ओढ़ लिया, फिर भी सर्दी से कलेजा कांप रहा था। थोड़ी ही देर में उसे जोर से ज्वर चढ़ आया, वह बेहोश हो गया। इस अचेत दशा में उसे भांति-भांति के स्वप्न दिखाई देने लगे। थोड़ी-थोड़ी देर के बाद चौंक पड़ता, आंखें खुल जाती, फिर बेहोश हो जाता।

सहसा वकील साहब की आवाज सुनकर वह चौंक पड़ा। हां, वकील साहब की आवाज थी। उसने लिहाफ फेंक दिया और चारपाई से उतरकर नीचे खड़ा हो गया। उसके मन में एक आवेग हुआ कि इस वक्त इनके सामने प्राण दे दूं। उसे ऐसा मालूम हुआ कि मैं मर जाऊं, तो इन्हें सच्ची खुशी होगी। शायद इसीलिए वह देखने आये हैं कि मेरे मरने में कितनी देर है। वकील साहब ने उसका हाथ पकड़ लिया, जिससे वह गिर न पड़े और पूछा—कैसी तबीयत है लल्लू। लेटे क्यों न रहे? लेट न जाओ, तुम खड़े क्यों हो गये?

मंसाराम—मेरी तबीयत तो बहुत अच्छी है। आपको व्यर्थ ही कष्ट हुआ। मुंशीजी ने कुछ जवाब न दिया। लड़के की दशा देखकर उनकी आंखों से आंसू निकल आये। वह हृष्ट-पुष्ट बालक, जिसे देखकर चित्त

प्रसन्न हो जाता था, अब सूखकर कांटा हो गया था। पांच-छः दिन में ही वह इतना दुबला हो गया था कि उसे पहचानना कठिन था।

मुंशीजी ने उसे आहिस्ता से चारपाई पर लिटा दिया और लिहाफ अच्छी तरह उसे उढ़ाकर सोचने लगे कि अब क्या करना चाहिए। कहीं लड़का हाथ से तो नहीं जाएगा। यह ख्याल करके वह शोक विह्वल हो गये और स्टूल पर बैठकर फूट-फूटकर रोने लगे।

मंसाराम भी लिहाफ में मुंह लपेटे रो रहा था। अभी थोड़े ही दिनों पहले उसे देखकर पिता का हृदय गर्व से फूल उठता था, लेकिन आज उसे इस दारुण दशा में देखकर भी वह सोच रहे हैं कि इसे घर ले चलूं या नहीं। क्या यहां दवा नहीं हो सकती? मैं यहां चौबीसों घण्टे बैठा रहूंगा। डॉक्टर साहब यहां हैं ही। कोई दिक्कत न होगी। घर ले चलने में उन्हें बाधाएं-ही-बाधाएं दिखाई देती थीं, सबसे बड़ा भय यह था कि वहां निर्मला इसके पास हरदम बैठी रहेगी और मैं मना न कर सकूंगा, यह उनके लिए असह्य था।

इतने में अध्यक्ष ने आकर कहा—मैं तो समझता हूं कि आप इन्हें अपने साथ ले जाएं। गाड़ी है ही, कोई तकलीफ न होगी। यहां अच्छी तरह देखभाल न हो सकेगी।

मुंशीजी—हां, आया तो मैं इसी खयाल से था, लेकिन इनकी हालत बहुत ही नाजुक मालूम होती है। जरा-सी असावधानी होने से सरसाम हो जाने का भय है।

अध्यक्ष—यहां से इन्हें ले जाने में थोड़ी-सी दिक्कत जरुर है, लेकिन यह तो आप खुद सोच सकते हैं कि घर पर जो आराम मिल सकता है, वह यहां किसी तरह नहीं मिल सकता। इसके अतिरिक्त किसी बीमार लड़के को यहां रखना नियम-विरुद्ध भी है।

मुंशीजी—कहिए तो मैं हेडमास्टर से आज्ञा ले लूं। मुझे इनका यहां से इस हालत में ले जाना किसी तरह मुनासिब नहीं मालूम होता।

अध्यक्ष ने हेडमास्टर का नाम सुना, तो समझे कि यह महाशय धमकी दे रहे हैं। जरा तिनककर बोले—हेडमास्टर नियम-विरुद्ध कोई बात नहीं कर सकते। मैं इतनी बड़ी जिम्मेदारी कैसे ले सकता हूं?

अब क्या हो? क्या घर ले जाना ही पड़ेगा? यहां रखने का तो यह बहाना था कि ले जाने से बीमारी बढ़ जाने की शंका है। यहां से ले जाकर अस्पताल में ठहराने का कोई बहाना नहीं है। जो सुनेगा, वह यही कहेगा कि डाक्टर की फीस बचाने के लिए लड़के को अस्पताल फेंक आये, पर अब ले जाने के सिवा और कोई उपाय न था। अगर अध्यक्ष महोदय इस वक्त रिश्वत लेने पर तैयार हो जाते, तो शायद दो-चार साल का वेतन ले लेते, लेकिन कायदे के पाबंद लोगों में इतनी बुद्धि, इतनी चतुराई कहां। अगर इस वक्त मुंशीजी को कोई आदमी ऐसा उज्र सुझा देता, जिसमें उन्हें मंसाराम को घर न ले जाना पड़े, तो वह आजीवन असका एहसान मानते। सोचने का समय भी न था। अध्यक्ष महोदय शैतान की तरह सिर पर सवार था। विवश होकर मुंशीजी ने दोनों साईसों को बुलाया और मंसाराम को उठाने लगे। मंसाराम अर्धचेतना की दशा में था, चौककर बोला, क्या है? कौन है?

मुंशीजी–कोई नहीं है बेटा, मैं तुम्हें घर ले चलना चाहता हूं, आओ, गोद में उठा लूं।

मंसाराम–मुझे क्यों घर ले चलते हैं? मैं वहां नहीं जाऊंगा।

मुंशीजी–यहां तो रह नहीं सकते, नियम ही ऐसा है।

मंसाराम–कुछ भी हो, वहां न जाऊंगा। मुझे और कहीं ले चलिए, किसी पेड़ के नीचे, किसी झोंपड़े में, जहां चाहे रखिए, पर घर पर न ले चलिए।

अध्यक्ष ने मुंशीजी से कहा–आप इन बातों का ख्याल न करें, यह तो होश में नहीं है।

मंसाराम–कौन होश में नहीं है? मैं होश में नहीं हूं? किसी को गालियां देता हूं? दांत काटता हूं? क्यों होश में नहीं हूं? मुझे यहीं पड़ा रहने दीजिए, जो कुछ होना होगा, यहीं होगा। अगर ऐसा है, तो मुझे अस्पताल ले चलिए, मैं वहां पड़ा रहूंगा। जीना होगा, जीऊंगा, मरना होगा मरुंगा, लेकिन घर किसी तरह भी न जाऊंगा।

यह जोर पाकर मुंशीजी फिर अध्यक्ष की मिन्नतें करने लगे, लेकिन वह कायदे का पाबंदी आदमी कुछ सुनता ही न था। अगर छूत की

बीमारी हुई और किसी दूसरे लड़के को छूत लग गयी, तो कौन उसका जवाबदेह होगा। इस तर्क के सामने मुंशीजी की कानूनी दलीलें भी मात हो गयीं।

आखिर मुंशीजी ने मंसाराम से कहा—बेटा, तुम्हें घर चलने से क्यों इंकार हो रहा है? वहां तो सभी तरह का आराम रहेगा।

मुंशीजी ने कहने को तो यह बात कह दी, लेकिन डर रहे थे कि कहीं सचमुच मंसाराम चलने पर राजी न हो जाए।

मंसाराम को अस्पताल में रखने का कोई बहाना खोज रहे थे और उसकी जिम्मेदारी मंसाराम ही के सिर डालना चाहते थे। यह अध्यक्ष के सामने की बात थी, वह इस बात की साक्षी दे सकते थे कि मंसाराम अपनी जिद से अस्पताल जा रहा है। मुंशीजी का इसमे लेशमात्र भी दोष नहीं है।

मंसाराम ने झल्लाकर नहीं-नहीं, नहीं सौ बार नहीं, मैं घर नहीं जाऊंगा। मुझे अस्पताल ले चलिए और घर के सब आदमियों को मना कर दीजिए कि मुझे देखने न आये। मुझे कुछ नहीं हुआ है, बिल्कुल बीमार नहीं हूं। आप मुझे छोड़ दीजिए, मैं अपने पांव से चल सकता हूं।

वह उठ खड़ा हुआ और उन्मत्त की भांति द्वार की ओर चला, लेकिन पैर लड़खड़ा गये। यदि मुंशीजी ने संभाल न लिया होता, तो उसे बड़ी चोट आती। दोनों नौकरों की मदद से मुंशीजी उसे बग्घी के पास लाये और अंदर बैठा दिया।

गाड़ी अस्पताल की ओर चली। वही हुआ जो मुंशीजी चाहते थे। इस शोक में भी उनका चित्त संतुष्ट था। लड़का अपनी इच्छा से अस्पताल जा रहा था क्या यह इस बात का प्रमाण नहीं था कि घर में इसे कोई स्नेह नहीं है? क्या इससे यह सिद्ध नहीं होता कि मंसाराम निर्दोष है? वह उसके उपर अकारण ही भ्रम कर रहे थे।

लेकिन जरा ही देर में इस तुष्टि की जगह उनके मन में ग्लानि का भाव जाग्रत हुआ। वह अपने प्राण-प्रिय पुत्र को घर न ले जाकर अस्पताल लिये जा रहे थे। उनके विशाल भवन में उनके पुत्र के लिए जगह न थी, इस दशा में भी जबकि उसकी जीवन संकट में पड़ा हुआ था। कितनी विडम्बना है!

एक क्षण के बाद एकाएक मुंशीजी के मन में प्रश्न उठा—कहीं मंसाराम उनके भावों को ताड़ तो नहीं गया? इसीलिए तो उसे घर से घृणा नहीं हो गयी है? अगर ऐसा है, तो गजब हो जाएगा।

उस अनर्थ की कल्पना ही से मुंशीजी के रोंए खड़े हो गये और कलेजा धकधक करने लगा। हृदय में एक धक्का-सा लगा। अगर इस ज्वर का यही कारण है, तो ईश्वर ही मालिक है। इस समय उनकी दशा अत्यन्त दयनीय थी। वह आग जो उन्होंने अपने ठिठुरे हुए हाथों को सेंकने के लिए जलाई थी, अब उनके घर में लगी जा रही थी। इस करुणा, शोक, पश्चाताप और शंका से उनका चित्त घबरा उठा। उनके गुप्त रोदन की ध्वनि बाहर निकल सकती, तो सुनने वाले रो पड़ते। उनके आंसू बाहर निकल सकते, तो उनका तार बंध जाता। उन्होंने पुत्र के वर्ण-हीन मुख की ओर एक वात्सल्यूपर्ण नेत्रों से देखा, वेदना से विकल होकर उसे छाती से लगा लिया और इतना रोये कि हिचकी बंध गयी।

सामने अस्पताल का फाटक दिखाई दे रहा था।

मुंशी तोताराम संध्या समय कचहरी से घर पहुँचे, तो निर्मला ने पूछा—उन्हें देखा, क्या हाल है?

मुंशीजी ने देखा कि निर्मला के मुख पर नाममात्र को भी शोक या चिन्ता का चिन्ह नहीं है। उसका बनाव-सिंगार और दिनों से भी कुछ गाढ़ा हुआ है। मसलन वह गले का हार न पहनती थी, पर आज वह भी गले मे शोभा दे रहा था। झूमर से भी उसे बहुत प्रेम न था, पर आज वह भी महीन रेशमी साड़ी के नीचे, काले-काले केशों के ऊपर, फानूस के दीपक की भांति चमक रहा था।

मुंशीजी ने मुंह फेरकर कहा—बीमार है और क्या हाल बताऊं?

निर्मला—तुम तो उन्हें यहां लाने गये थे?

मुंशीजी ने झुंझलाकर कहा—वह नहीं आता, तो क्या मैं जबरदस्ती उठा लाता? कितना समझाया कि बेटा घर चलो, वहां तुम्हें कोई तकलीफ

न होने पावेगी, लेकिन घर का नाम सुनकर उसे जौरो दूना ज्वर हो जाता था। कहने लगा–मैं यहां मर जाऊंगा, लेकिन घर न जाऊंगा। आखिर मजबूर होकर अस्पताल पहुंचा आया और क्या करता?

रुक्मिणी भी आकर बरामदे में खड़ी हो गई थी। बोलीं–वह जन्म का हठी है, यहां किसी तरह न आयेगा और यह भी देख लेना, वहां अच्छा भी न होगा?

मुंशीजी ने कातर स्वर में कहा–तुम दो-चार दिन के लिए वहां चली जाओ, तो बड़ा अच्छा हो बहन, तुम्हारे रहने से उसे तस्कीन होती रहेगी। मेरी बहन, मेरी यह विनय मान लो। अकेले वह रो-रोकर प्राण दे देगा। बस हाय अम्मां! हाय अम्मां! की रट लगाकर रोया करता है। मैं वहीं जा रहा हूं, मेरे साथ ही चलो। उसकी दशा अच्छी नहीं। बहन, वह सूरत ही नहीं रही। देखें ईश्वर क्या करते हैं?

यह कहते-कहते मुंशीजी की आंखों से आंसू बहने लगे, लेकिन रुक्मिणी अविचलित भाव से बोली–मैं जाने को तैयार हूं। मेरे वहां रहने से अगर मेरे लाल के प्राण बच जाएं, तो मैं सिर के बल दौड़ी जाऊं, लेकिन मेरा कहना गिरह में बांध लो भैया, वहां वह अच्छा न होगा। मैं उसे खूब पहचानती हूं। उसे कोई बीमारी नहीं है, केवल घर से निकाले जाने का शोक है। यही दुःख ज्वर के रुप में प्रकट हुआ है। तुम एक नहीं, लाख दवा करो, सिविल सर्जन को ही क्यों न दिखाओ, उसे कोई दवा असर न करेगी।

मुंशीजी–बहन, उसे घर से निकाला किसने है? मैंने तो केवल उसकी पढ़ाई के खयाल से उसे वहां भेजा था।

रुक्मिणी–तुमने चाहे जिस खयाल से भेजा हो, लेकिन यह बात उसे लग गयी। मैं तो अब किसी गिनती में नहीं हूं, मुझे किसी बात में बोलने का कोई अधिकार नहीं। मालिक तुम, मालकिन तुम्हारी स्त्री। मैं तो केवल तुम्हारी रोटियों पर पड़ी हुई अभगिनी विधवा हूं। मेरी कौन सुनेगा और कौन परवाह करेगा? लेकिन बिना बोले रहा नहीं जाता। मंसा तभी अच्छा होगाः जब घर आयेगा, जब तुम्हारा ह्रदय वही हो जाएगा, जो पहले था।

यह कहकर रुक्मिणी वहां से चली गयीं, उनकी ज्योतिहीन, पर अनुभवपूर्ण आंखों के सामने जो चरित्र हो रहे थे, उनका रहस्य वह खूब समझती थीं और उनका सारा क्रोध निरपराधिनी निर्मला ही पर उतरता था। इस समय भी वह कहते-कहते रुक गयीं, कि जब तक यह लक्ष्मी इस घर में रहेंगी, इस घर की दशा बिगड़ती ही जाएगी। उसको प्रगट रुप से न कहने पर भी उसका आशय मुंशीजी से छिपा नहीं रहा। उनके चले जाने पर मुंशीजी ने सिर झुका लिया और सोचने लगे। उन्हें अपने ऊपर इस समय इतना क्रोध आ रहा था कि दीवार से सिर पटककर प्राणों का अन्त कर दें। उन्होंने क्यों विवाह किया था? विवाह करने की क्या जरुरत थी? ईश्वर ने उन्हें एक नहीं, तीन-तीन पुत्र दिये थे? उनकी अवस्था भी पचास के लगभग पहुंच गयी थी फिर उन्होंने क्यों विवाह किया? क्या इसी बहाने ईश्वर को उनका सर्वनाश करना मंजूर था? उन्होंने सिर उठाकर एक बार निर्मला की सहास, पर निश्चल मूर्ति देखी और अस्पताल चले गये। निर्मला की सहास, छवि ने उनका चित्त शान्त कर दिया था।

आज कई दिनों के बाद उन्हें शान्ति मयस्सर हुई थी। प्रेम-पीड़ित ह्रदय इस दशा में क्या इतना शान्त और अविचलित रह सकता है? नहीं, कभी नहीं। ह्रदय की चोट भाव-कौशल से नहीं छिपाई जा सकती। अपने चित्त की दुर्बलता पर इस समय उन्हें अत्यन्त क्षोभ हुआ। उन्होंने अकारण ही सन्देह को ह्रदय में स्थान देकर इतना अनर्थ किया। मंसाराम की ओर से भी उनका मन निःशंक हो गया। हां उसकी जगह अब एक नयी शंका उत्पन्न हो गयी। क्या मंसाराम भांप तो नहीं गया? क्या भांपकर ही तो घर आने से इन्कार नहीं कर रहा है? अगर वह भांप गया है, तो महान् अनर्थ हो जाएगा। उसकी कल्पना ही से उनका मन दहल उठा। उनकी देह की सारी हड्डियां मानों इस हाहाकार पर पानी डालने के लिए व्याकुल हो उठीं। उन्होंने कोचवान से घोड़े को तेज चलाने को कहा।

आज कई दिनों के बाद उनके ह्रदय मंडल पर छाया हुआ सघन अंधेरा फट गया था और प्रकाश की लहरें अन्दर से निकलने के लिए

व्यग्र हो रही थीं। उन्होंने बाहर सिर निकाल कर देखा, कोचवान सो तो नहीं रहा है। घोड़े की चाल उन्हें इतनी मन्द कभी न मालूम हुई थी।

अस्पताल पहुंचकर वह लपके हुए मंसाराम के पास गये। देखा तो डॉक्टर साहब उसके सामने चिन्ता में मग्न खड़े थे। मुंशीजी के हाथ-पांव फूल गये। मुंह से शब्द न निकल सका। भरभराई हुई आवाज में बड़ी मुश्किल से बोले—क्या हाल है, डॉक्टर साहब? यह कहते-कहते वह रो पड़े और जब डॉक्टर साहब को उनके प्रश्न का उत्तर देने में एक क्षण का विलम्ब हुआ, तब तो उनके प्राण नहों में समा गये। उन्होंने पलंग पर बैठकर अचेत बालक को गोद में उठा लिया और बालक की भांति सिसक-सिसककर रोने लगे। मंसाराम की देह तवे की तरह जल रही थी। मंसाराम ने एक बार आंखें खोलीं। आह, कितनी भयंकर और उसके साथ ही कितनी दीन दृष्टि थी।

मुंशीजी ने बालक को कण्ठ से लगाकर डॉक्टर से पूछा—क्या हाल है, साहब! आप चुप क्यों हैं?

डॉक्टर ने संदिग्ध स्वर से कहा—हाल जो कुछ है, वह आप देख ही रहे हैं। 106 डिग्री का ज्वर है और मैं क्या बताऊं? अभी ज्वर का प्रकोप बढ़ता ही जाता है। मेरे किये जो कुछ हो सकता है, कर रहा हूं। ईश्वर मालिक है। जबसे आप गये हैं, मैं एक मिनट के लिए भी यहां से नहीं हिला। भोजन तक नहीं कर सका। हालत इतनी नाजुक है कि एक मिनट में क्या हो जाएगा, नहीं कहा जा सकता? यह महाज्वर है, बिलकुल होश नहीं है। रह-रहकर 'डिलीरियम' का दौरा-सा हो जाता है। क्या घर में इन्हें किसी ने कुछ कहा है! बार-बार, अम्मांजी, तुम कहां हो! यही आवाज मुंह से निकलती है।

डॉक्टर साहब यह कह ही रहे थे कि सहसा मंसाराम उठकर बैठ गया और धक्के से मुंशीजी को चारपाई के नीचे ढकेलकर उन्मत्त स्वर से बोला—क्यों धमकाते हैं, आप! मार डालिए, मार डालिए, अभी मार डालिए। तलवार नहीं मिलती! रस्सी का फन्दा है या वह भी नहीं। मैं अपने गले में लगा लूंगा। हाय अम्मांजी, तुम कहां हो! यह कहते-कहते वह फिर अचेत होकर गिर पड़ा।

मुंशीजी एक क्षण तक मंसाराम की शिथिल मुद्रा की ओर व्यथित नेत्रों से ताकते रहे, फिर सहसा उन्होंने डॉक्टर साहब का हाथ पकड़ लिया और अत्यन्त दीनतापूर्ण आग्रह से बोले—डॉक्टर साहब, इस लड़के को बचा लीजिए, ईश्वर के लिए बचा लीजिए, नहीं मेरा सर्वनाश हो जाएगा। मैं अमीर नहीं हूं लेकिन आप जो कुछ कहेंगे, वह हाजिर करुंगा, इसे बचा लीजिए। आप बड़े-से-बड़े डॉक्टर को बुलाइए और उनकी राय लीजिए, मैं सब खर्च दूंगा। इसकी यह दशा अब नहीं देखी जाती। हाय, मेरा होनहार बेटा!

डॉक्टर साहब ने करुण स्वर में कहा—बाबू साहब, मैं आपसे सत्य कह रहा हूं कि मैं इनके लिए अपनी तरफ से कोई बात उठा नहीं रख रहा हूं। अब आप दूसरे डॉक्टरों से सलाह लेने को कहते हैं। अभी डॉक्टर लाहिरी, डॉक्टर भाटिया और डॉक्टर माथुर को बुलाता हूं। विनायक शास्त्री को भी बुलाये लेता हूं, लेकिन मैं आपको व्यर्थ का आश्वासन नहीं देना चाहता, हालत नाजुक है।

मुंशीजी ने रोते हुए कहा—नहीं, डॉक्टर साहब, यह शब्द मुंह से न निकालिए। हालत इसके दुश्मनों की नाजुक हो। ईश्वर मुझ पर इतना कोप न करेंगे। आप कलकत्ता और बम्बई के डॉक्टरों को तार दीजिए, मैं जिन्दगी भर आपकी गुलामी करुंगा। यही मेरे कुल का दीपक है। यही मेरे जीवन का आधार है। मेरा ह्रदय फटा जा रहा है। कोई ऐसी दवा दीजिए, जिससे इसे होश आ जाए। मैं जरा अपने कानों से उसकी बातें सुनूं जानूं कि उसे क्या कष्ट हो रहा है? हाय, मेरा बच्चा!

डॉक्टर—आप जरा दिल को तस्कीन दीजिए। आप बुजुर्ग आदमी हैं, यों हाय-हाय करने और डॉक्टरों की फौज जमा करने से कोई नतीजा न निकलेगा। शान्त होकर बैठिए, मैं शहर के लोगों को बुला रहा हूं, देखिए क्या कहते हैं? आप तो खुद ही बदहवास हुए जाते हैं।

मुंशीजी—अच्छा, डॉक्टर साहब! मैं अब न बोलूंगा, जबान तब तक न खोलूंगा, आप जो चाहे करें, बच्चा अब आपके हाथ में है। आप ही उसकी रक्षा कर सकते हैं। मैं इतना ही चाहता हूं कि जरा इसे होश आ

जाए, मुझे पहचान ले, मेरी बातें समझने लगे। क्या कोई ऐसी संजीवनी बूटी नहीं? मैं इससे दो-चार बातें कर लेता।

यह कहते–कहते मुंशीजी आवेश में आकर मंसाराम से बोले–बेटा, जरा आंखें खोलो, कैसा जी है? मैं तुम्हारे पास बैठा रो रहा हूं, मुझे तुमसे कोई शिकायत नहीं है, मेरा दिल तुम्हारी ओर से साफ है।

डॉक्टर–फिर आपने अनर्गल बातें करनी शुरु कीं। अरे साहब, आप बच्चे नहीं हैं, बुजुर्ग है, जरा धैर्य से काम लीजिए।

मुंशीजी–अच्छा, डॉक्टर साहब, अब न बोलूंगा, खता हुई। आप जो चाहें कीजिए। मैंने सब कुछ आप पर छोड़ दिया। कोई ऐसा उपाय नहीं, जिससे मैं इसे इतना समझा सकूं कि मेरा दिल साफ है? आप ही कह दीजिए डॉक्टर साहब, कह दीजिए, तुम्हारा अभागा पिता बैठा रो रहा है। उसका दिल तुम्हारी तरफ से बिलकुल साफ है। उसे कुछ भ्रम हुआ था। वह अब दूर हो गया। बस, इतना ही कर दीजिए। मैं और कुछ नहीं चाहता। मैं चुपचाप बैठा हूं। जबान को नहीं खोलता, लेकिन आप इतना जरुर कह दीजिए।

डॉक्टर–ईश्वर के लिए बाबू साहब, जरा सब्र कीजिए, वरना मुझे मजबूर होकर आपसे कहना पड़ेगा कि घर जाइए। मैं जरा दफ्तर में जाकर डॉक्टरों को खत लिख रहा हूं। आप चुपचाप बैठे रहिएगा।

निर्दयी डॉक्टर! जवान बेटे की यहा दशा देखकर कौन पिता है, जो धैर्य से काम लेगा? मुंशीजी बहुत गम्भीर स्वभाव के मनुष्य थे। यह भी जानते थे कि इस वक्त हाय-हाय मचाने से कोई नतीजा नहीं, लेकिन फिर भी इस समय शान्त बैठना उनके लिए असम्भव था। अगर दैव-गति से यह बीमारी होती, तो वह शान्त हो सकते थे, दूसरों को समझा सकते थे, खुद डॉक्टरों को बुला सकते थे, लेकिन क्या यह जानकर भी धैर्य रख सकते थे कि यह सब आग मेरी ही लगाई हुई है? कोई पिता इतना वज्र-हृदय हो सकता है? उनका रोम-रोम इस समय उन्हें धिक्कार रहा था। उन्होंने सोचा, मुझे यह दुर्भावना उत्पन्न ही क्यों हुई? मैंने क्यों बिना किसी प्रत्यक्ष प्रमाण के ऐसी भीषण कल्पना कर डाली?

अच्छा मुझे उस दशा में क्या करना चाहिए था। जो कुछ उन्होंने किया उसके सिवा वह और क्या करते, इसका वह निश्चय न कर सके। वास्तव में विवाह के बन्धन में पड़ना ही अपने पैरों में कुल्हाड़ी मारना था। हां, यही सारे उपद्रव की जड़ है।

मगर मैंने यह कोई अनोखी बात नहीं की। सभी स्त्री-पुरुष विवाह करते हैं। उनका जीवन आनन्द से कटता है। आनन्द की इच्छा से ही तो हम विवाह करते हैं। मुहल्ले में सैकड़ों आदमियों ने दूसरी, तीसरी, चौथी यहां तक कि सातवीं शादियां की हैं और मुझसे भी कहीं अधिक अवस्था में। वह जब तक जिये आराम ही से जिये। यह भी नहीं हुआ कि सभी स्त्री से पहले मर गये हों। दुहाज-तिहाज होने पर भी कितने ही फिर रंडुए हो गये। अगर मेरी-जैसी दशा सबकी होती, तो विवाह का नाम ही कौन लेता? मेरे पिताजी ने पचपनवें वर्ष में विवाह किया था और मेरे जन्म के समय उनकी अवस्था साठ से कम न थी। हां, इतनी बात जरुर है कि तब और अब में कुछ अंतर हो गया है।

पहले स्त्रियां पढ़ी-लिखी न होती थीं। पति चाहे कैसा ही हो, उसे पूज्य समझती थीं, चाहे यह बात हो कि पुरुष सब कुछ देखकर भी बेहयाई से काम लेता हो, अवश्य यही बात है।

जब युवक वृद्धा के साथ प्रसन्न नहीं रह सकता, तो युवती क्यों किसी वृद्ध के साथ प्रसन्न रहने लगी? लेकिन मैं तो कुछ ऐसा बुड्ढा न था। मुझे देखकर कोई चालीस से अधिक नहीं बता सकता। कुछ भी हो, जवानी ढल जाने पर जवान औरत से विवाह करके कुछ-न-कुछ बेहयाई जरुर करनी पड़ती है, इसमें सन्देह नहीं। स्त्री स्वभाव से लज्जाशील होती है। कुलटाओं की बात तो दूसरी है, पर साधारणतः स्त्री पुरुष से कहीं ज्यादा संयमशील होती है। जोड़ का पति पाकर वह चाहे पर-पुरुष से हंसी-दिल्लगी कर ले, पर उसका मन शुद्ध रहता है। बेजोड़ विवाह हो जाने से वह चाहे किसी की ओर आंखे उठाकर न देखे, पर उसका चित्त दुखी रहता है। वह पक्की दीवार है, उसमें सबरी का असर नहीं होता, यह कच्ची दीवार है और उसी वक्त तक खड़ी रहती है, जब तक इस पर सबरी न चलाई जाए।

इन्हीं विचारों में पड़े-पड़े मुंशीजी को एक झपकी आ गयी। मन के भावों ने तत्काल स्वप्न का रुप धारण कर लिया। क्या देखते हैं कि उनकी पहली स्त्री मंसाराम के सामने खड़ी कह रही है–'स्वामी, यह तुमने क्या किया? जिस बालक को मैंने अपना रक्त पिला-पिलाकर पाला, उसको तुमने इतनी निर्दयता से मार डाला। ऐसे आदर्श चरित्र बालक पर तुमने इतना घोर कलंक लगा दिया? अब बैठे क्या बिसूरते हो। तुमने उससे हाथ धो लिया। मैं तुम्हारे निर्दयी हाथों से छीनकर उसे अपने साथ लिए जाती हूं। तुम तो इतने शक्की कभी न थे। क्या विवाह करते ही शक को भी गले बांध लाये? इस कोमल हृदय पर इतना कठोर आघात! इतना भीषण कलंक! इतना बड़ा अपमान सहकर जीनेवाले कोई बेहया होंगे। मेरा बेटा नहीं सह सकता!' यह कहते-कहते उसने बालक को गोद में उठा लिया और चली।

मुंशीजी ने रोते हुए उसकी गोद से मंसाराम को छीनने के लिए हाथ बढ़ाया, तो आंखे खुल गयीं और डॉक्टर लाहिरी, डॉक्टर भाटिया आदि आधे दर्जन डॉक्टर उनको सामने खड़े दिखायी दिये।

8

तीन दिन गुजर गये और मुंशीजी घर न आये। रुक्मिणी दोनों वक्त अस्पताल जातीं और मंसाराम को देख आती थीं। दोनों लड़के भी जाते थे, पर निर्मला कैसे जाती? उनके पैरों में तो बेड़ियां पड़ी हुई थीं। वह मंसाराम की बीमारी का हाल-चाल जानने के लिए व्यग्र रहती थी, यदि रुक्मिणी से कुछ पूछती थीं, तो ताने मिलते थे और लड़को से पूछती तो बेसिर-पैर की बातें करने लगते थे।

एक बार खुद जाकर देखने के लिए उसका चित्त व्याकुल हो रहा था। उसे यह भय होता था कि सन्देह ने कहीं मुंशीजी के पुत्र-प्रेम को शिथिल न कर दिया हो, कहीं उनकी कृपणता ही तो मंसाराम के अच्छे होने में बाधक नहीं हो रही है? डॉक्टर किसी के सगे नहीं होते, उन्हें तो अपने पैसों से काम है, मुर्दा दोजख में जाए या बहिश्त में। उसके मन मे प्रबल इच्छा होती थी कि जाकर अस्पताल के डॉक्टरों को एक हजार की थैली देकर कहे—इन्हें बचा लीजिए, यह थैली आपकी भेंट हैं, पर उसके पास न तो इतने रुपये ही थे, न इतना साहस ही था। अब भी यदि वह वहां पहुंच सकती, तो मंसाराम अच्छा हो जाता। उसकी जैसी सेवा-शुश्रूषा होनी चाहिए, वैसी नहीं हो रही है। नहीं तो क्या तीन दिन तक ज्वर ही न उतरता? यह दैहिक ज्वर नहीं, मानसिक ज्वर है और चित्त के शान्त होने ही से इसका प्रकोप उतर सकता है।

अगर वह वहां रात भर बैठी रह सकती और मुंशीजी जरा भी मन मैला न करते, तो कदाचित् मंसाराम को विश्वास हो जाता कि पिताजी का दिल साफ है और फिर अच्छे होने में देर न लगती, लेकिन ऐसा होगा? मुंशीजी उसे वहां देखकर प्रसन्नचित्त रह सकेंगे? क्या अब भी

उनका दिल साफ नहीं हुआ? यहां से जाते समय तो ऐसा ज्ञात हुआ था कि वह अपने प्रमाद पर पछता रहे हैं। ऐसा तो न होगा कि उसके वहां जाते ही मुंशीजी का सन्देह फिर भड़क उठे और वह बेटे की जान लेकर ही छोड़ें?

इस दुविधा में पड़े-पड़े तीन दिन गुजर गये और न घर में चूल्हा जला, न किसी ने कुछ खाया। लड़को के लिए बाजार से पूरियां ली जाती थीं, रुक्मिणी और निर्मला भूखी ही सो जाती थीं। उन्हें भोजन की इच्छा ही न होती।

चौथे दिन जियाराम स्कूल से लौटा, तो अस्पताल होता हुआ घर आया। निर्मला ने पूछा–क्यों भैया, अस्पताल भी गये थे? आज क्या हाल है? तुम्हारे भैया उठे या नहीं?

जियाराम रुआंसा होकर बोला–अम्मांजी, आज तो वह कुछ बोलते-चालते ही न थे। चुपचाप चारपाई पर पड़े जोर-जोर से हाथ-पांव पटक रहे थे।

निर्मला के चेहरे का रंग उड़ गया। घबराकर पूछा–तुम्हारे बाबूजी वहां न थे?

जियाराम–थे क्यों नहीं? आज वह बहुत रोते थे।

निर्मला का कलेजा धक्-धक् करने लगा। पूछा–डॉक्टर लोग वहां न थे?

जियाराम–डॉक्टर भी खड़े थे और आपस में कुछ सलाह कर रहे थे। सबसे बड़ा सिविल सर्जन अंगरेजी में कह रहा था कि मरीज की देह में कुछ ताजा खून डालना चाहिए। इस पर बाबूजी ने कहा–मेरी देह से जितना खून चाहें ले लीजिए। सिविल सर्जन ने हंसकर कहा–आपके ब्लड से काम नहीं चलेगा, किसी जवान आदमी का ब्लड चाहिए। आखिर उसने पिचकारी से कोई दवा भैया के बाजू में डाल दी। चार अंगुल से कम के सुई न रही होगी, पर भैया मिनके तक नहीं। मैंने तो मारे डरके आंखें बन्द कर लीं।

बड़े–बड़े महान संकल्प आवेश में ही जन्म लेते हैं। कहां तो निर्मला भय से सूखी जाती थी, कहां उसके मुंह पर दृढ़ संकल्प की

आभा झलक पड़ी। उसने अपनी देह का ताजा खून देने का निश्चय किया। अगर उसके रक्त से मंसाराम के प्राण बच जाएं, तो वह बड़ी खुशी से उसकी अन्तिम बूंद तक दे डालेगी। अब जिसका जो जी चाहे समझे, वह कुछ परवाह न करेगी। उसने जियाराम से कहा–तुम लपककर एक एक्का बुला लो, मैं अस्पताल जाऊंगी।

जियाराम–वहां तो इस वक्त बहुत से आदमी होंगे। जरा रात हो जाने दीजिए।

निर्मला–नहीं, तुम अभी एक्का बुला लो।

जियाराम–कहीं बाबूजी बिगड़ें न?

निर्मला–बिगड़ने दो। तुम अभी जाकर सवारी लाओ।

जियाराम–मैं कह दूंगा, अम्मांजी ही ने मुझसे सवारी मंगाई थी।

निर्मला–कह देना।

जियाराम तो उधर तांगा लाने गया, इतनी देर में निर्मला ने सिर में कंघी की, जूड़ा बांधा, कपड़े बदले, आभूषण पहने, पान खाया और द्वार पर आकर तांगे की राह देखने लगी।

रुक्मिणी अपने कमरे में बैठी हुई थीं उसे इस तैयारी से आते देखकर बोलीं–कहां जाती हो, बहू?

निर्मला–जरा अस्पताल तक जाती हूं।

रुक्मिणी–वहां जाकर क्या करोगी?

निर्मला–कुछ नहीं, करुंगी क्या? करने वाले तो भगवान हैं। देखने को जी चाहता है।

रुक्मिणी–मैं कहतीं हूं, मत जाओ।

निर्मला ने विनीत भाव से कहा–अभी चली आऊंगी, दीदीजी। जियाराम कह रहे हैं कि इस वक्त उनकी हालत अच्छी नहीं है। जी नहीं मानता, आप भी चलिए न?

रुक्मिणी–मैं देख आई हूं। इतना ही समझ लो कि, अब बाहरी खून पहुंचाने पर ही जीवन की आशा है। कौन अपना ताजा खून देगा और क्यों देगा? उसमें भी तो प्राणों का भय है।

निर्मला–इसीलिए तो मैं जाती हूं। मेरे खून से क्या काम न चलेगा?

रुक्मिणी–चलेगा क्यों नहीं, जवान ही का तो खून चाहिए, लेकिन तुम्हारे खून से मंसाराम की जान बचे, इससे यह कहीं अच्छा है कि उसे पानी में बहा दिया जाए।

तांगा आ गया। निर्मला और जियाराम दोनों जा बैठे। तांगा चला।

रुक्मिणी द्वार पर खड़ी देर तक रोती रही। आज पहली बार उसे निर्मला पर दया आई, उसका बस होता तो वह निर्मला को बांध रखती। करुणा और सहानुभूति का आवेश उसे कहां लिये जाता है, वह अप्रकट रुप से देख रही थी। आह! यह दुर्भाग्य की प्रेरणा है। यह सर्वनाश का मार्ग है।

निर्मला अस्पताल पहुंची, तो दीपक जल चुके थे। डॉक्टर लोग अपनी राय देकर विदा हो चुके थे। मंसाराम का ज्वर कुछ कम हो गया था वह टकटकी लगाए हुए द्वार की ओर देख रहा था। उसकी दृष्टि उन्मुक्त आकाश की ओर लगी हुई थी, मानों किसी देवता की प्रतीक्षा कर रहा हो! वह कहां है, जिस दशा में है, इसका उसे कुछ ज्ञान न था।

सहसा निर्मला को देखते ही वह चौंककर उठ बैठा। उसकी समाधि टूट गई। उसकी विलुप्त चेतना प्रदीप्त हो गई। उसे अपने स्थिति का, अपनी दशा का ज्ञान हो गया, मानो कोई भूली हुई बात याद हो गई हो। उसने आंखें फाड़कर निर्मला को देखा और मुंह फेर लिया।

एकाएक मुंशीजी तीव्र स्वर से बोले–तुम, यहां क्या करने आईं?

निर्मला अवाक् रह गई। वह बतलाये कि क्या करने आई? इतने सीधे से प्रश्न का भी वह कोई जवाब न दे सकी? वह क्या करने आई थी? इतना जटिल प्रश्न किसके सामने आया होगा? घर का आदमी बीमार है, उसे देखने आई है, यह बात क्या बिना पूछे मालूम न हो सकती थी? फिर प्रश्न क्यों? वह हतबुद्धि-सी खड़ी रही, मानो संज्ञाहीन हो गई हो उसने दोनों लड़को से मुंशीजी के शोक और संताप की बातें सुनकर यह अनुमान किया था कि अब उनका दिल साफ हो गया है। अब उसे ज्ञात हुआ कि वह भ्रम था। हां, वह महाभ्रम था। अगर वह जानती कि आंसुओं की दृष्टि ने भी संदेह की अग्नि शांत नहीं की, तो वह कदापि न आती। वह कुढ़-कुढ़ाकर मर जाती, घर से पांव न निकालती।

मुंशीजी ने फिर वही प्रश्न किया—तुम यहां क्यों आईं?

निर्मला ने निःशंक भाव से उत्तर दिया—आप यहां क्या करने आये हैं?

मुंशीजी के नथुने फड़कने लगे। वह झल्लाकर चारपाई से उठे और निर्मला का हाथ पकड़कर बोले—तुम्हारे यहां आने की कोई जरुरत नहीं। जब मैं बुलाऊं तब आना। समझ गईं?

अरे! यह क्या अनर्थ हुआ! मंसाराम जो चारपाई से हिल भी न सकता था, उठकर खड़ा हो गया और निर्मला के पैरों पर गिरकर रोते हुए बोला—अम्मांजी, इस अभागे के लिए आपको व्यर्थ इतना कष्ट हुआ। मैं आपका स्नेह कभी भी न भूलंगा। ईश्वर से मेरी यही प्रार्थना है कि मेरा पुर्नजन्म आपके गर्भ से हो, जिससे मैं आपके ऋण से उऋण हो सकूं। ईश्वर जानता है, मैंने आपको विमाता नहीं समझा। मैं आपको अपनी माता समझता रहा। आपकी उम्र मुझसे बहुत ज्यादा न हो, लेकिन आप, मेरी माता के स्थान पर थी और मैंने आपको सदैव इसी दृष्टि से देखा...अब नहीं बोला जाता अम्मांजी, क्षमा कीजिए! यह अंतिम भेंट है।

निर्मला ने अश्रु-प्रवाह को रोकते हुए कहा—तुम ऐसी बातें क्यों करते हो? दो-चार दिन में अच्छे हो जाओगे।

मंसाराम ने क्षीण स्वर में कहा—अब जीने की इच्छा नहीं और न बोलने की शक्ति ही है। यह कहते-कहते मंसाराम अशक्त होकर वहीं जमीन पर लेट गया।

निर्मला ने पति की ओर निर्भय नेत्रों से देखते हुए कहा—डॉक्टर ने क्या सलाह दी?

मुंशीजी—सब-के-सब भंग खा गए हैं, कहते हैं, ताजा खून चाहिए।

निर्मला—ताजा खून मिल जाए, तो प्राण-रक्षा हो सकती है?

मुंशीजी ने निर्मला की ओर तीव्र नेत्रों से देखकर कहा—मैं ईश्वर नहीं हूं और न डॉक्टर ही को ईश्वर समझता हूं।

निर्मला—ताजा खून तो ऐसी अलभ्य वस्तु नहीं!

मुंशीजी—आकाश के तारे भी तो अलभ्य नही! मुंह के सामने खंदक क्या चीज है?

निर्मला–मैं आपना खून देने को तैयार हूं। डॉक्टर को बुलाइए।

मुंशीजी ने विस्मित होकर कहा–तुम!

निर्मला–हां, क्या मेरे खून से काम न चलेगा?

मुंशीजी–तुम अपना खून दोगी? नहीं, तुम्हारे खून की जरुरत नहीं। इसमें प्राणों का भय है।

निर्मला–मेरे प्राण और किस दिन काम आयेंगे?

मुंशीजी ने सजल-नेत्र होकर कहा–नहीं निर्मला, उसका मूल्य अब मेरी निगाहों में बहुत बढ़ गया है। आज तक वह मेरे भोग की वस्तु थी, आज से वह मेरी भक्ति की वस्तु है। मैंने तुम्हारे साथ बड़ा अन्याय किया है, क्षमा करो।

जो कुछ होना था हो गया, किसी की कुछ न चली। डॉक्टर साहब निर्मला की देह से रक्त निकालने की चेष्टा कर ही रहे थे कि मंसाराम अपने उज्ज्वल चरित्र की अन्तिम झलक दिखाकर इस भ्रम-लोक से विदा हो गया। कदाचित् इतनी देर तक उसके प्राण निर्मला ही की राह देख रहे थे। उसे निष्कलंक सिद्ध किये बिना वे देह को कैसे त्याग देते? अब उनका उद्देश्य पूरा हो गया था।

मुंशीजी को निर्मला के निर्दोष होने का विश्वास हो गया, पर कब? जब हाथ से तीर निकल चुका था, जब मुसाफिर ने रकाब में पांव डाल लिया था।

पुत्र-शोक में मुंशीजी का जीवन भार-स्वरुप हो गया। उस दिन से फिर उनके होठों पर हंसी न आई। यह जीवन अब उन्हें व्यर्थ-सा जान पड़ता था। कचहरी जाते, मगर मुकदमों की पैरवी करने के लिए नहीं, केवल दिल बहलाने के लिए घंटे-दो-घंटे में वहां से उकताकर चले आते। खाने बैठते तो कौर मुंह में न जाता। निर्मला अच्छी से अच्छी चीज पकाती पर मुंशीजी दो-चार कौर से अधिक न खा सकते। ऐसा जान पड़ता कि कौर मुंह से निकला आता है! मंसाराम के कमरे की ओर जाते ही उनका हृदय टूक-टूक हो जाता था। जहां उनकी

आशाओं का दीपक जलता रहता था, वहां अब अंधकार छाया हुआ था। उनके दो पुत्र अब भी थे, लेकिन दूध देती हुई गाय मर गई, तो बछिया का क्या भरोसा? जब फूलने-फलनेवाला वृक्ष गिर पड़ा, नन्हे-नन्हे पौधों से क्या आशा? यों तो जवान-बूढ़े सभी मरते हैं, लेकिन दुःख इस बात का था कि उन्होंने स्वयं लड़के की जान ली। जिस दम बात याद आ जाती, तो ऐसा मालूम होता था कि उनकी छाती फट जाएगी--मानो हृदय बाहर निकल पड़ेगा।

निर्मला को पति से सच्ची सहानुभूति थी। जहां तक हो सकता था, वह उनको प्रसन्न रखने का फिक्र रखती थी और भूलकर भी पिछली बातें जबान पर न लाती थी। मुंशीजी उससे मंसाराम की कोई चर्चा करते शरमाते थे। उनकी कभी-कभी ऐसी इच्छा होती कि एक बार निर्मला से अपने मन के सारे भाव खोलकर कह दूं, लेकिन लज्जा रोक लेती थी। इस भांति उन्हें सान्त्वना भी न मिलती थी, जो अपनी व्यथा कह डालने से, दूसरो को अपने गम में शरीक कर लेने से, प्राप्त होती है। मवाद बाहर न निकलकर अन्दर-ही-अन्दर अपना विष फैलाता जाता था, दिन-दिन देह घुलती जाती थी।

इधर कुछ दिनों से मुंशीजी और उन डॉक्टर साहब में जिन्होंने मंसाराम की दवा की थी, याराना हो गया था, बेचारे कभी-कभी आकर मुंशीजी को समझाया करते, कभी-कभी अपने साथ हवा खिलाने के लिए खींच ले जाते। उनकी स्त्री भी दो-चार बार निर्मला से मिलने आई थीं। निर्मला भी कई बार उनके धर गई थी, मगर वहां से जब लौटती, तो कई दिन तक उदास रहती। उस दम्पत्ति का सुखमय जीवन देखकर उसे अपनी दशा पर दुःख हुए बिना न रहता था।

डॉक्टर साहब को कुल दो सौ रुपये मिलते थे, पर इतने में ही दोनों आनन्द से जीवन व्यतीत करते थे। घर में केवल एक महरी थी, गृहस्थी का बहुत-सा काम स्त्री को अपने ही हाथों करना पड़ता था। गहने भी उसकी देह पर बहुत कम थे, पर उन दोनों में वह प्रेम था, जो धन की तृण के बराबर परवाह नहीं करता। पुरुष को देखकर स्त्री का चेहरा खिल उठता था। स्त्री को देखकर पुरुष निहाल हो जाता था।

निर्मला के घर में धन इससे कहीं अधिक था, आभूषणों से उनकी देह फटी पड़ती थी, घर का कोई काम उसे अपने हाथ से न करना पड़ता था। पर निर्मला सम्पन्न होने पर भी अधिक दुखी थी, और सुधा विपन्न होने पर भी सुखी। सुधा के पास कोई ऐसी वस्तु थी, जो निर्मला के पास न थी, जिसके सामने उसे अपना वैभव तुच्छ जान पड़ता था। यहां तक कि वह सुधा के घर गहने पहनकर जाते शरमाती थी।

एक दिन निर्मला डॉक्टर साहब के घर आई, तो उसे बहुत उदास देखकर सुधा ने पूछा–बहिन, आज बहुत उदास हो, वकील साहब की तबीयत तो अच्छी है, न?

निर्मला–क्या कहूं, सुधा? उनकी दशा दिन-दिन खराब होती जाती है, कुछ कहते नहीं बनता। न जाने ईश्वर को क्या मंजूर है?

सुधा–हमारे बाबूजी तो कहते हैं कि उन्हें कहीं जलवायु बदलने के लिए जाना जरुरी है, नहीं तो, कोई भंयकर रोग खड़ा हो जाएगा। कई बार वकील साहब से कह भी चुके हैं पर वह यही कह दिया करते हैं कि मैं तो बहुत अच्छी तरह हूं, मुझे कोई शिकायत नहीं। आज तुम कहना।

निर्मला–जब डॉक्टर साहब की नहीं सुनी, तो मेरी सुनेंगे?

यह कहते-कहते निर्मला की आंखें डबडबा गई और जो शंका, इधर महीनों से उसके हृदय को विकल करती रहती थी, मुंह से निकल पड़ी। अब तक उसने उस शंका को छिपाया था, पर अब न छिपा सकी। बोली-बहिन मुझे लक्षण कुछ अच्छे नहीं मालूम होते। देखें, भगवान् क्या करते हैं?

सुधा–तुम आज उनसे खूब जोर देकर कहना कि कहीं जलवायु बदलने चलिए। दो चार महीने बाहर रहने से बहुत सी बातें भूल जाएंगी। मैं तो समझती हूं, शायद मकान बदलने से भी उनका शोक कुछ कम हो जाएगा। तुम कहीं बाहर जा भी न सकोगी। यह कौन-सा महीना है?

निर्मला–आठवां महीना बीत रहा है। यह चिन्ता तो मुझे और भी मारे डालती है। मैंने तो इसके लिए ईश्वर से कभी प्रार्थना न की थी। यह बला मेरे सिर न जाने क्यों मढ़ दी? मैं बड़ी अभागिनी हूं, बहिन, विवाह के एक महीने पहले पिताजी का देहान्त हो गया। उनके मरते

ही मेरे सिर शनीचर सवार हुए। जहां पहले विवाह की बातचीत पक्की हुई थी, उन लोगों ने आंखें फेर लीं। बेचारी अम्मां को हारकर मेरा विवाह यहां करना पड़ा। अब छोटी बहिन का विवाह होने वाला है। देखें, उसकी नाव किस घाट जाती है!

सुधा–जहां पहले विवाह की बातचीत हुई थी, उन लोगों ने इन्कार क्यों कर दिया?

निर्मला–यह तो वे ही जानें। पिताजी न रहे, तो सोने की गठरी कौन देता?

सुधा–यह तो नीचता है। कहां के रहने वाले थे?

निर्मला–लखनऊ के। नाम तो याद नहीं, आबकारी के कोई बड़े अफसर थे।

सुधा ने गम्भीर भाव से पूछा–और उनका लड़का क्या करता था?

निर्मला–कुछ नहीं, कहीं पढ़ता था, पर बड़ा होनहार था।

सुधा ने सिर नीचा करके कहा–उसने अपने पिता से कुछ न कहा था? वह तो जवान था, अपने बाप को दबा न सकता था?

निर्मला–अब यह मैं क्या जानूं बहिन? सोने की गठरी किसे प्यारी नहीं होती? जो पण्डित मेरे यहां से सन्देश लेकर गया था, उसने तो कहा था कि लड़का ही इन्कार कर रहा है। लड़के की मां अलबत्ता देवी थी। उसने पुत्र और पति दोनों ही को समझाया, पर उसकी कुछ न चली।

सुधा–मैं तो उस लड़के को पाती, तो खूब आड़े हाथों लेती।

निर्मला–मेरे भाग्य में जो लिखा था, वह हो चुका। बेचारी कृष्णा पर न जाने क्या बीतेगी?

संध्या समय निर्मला ने जाने के बाद जब डॉक्टर साहब बाहर से आये, तो सुधा ने कहा–क्यों जी, तुम उस आदमी का क्या कहोगे, जो एक जगह विवाह ठीक कर लेने बाद फिर लोभवश किसी दूसरी जगह संबंध कर ले?

डॉक्टर सिन्हा ने स्त्री की ओर कुतूहल से देखकर कहा–ऐसा नहीं करना चाहिए, और क्या?

सुधा–यह क्यों नहीं कहते कि ये घोर नीचता है, पहले सिरे का कमीनापन है!

सिन्हा–हां, यह कहने में भी मुझे इन्कार नहीं।

सुधा–किसका अपराध बड़ा है? वर का या वर के पिता का?

सिन्हा की समझ में अभी तक नहीं आया कि सुधा के इन प्रश्नों का आशय क्या है? विस्मय से बोले–जैसी स्थिति हो अगर वह पिता के अधीन हो, तो पिता का ही अपराध समझो।

सुधा–अधीन होने पर भी क्या जवान आदमी का अपना कोई कर्त्तव्य नहीं है? अगर उसे अपने लिए नये कोट की जरुरत हो, तो वह पिता के विरोध करने पर भी उसे रो-धोकर बनवा लेता है। क्या ऐसे महत्त्व के विषय में वह अपनी आवाज पिता के कानों तक नहीं पहुंचा सकता? यह कहो कि वह और उसका पिता दोनों अपराधी हैं, परन्तु वर अधिक। बूढ़ा आदमी सोचता है–मुझे तो सारा खर्च संभालना पड़ेगा, कन्या पक्ष से जितना ऐंठ सकूं, उतना ही अच्छा। मगर वर का धर्म है कि यदि वह स्वार्थ के हाथों बिलकुल बिक नहीं गया है, तो अपने आत्मबल का परिचय दे। अगर वह ऐसा नहीं करता, तो मैं कहूंगी कि वह लोभी है और कायर भी। दुर्भाग्यवश ऐसा ही एक प्राणी मेरा पति है और मेरी समझ में नहीं आता कि किन शब्दों में उसका तिरस्कार करुं!

सिन्हा ने हिचकिचाते हुए कहा–वह...वह...वह...दूसरी बात थी। लेन-देन का कारण नहीं था, बिलकुल दूसरी बात थी। कन्या के पिता का देहान्त हो गया था। ऐसी दशा में हम लोग क्या करते? यह भी सुनने में आया था कि कन्या में कोई ऐब है। वह बिलकुल दूसरी बात थी, मगर तुमसे यह कथा किसने कही?

सुधा–कह दो कि वह कन्या कानी थी, या कुबड़ी थी या नाइन के पेट की थी या भ्रष्टा थी। इतनी कसर क्यों छोड़ दी? भला सुनूं तो, उस कन्या में क्या ऐब था?

सिन्हा–मैंने देखा तो था नहीं, सुनने में आया था कि उसमें कोई ऐब है।

सुधा–सबसे बड़ा ऐब यही था कि उसके पिता का स्वर्गवास हो गया था और वह कोई लंबी-चौड़ी रकम न दे सकती थी। इतना स्वीकार करते क्यों झेंपते हो? मैं कुछ तुम्हारे कान तो काट न लूंगी! अगर दो-चार फिकरे कहूं, तो इस कान से सुनकर उसक कान से उड़ा देना। ज्यादा-चीं-चपड़ करुं, तो छड़ी से काम ले सकते हो। औरत जात डण्डे ही से ठीक रहती है। अगर उस कन्या में कोई ऐब था, तो मैं कहूंगी, लक्ष्मी भी बे-ऐब नहीं। तुम्हारी खोटी थी, बस! और क्या? तुम्हें तो मेरे पाले पड़ना था।

सिन्हा–तुमसे किसने कहा कि वह ऐसी थी वैसी थी? जैसे तुमने किसी से सुनकर मान लिया।

सुधा–मैंने सुनकर नहीं मान लिया। अपनी आंखों देखा। ज्यादा बखान क्या करुं, मैंने ऐसी सुन्दर स्त्री कभी नहीं देखी थी।

सिन्हा ने व्यग्र होकर पूछा–क्या वह यहीं कहीं है? सच बताओ, उसे कहां देखा! क्या तुम्हारे घर आई थी?

सुधा–हां, मेरे घर में आई थी और एक बार नहीं, कई बार आ चुकी है। मैं भी उसके यहां कई बार जा चुकी हूं, वकील साहब की बीवी वही कन्या है, जिसे आपने ऐबों के कारण त्याग दिया।

सिन्हा–सच!

सुधा–बिलकुल सच। आज अगर उसे मालूम हो जाए कि आप वही महापुरुष हैं, तो शायद फिर इस घर मे कदम न रखे। ऐसी सुशीला, घर के कामों में ऐसी निपुण और ऐसी परम सुन्दरी स्त्री इस शहर मे दो ही चार होंगी। तुम मेरा बखान करते हो। मै उसकी लौंडी बनने के योग्य भी नहीं हूं। घर में ईश्वर का दिया हुआ सब कुछ है, मगर जब प्राणी ही मेल का नहीं, तो और सब रहकर क्या करेगा? धन्य है उसके धैर्य को कि उस बुड्ढे खूसट वकील के साथ जीवन के दिन काट रही है। मैंने तो कब का जहर खा लिया होता। मगर मन की व्यथा कहने से ही थोड़े प्रकट होती है। हंसती है, बोलती है, गहने-कपड़े पहनती है, पर रोयां-रोयां रोया करता है।

सिन्हा–वकील साहब की खूब शिकायत करती होगी?

सुधा–शिकायत क्यों करेगी? क्या वह उसके पति नहीं हैं? संसार मे अब उसके लिए जो कुछ हैं, वकील साहब। वह बुड्ढे हों या रोगी, पर हैं तो उसके स्वामी ही। कुलवंती स्त्रियां पति की निन्दा नहीं करतीं, यह कुलटाओं का काम है। वह उनकी दशा देखकर कुढ़ती हैं, पर मुंह से कुछ नहीं कहती।

सिन्हा–इन वकील साहब को क्या सूझी थी, जो इस उम्र में ब्याह करने चले?

सुधा–ऐसे आदमी न हों, तो गरीब क्वारियों की नाव कौन पार लगाये? तुम और तुम्हारे साथी बिना भारी गठरी लिए बात नहीं करते, तो फिर ये बेचारी किसके घर जाएं? तुमने यह बड़ा भारी अन्याय किया है, और तुम्हें इसका प्रायश्चित करना पड़ेगा। ईश्वर उसका सुहाग अमर करे, लेकिन वकील साहब को कहीं कुछ हो गया, तो बेचारी का जीवन ही नष्ट हो जाऐगा। आज तो वह बहुत रोती थी। तुम लोग सचमुच बड़े निर्दयी हो। मैं तो अपने सोहन का विवाह किसी गरीब लड़की से करुंगी।

डॉक्टर साहब ने यह पिछला वाक्य नहीं सुना। वह घोर चिन्ता में पड़ गये। उनके मन में यह प्रश्न उठ-उठकर उन्हें विकल करने लगा–कहीं वकील साहब को कुछ हो गया तो? आज उन्हें अपने स्वार्थ का भंयकर स्वरुप दिखायी दिया। वास्तव में यह उन्हीं का अपराध था। अगर उन्होंने पिता से जोर देकर कहा होता कि मै और कहीं विवाह न करुंगा, तो क्या वह उनकी इच्छा के विरुद्व उनका विवाह कर देते?

सहसा सुधा ने कहा–कहो तो कल निर्मला से तुम्हारी मुलाकात करा दूं? वह भी जरा तुम्हारी सूरत देख ले। वह कुछ बोलेगी तो नहीं, पर कदाचित् एक दृष्टि से वह तुम्हारा इतना तिरस्कार कर देगी, जिसे तुम कभी न भूल सकोगे। बोलो, कल मिला दूँ? तुम्हारा बहुत संक्षिप्त परिचय भी करा दूंगी।

सिन्हा ने कहा–नहीं सुधा, तुम्हारे हाथ जोड़ता हूं, कहीं ऐसा गजब न करना! नहीं तो सच कहता हूं, घर छोड़कर भाग जाऊंगा।

सुधा–जो कांटा बोया है, उसका फल खाते क्यों इतना डरते हो? जिसकी गर्दन पर कटार चलाई है, जरा उसे तड़पते भी तो देखो।

मेरे दादा जी ने पांच हजार दिये न! अभी छोटे भाई के विवाह में पांच-छः हजार और मिल जाएंगे। फिर तो तुम्हारे बराबर धनी संसार में कोई दूसरा न होगा। ग्यारह हजार बहुत होते हैं। बाप-रे-बाप! ग्यारह हजार! उठा-उठाकर रखने लगे, तो महीनों लग जाएं अगर लड़के उड़ाने लगें, तो पीढ़ियों तक चले। कहीं से बात हो रही है या नहीं?

इस परिहास से डॉक्टर साहब इतना झेंपे कि सिर तक न उठा सके। उनका सारा वाक्-चातुर्य गायब हो गया। नन्हा-सा मुंह निकल आया, मानो मार पड़ गई हो। इसी वक्त किसी ने डॉक्टर साहब को बाहर से पुकारा बेचारे जान लेकर भागे। स्त्री कितनी परिहास कुशल होती है, इसका आज परिचय मिल गया।

रात को डॉक्टर साहब शयन करते हुए सुधा से बोले–निर्मला की तो कोई बहिन है न?

सुधा–हां, आज उसकी चर्चा तो करती थी। इसकी चिन्ता अभी से सवार हो रही है। अपने ऊपर तो जो कुछ बीतना था, बीत चुका, बहिन की फिक्र में पड़ी हुई थी। मां के पास तो अब और भी कुछ नहीं रहा, मजबूरन किसी ऐसे ही बूढ़े बाबा के गले वह भी मढ़ दी जायेगी।

सिन्हा–निर्मला तो अपनी मां की मदद कर सकती है।

सुधा ने तीक्ष्ण स्वर में कहा–तुम भी कभी-कभी बिलकुल बेसिर-पैर की बातें करने लगते हो। निर्मला बहुत करेगी, तो दो-चार सौ रुपये दे देगी, और क्या कर सकती है? वकील साहब का यह हाल हो रहा है, उसे अभी पहाड़-सी उम्र काटनी है। फिर कौन जाने उनके घर का क्या हाल है? इधर छः महीने से बेचारे घर बैठे हैं। रुपये आकाश से थोड़े ही बरसते है। दस–बीस हजार होंगे भी तो बैंक में होंगे, कुछ निर्मला के पास तो रखे न होंगे। हमारा दो सौ रुपया महीने का खर्च है, तो क्या इनका चार सौ रुपये महीने का भी न होगा?

सुधा को तो नींद आ गई, पर डॉक्टर साहब बहुत देर तक करवट बदलते रहे, फिर कुछ सोचकर उठे और मेज पर बैठकर एक पत्र लिखने लगे।

9

तीन बाते एक ही साथ हुईं—निर्मला की कन्या ने जन्म लिया, कृष्णा का विवाह निश्चित हुआ और मुंशी तोताराम का मकान नीलाम हो गया।

कन्या का जन्म तो साधारण बात थी, यद्यपि निर्मला की दृष्टि में यह उसके जीवन की सबसे महान घटना थी, लेकिन शेष दोनों घटनाएं असाधारण थीं।

कृष्णा का विवाह ऐसे सम्पन्न घराने में क्योंकर ठीक हुआ? उसकी माता के पास तो दहेज के नाम को कौड़ी भी न थी और इधर बूढ़े सिन्हा साहब जो अब पेंशन लेकर घर आ गये थे, बिरादरी में महालोभी मशहूर थे। वह अपने पुत्र का विवाह ऐसे दरिद्र घराने में करने पर कैसे राजी हुए। किसी को सहसा विश्वास न आता था।

इससे भी बड़े आश्चर्य की बात मुंशीजी के मकान का नीलाम होना था।

लोग मुंशीजी को अगर लखपती नहीं, तो बड़ा आदमी अवश्य समझते थे। उनका मकान कैसे नीलाम हुआ?

बात यह थी कि मुंशीजी ने एक महाजन से कुछ रुपये कर्ज लेकर एक गांव रेहन रखा था। उन्हें आशा थी कि साल-आध-साल में यह रुपये पाट देंगे, फिर दस—पांच साल में उस गांव पर कब्जा कर लेंगे।

वह जमींदार असल और सूद के कुल रुपये अदा करने में असमर्थ हो जाएगा। इसी भरोसे पर मुंशीजी ने यह मामला किया था।

गांव बहुत बड़ा था, चार-पांच सौ रुपये नफा होता था, लेकिन मन की सोची मन ही में रह गई।

मुंशीजी दिल को बहुत समझाने पर भी कचहरी न जा सके। पुत्रशोक ने उनमें कोई काम करने की शक्ति ही नहीं छोड़ी।

कौन ऐसा हृदय-शून्य पिता है, जो पुत्र की गर्दन पर तलवार चलाकर चित्त को शान्त कर ले?

महाजन के पास जब साल भर तक सूद न पहुंचा और न उसके बार-बार बुलाने पर मुंशीजी उसके पास गये।

यहां तक कि पिछली बार उन्होंने साफ-साफ कह दिया कि हम किसी के गुलाम नहीं हैं, साहूजी जो चाहे करें तब साहूजी को गुस्सा आ गया। उसने नालिश कर दी।

मुंशीजी पैरवी करने भी न गये।

एकाएक डिग्री हो गई। यहां घर में रुपये कहां रखे थे? इतने ही दिनों में मुंशीजी की साख भी उठ गई थी। वह रुपये का कोई प्रबन्ध न कर सके। आखिर मकान नीलाम पर चढ़ गया।

निर्मला सौर में थी। यह खबर सुनी, तो कलेजा सन्न-सा हो गया। जीवन में कोई सुख न होने पर भी धनाभाव की चिन्ताओं से मुक्त थी।

धन मानव जीवन में अगर सर्वप्रधान वस्तु नहीं, तो वह उसके बहुत निकट की वस्तु अवश्य है। अब और अभावों के साथ यह चिन्ता भी उसके सिर सवार हुई। उसने दाई द्वारा कहला भेजा, मेरे सब गहने बेचकर घर को बचा लीजिए, लेकिन मुंशीजी ने यह प्रस्ताव किसी तरह स्वीकार न किया।

उस दिन से मुंशीजी और भी चिन्ताग्रस्त रहने लगे। जिस धन का सुख भोगने के लिए उन्होंने विवाह किया था, वह अब अतीत की स्मृति मात्र था। वह मारे ग्लानि के अब निर्मला को अपना मुंह तक न दिखा सकते। उन्हें अब उस अन्याय का अनुमान हो रहा था, जो उन्होंने निर्मला के साथ किया था और कन्या के जन्म ने तो रही-सही कसर भी पूरी कर दी, सर्वनाश ही कर डाला!

बारहवें दिन सौर से निकलकर निर्मला नवजात शिशु को गोद लिये पति के पास गई। वह इस अभाव में भी इतनी प्रसन्न थी, मानो उसे कोई चिन्ता नहीं है।

बालिका को हृदय से लगार वह अपनी सारी चिन्ताएं भूल गई थी। शिशु के विकसित और हर्ष प्रदीप्त नेत्रों को देखकर उसका हृदय प्रफुल्लित हो रहा था।

मातृत्व के इस उद्‌गार में उसके सारे क्लेश विलीन हो गये थे। वह शिशु को पति की गोद में देकर निहाल हो जाना चाहती थी, लेकिन मुंशीजी कन्या को देखकर सहम उठे। गोद लेने के लिए उनका हृदय हुलसा नहीं, पर उन्होंने एक बार उसे करुण नेत्रों से देखा और फिर सिर झुका लिया, शिशु की सूरत मंसाराम से बिलकुल मिलती थी।

निर्मला ने उसके मन का भाव और ही समझा। उसने शतगुण स्नेह से लड़की को हृदय से लगा लिया मानो उनसे कह रही है–अगर तुम इसके बोझ से दबे जाते हो, तो आज से मैं इस पर तुम्हारा साया भी नहीं पड़ने दूंगी। जिस रतन को मैंने इतनी तपस्या के बाद पाया है, उसका निरादर करते हुए तुम्हार हृदय फट नहीं जाता?

वह उसी क्षण शिशु को गोद से चिपकाते हुए अपने कमरे में चली आई और देर तक रोती रही। उसने पति की इस उदासीनता को समझने की जरा भी चेष्टा न की, नहीं तो शायद वह उन्हें इतना कठोर न समझती। उसके सिर पर उत्तरदायित्व का इतना बड़ा भार कहां था, जो उसके पति पर आ पड़ा था? वह सोचने की चेष्टा करती, तो क्या इतना भी उसकी समझ में न आता?

मुंशीजी को एक ही क्षण में अपनी भूल मालूम हो गई। माता का हृदय प्रेम में इतना अनुरक्त रहता है कि भविष्य की चिन्ता और बाधाएं उसे जरा भी भयभीत नहीं करतीं। उसे अपने अंतःकरण में एक अलौकिक शक्ति का अनुभव होता है, जो बाधाओं को उनके सामने परास्त कर देती है।

मुंशीजी दौड़े हुए घर मे आये और शिशु को गोद में लेकर बोले मुझे याद आता है, मंसा भी ऐसा ही था–बिलकुल ऐसा ही!

निर्मला–दीदीजी भी तो यही कहती है।

मुंशीजी–बिलकुल वही बड़ी-बड़ी आंखे और लाल-लाल ओंठ हैं। ईश्वर ने मुझे मेरा मंसाराम इस रुप में दे दिया। वही माथा है, वही मुंह, वही हाथ-पांव! ईश्वर तुम्हारी लीला अपार है।

सहसा रुक्मिणी भी आ गई। मुंशीजी को देखते ही बोली—देखो बाबू, मंसाराम है कि नहीं? वही आया है। कोई लाख कहे, मैं न मानूंगी। साफ मंसाराम है। साल भर के लगभग हो भी तो गया।

मुंशीजी—बहिन, एक-एक अंग तो मिलता है। बस, भगवान् ने मुझे मेरा मंसाराम दे दिया। (शिशु से) क्यों री, तू मंसाराम ही है? छोड़कर जाने का नाम न लेना, नहीं फिर खींच लाऊंगा। कैसे निष्ठुर होकर भागे थे। आखिर पकड़ लाया कि नहीं? बस, कह दिया, अब मुझे छोड़कर जाने का नाम न लेना। देखो बहिन, कैसी टुकुर-टुकुर ताक रही है?

उसी क्षण मुंशीजी ने फिर से अभिलाषाओं का भवन बनाना शुरु कर दिया। मोह ने उन्हें फिर संसार की ओर खींचा।

मानव जीवन! तू इतना क्षणभंगुर है, पर तेरी कल्पनाएं कितनी दीर्घायु!

वही तोताराम जो संसार से विरक्त हो रह थे, जो रात-दिन मुत्यु का आवाहन किया करते थे, तिनके का सहारा पाकर तट पर पहुंचने के लिए पूरी शक्ति से हाथ-पांव मार रहे हैं।

मगर तिनके का सहारा पाकर कोई तट पर पहुंचा है?

10

निर्मला को यद्यपि अपने घर के झंझटों से अवकाश न था, पर कृष्णा के विवाह का संदेश पाकर वह किसी तरह न रुक सकी। उसकी माता ने बहुत आग्रह करके बुलाया था। सबसे बड़ा आकर्षण यह था कि कृष्णा का विवाह उसी घर में हो रहा था, जहां निर्मला का विवाह पहले तय हुआ था। आश्चर्य यही था कि इस बार ये लोग बिना कुछ दहेज लिए कैसे विवाह करने पर तैयार हो गए!

निर्मला को कृष्णा के विषय में बड़ी चिन्ता हो रही थी। समझती थी–मेरी ही तरह वह भी किसी के गले मढ़ दी जाएगी। बहुत चाहती थी कि माता की कुछ सहायता करुं, जिससे कृष्णा के लिए कोई योग्य वर मिले, लेकिन इधर वकील साहब के घर बैठ जाने और महाजन के नालिश कर देने से उसका हाथ भी तंग था। ऐसी दशा में यह खबर पाकर उसे बड़ी शान्ति मिली। चलने की तैयारी कर ली। वकील साहब स्टेशन तक पहुंचाने आये। नन्हीं बच्ची से उन्हें बहुत प्रेम था। छोड़ते ही न थे, यहां तक कि निर्मला के साथ चलने को तैयार हो गये, लेकिन विवाह से एक महीने पहले उनका ससुराल जा बैठना निर्मला को उचित न मालूम हुआ।

निर्मला ने अपनी माता से अब तक अपनी विपत्ति कथा न कही थी। जो बात हो गई, उसका रोना रोकर माता को कष्ट देने और रुलाने से क्या फायदा? इसलिए उसकी माता समझती थी, निर्मला बड़े आनन्द से है। अब जो निर्मला की सूरत देखी, तो मानो उसके हृदय पर धक्का-सा लग गया। लड़कियां सुसुराल से घुलकर नहीं आतीं, फिर निर्मला जैसी लड़की, जिसको सुख की सभी सामग्रियां प्राप्त थीं। उसने

कितनी लड़कियों को दूज की चन्द्रमा की भांति ससुराल जाते और पूर्ण चन्द्र बनकर आते देखा था। मन में कल्पना कर रही थी, निर्मला का रंग निखर गया होगा, देह भरकर सुडौल हो गई होगी, अंग-प्रत्यंग की शोभा कुछ और ही हो गई होगी। अब जो देखा, तो वह आधी भी न रही थीं न यौवन की चंचलता थी न वह विहसित छवि जो हृदय को मोह लेती है। वह कमनीयता, सुकुमारता, जो विलासमय जीवन से आ जाती है, यहां नाम को न थी। मुख पीला, चेष्टा गिरी हुईं, तो माता ने पूछा—क्यों री, तुझे वहां खाने को न मिलता था? इससे कहीं अच्छी तो तू यहीं थी। वहां तुझे क्या तकलीफ थी?

कृष्णा ने हंसकर कहा—वहां मालकिन थीं कि नहीं। मालकिन को दुनिया भर की चिन्ताएं रहती हैं, भोजन कब करें?

निर्मला—नहीं अम्मां, वहां का पानी मुझे रास नही आया। तबीयत भारी रहती है।

माता—वकील साहब न्योते में आयेंगे न? तब पूछूंगी कि आपने फूल-सी लड़की ले जाकर उसकी यह गत बना डाली। अच्छा, अब यह बता कि तूने यहां रुपये क्यों भेजे थे? मैंने तो तुमसे कभी न मांगे थे। लाख गई-गुजरी हूं, लेकिन बेटी का धन खाने की नीयत नहीं।

निर्मला ने चकित होकर पूछा—किसने रुपये भेजे थे। अम्मां, मैंने तो नहीं भेजे।

माता—झूठ न बोल! तूने पांच सौ रुपये के नोट नहीं भेजे थे?

कृष्णा—भेजे नहीं थे, तो क्या आसमान से आ गये? तुम्हारा नाम साफ लिखा था। मोहर भी वहीं की थी।

निर्मला—तुम्हारे चरण छूकर कहती हूं, मैंने रुपये नहीं भेजे। यह कब की बात है?

माता—अरे, दो-ढाई महीने हुए होंगे। अगर तूने नहीं भेजे, तो आये कहां से?

निर्मला—यह मैं क्या जानूं? मगर मैंने रुपये नहीं भेजे। हमारे यहां तो जब से जवान बेटा मरा है, कचहरी ही नहीं जाते। मेरा हाथ तो आप ही तंग था, रुपये कहां से आते?

माता–यह तो बड़े आश्चर्य की बात है। वहां और कोई तेरा सगा सम्बन्धी तो नहीं है? वकील साहब ने तुमसे छिपाकर तो नहीं भेजे?

निर्मला–नहीं अम्मां, मुझे तो विश्वास नहीं।

माता–इसका पता लगाना चाहिए। मैंने सारे रुपये कृष्णा के गहने-कपड़े में खर्च कर डाले। यही बड़ी मुश्किल हुई।

दोनों लड़को में किसी विषय पर विवाद उठ खड़ा हुआ और कृष्णा उधर फैसला करने चली गई, तो निर्मला ने माता से कहा–इस विवाह की बात सुनकर मुझे बड़ा आश्चर्य हुआ। यह कैसे हुआ अम्मां?

माता–यहां जो सुनता है, दांतों उंगली दबाता हैं। जिन लोगों ने पक्की की-कराई बात फेर दी और केवल थोड़े से रुपये के लोभ से, वे अब बिना कुछ लिए कैसे विवाह करने पर तैयार हो गये, समझ में नहीं आता। उन्होंने खुद ही पत्र भेजा। मैंने साफ लिख दिया कि मेरे पास देने-लेने को कुछ नहीं है, कुश-कन्या ही से आपकी सेवा कर सकती हूं।

निर्मला–इसका कुछ जवाब नहीं दिया?

माता–शास्त्रीजी पत्र लेकर गये थे। वह तो यही कहते थे कि अब मुंशीजी कुछ लेने के इच्छुक नहीं है। अपनी पहली वादा-खिलाफी पर कुछ लज्जित भी हैं। मुंशीजी से तो इतनी उदारता की आशा न थी, मगर सुनती हूं, उनके बड़े पुत्र बहुत सज्जन आदमी हैं। उन्होंने कह सुनकर बाप को राजी किया है।

निर्मला–पहले तो वह महाशय भी थैली चाहते थे न?

माता–हां, मगर अब तो शास्त्रीजी कहते थे कि दहेज के नाम से चिढ़ते हैं। सुना है यहां विवाह न करने पर पछताते भी थे। रुपये के लिए बात छोड़ी थी और रुपये खूब पाये, स्त्री पसंन्द नहीं।

निर्मला के मन में उस पुरुष को देखने की प्रबल उत्कंठा हुई, जो उसकी अवहेलना करके अब उसकी बहिन का उद्वार करना चाहता है। प्रायश्चित सही, लेकिन कितने ऐसे प्राणी हैं, जो इस तरह प्रायश्चित करने को तैयार हैं? उनसे बातें करने के लिए, नम्र शब्दों से उनका तिरस्कार करने के लिए, अपनी अनुपम छवि दिखाकर उन्हें और भी जलाने के लिए निर्मला का हृदय अधीर हो उठा। रात को दोनों बहिनें एक ही कमरे में सोईं।

मुहल्ले में किन-किन लड़कियों का विवाह हो गया, कौन-कौन लड़कोरी हुईं, किस-किस का विवाह धूम-धाम से हुआ। किस-किस के पति कम इच्छानुकूल मिले, कौन कितने और कैसे गहने चढ़ावे में लाया, इन्हीं विषयों में दोनों में बड़ी देर तक बातें होती रही। कृष्णा बार-बार चाहती थी कि बहिन के घर का कुछ हाल पूछे, मगर निर्मला उसे पूछने का अवसर न देती थी। जानती थी कि यह जो बातें पूछेगी उसके बताने में मुझे संकोच होगा। आखिर एक बार कृष्णा पूछ ही बैठी—जीजाजी भी आयेंगे न?

निर्मला—आने को कहा तो है।

कृष्णा—अब तो तुमसे प्रसन्न रहते हैं न या अब भी वही हाल है? मैं तो सुना करती थी दुहाजू पति स्त्री को प्राणों से भी प्रिया समझते हैं, वहां बिलकुल उल्टी बात देखी। आखिर किस बात पर बिगड़ते रहते हैं?

निर्मला—अब मैं किसी के मन की बात क्या जानूं?

कृष्णा—मैं तो समझती हूं, तुम्हारी रुखाई से वह चिढ़ते होंगे। तुम तो यहीं से जली हुई गई थी। वहां भी उन्हें कुछ कहा होगा।

निर्मला—यह बात नहीं है, कृष्णा, मैं सौगन्ध खाकर कहती हूं, जो मेरे मन में उनकी ओर से जरा भी मैल हो। मुझसे जहां तक हो सकता है, उनकी सेवा करती हूं, अगर उनकी जगह कोई देवता भी होता, तो भी मैं इससे ज्यादा और कुछ न कर सकती। उन्हें भी मुझसे प्रेम है। बराबर मेरा मुख देखते रहते हैं, लेकिन जो बात उनके और मेरे काबू के बाहर है, उसके लिए वह क्या कर सकते हैं और मैं क्या कर सकती हूं? न वह जवान हो सकते हैं, न मैं बुढ़िया हो सकती हूं। जवान बनने के लिए वह न जाने कितने रस और भस्म खाते रहते हैं, मैं बुढ़िया बनने के लिए दूध-घी सब छोड़े बैठी हूं। सोचती हूं, मेरे दुबलेपन ही से अवस्था का भेद कुछ कम हो जाए, लेकिन न उन्हें पौष्टिक पदार्थों से कुछ लाभ होता है, न मुझे उपवासों से। जब से मंसाराम का देहान्त हो गया है, तब से उनकी दशा और खराब हो गयी है।

कृष्णा—मंसाराम को तुम भी बहुत प्यार करती थीं?

निर्मला—वह लड़का ही ऐसा था कि जो देखता था, प्यार करता था। ऐसी बड़ी-बड़ी डोरेदार आंखें मैंने किसी की नहीं देखीं। कमल की

भांति मुख हरदम खिला रहता था। ऐसा साहसी कि अगर अवसर आ पड़ता, तो आग में फांद जाता। कृष्णा, मैं तुमसे कहती हूं, जब वह मेरे पास आकर बैठ जाता, तो मैं अपने को भूल जाती थी। जी चाहता था, वह हरदम सामने बैठा रहे और मैं देखा करुं। मेरे मन में पाप का लेश भी न था। अगर एक क्षण के लिए भी मैंने उसकी ओर किसी और भाव से देखा हो, तो मेरी आंखें फूट जाएं, पर न जाने क्यों उसे अपने पास देखकर मेरा हृदय फूला न समाता था। इसीलिए मैंने पढ़ने का स्वांग रचा नहीं तो वह घर में आता ही न था। यह मै जानती हूं कि अगर उसके मन में पाप होता, तो मैं उसके लिए सब कुछ कर सकती थी।

कृष्णा–अरे बहिन, चुप रहो, कैसी बातें मुंह से निकालती हो?

निर्मला–हां, यह बात सुनने में बुरी मालूम होती है और है भी बुरी, लेकिन मनुष्य की प्रकृति को तो कोई बदल नहीं सकता। तू ही बता–एक पचास वर्ष के मर्द से तेरा विवाह हो जाए, तो तू क्या करेगी?

कृष्णा–बहिन, मैं तो जहर खाकर सो रहूं। मुझसे तो उसका मुंह भी न देखते बने।

निर्मला–तो बस यही समझ ले। उस लड़के ने कभी मेरी ओर आंख उठाकर नहीं देखा, लेकिन बुड्ढे तो शक्की होते ही हैं, तुम्हारे जीजा उस लड़के के दुश्मन हो गए और आखिर उसकी जान लेकर ही छोड़ी। जिसे दिन उसे मालूम हो गया कि पिताजी के मन में मेरी ओर से सन्देह है, उसी दिन से उसे ज्वर चढ़ा, जो जान लेकर ही उतरा। हाय! उस अन्तिम समय का दृश्य आंखों से नहीं उतरता। मैं अस्पताल गई थी, वह ज्वर में बेहोश पड़ा था, उठने की शक्ति न थी, लेकिन ज्यों ही मेरी आवाज सुनी, चौंककर उठ बैठा और 'माता-माता' कहकर मेरे पैरों पर गिर पड़ा (रोकर) कृष्णा, उस समय ऐसा जी चाहता था अपने प्राण निकाल कर उसे दे दूं। मेरे पैरों पर ही वह मूर्छित हो गया और फिर आंखें न खोली। डॉक्टर ने उसकी देह मे ताजा खून डालने का प्रस्ताव किया था, यही सुनकर मैं दौड़ी गई थी लेकिन जब तक डॉक्टर लोग वह प्रक्रिया आरम्भ करें, उसके प्राण, निकल गए।

कृष्णा–ताजा रक्त पड़ जाने से उसकी जान बच जाती?

निर्मला–कौन जानता है? लेकिन मैं तो अपने रुधिर की अन्तिम बूंद तक देने का तैयार थी उस दशा में भी उसका मुखमण्डल दीपक की भांति चमकता था। अगर वह मुझे देखते ही दौड़कर मेरे पैरों पर न गिर पड़ता, पहले कुछ रक्त देह में पहुंच जाता, तो शायद बच जाता।

कृष्णा–तो तुमने उन्हें उसी वक्त लिटा क्यों न दिया?

निर्मला–अरे पगली, तू अभी तक बात न समझी। वह मेरे पैरों पर गिरकर और माता-पुत्र का सम्बन्ध दिखाकर अपने बाप के दिल से वह सन्देह निकाल देना चाहता था। केवल इसीलिए वह उठा था। मेरा क्लेश मिटाने के लिए उसने प्राण दिये और उसकी वह इच्छा पूरी हो गई। तुम्हारे जीजाजी उसी दिन से सीधे हो गये। अब तो उनकी दशा पर मुझे दया आती है। पुत्र-शोक उनके प्राण लेकर छोड़ेगा। मुझ पर सन्देह करके मेरे साथ ज़ो अन्याय किया है, अब उसका प्रतिशोध कर रहे हैं। अबकी उनकी सूरत देखकर तू डर जाएगी। बूढ़े बाबा हो गये हैं, कमर भी कुछ झुक चली है।

कृष्णा–बुड्ढे लोग इतनी शक्की क्यों होते हैं, बहिन?

निर्मला–यह जाकर बुड्ढों से पूछो।

कृष्णा–मैं समझती हूं, उनके दिल में हरदम एक चोर-सा बैठा रहता होगा कि इस युवती को प्रसन्न नहीं रख सकता। इसलिए जरा–जरा–सी बात पर उन्हें शक होने लगता है।

निर्मला–जानती तो है, फिर मुझसे क्यों पूछती है?

कृष्णा–इसीलिए बेचारा स्त्री से दबता भी होगा। देखने वाले समझते होंगे कि यह बहुत प्रेम करता है।

निर्मला–तूने इतने ही दिनों में इतनी बातें कहां सीख लीं? इन बातों को जाने दे, बता, तुझे अपना वर पसन्द है? उसकी तस्वीर तो देखी होगी?

कृष्णा–हां, आई तो थी, लाऊं, देखोगी?

एक क्षण में कृष्णा ने तस्वीर लाकर निर्मला के हाथ में रख दी।

निर्मला ने मुस्कराकर कहा–तू बड़ी भाग्यवान् है।

कृष्णा–अम्माजी ने भी बहुत पसन्द किया।

निर्मला–तुझे पसन्द है कि नहीं, सो कह, दूसरों की बात न चला।

कृष्णा–(लजाती हुई) शकल-सूरत तो बुरी नहीं है, स्वभाव का हाल ईश्वर जाने। शास्त्रीजी तो कहते थे, ऐसे सुशील और चरित्रवान् युवक कम होंगे।

निर्मला–यहां से तेरी तस्वीर भी गई थी?

कृष्णा–गई तो थी, शास्त्रीजी ही तो ले गए थे।

निर्मला–उन्हें पसन्द आई?

कृष्णा–अब किसी के मन की बात मैं क्या जानूं? शास्त्री जी कहते थे, बहुत खुश हुए थे।

निर्मला–अच्छा, बता, तुझे क्या उपहार दूं? अभी से बता दे, जिससे बनवा रखूं।

कृष्णा–जो तुम्हारा जी चाहे, देना। उन्हें पुस्तकों से बहुत प्रेम है। अच्छी-अच्छी पुस्तकें मंगवा देना।

निर्मला–उनके लिए नहीं पूछती तेरे लिए पूछती हूं।

कृष्णा–अपने ही लिये तो मैं कह रही हूं।

निर्मला–(तस्वीर की तरफ देखती हुई) कपड़े सब खद्दर के मालूम होते हैं।

कृष्णा–हां, खद्दर के बड़े प्रेमी हैं। सुनती हूं कि पीठ पर खद्दर लाद कर देहातों में बेचने जाया करते हैं। व्याख्यान देने में भी चतुर हैं।

निर्मला–तब तो तुझे भी खद्दर पहनना पड़ेगा। तुझे तो मोटे कपड़ों से चिढ़ है।

कृष्णा–जब उन्हें मोटे कपड़े अच्छे लगते हैं, तो मुझे क्यों चिढ़ होगी, मैंने तो चर्खा चलाना सीख लिया है।

निर्मला–सच! सूत निकाल लेती है?

कृष्णा–हां, बहिन, थोड़ा-थोड़ा निकाल लेती हूं। जब वह खद्दर के इतने प्रेमी हैं, तो चर्खा भी जरुर चलाते होंगे। मैं न चला सकूंगी, तो मुझे कितना लज्जित होना पड़ेगा।

इस तरह बात करते-करते दोनों बहिनों सोईं। कोई दो बजे रात को बच्ची रोई तो निर्मला की नींद खुली। देखा तो कृष्णा की चारपाई खाली पड़ी थी। निर्मला को आश्चर्य हुआ कि इतना रात गये कृष्णा कहां

चली गई। शायद पानी-वानी पीने गई हो। मगर पानी तो सिरहाने रखा हुआ है, फिर कहां गई है? उसे दो-तीन बार उसका नाम लेकर आवाज दी, पर कृष्णा का पता न था। तब तो निर्मला घबरा उठी। उसके मन में भांति-भांति की शंकाएं होने लगी। सहसा उसे ख्याल आया कि शायद अपने कमरे में न चली गई हो। बच्ची सो गई, तो वह उठकर कृष्णा के कमरे के द्वार पर आई। उसका अनुमान ठीक था, कृष्णा अपने कमरे में थी। सारा घर सो रहा था और वह बैठी चर्खा चला रही थी। इतनी तन्मयता से शायद उसने थिऐटर भी न देखा होगा।

निर्मला दंग रह गई। अन्दर जाकर बोली–यह क्या कर रही है रे! यह चर्खा चलाने का समय है?

कृष्णा चौंककर उठ बैठी और संकोच से सिर झुकाकर बोली–तुम्हारी नींद कैसे खुल गई? पानी-वानी तो मैंने रख दिया था।

निर्मला–मैं कहती हूं, दिन को तुझे समय नहीं मिलता, जो पिछली रात को चर्खा लेकर बैठी है?

कृष्णा–दिन को फुरसत ही नहीं मिलती?

निर्मला–(सूत देखकर) सूत तो बहुत महीन है।

कृष्णा–कहां बहिन, यह सूत तो मोटा है। मैं बारीक सूत कातकर उनके लिए साफा बनाना चाहती हूं। यही मेरा उपहार होगा।

निर्मला–बात तो तूने खूब सोची है। इससे अधिक मूल्यवान वस्तु उनकी दृष्टि में और क्या होगी? अच्छा, उठ इस वक्त, कल कातना! कहीं बीमार पड़ जाएगी, तो सब धरा रह जाएगा।

कृष्णा–नहीं मेरी बहिन, तुम चलकर सोओ, मैं अभी आती हूं।

निर्मला ने अधिक आग्रह न किया, लेटने चली गई। मगर किसी तरह नींद न आई। कृष्णा की उत्सुकता और यह उमंग देखकर उसका हृदय किसी अलक्षित आकांक्षा से आन्दोलित हो उठा ओह! इस समय इसका हृदय कितना प्रफुल्लित हो रहा है। अनुराग ने इसे कितना उन्मत्त कर रखा है। तब उसे अपने विवाह की याद आई। जिस दिन तिलक गया था, उसी दिन से उसकी सारी चंचलता, सारी सजीवता विदा हो गई थी। अपनी कोठरी में बैठी वह अपनी किस्मत को रोती थी और ईश्वर से विनय करती थी कि प्राण निकल जाए।

अपराधी जैसे दंड की प्रतीक्षा करता है, उसी भांति वह विवाह की प्रतीक्षा करती थी, उस विवाह की, जिसमें उसके जीवन की सारी अभिलाषाएं विलीन हो जाएंगी, जब मण्डप के नीचे बने हुए हवन-कुण्ड में उसकी आशाएं जलकर भस्म हो जाएंगी।

महीना कटते देर न लगी। विवाह का शुभ मुहूर्त आ पहुंचा मेहमानों से घर भर गया। मुंशी तोताराम एक दिन पहले आ गये और उनके साथ निर्मला की सहेली भी आई। निर्मला ने बहुत आग्रह न किया था, वह खुद आने को उत्सुक थी। निर्मला की सबसे बड़ी उत्कंठा यही थी कि वर के बड़े भाई के दर्शन करुंगी और हो सका तो उसकी सुबुद्धि पर धन्यवाद दूंगी। सुधा ने हंस कर कहा–तुम उनसे बोल सकोगी?

निर्मला–क्यों, बोलने में क्या हानि है? अब तो दूसरा ही सम्बन्ध हो गया और मैं न बोल सकूंगी, तो तुम तो हो ही।

सुधा–न भाई, मुझसे यह न होगा। मैं पराये मर्द से नहीं बोल सकती। न जाने कैसे आदमी हों।

निर्मला–आदमी तो बुरे नहीं है, और फिर उनसे कुछ विवाह तो करना नहीं, जरा-सा बोलने में क्या हानि है? डॉक्टर साहब यहां होते, तो मैं तुम्हें आज्ञा दिला देती।

सुधा–जो लोग हुदय के उदार होते हैं, क्या चरित्र के भी अच्छे होते है? पराई स्त्री की घूरने में तो किसी मर्द को संकोच नहीं होता।

निर्मला–अच्छा न बोलना, मैं ही बातें कर लूंगी, घूर लेंगे जितना उनसे घूरते बनेगा, बस, अब तो राजी हुई।

इतने में कृष्णा आकर बैठ गई। निर्मला ने मुस्कराकर कहा–सच बता कृष्णा, तेरा मन इस वक्त क्यों उचाट हो रहा है?

कृष्णा–जीजाजी बुला रहे हैं, पहले जाकर सुन आओ, पीछे गप्पें लड़ाना बहुत बिगड़ रहे हैं।

निर्मला–क्या है, तूने कुछ पूछा नहीं?

कृष्णा–कुछ बीमार से मालूम होते हैं। बहुत दुबले हो गए हैं।

निर्मला—तो जरा बैठकर उनका मन बहला देती। यहां दौड़ी क्यों चली आई? यह कहो, ईश्वर ने कृपा की, नहीं तो ऐसा ही पुरुष तुझे भी मिलता। जरा बैठकर बातें करो। बुड्ढे बातें बड़ी लच्छेदार करते हैं। जवान इतने डींगियल नहीं होते।

कृष्णा—नहीं बहिन, तुम जाओ, मुझसे तो वहां बैठा नहीं जाता।

निर्मला चली गई, तो सुधा ने कृष्णा से कहा—अब तो बारात आ गई होगी। द्वार-पूजा क्यों नही होती?

कृष्णा—क्या जाने बहिन, शास्त्रीजी सामान इकट्ठा कर रहे हैं?

सुधा—सुना है, दूल्हे की भावज बड़े कड़े स्वाभाव की स्त्री है।

कृष्णा—कैसे मालूम?

सुधा—मैंने सुना है, इसीलिए चेताये देती हूं। चार बातें गम खाकर रहना होगा।

कृष्णा—मेरी झगड़ने की आदत नहीं। जब मेरी तरफ से कोई शिकायत ही न पायेंगी तो क्या अनायास ही बिगड़ेगी!

सुधा—हां, सुना तो ऐसा ही है। झूठ-मूठ लड़ा करती है।

कृष्णा—मैं तो सौ बात की एक बात जानती हूं, नम्रता पत्थर को भी मोम कर देती है।

सहसा शोर मचा—बारात आ रही है। दोनों रमणियां खिड़की के सामने आ बैठीं। एक क्षण में निर्मला भी आ पहुंची।

वर के बड़े भाई को देखने की उसे बड़ी उत्सुकता हो रही थी।

सुधा ने कहा—कैसे पता चलेगा कि बड़े भाई कौन हैं?

निर्मला—शास्त्रीजी से पूछूं, तो मालूम हो। हाथी पर तो कृष्णा के ससुर महाशय हैं। अच्छा डॉक्टर साहब यहां कैसे आ पहुँचे! वह घोड़े पर क्या हैं, देखती नहीं हो?

सुधा—हां, हैं तो वही।

निर्मला—उन लोगों से मित्रता होगी। कोई सम्बन्ध तो नहीं है।

सुधा—अब भेंट हो तो पूछूं, मुझे तो कुछ नहीं मालूम।

निर्मला—पालकी मे जो महाशय बैठे हुए हैं, वह तो दूल्हा के भाई जैसे नहीं दीखते।

सुधा–बिलकुल नहीं। मालूम होता है, सारी देह मे पेट-ही-पेट है।

निर्मला–दूसरे हाथी पर कौन बैठा है, समझ में नही आता।

सुधा–कोई हो, दूल्हा का भाई नहीं हो सकता। उसकी उम्र नहीं देखती हो, चालीस के ऊपर होगी।

निर्मला–शास्त्रीजी तो इस वक्त द्वार-पूजा कि फिक्र में हैं, नहीं तो उनसे पूछती।

संयोग से नाई आ गया। सन्दूकों की कुंजियां निर्मला के पास थीं। इस वक्त द्वारचार के लिए कुछ रुपये की जरुरत थी, माता ने भेजा था, यह नाई भी पण्डित मोटेराम जी के साथ तिलक लेकर गया था।

निर्मला ने कहा–क्या अभी रुपये चाहिए?

नाई–हां बहिनजी, चलकर दे दीजिए।

निर्मला–अच्छा चलती हूं। पहले यह बता, तू दूल्हा के बड़े भाई को पहचानता है?

नाई–पहचानता काहे नहीं, वह क्या सामने हैं।

निर्मला–कहां, मैं तो नहीं देखती?

नाई–अरे वह क्या घोड़े पर सवार हैं। वही तो हैं।

निर्मला ने चकित होकर कहा–क्या कहता है, घोड़े पर दूल्हा के भाई हैं! पहचानता है या अटकल से कह रहा है?

नाई–अरे बहिनजी, क्या इतना भूल जाऊंगा अभी तो जलपान का सामान दिये चला आता हूं।

निर्मल–अरे, यह तो डॉक्टर साहब हैं। मेरे पड़ोस में रहते हैं।

नाई–हां-हां, वही तो डॉक्टर साहब हैं।

निर्मला ने सुधा की ओर देखकर कहा–सुनती हो बहिन, इसकी बातें? सुधा ने हंसी रोककर कहा–झूठ बोलता है।

नाई–अच्छा साहब, झूठ ही सही, अब बड़ों के मुंह कौन लगे! अभी शास्त्रीजी से पूछवा दूंगा, तब तो मानिएगा?

नाई के आने में देर हुई, मोटेराम खुद आंगन में आकर शोर मचाने लगे–इस घर की मर्यादा रखना ईश्वर ही के हाथ है। नाई घण्टे भर से आया हुआ है, और अभी तक रुपये नहीं मिले।

निर्मला–जरा यहां चले आइएगा शास्त्रीजी, कितने रुपये दरकरार हैं, निकाल दूं?

शास्त्रीजी भुनभुनाते और जोर-जोर से हांफते हुए ऊपर आये और एक लम्बी सांस लेकर बोले–क्या है? यह बातों का समय नहीं है, जल्दी से रुपये निकाल दो।

निर्मला–लीजिए, निकाल तो रहीं हूं। अब क्या मुंह के बल गिर पड़ूं? पहले यह बताइए कि दूल्हा के बड़े भाई कौन हैं?

शास्त्रीजी–राम–राम, इतनी-सी बात के लिए मुझे आकाश पर लटका दिया। नाई क्या न पहचानता था?

निर्मला–नाई तो कहता है कि वह जो घोड़े पर सवार है, वही हैं।

शास्त्रीजी–तो फिर किसे बता दे? वही तो हैं ही।

नाई–घड़ी भर से कह रहा हूं, पर बहिनजी मानती ही नहीं।

निर्मला ने सुधा की ओर स्नेह, ममता, विनोद कृत्रिम तिरस्कार की दृष्टि से देखकर कहा–अच्छा, तो तुम्ही अब तक मेरे साथ यह त्रिया-चरित्र खेल रही थी! मैं जानती, तो तुम्हें यहां बुलाती ही नहीं। ओफ्फोह! बड़ा गहरा पेट है तुम्हारा! तुम महीनों से मेरे साथ शरारत करती चली आती हो, और कभी भूल से भी इस विषय का एक शब्द तुम्हारे मुंह से नहीं निकला। मैं तो दो-चार ही दिन में उबल पड़ती।

सुधा–तुम्हें मालूम हो जाता, तो तुम मेरे यहां आती ही क्यों?

निर्मला–गजब-रे-गजब, मैं डॉक्टर साहब से कई बार बातें कर चुकी हूं। तुम्हारे ऊपर यह सारा पाप पड़ेगा। देखा कृष्णा, तूने अपनी जेठानी की शरारत! यह ऐसी मायाविनी है, इनसे डरती रहना।

कृष्णा–मैं तो ऐसी देवी के चरण धो-धोकर माथे चढ़ाऊंगी। धन्य-भाग कि इनके दर्शन हुए।

निर्मला–अब समझ गई। रुपये भी तुम्हीं ने भिजवाये होंगे। अब सिर हिलाया तो सच कहती हूं, मार बैठूंगी।

सुधा–अपने घर बुलाकर के मेहमान का अपमान नहीं किया जाता।

निर्मला–देखो तो अभी कैसी-कैसी खबरे लेती हूं। मैंने तुम्हारा मान रखने को जरा-सा लिख दिया था और तुम सचमुच आ पहुंची। भला वहां वाले क्या कहते होंगे?

सुधा–सबसे कहकर आई हूं।

निर्मला–अब तुम्हारे पास कभी न आऊंगी। इतना तो इशारा कर देतीं कि डॉक्टर साहब से पर्दा रखना।

सुधा–उनके देख लेने ही से कौन बुराई हो गई? न देखते तो अपनी किस्मत को रोते कैसे? जानते कैसे कि लोभ में पड़कर कैसी चीज खो दी? अब तो तुम्हें देखकर लालाजी हाथ मलकर रह जाते हैं। मुंह से तो कुछ नहीं कहते, पर मन में अपनी भूल पर पछताते हैं।

निर्मला–अब तुम्हारे घर कभी न आऊंगी।

सुधा–अब पिण्ड नहीं छूट सकता। मैंने कौन तुम्हारे घर की राह नहीं देखी है।

द्वार-पूजा समाप्त हो चुकी थी। मेहमान लोग बैठे जलपान कर रहे थे। मुंशीजी की बगल में ही डॉक्टर सिन्हा बैठे हुए थे। निर्मला ने कोठे पर चिक की आड़ से उन्हें देखा और कलेजा थामकर रह गई। एक आरोग्य, यौवन और प्रतिभा का देवता था, पर दूसरा...इस विषय में कुछ न कहना ही उचित है। निर्मला ने डॉक्टर साहब को सैकड़ों ही बार देखा था, पर आज उसके हृदय में जो विचार उठे, वे कभी न उठे थे। बार-बार यह जी चाहता था कि बुलाकर खूब फटकारुं, ऐसे-ऐसे ताने मारुं कि वह भी याद करें, रुला-रुलाकर छोड़ूं, मगर रहम करके रह जाती थी।

बारात जनवासे चली गई थी। भोजन की तैयारी हो रही थी। निर्मला भोजन के थाल चुनने में व्यस्त थी। सहसा महरी ने आकर कहा–बिट्टी, तुम्हें सुधा रानी बुला रही है। तुम्हारे कमरे में बैठी हैं।

निर्मला ने थाल छोड़ दिये और घबराई हुई सुधा के पास आई, मगर अन्दर कदम रखते ही ठिठक गई, डॉक्टर सिन्हा खड़े थे।

सुधा ने मुस्कराकर कहा–लो बहिन, बुला दिया। अब जितना चाहो, फटकारो। मैं दरवाजा रोके खड़ी हूं, भाग नहीं सकते।

डॉक्टर साहब ने गम्भीर भाव से कहा–भागता कौन है? यहां तो सिर झुकाए खड़ा हूं।

निर्मला ने हाथ जोड़कर कहा–इसी तरह सदा कृपा-दृष्टि रखिएगा, भूल न जाइएगा। यह मेरी विनय है।

11

कृष्णा के विवाह के बाद सुधा चली गई, लेकिन निर्मला मैके ही में रह गई। वकील साहब बार-बार लिखते थे, पर वह न जाती थी। वहां जाने को उसका जी न चाहता था। वहां कोई ऐसी चीज न थी, जो उसे खींच ले जाए। यहां माता की सेवा और छोटे भाइयों की देखभाल में उसका समय बड़े आनन्द के कट जाता था।

वकील साहब खुद आते तो शायद वह जाने पर राजी हो जाती, लेकिन इस विवाह में, मुहल्ले की लड़कियों ने उनकी वह दुर्गत की थी कि बेचारे आने का नाम ही न लेते थे। सुधा ने भी कई बार पत्र लिखा, पर निर्मला ने उससे भी हीले-हवा़ले किये। आखिर एक दिन सुधा ने नौकर को साथ लिया और स्वयं आ धमकी।

जब दोनों गले मिल चुकीं, तो सुधा ने कहा–तुम्हें तो वहां जाते मानो डर लगता है।

निर्मला–हां बहिन, डर तो लगता है। ब्याह की गई तीन साल में आई, अब की तो वहां उम्र ही खत्म हो जाएगी, फिर कौन बुलाता है और कौन आता है?

सुधा–आने को क्या हुआ, जब जी चाहे चली आना। वहां वकील साहब बहुत बेचैन हो रहे हैं।

निर्मला–बहुत बेचैन, रात को शायद नींद न आती हो।

सुधा–बहिन, तुम्हारा कलेजा पत्थर का है। उनकी दशा देखकर तरस आता है। कहते थे, घर मे कोई पूछने वाला नहीं, न कोई लड़का, न बाला, किससे जी बहलायें? जब से दूसरे मकान में उठ आए हैं, बहुत दुखी रहते हैं।

निर्मला–लड़के तो ईश्वर के दिये दो-दो हैं।

सुधा–उन दोनों की तो बड़ी शिकायत करते थे। जियाराम तो अब बात ही नहीं सुनता–तुर्की-बतुर्की जवाब देता है। रहा छोटा, वह भी उसी के कहने में है। बेचारे बड़े लड़के की याद करके रोया करते हैं।

निर्मला–जियाराम तो शरीर न था, वह बदमाशी कब से सीख गया? मेरी तो कोई बात न टालता था, इशारे पर काम करता था।

सुधा–क्या जाने बहिन, सुना, कहता है, आप ही ने भैया को जहर देकर मार डाला, आप हत्यारे हैं। कई बार तुमसे विवाह करने के लिए ताने दे चुका है। ऐसी-ऐसी बातें कहता है कि वकील साहब रो पड़ते हैं। अरे, और तो क्या कहूं, एक दिन पत्थर उठाकर मारने दौड़ा था।

निर्मला ने गम्भीर चिन्ता में पड़कर कहा–यह लड़का तो बड़ा शैतान निकला। उसे यह किसने कहा कि उसके भाई को उन्होंने जहर दे दिया है?

सुधा–वह तुम्हीं से ठीक होगा।

निर्मला को यह नई चिन्ता पैदा हुई। अगर जिया का यही रंग है, अपने बाप से लड़ने पर तैयार रहता है, तो मुझसे क्यों दबने लगा? वह रात को बड़ी देर तक इसी फिक्र मे डूबी रही।

मंसाराम की आज उसे बहुत याद आई। उसके साथ जिन्दगी आराम से कट जाती। इस लड़के का जब अपने पिता के सामने ही वह हाल है, तो उनके पीछे उसके साथ कैसे निर्वाह होगा! घर हाथ से निकल ही गया। कुछ-न-कुछ कर्ज अभी सिर पर होगा ही, आमदनी का यह हाल। ईश्वर ही बेड़ा पार लगायेंगे।

आज पहली बार निर्मला को बच्चों की फिक्र पैदा हुई। इस बेचारी का न जाने क्या हाल होगा? ईश्वर ने यह विपत्ति सिर डाल दी। मुझे तो इसकी जरुरत न थी। जन्म ही लेना था, तो किसी भाग्यवान के घर जन्म लेती। बच्ची उसकी छाती से लिपटी हुई सो रही थी। माता ने उसको और भी चिपटा लिया, मानो कोई उसके हाथ से उसे छीने लिये जाता है।

निर्मला के पास ही सुधा की चारपाई भी थी। निर्मला तो चिन्ता सागर मे गोता खा रही थी और सुधा मीठी नींद का आनन्द उठा रही थी। क्या उसे अपने बालक की फिक्र सताती है? मृत्यु तो बूढ़े और

जवान का भेद नहीं करती, फिर सुधा को कोई चिन्ता क्यों नहीं सताती? उसे तो कभी भविष्य की चिन्ता से उदास नहीं देखा।

सहसा सुधा की नींद खुल गई। उसने निर्मला को अभी तक जागते देखा, तो बोली–अरे अभी तुम सोई नहीं?

निर्मला–नींद ही नहीं आती।

सुधा–आंखें बन्द कर लो, आप ही नींद आ जाएगी। मैं तो चारपाई पर आते ही मर-सी जाती हूं। वह जागते भी हैं, तो खबर नहीं होती। न जाने मुझे क्यों इतनी नींद आती है। शायद कोई रोग है।

निर्मला–हां, बड़ा भारी रोग है। इसे राज-रोग कहते हैं। डॉक्टर साहब से कहो–दवा शुरु कर दें।

सुधा–तो आखिर जागकर क्या सोचूं? कभी-कभी मैके की याद आ जाती है, तो उस दिन जरा देर में आंख लगती है।

निर्मला–डॉक्टर साहब की याद नहीं आती?

सुधा–कभी नहीं, उनकी याद क्यों आये? जानती हूं कि टेनिस खेलकर आए होंगे, खाना खाया होगा और आराम से लेटे होंगे।

निर्मला–लो, सोहन भी जाग गया। जब तुम जाग गईं तो भला यह क्यों सोने लगा?

सुधा–हां बहिन, इसकी अजीब आदत है। मेरे साथ सोता और मेरे ही साथ जागता है। उस जन्म का कोई तपस्वी है। देखो, इसके माथे पर तिलक का कैसा निशान है। बांहों पर भी ऐसे ही निशान हैं। जरुर कोई तपस्वी है।

निर्मला–तपस्वी लोग तो चन्दन-तिलक नहीं लगाते। उस जन्म का कोई धूर्त पुजारी होगा। क्यों रे, तू कहां का पुजारी था? बता?

सुधा–इसका ब्याह मैं बच्ची से करुंगी।

निर्मला–चलो बहिन, गाली देती हो। बहिन से भी भाई का ब्याह होता है?

सुधा–मैं तो करुंगी, चाहे कोई कुछ कहे। ऐसी सुन्दर बहू और कहां पाऊंगी? जरा देखो तो बहन, इसकी देह कुछ गर्म है या मुझे ही मालूम होती है।

निर्मला ने सोहन का माथा छूकर कहा–नहीं-नहीं, देह गर्म है। यह ज्वर कब आ गया! दूध तो पी रहा है न?

सुधा–अभी सोया था, तब तो देह ठंडी थी। शायद सर्दी लग गई, उढ़ाकर सुलाये देती हूं। सबेरे तक ठीक हो जाएगा।

सबेरा हुआ तो सोहन की दशा और भी खराब हो गई। उसकी नाक बहने लगी और बुखार और भी तेज हो गया। आंखें चढ़ गईं और सिर झुक गया। न वह हाथ-पैर हिलाता था, न हंसता-बोलता था, बस, चुपचाप पड़ा था। ऐसा मालूम होता था कि उसे इस वक्त किसी का बोलना अच्छा नहीं लगता। कुछ-कुछ खांसी भी आने लगी। अब तो सुधा घबराई।

निर्मला की भी राय हुई कि डॉक्टर साहब को बुलाया जाए, लेकिन उसकी बूढ़ी माता ने कहा–डॉक्टर-हकीम साहब का यहां कुछ काम नहीं। साफ तो देख रही हूं कि बच्चे को नजर लग गई है। भला डॉक्टर आकर क्या करेंगे?

सुधा–अम्मांजी, भला यहां नजर कौन लगा देगा? अभी तक तो बाहर कहीं गया भी नहीं।

माता–नजर कोई लगाता नहीं बेटी, किसी-किसी आदमी की दीठ बुरी होती है, आप-ही-आप लग जाती है। कभी-कभी मां-बाप तक की नजर लग जाती है। जब से आया है, एक बार भी नहीं रोया। चोंचले बच्चों की यही गति होती है। मैं इसे हुमकते देखकर डरी थी कि कुछ-न-कुछ अनिष्ट होने वाला है। आंखें नहीं देखती हो, कितनी चढ़ गई हैं। यही नजर की सबसे बड़ी पहचान है।

बुढ़िया महरी और पड़ोस की पंडिताइन ने इस कथन का अनुमोदन कर दिया। बस महंगू ने आकर बच्चे का मुंह देखा और हंस कर बोला–मालकिन, यह दीठ है और कुछ नहीं। जरा पतली-पतली तीलियां मंगवा दीजिए। भगवान ने चाहा तो संझा तक बच्चा हंसने लगेगा।

सरकण्डे के पांच टुकड़े लाये गये। महगूं ने उन्हें बराबर करके एक डोरे से बांध दिया और कुछ बुदबुदाकर उसी पोले हाथों से पांच बार सोहन का सिर सहलाया। अब जो देखा, तो पांचों तीलियां छोटी-बड़ी

हो गई थी। सब स्त्रियां यह कौतुक देखकर दंग रह गईं। अब नजर में किसे सन्देह हो सकता था। महगूं ने फिर बच्चे को तीलियों से सहलाना शुरु किया। अब की तीलियां बराबर हो गईं। केवल थोड़ा-सा अन्तर रह गया। यह सब इस बात का प्रमाण था कि नजर का असर अब थोड़ा-सा और रह गया है। महगूं सबको दिलासा देकर शाम को फिर आने का वायदा करके चला गया।

बालक की दशा दिन को और खराब हो गई। खांसी का जोर हो गया। शाम के समय महगूं ने आकर फिर तीलियों का तमाशा किया। इस वक्त पांचों तीलियों बराबर निकलीं। स्त्रियां निश्चिंत हो गईं लेकिन सोहन को सारी रात खांसते गुजरी। यहां तक कि कई बार उसकी आंखें उलट गईं।

सुधा और निर्मला दोनों ने बैठकर सबेरा किया। खैर, रात कुशल से कट गई। अब वृद्वा माताजी नया रंग लाईं। महगूं नजर न उतार सका, इसलिए अब किसी मौलवी से फूंक डलवाना जरुरी हो गया। सुधा फिर भी अपने पति को सूचना न दे सकी। मेहरी सोहन को एक चादर से लपेट कर एक मस्जिद में ले गई और फूंक डलवा लाई, शाम को भी फूंक छोड़ी, पर सोहन ने सिर न उठाया। रात आ गई, सुधा ने मन मे निश्चय किया कि रात कुशल से बीतेगी, तो प्रातःकाल पति को तार दूंगी। लेकिन रात कुशल से न बीतने पाई।

आधी रात जाते-जाते बच्चा हाथ से निकल गया। सुधा की जीवन सम्पति देखते-देखते उसके हाथों से छिन गई।

वही जिसके विवाह का दो दिन पहले विनोद हो रहा था, आज सारे घर को रुला रहा है। जिसकी भोली-भाली सूरत देखकर माता की छाती फूल उठती थी, उसी को देखकर आज माता की छाती फटी जाती है। सारा घर सुधा को समझाता था, पर उसके आंसू न थमते थे, सब्र न होता था। सबसे बड़ा दुःख इस बात का था का पति को कौन मुंह दिखलाऊंगी! उन्हें खबर तक न दी।

रात ही को तार दे दिया गया और दूसरे दिन डॉक्टर सिन्हा नौ बजते-बजते मोटर पर आ पहुंचे। सुधा ने उनके आने की खबर पाई,

तो और भी फूट-फूटकर रोने लगी। बालक की जल-क्रिया हुई, डॉक्टर साहब कई बार अन्दर आये, किन्तु सुधा उनके पास न गई। उनके सामने कैसे जाए? कौन मुंह दिखाये? उसने अपनी नादानी से उनके जीवन का रत्न छीनकर दरिया में डाल दिया।

अब उनके पास जाते उसकी छाती के टुकड़े-टुकड़े हुए जाते थे। बालक को उसकी गोद में देखकर पति की आंखे चमक उठती थीं। बालक हुमककर पिता की गोद में चला जाता था। माता फिर बुलाती, तो पिता की छाती से चिपट जाता था और लाख चुमकारने-दुलारने पर भी बाप की गोद न छोड़ता था। तब मां कहती थी–बड़ा मतलबी है।

आज वह किसे गोद मे लेकर पति के पास जाएगी? उसकी सूनी गोद देखकर कहीं वह चिल्लाकर रो न पड़ें। पति के सम्मुख जाने की अपेक्षा उसे मर जाना कहीं आसान जान पड़ता था। वह एक क्षण के लिए भी निर्मला को न छोड़ती थी कि कहीं पति से सामना न हो जाए।

निर्मला ने कहा–बहिन, जो होना था वह हो चुका, अब उनसे कब तक भागती फिरोगी। रात ही को चले जाएंगे। अम्मां कहती थीं।

सुधा से सजल नेत्रों से ताकते हुए कहा–कौन मुंह लेकर उनके पास जाऊं? मुझे डर लग रहा है कि उनके सामने जाते ही मेरे पैर न थर्राने लगे और मैं गिर पडूं।

निर्मला–चलो, मैं तुम्हारे साथ चलती हूं। तुम्हें संभाले रहूंगी।

सुधा–मुझे छोड़कर भाग तो न जाओगी?

निर्मला–नहीं-नहीं, भागूंगी नहीं।

सुधा–मेरा कलेजा तो अभी से उमड़ा आता है। मैं इतना घोर व्रजपात होने पर भी बैठी हूं, मुझे यही आश्चर्य हो रहा है। सोहन को वह बहुत प्यार करते थे बहिन। न जाने उनके चित्त की क्या दशा होगी। मैं उन्हें ढाढ़स क्या दूंगी, आप ही रोती रहूंगी। क्या रात ही को चले जाएंगे?

निर्मला–हां, अम्मांजी तो कहती थी छुट्टी नहीं ली है।

दोनो सहेलियां मर्दाने कमरे की ओर चलीं, लेकिन कमरे के द्वार पर पहुंचकर सुधा ने निर्मला को विदा कर दिया। अकेली कमरे मे दाखिल हुई।

डॉक्टर साहब घबरा रहे थे कि न जाने सुधा की क्या दशा हो रही है। भांति-भांति की शंकाएं मन मे आ रही थीं। जाने को तैयार बैठे थे, लेकिन जी न चाहता था। जीवन शून्य-सा मालूम होता था। मन-ही-मन कुढ़ रहे थे, अगर ईश्वर को इतनी जल्दी यह पदार्थ देकर छीन लेना था, तो दिया ही क्यों था? उन्होंने तो कभी सन्तान के लिए ईश्वर से प्रार्थना न की थी। वह आजन्म निःसन्तान रह सकते थे, पर सन्तान पाकर उससे वंचित हो जाना उन्हें असह्य जान पड़ता था।

क्या सचमुच मनुष्य ईश्वर का खिलौना है? यही मानव जीवन का महत्व है? यह केवल बालकों का घरौंदा है, जिसके बनने का न कोई हेतु है न बिगड़ने का? फिर बालकों को भी तो अपने घरौंदे से अपनी कागज की नावों से, अपनी लकड़ी के घोड़ों से ममता होती है। अच्छे खिलौने को वह जान के पीछे छिपाकर रखते हैं।

अगर ईश्वर बालक ही है तो वह विचित्र बालक है। किन्तु बुद्वि तो ईश्चर का यह रुप स्वीकार नहीं करती। अनन्त सृष्टि का कर्ता उद्दण्ड बालक नहीं हो सकता है। हम उसे उन सारे गुणों से विभूषित करते हैं, जो हमारी बुद्वि की पहुंच से बाहर हैं। खिलाड़ीपन तो उन महान् गुणों मे नहीं! क्या हंसते-खेलते बालकों का प्राण हर लेना खेल है? क्या ईश्वर ऐसा पैशाचिक खेल खेलता है?

सहसा सुधा दबे-पांव कमरे में दाखिल हुई। डॉक्टर साहब उठ खड़े हुए और उसके समीप आकर बोले—तुम कहां थी, सुधा? मैं तुम्हारी राह देख रहा था।

सुधा की आंखों से कमरा तैरता हुआ जान पड़ा। पति की गर्दन मे हाथ डालकर उसने उनकी छाती पर सिर रख दिया और रोने लगी, लेकिन इस अश्रु-प्रवाह में उसे असीम धैर्य और सांत्वना का अनुभव हो रहा था। पति के वक्ष-स्थल से लिपटी हुई वह अपने ह्रदय में एक विचित्र स्फूर्ति और बल का संचार होते हुए पाती थी, मानो पवन से थरथराता हुआ दीपक आंचल की आड़ में आ गया हो।

डॉक्टर साहब ने रमणी के अश्रु-सिंचित कपोलों को दोनो हाथो में लेकर कहा—सुधा, तुम इतना छोटा दिल क्यों करती हो? सोहन अपने

जीवन में जो कुछ करने आया था, वह कर चुका था, फिर वह क्यों बैठा रहता?

जैसे कोई वृक्ष जल और प्रकाश से बढ़ता है, लेकिन पवन के प्रबल झोकों ही से सुदृढ़ होता है, उसी भांति प्रणय भी दुःख के आघातों ही से विकास पाता है। खुशी के साथ हंसनेवाले बहुतेरे मिल जाते हैं, रंज में जो साथ रोये, वह हमारा सच्चा मित्र है। जिन प्रेमियों को साथ रोना नहीं नसीब हुआ, वे मुहब्बत के मजे क्या जानें?

सोहन की मृत्यु ने आज हमारे द्वैत को बिलकुल मिटा दिया। आज ही हमने एक दूसरे का सच्चा स्वरुप देखा है।

सुधा ने सिसकते हुए कहा—मैं नजर के धोखे में थी। हाय! तुम उसका मुंह भी न देखने पाये। न जाने इन दिनों उसे इतनी समझ कहां से आ गई थी। जब मुझे रोते देखता, तो अपने कष्ट भूलकर मुस्करा देता। तीसरे ही दिन मेरे लाडले की आंख बन्द हो गई। कुछ दवा-दर्पन भी न करने पाई।

यह कहते-कहते सुधा के आंसू फिर उमड़ आये।

डॉक्टर सिन्हा ने उसे सीने से लगाकर करुणा से कांपती हुई आवाज में कहा—प्रिये, आज तक कोई ऐसा बालक या वृद्ध न मरा होगा, जिससे घरवालों की दवा-दर्पन की लालसा पूरी हो गई।

सुधा—निर्मला ने मेरी बड़ी मदद की। मैं तो एकाध झपकी ले भी लेती थी, पर उसकी आंखें नहीं झपकी। रात-रात लिये बैठी या टहलती रहती थी। उसके अहसान कभी न भूलंगी। क्या तुम आज ही जा रहे हो?

डॉक्टर—हां, छुट्टी लेने का मौका न था। सिविल सर्जन शिकार खेलने गया हुआ था।

सुधा—यह सब हमेशा शिकार ही खेला करते हैं?

डॉक्टर—राजाओं को और काम ही क्या है?

सुधा—मैं तो आज न जाने दूंगी।

डॉक्टर—जी तो मेरा भी नहीं चाहता।

सुधा—तो मत जाओ, तार दे दो। मैं भी तुम्हारे साथ चलूंगी। निर्मला को भी लेती चलूंगी।

सुधा वहां से लौटी, तो उसके हृदय का बोझ हल्का हो गया था। पति की प्रेमपूर्ण कोमल वाणी ने उसके सारे शोक और संताप का हरण कर लिया था। प्रेम में असीम विश्वास है, असीम धैर्य है और असीम बल है।

जब हमारे ऊपर कोई बड़ी विपत्ति आ पड़ती है, तो उससे हमें केवल दुःख ही नहीं होता, हमें दूसरों के ताने भी सहने पड़ते हैं। जनता को हमारे ऊपर टिप्पणियां करने का वह सुअवसर मिल जाता है, जिसके लिए वह हमेशा बेचैन रहती है। मंसाराम क्या मरा, मानों समाज को उन पर आवाजें कसने का बहाना मिल गया। भीतर की बातें कौन जाने, प्रत्यक्ष बात यह थी कि यह सब सौतेली मां की करतूत है चारों तरफ यही चर्चा थी,

ईश्वर न करे लड़कों का सौतेली मां से पाला पड़े। जिसे अपना बना-बनाया घर उजाड़ना हो, अपने प्यारे बच्चों की गर्दन पर छुरी फेरनी हो, वह बच्चों के रहते हुए अपना दूसरा ब्याह करे। ऐसा कभी नहीं देखा कि सौत के आने पर घर तबाह न हो गया हो, वही बाप जो बच्चों पर जान देता था सौत के आते ही उन्हीं बच्चों का दुश्मन हो जाता है, उसकी मति ही बदल जाती है। ऐसी देवी ने जन्म ही नहीं लिया, जिसने सौत के बच्चों को अपना समझा हो।

मुश्किल यह थी कि लोग टिप्पणियों पर सन्तुष्ट न होते थे। कुछ ऐसे सज्जन भी थे, जिन्हें अब जियाराम और सियाराम से विशेष स्नेह हो गया था। वे दानों बालकों से बड़ी सहानुभूति प्रकट करते, यहां तक कि दो-एक महिलाएं तो उसकी माता के शील और स्वभाव को याद कर आंसू बहाने लगती थीं। हाय-हाय! बेचारी क्या जानती थी कि उसके मरते ही लाड़लों की यह दुर्दशा होगी! अब दूध-मक्खन काहे को मिलता होगा!

जियाराम कहता—मिलता क्यों नहीं?

महिला कहती—मिलता है! अरे बेटा, मिलना भी कई तरह का होता है। पानीवाला दूध टके सेर का मंगाकर रख दिया, पियो चाहे न पियो,

कौन पूछता है? नहीं तो बेचारी नौकर से दूध दुहवा कर मंगवाती थी। वह तो चेहरा ही कहे देता है। दूध की सूरत छिपी नहीं रहती, वह सूरत ही नहीं रहीं।

जिया को अपनी मां के समय के दूध का स्वाद तो याद था नहीं, जो इस आक्षेप का उत्तर देता और न उस समय की अपनी सूरत ही याद थी, चुप रह जाता। इन शुभाकांक्षाओं का असर भी पड़ना स्वाभाविक था। जियाराम को अपने घरवालों से चिढ़ होती जाती थी।

मुंशीजी मकान नीलामी हो जोने के बाद दूसरे घर में उठ आए, तो किराये की फिक्र हुई। निर्मला ने मक्खन बन्द कर दिया। वह आमदनी ही नहीं रही, तो खर्च कैसे रहता। दोनों कहार अलग कर दिये गये। जियाराम को यह कतर-व्योंत बुरी लगती थी। जब निर्मला मैके चली गयी, तो मुंशीजी ने दूध भी बन्द कर दिया। नवजात कन्या की चिन्ता अभी से उनके सिर पर सवार हो गयी थी।

सियाराम ने बिगड़कर कहा–दूध बन्द रहने से तो आपका महल बन रहा होगा, भोजन भी बंद कर दीजिए!

मुंशीजी–दूध पीने का शौक है, तो जाकर दुहा क्यों नही लाते? पानी के पैसे तो मुझसे न दिये जाएंगे।

जियाराम–मैं दूध दुहाने जाऊं, कोई स्कूल का लड़का देख ले तब?

मुंशीजी–तब कुछ नहीं। कह देना अपने लिए दूध लिए जाता हूं। दूध लाना कोई चोरी नहीं है।

जियाराम–चोरी नहीं है! आप ही को कोई दूध लाते देख ले, तो आपको शर्म न आयेगी।

मुंशीजी–बिल्कुल नहीं। मैंने तो इन्हीं हाथों से पानी खींचा है, अनाज की गठरियां लाया हूं। मेरे बाप लखपति नहीं थे।

जियाराम–मेरे बाप तो गरीब नहीं, मैं क्यों दूध दुहाने जाऊं? आखिर आपने कहारों को क्यों जवाब दे दिया?

मुंशीजी–क्या तुम्हें इतना भी नहीं सूझता कि मेरी आमदनी अब पहले सी नहीं रही इतने नादान तो नहीं हो?

जियाराम–आखिर आपकी आमदनी क्यों कम हो गयी?

मुंशीजी–जब तुम्हें अकल ही नहीं है, तो क्या समझाऊं। यहां जिन्दगी से तंग आ गया हूं, मुकदमें कौन ले और ले भी तो तैयार कौन करे? वह दिल ही नहीं रहा। अब तो जिंदगी के दिन पूरे कर रहा हूं। सारे अरमान लल्लू के साथ चले गये।

जियाराम–अपने ही हाथों न।

मुंशीजी ने चीखकर कहा–अरे अहमक! यह ईश्वर की मर्जी थी। अपने हाथों कोई अपना गला काटता है।

जियाराम–ईश्वर तो आपका विवाह करने न आया था।

मुंशीजी अब जब्त न कर सके, लाल-लाल आंखें निकालकर बोले–क्या तुम आज लड़ने के लिए कमर बांधकर आये हो? आखिर किस बिरते पर? मेरी रोटियां तो नहीं चलाते? जब इस काबिल हो जाना, मुझे उपदेश देना। तब मैं सुन लूंगा। अभी तुमको मुझे उपदेश देने का अधिकार नहीं है। कुछ दिनों अदब और तमीज़ सीखो। तुम मेरे सलाहकार नहीं हो कि मैं जो काम करुं, उसमें तुमसे सलाह लूं। मेरी पैदा की हुई दौलत है, उसे जैसे चाहूं खर्च कर सकता हूं। तुमको जबान खोलने का भी हक नहीं है। अगर फिर तुमने मुझसे बेअदबी की, तो नतीजा बुरा होगा। जब मंसाराम जैसा रत्न खोकर मेरे प्राण न निकले, तो तुम्हारे बगैर मैं मर न जाऊंगा, समझ गये?

यह कड़ी फटकार पाकर भी जियाराम वहां से न टला। निःशंक भाव से बोला–तो आप क्या चाहते हैं कि हमें चाहे कितनी ही तकलीफ हो मुंह न खोले? मुझसे तो यह न होगा। भाई साहब को अदब और तमीज का जो इनाम मिला, उसकी मुझे भूख नहीं। मुझमें जहर खाकर प्राण देने की हिम्मत नहीं। ऐसे अदब को दूर से दंडवत करता हूं।

मुंशीजी–तुम्हें ऐसी बातें करते हुए शर्म नहीं आती?

जियाराम–लड़के अपने बुजुर्गों ही की नकल करते हैं।

मुंशीजी का क्रोध शान्त हो गया। जियाराम पर उसका कुछ भी असर न होगा, इसका उन्हें यकीन हो गया। उठकर टहलने चले गये। आज उन्हें सूचना मिल गयी कि इस घर का शीघ्र ही सर्वनाश होने वाला है।

उस दिन से पिता और पुत्र मे किसी न किसी बात पर रोज ही एक झपट हो जाती है। मुंशीजी ज्यों-त्यों तरह देते थे, जियाराम और भी शेर होता जाता था।

एक दिन जियाराम ने रुक्मिणी से यहां तक कह डाला–बाप हैं, यह समझकर छोड़ देता हूं, नहीं तो मेरे ऐसे-ऐसे साथी हैं कि चाहूं तो भरे बाजार मे पिटवा दूं।

रुक्मिणी ने मुंशीजी से कह दिया। मुंशीजी ने प्रकट रुप से तो बेपरवाही ही दिखायी, पर उनके मन में शंका समा गई। शाम को सैर करना छोड़ दिया। यह नयी चिन्ता सवार हो गयी। इसी भय से निर्मला को भी न लाते थे कि शैतान उसके साथ भी यही बर्ताव करेगा।

जियाराम एक बार दबी जबान में कह भी चुका था–देखूं, अबकी कैसे इस घर में आती है?

मुंशीजी भी खूब समझ गये थे कि मैं इसका कुछ भी नहीं कर सकता। कोई बाहर का आदमी होता, तो उसे पुलिस और कानून के शिकंजे में कसते। अपने लड़के को क्या करें? सच कहा है–आदमी हारता है, तो अपने लड़कों ही से।

एक दिन डॉक्टर सिन्हा ने जियाराम को बुलाकर समझाना शुरु किया। जियाराम उनका अदब करता था। चुपचाप बैठा सुनता रहा। जब डॉक्टर साहब ने अन्त में पूछा, आखिर तुम चाहते क्या हो? तो वह बोला–साफ-साफ कह दूं? बूरा तो न मानिएगा?

सिन्हा–नहीं, जो कुछ तुम्हारे दिल में हो साफ-साफ कह दो।

जियाराम–तो सुनिए, जब से भैया मरे हैं, मुझे पिताजी की सूरत देखकर क्रोध आता है। मुझे ऐसा मालूम होता है कि इन्हीं ने भैया की हत्या की है और एक दिन मौका पाकर हम दोनों भाइयों की भी हत्या करेंगे। अगर उनकी यह इच्छा न होती तो ब्याह ही क्यों करते?

डॉक्टर साहब ने बड़ी मुश्किल से हंसी रोककर कहा–तुम्हारी हत्या करने के लिए उन्हें ब्याह करने की क्या जरुरत थी, यह बात मेरी समझ में नहीं आयी। बिना विवाह किये भी तो वह हत्या कर सकते थे।

जियाराम–कभी नहीं, उस वक्त तो उनका दिल ही कुछ और था, हम लोगों पर जान देते थे अब मुंह तक नहीं देखना चाहते। उनकी यही इच्छा है कि उन दोनों प्राणियों के सिवा घर में और कोई न रहे। अब जो लड़के होंगे उनके रास्ते से हम लोगों का हटा देना चाहते है। यही उन दोनों आदमियों की दिली मंशा है। हमें तरह-तरह की तकलीफें देकर भगा देना चाहते हैं। इसीलिए आजकल मुकदमे नहीं लेते। हम दोनों भाई आज मर जाएं, तो फिर देखिए कैसी बहार होती है।

डॉक्टर–अगर तुम्हें भगाना ही होता, तो कोई इल्जाम लगाकर घर से निकाल न देते?

जियाराम–इसके लिए पहले ही से तैयार बैठा हूं।

डॉक्टर–सुनूं, क्या तैयारी की है?

जियाराम–जब मौका आएगा, देख लीजिएगा।

यह कहकर जियाराम चलता हुआ। डॉक्टर सिन्हा ने बहुत पुकारा, पर उसने फिर कर देखा भी नहीं।

कई दिन के बाद डॉक्टर साहब की जियाराम से फिर मुलाकात हो गयी। डॉक्टर साहब सिनेमा के प्रेमी थे और जियाराम की तो जान ही सिनेमा में बसती थी।

डॉक्टर साहब ने सिनेमा पर आलोचना करके जियाराम को बातों में लगा लिया और अपने घर लाये। भोजन का समय आ गया था,, दोनों आदमी साथ ही भोजन करने बैठे।

जियाराम को वहां भोजन बहुत स्वादिष्ट लगा, बोला–मेरे यहां तो जब से महाराज अलग हुआ खाने का मजा ही जाता रहा। बुआजी पक्का वैष्णवी भोजन बनाती हैं। जबरदस्ती खा लेता हूं, पर खाने की तरफ ताकने को जी नहीं चाहता।

डॉक्टर–मेरे यहां तो जब घर में खाना पकता है, तो इससे कहीं स्वादिष्ट होता है। तुम्हारी बुआजी प्याज-लहसुन न छूती होंगी?

जियाराम–हां साहब, उबालकर रख देती हैं। लालाजी को इसकी परवाह ही नहीं कि कोई खाता है या नहीं। इसीलिए तो महाराज को अलग किया है। अगर रुपये नहीं है, तो गहने कहां से बनते हैं?

डॉक्टर–यह बात नहीं है जियाराम, उनकी आमदनी सचमुच बहुत कम हो गयी है। तुम उन्हें बहुत दिक करते हो।

जियाराम–(हंसकर) मैं उन्हें दिक करता हूं? मुझसे कसम ले लीजिए, जो कभी उनसे बोलता भी हूं। मुझे बदनाम करने का उन्होंने बीड़ा उठा लिया है। बेसबब, बेवजह पीछे पड़े रहते हैं। यहां तक कि मेरे दोस्तों से भी उन्हें चिढ़ है। आप ही सोचिए, दोस्तों के बगैर कोई जिन्दा रह सकता है? मैं कोई लुच्चा नहीं हू कि लुच्चों की सोहबत रखूं, मगर आप दोस्तों ही के पीछे मुझे रोज सताया करते हैं। कल तो मैंने साफ कह दिया–मेरे दोस्त घर आयेंगे, किसी को अच्छा लगे या बुरा। जनाब, कोई हो, हर वक्त की धौंस नहीं सह सकता।

डॉक्टर–मुझे तो भाई, उन पर बड़ी दया आती है। यह जमाना उनके आराम करने का था। एक तो बुढ़ापा, उस पर जवान बेटे का शोक, स्वास्थ्य भी अच्छा नहीं। ऐसा आदमी क्या कर सकता है? वह जो कुछ थोड़ा-बहुत करते हैं, वही बहुत है। तुम अभी और कुछ नहीं कर सकते, तो कम-से-कम अपने आचरण से तो उन्हें प्रसन्न रख सकते हो। बुड्ढों को प्रसन्न करना बहुत कठिन काम नहीं। यकीन मानो, तुम्हारा हंसकर बोलना ही उन्हें खुश करने को काफी है। इतना पूछने में तुम्हारा क्या खर्च होता है। बाबूजी, आपकी तबीयत कैसी है? वह तुम्हारी यह उद्दण्डता देखकर मन-ही-मन कुढ़ते रहते हैं। मैं तुमसे सच कहता हूं, कई बार रो चुके हैं। उन्होंने मान लो शादी करने में गलती की। इसे वह भी स्वीकार करते हैं, लेकिन तुम अपने कर्त्तव्य से क्यों मुंह मोड़ते हो? वह तुम्हारे पिता है, तुम्हें उनकी सेवा करनी चाहिए। एक बात भी ऐसी मुंह से न निकालनी चाहिए, जिससे उनका दिल दुखे। उन्हें यह खयाल करने का मौका ही क्यों दे कि सब मेरी कमाई खाने वाले हैं, बात पूछने वाला कोई नहीं। मेरी उम्र तुमसे कहीं ज्यादा है, जियाराम, पर आज तक मैंने अपने पिताजी की किसी बात का जवाब नहीं दिया। वह आज भी मुझे डांटते है, सिर झुकाकर सुन लेता हूं। जानता हूं, वह जो कुछ कहते हैं, मेरे भले ही को कहते हैं। माता-पिता से बढ़कर हमारा हितैषी और कौन हो सकता है? उसके ऋण से कौन मुक्त हो सकता है?

जियाराम बैठा रोता रहा। अभी उसके सद्‌भावों का सम्पूर्णतः लोप न हुआ था, अपनी दुर्जनता उसे साफ नजर आ रही थी। इतनी ग्लानि उसे बहुत दिनों से न आयी थी। रोकर डॉक्टर साहब से कहा–मैं बहुत लज्जित हूं। दूसरों के बहकाने में आ गया। अब आप मेरी जरा भी शिकायत न सुनेंगे। आप पिताजी से मेरे अपराध क्षमा करा दीजिए। मैं सचमुच बड़ा अभागा हूं। उन्हें मैंने बहुत सताया। उनसे कहिए–मेरे अपराध क्षमा कर दें, नहीं मैं मुंह में कालिख लगाकर कहीं निकल जाऊंगा, डूब मरुंगा।

डॉक्टर साहब अपनी उपदेश-कुशलता पर फूले न समाये। जियाराम को गले लगाकर विदा किया। जियाराम घर पहुंचा, तो ग्यारह बज गये थे। मुंशीजी भोजन करके अभी बाहर आये थे। उसे देखते ही बोले–जानते हो कै बजे है? बारह का वक्त है।

जियाराम ने बड़ी नम्रता से कहा–डॉक्टर सिन्हा मिल गये। उनके साथ उनके घर तक चला गया। उन्होंने खाने के लिए जिद की, मजबूरन खाना पड़ा। इसी सें देर हो गयी।

मुंशीजी–डॉक्टर सिन्हा से दुखड़े रोने गये होंगे या और कोई काम था।

जियाराम की नम्रता का चौथा भाग उड़ गया, बोला–दुखड़े रोने की मेरी आदत नहीं है।

मुंशीजी–जरा भी नहीं, तुम्हारे मुंह मे तो जबान ही नहीं। मुझसे जो लोग तुम्हारी बातें करते हैं, वह गढ़ा करते होंगे?

जियाराम–और दिनों की मैं नहीं कहता, लेकिन आज डॉक्टर सिन्हा के यहां मैंने कोई बात ऐसी नहीं की, जो इस वक्त आपके सामने न कर सकूं।

मुंशीजी–बड़ी खुशी की बात है। बेहद खुशी हुई। आज से गुरुदीक्षा ले ली है क्या?

जियाराम की नम्रता का एक चतुर्थांश और गायब हो गया। सिर उठाकर बोला–आदमी बिना गुरुदीक्षा लिए हुए भी अपनी बुराइयों पर लज्जित हो सकता है। अपना सुधार करने के लिए गुरुमन्त्र कोई जरुरी चीज नहीं।

मुंशीजी–अब तो लुच्चे न जमा होंगे?

जियाराम–आप किसी को लुच्चा क्यों कहते हैं, जब तक ऐसा कहने के लिए आपके पास कोई प्रमाण नहीं?

मुंशीजी–तुम्हारे दोस्त सब लुच्चे-लफंगे हैं। एक भी भला आदमी नही। मैं तुमसे कई बार कह चुका कि उन्हें यहां मत जमा किया करो, पर तुमने सुना नहीं। आज मैं आखिर बार कहे देता हूं कि अगर तुमने उन शोहदों को जमा किया, तो मुझे पुलिस की सहायता लेनी पड़ेगी।

जियाराम की नम्रता का एक चतुर्थांश और गायब हो गया। फड़ककर बोला–अच्छी बात है, पुलिस की सहायता लीजिए। देखें क्या करती है? मेरे दोस्तों में आधे से ज्यादा पुलिस के अफसरों ही के बेटे हैं। जब आप ही मेरा सुधार करने पर तुले हुए है, तो मैं व्यर्थ क्यों कष्ट उठाऊं?

यह कहता हुआ जियाराम अपने कमरे मे चला गया और एक क्षण के बाद हारमोनिया के मीठे स्वरों की आवाज बाहर आने लगी।

12

अबकी सुधा के साथ निर्मला को भी आना पड़ा। वह तो मैके में कुछ दिन और रहना चाहती थी, लेकिन शोकातुर सुधा अकेले कैसे रहती! उसको आखिर आना ही पड़ा।

रुक्मिणी ने भूंगी से कहा–देखती है, बहू मैके से कैसा निखरकर आयी है!

भूंगी ने कहा–दीदी, मां के हाथ की रोटियां लड़कियों को बहुत अच्छी लगती है।

रुक्मिणी–ठीक कहती है भूंगी, खिलाना तो बस मां ही जानती है।

निर्मला को ऐसा मालूम हुआ कि घर का कोई आदमी उसके आने से खुश नहीं। मुंशीजी ने खुशी तो बहुत दिखाई, पर हृदयगत चिन्ता को न छिपा सके। बच्ची का नाम सुधा ने आशा रख दिया था। वह आशा की मूर्ति-सी थी भी। देखकर सारी चिन्ता भाग जाती थी।

मुंशीजी ने उसे गोद में लेना चाहा, तो रोने लगी, दौड़कर मां से लिपट गयी, मानो पिता को पहचानती ही नहीं। मुंशीजी ने मिठाइयों से उसे परचाना चाहा। घर में कोई नौकर तो था नहीं, जाकर सियाराम से दो आने की मिठाइयां लाने को कहा।

जियाराम भी बैठा हुआ था। बोल उठा–हम लोगों के लिए तो कभी मिठाइयां नहीं आतीं।

मुंशीजी ने झुंझलाकर कहा–तुम लोग बच्चे नहीं हो।

जियाराम–और क्या बूढ़े हैं? मिठाइयां मंगवाकर रख दीजिए, तो मालूम हो कि बच्चे हैं या बूढ़े। निकालिए चार आना और आशा के बदौलत हमारे नसीब भी जागें।

मुंशीजी—मेरे पास इस वक्त पैसे नहीं है। जाओ सिया, जल्द आना।

जियाराम—सिया नहीं जाएगा। किसी का गुलाम नहीं है। आशा अपने बाप की बेटी है, तो वह भी अपने बाप का बेटा है।

मुंशीजी—क्या फजूल की बातें करते हो। नन्हीं-सी बच्ची की बराबरी करते तुम्हें शर्म नही आती? जाओ सियाराम, ये पैसे लो।

जियाराम—मत जाना सिया! तुम किसी के नौकर नहीं हो।

सिया बड़ी दुविधा में पड़ गया। किसका कहना माने? अन्त में उसने जियाराम का कहना मानने का निश्चय किया। बाप ज्यादा-से-ज्यादा घुड़क देंगे, जिया तो मारेगा, फिर वह किसके पास फरियाद लेकर जाएगा। बोला—मैं न जाऊंगा।

मुंशीजी ने धमकाकर कहा—अच्छा, तो मेरे पास फिर कोई चीज मांगने मत आना।

मुंशीजी खुद बाजार चले गये और एक रुपये की मिठाई लेकर लौटे। दो आने की मिठाई मांगते हुए उन्हें शर्म आयी। हलवाई उन्हें पहचानता था। दिल में क्या कहेगा?

मिठाई लिए हुए मुंशीजी अन्दर चले गये। सियाराम ने मिठाई का बड़ा-सा दोना देखा, तो बाप का कहना न मानने का उसे दुख हुआ। अब वह किस मुंह से मिठाई लेने अन्दर जाएगा। बड़ी भूल हुई। वह मन-ही-मन जियाराम के चांटों की चोट और मिठाई की मिठास में तुलना करने लगा।

सहसा भूंगी ने दो तश्तरियां दोनो के सामने लाकर रख दीं। जियाराम ने बिगड़कर कहा—इसे उठा ले जा!

भूंगी—काहे को बिगड़ते हो बाबू क्या मिठाई अच्छी नहीं लगती?

जियाराम—मिठाई आशा के लिए आयी है, हमारे लिए नहीं आयी? ले जा, नहीं तो सड़क पर फेंक दूंगा। हम तो पैसे-पैसे के लिए रटते रहते हैं। और यहां रुपये की मिठाई आती है।

भूंगी—तुम ले लो सिया बाबू, यह न लेंगे न सही।

सियाराम ने डरते-डरते हाथ बढ़ाया था कि जियाराम ने डांटकर कहा—मत छूना मिठाई, नहीं तो हाथ तोड़कर रख दूंगा। लालची कहीं का!

सियाराम यह धुड़की सुनकर सहम उठा, मिठाई खाने की हिम्मत न पड़ी। निर्मला ने यह कथा सुनी, तो दोनों लड़कों को मनाने चली। मुंशीजी ने कड़ी कसम रख दी।

निर्मला–आप समझते नहीं है। यह सारा गुस्सा मुझ पर है।

मुंशीजी–गुस्ताख हो गया है। इस खयाल से कोई सख्ती नहीं करता कि लोग कहेंगे, बिना मां के बच्चों को सताते हैं, नहीं तो सारी शरारत घड़ी-भर में निकाल दूं।

निर्मला–इसी बदनामी का तो मुझे डर है।

मुंशीजी–अब न डरुंगा, जिसके जी में जो आये कहे।

निर्मला–पहले तो ये ऐसे न थे।

मुंशीजी–अजी, कहता है कि आपके लड़के मौजूद थे, आपने शादी क्यों की! यह कहते भी इसे संकोच नहीं होता कि आप लोगों ने मंसाराम को विष दे दिया। लड़का नहीं है, शत्रु है।

जियाराम द्वार पर छिपकर खड़ा था। स्त्री-पुरुष मे मिठाई के विषय मे क्या बातें होती हैं, यही सुनने वह आया था।

मुंशीजी का अन्तिम वाक्य सुनकर उससे न रहा गया। बोल उठा–शत्रु न होता, तो आप उसके पीछे क्यों पड़ते? आप जो इस वक्त कर रहे हैं, वह मैं बहुत पहले समझे बैठा हूं। भैया नासमझ थे, धोखा खा गये। हमारे साथ आपकी दाल न गलेगी। सारा जमाना कह रहा है कि भाई साहब को जहर दिया गया है। मैं कहता हूं तो आपको क्यों गुस्सा आता है?

निर्मला तो सन्नाटे में आ गयी। मालूम हुआ, किसी ने उसकी देह पर अंगारे डाल दिये। मुंशीजी ने डांटकर जियाराम को चुप कराना चाहा, जियाराम निःशंक खड़ा ईंट का जवाब पत्थर से देता रहा।

यहां तक कि निर्मला को भी उस पर क्रोध आ गया। यह कल का छोकरा, किसी काम का न काज का, यों खड़ा टर्रा रहा है, जैसे घर भर का पालन-पोषण यही करता हो। त्योंरियां चढ़ाकर बोली–बस, अब बहुत हुआ जियाराम, मालूम हो गया, तुम बड़े लायक हो, बाहर जाकर बैठो।

मुंशीजी अब तक तो कुछ दब-दबकर बोलते रहे, निर्मला की शह पाई तो दिल बढ़ गया। दांत पीसकर लपके और इसके पहले कि निर्मला उनके हाथ पकड़ सकें, एक थप्पड़ चला ही दिया। थप्पड़ निर्मला के मुंह पर पड़ा, वही सामने पड़ी। माथा चकरा गया।

मुंशीजी ने सूखे हाथों में इतनी शक्ति है, इसका वह अनुमान न कर सकती थी। सिर पकड़कर बैठ गयी। मुंशीजी का क्रोध और भी भड़क उठा, फिर घूंसा चलाया पर अबकी जियाराम ने उनका हाथ पकड़ लिया और पीछे ढकेलकर बोला–दूर से बातें कीजिए, क्यों नाहक अपनी बेइज्जती करवाते हैं? अम्मांजी का लिहाज कर रहा हूं, नहीं तो दिखा देता।

यह कहता हुआ वह बाहर चला गया।

मुंशीजी संज्ञा-शून्य से खड़े रहे।

इस वक्त अगर जियाराम पर दैवी वज्र गिर पड़ता, तो शायद उन्हें हार्दिक आनन्द होता। जिस पुत्र को कभी गोद में लेकर निहाल हो जाते थे, उसी के प्रति आज भांति-भांति की दुष्कल्पनाएं मन में आ रही थीं।

रुक्मिणी अब तक तो अपनी कोठरी में थी। अब आकर बोली–बेटा अपने बराबर का हो जाए तो उस पर हाथ न छोड़ना चाहिए।

मुंशीजी ने ओंठ चबाकर कहा–मैं इसे घर से निकालकर छोडूंगा। भीख मांगे या चोरी करे, मुझसे कोई मतलब नहीं।

रुक्मिणी–नाक किसकी कटेगी?

मुंशीजी–इसकी चिन्ता नहीं।

निर्मला–मैं जानती कि मेरे आने से यह तूफान खड़ा हो जाएगा, तो भूलकर भी न आती। अब भी भला है, मुझे भेज दीजिए। इस घर में मुझसे न रहा जाएगा।

रुक्मिणी–तुम्हारा बहुत लिहाज करता है बहू, नहीं तो आज अनर्थ ही हो जाता।

निर्मला–अब और क्या अनर्थ होगा दीदीजी? मैं तो फूंक-फूंककर पांव रखती हूं, फिर भी अपयश लग ही जाता है। अभी घर में पांव रखते देर नहीं हुई और यह हाल हो गया। ईश्वर ही कुशल करे।

रात को भोजन करने कोई न उठा, अकेले मुंशीजी ने खाया। निर्मला को आज नयी चिन्ता हो गयी–जीवन कैसे पार लगेगा? अपना ही पेट होता तो विशेष चिन्ता न थी। अब तो एक नयी विपत्ति गले पड़ गयी थी। वह सोच रही थी–मेरी बच्ची के भाग्य में क्या लिखा है राम?

13

चिन्ता में नींद कब आती है? निर्मला चारपाई पर करवटें बदल रही थी। कितना चाहती थी कि नींद आ जाए, पर नींद ने न आने की कसम सी खा ली थी। चिराग बुझा दिया था, खिड़की के दरवाजे खोल दिये थे, टिक-टिक करने वाली घड़ी भी दूसरे कमरे में रख आयी थी, पर नींद का नाम न था। जितनी बातें सोचनी थीं, सब सोच चुकी, चिन्ताओं का भी अन्त हो गया, पर पलकें न झपकीं। तब उसने फिर लैम्प जलाया और एक पुस्तक पढ़ने लगी। दो-चार ही पृष्ठ पढ़े होंगे कि झपकी आ गयी। किताब खुली रह गयी।

सहसा जियाराम ने कमरे में कदम रखा। उसके पांव थर-थर कांप रहे थे। उसने कमरे मे ऊपर-नीचे देखा। निर्मला सोई हुई थी, उसके सिरहाने ताक पर, एक छोटा-सा पीतल का सन्दूकचा रक्खा हुआ था।

जियाराम दबे पांव गया, धीरे से सन्दूकचा उतारा और बड़ी तेजी से कमरे के बाहर निकला। उसी वक्त निर्मला की आंखें खुल गयीं। चौंककर उठ खड़ी हुई। द्वार पर आकर देखा। कलेजा धक् से हो गया। क्या यह जियाराम है? मेरे कमरे मे क्या करने आया था। कहीं मुझे धोखा तो नहीं हुआ? शायद दीदीजी के कमरे से आया हो। यहां उसका काम ही क्या था? शायद मुझसे कुछ कहने आया हो, लेकिन इस वक्त क्या कहने आया होगा? इसकी नीयत क्या है? उसका दिल कांप उठा।

मुंशीजी ऊपर छत पर सो रहे थे। मुंडेर न होने के कारण निर्मला ऊपर न सो सकती थी। उसने सोचा चलकर उन्हें जगाऊं, पर जाने की हिम्मत न पड़ी। शक्की आदमी हैं, न जाने क्या समझ बैठें और क्या करने पर तैयार हो जाएं? आकर फिर पुस्तक पढ़ने लगी। सबेरे पूछने

पर आप ही मालूम हो जाएगा। कौन जाने मुझे धोखा ही हुआ हो। नींद मे कभी-कभी धोखा हो जाता है, लेकिन सबेरे पूछने का निश्चय कर भी उसे फिर नींद नहीं आयी। सबेरे वह जलपान लेकर स्वयं जियाराम के पास गयी, तो वह उसे देखकर चौंक पड़ा। रोज तो भूंगी आती थी आज यह क्यों आ रही है? निर्मला की ओर ताकने की उसकी हिम्मत न पड़ी।

निर्मला ने उसकी ओर विश्वासपूर्ण नेत्रों से देखकर पूछा–रात को तुम मेरे कमरे में गये थे?

जियाराम ने विस्मय दिखाकर कहा–मैं? भला मैं रात को क्या करने जाता? क्या कोई गया था?

निर्मला ने इस भाव से कहा, मानो उसे उसकी बात का पूरी विश्वास हो गया–हां, मुझे ऐसा मालूम हुआ कि कोई मेरे कमरे से निकला। मैंने उसका मुंह तो न देखा, पर उसकी पीठ देखकर अनुमान किया कि शायद तुम किसी काम से आये हो। इसका पता कैसे चले कौन था? कोई था जरुर इसमें कोई सन्देह नहीं।

जियाराम अपने को निरपराध सिद्व करने की चेष्टा कर कहने लगा–मैं तो रात को थियेटर देखने चला गया था। वहां से लौटा तो एक मित्र के घर लेट रहा। थोड़ी देर हुई लौटा हूं। मेरे साथ और भी कई मित्र थे। जिससे जी चाहे, पूछ लें। हां, भाई मैं बहुत डरता हूं। ऐसा न हो, कोई चीज गायब हो गयी, तो मेरा नाम लगे। चोर को तो कोई पकड़ नहीं सकता, मेरे मत्थे जाएगी। बाबूजी को आप जानती हैं। मुझे मारने दौड़ेंगे।

निर्मला–तुम्हारा नाम क्यों लगेगा? अगर तुम्हीं होते तो भी तुम्हें कोई चोरी नहीं लगा सकता। चोरी दूसरे की चीज की जाती है, अपनी चीज की चोरी कोई नहीं करता।

अभी तक निर्मला की निगाह अपने सन्दूकचे पर न पड़ी थी। भोजन बनाने लगी। जब वकील साहब कचहरी चले गये, तो वह सुधा से मिलने चली। इधर कई दिनों से मुलाकात न हुई थी, फिर रातवाली घटना पर विचार परिवर्तन भी करना था। भूंगी से कहा–कमरे में से गहनों का बक्स उठा ला।

भूंगी ने लौटकर कहा–वहां तो कहीं सन्दूक नहीं हैं। कहां रखा था?

निर्मला ने चिढ़कर कहा–एक बार में तो तेरा काम ही कभी नहीं होता। वहां छोड़कर और जाएगा कहां। आलमारी में देखा था?

भूंगी–नहीं बहूजी, आलमारी में तो नहीं देखा, झूठ क्यों बोलूं?

निर्मला मुस्करा पड़ी। बोली–जा देख, जल्दी आ।

एक क्षण में भूंगी फिर खाली हाथ लौट आयी–आलमारी में भी तो नहीं है। अब जहां बताओ वहां देखूं।

निर्मला झुंझलाकर यह कहती हुई उठ खड़ी हुई–तुझे ईश्वर ने आंखें ही न जाने किसलिए दीं! देख, उसी कमरे में से लाती हूं कि नहीं।

भूंगी भी पीछे–पीछे कमरे में गयी। निर्मला ने ताक पर निगाह डाली, अलमारी खोलकर देखी। चारपाई के नीचे झांककर देखा, फिर कपड़ों का बड़ा संदूक खोलकर देखा। सन्दूकचे का कहीं पता नहीं। आश्चर्य हुआ, आखिर सन्दूकचा गया कहां?

सहसा रातवाली घटना बिजली की भांति उसकी आंखों के सामने चमक गयी। कलेजा उछल पड़ा। अब तक निश्चिन्त होकर खोज रही थी। अब ताप-सा चढ़ आया। बड़ी उतावली से चारों ओर खोजने लगी। कहीं पता नहीं। जहां खोजना चाहिए था, वहां भी खोजा और जहां नहीं खोजना चाहिए था, वहां भी खोजा। इतना बड़ा सन्दूकचा बिछावन के नीचे कैसे छिप जाता? पर बिछावन भी झाड़कर देखा। क्षण-क्षण मुख की कान्ति मलिन होती जाती थी। प्राण कंठ में समाते जाते थे। अन्त में निराश होकर उसने छाती पर एक घूंसा मारा और रोने लगी।

गहने ही स्त्री की सम्पत्ति होते हैं। पति की और किसी सम्पत्ति पर उसका अधिकार नहीं होता। इन्हीं का उसे बल और गौरव होता है। निर्मला के पास पांच-छः हजार के गहने थे। जब उन्हें पहनकर वह निकलती थी, तो उतनी देर के लिए उल्लास से उसका हृदय खिला रहता था। एक-एक गहना मानो विपत्ति और बाधा से बचाने के लिए एक-एक रक्षास्त्र था। अभी रात ही उसने सोचा था, जियाराम की लौंडी बनकर वह न रहेगी। ईश्वर न करे कि वह किसी के सामने हाथ फैलाये। इसी खेवे से वह अपनी नाव को भी पार लगा

देगी और अपनी बच्ची को भी किसी-न-किसी घाट पहुंचा देगी। उसे किस बात की चिन्ता है! उन्हें तो कोई उससे न छीन लेगा। आज ये मेरे सिंगार हैं, कल को मेरे आधार हो जाएंगे। इस विचार से उसके हृदय को कितनी सान्त्वना मिली थी! वह सम्पत्ति आज उसके हाथ से निकल गयी।

अब वह निराधार थी। संसार उसका कोई अवलम्ब कोई सहारा न था। उसकी आशाओं का आधार जड़ से कट गया, वह फूट-फूटकर रोने लगी। ईश्वर! तुमसे इतना भी न देखा गया? मुझ दुखिया को तुमने यों ही अपंग बना दिया थ, अब आंखे भी फोड़ दीं। अब वह किसके सामने हाथ फैलायेगी, किसके द्वार पर भीख मांगेगी। पसीने से उसकी देह भीग गयी, रोते-रोते आंखे सूज गयीं। निर्मला सिर नीचा किये रो रही थी। रुक्मिणी उसे धीरज दिला रही थीं, लेकिन उसके आंसू न रुकते थे, शोक की ज्वाला कम न होती थी।

तीन बजे जियाराम स्कूल से लौटा। निर्मला उसके आने की खबर पाकर विक्षिप्त की भांति उठी और उसके कमरे के द्वार पर आकर बोली—भैया, दिल्लगी की हो तो दे दो। दुखिया को सताकर क्या पाओगे?

जियाराम एक क्षण के लिए कातर हो उठा। चोर-कला में उसका यह पहला ही प्रयास था। यह कठोरता, जिससे हिंसा में मनोरंजन होता है अभी तक उसे प्राप्त न हुई थी। यदि उसके पास सन्दूकचा होता और फिर इतना मौका मिलता कि उसे ताक पर रख आवे, तो कदाचित् वह उस मौके को न छोड़ता, लेकिन सन्दूक उसके हाथ से निकल चुका था। यारों ने उसे सराफे में पहुंचा दिया था और औने-पौने बेच भी डाला था। चोरों की झूठ के सिवा और कौन रक्षा कर सकता है। बोला—भला अम्मांजी, मैं आपसे ऐसी दिल्लगी करुंगा? आप अभी तक मुझ पर शक करती जा रही हैं। मैं कह चुका कि मैं रात को घर पर न था, लेकिन आपको यकीन ही नहीं आता। बड़े दुःख की बात है कि मुझे आप इतना नीच समझती हैं।

निर्मला ने आंसू पोंछते हुए कहा—मैं तुम्हारे पर शक नहीं करती भैया, तुम्हें चोरी नहीं लगाती। मैंने समझा, शायद दिल्लगी की हो।

जियाराम पर वह चोरी का संदेह कैसे कर सकती थी? दुनिया यही तो कहेगी कि लड़के की मां मर गई है, तो उस पर चोरी का इलजाम लगाया जा रहा है। मेरे मुंह मे ही तो कालिख लगेगी!

जियाराम ने आश्वासन देते हुए कहा–चलिए, मैं देखूं, आखिर ले कौन गया? चोर आया किस रास्ते से?

भूंगी–भैया, तुम चोरों के आने को कहते हो। चूहे के बिल से तो निकल ही आते हैं, यहां तो चारो ओर ही खिड़कियां हैं।

जियाराम–खूब अच्छी तरह तलाश कर लिया है?

निर्मला–सारा घर तो छान मारा, अब कहां खोजने को कहते हो?

जियाराम-–आप लोग सो भी तो जाती हैं मुर्दों से बाजी लगाकर।

चार बजे मुंशीजी घर आये, तो निर्मला की दशा देखकर पूछा–कैसी तबीयत है? कहीं दर्द तो नहीं है? कह कहकर उन्होंने आशा को गोद में उठा लिया।

निर्मला कोई जवाब न दे सकी, फिर रोने लगी।

भूंगी ने कहा–ऐसा कभी नहीं हुआ था। मेरी सारी उम्र इसी घर में कट गयी। आज तक एक पैसे की चोरी नहीं हुई। दुनिया यही कहेगी कि भूंगी का काम है, अब तो भगवान ही पत-पानी रखें।

मुंशीजी अचकन के बटन खोल रहे थे, फिर बटन बन्द करते हुए बोले–क्या हुआ? कोई चीज चोरी हो गयी?

भूंगी–बहूजी के सारे गहने उठ गये।

मुंशीजी–रखे कहां थे?

निर्मला ने सिसकियां लेते हुए रात की सारी घटना बयान कर दी, पर जियाराम की सूरत के आदमी के अपने कमरे से निकलने की बात न कही।

मुंशीजी ने ठंडी सांस भरकर कहा–ईश्वर भी बड़ा अन्यायी है। जो मरे उन्हीं को मारता है। मालूम होता है, अदिन आ गये हैं। मगर चोर आया तो किधर से? कहीं सेंध नहीं पड़ी और किसी तरफ से आने का रास्ता नहीं। मैंने तो कोई ऐसा पाप नहीं किया, जिसकी मुझे यह सजा मिल रही है। बार-बार कहता रहा, गहने का सन्दूकचा ताक पर मत रखो, मगर कौन सुनता है।

निर्मला—मैं क्या जानती थी कि यह गजब टूट पड़ेगा!

मुंशीजी—इतना तो जानती थी कि सब दिन बराबर नहीं जाते। आज बनवाने जाऊं, तो दस हजार से कम न लगेंगे। आजकल अपनी जो दशा है, वह तुमसे छिपी नहीं, खर्च भर का मुश्किल से मिलता है, गहने कहां से बनेंगे। जाता हूं, पुलिस में इत्तिला कर आता हूं, पर मिलने की उम्मीद न समझो।

निर्मला ने आपत्ति के भाव से कहा—जब जानते हैं कि पुलिस में इत्तिला करने से कुछ न होगा, तो क्यों जा रहे हैं?

मुंशीजी—दिल नहीं मानता और क्या? इतना बड़ा नुकसान उठाकर चुपचाप तो नहीं बैठ जाता।

निर्मला—मिलनेवाले होते, तो जाते ही क्यों? तकदीर में न थे, तो कैसे रहते?

मुंशीजी—तकदीर मे होंगे, तो मिल जाएंगे, नहीं तो गये तो हैं ही।

मुंशीजी कमरे से निकले। निर्मला ने उनका हाथ पकड़कर कहा—मैं कहती हूं, मत जाओ, कहीं ऐसा न हो, लेने के देने पड़ जाएं।

मुंशीजी ने हाथ छुड़ाकर कहा—तुम भी बच्चों की-सी जिद्द कर रही हो। दस हजार का नुकसान ऐसा नहीं है, जिसे मैं यों ही उठा लूं। मैं रो नहीं रहा हूं, पर मेरे हृदय पर जो बीत रही है, वह मैं ही जानता हूं। यह चोट मेरे कलेजे पर लगी है।

मुंशीजी और कुछ न कह सके। गला फंस गया। वह तेजी से कमरे से निकल आये और थाने पर जा पहुँचे। थानेदार उनका बहुत लिहाज करता था। उसे एक बार रिश्वत के मुकदमे से बरी करा चुके थे। उनके साथ ही तफ्तीश करने आ पहुंचा। नाम था अलायार खां।

शाम हो गयी थी। थानेदार ने मकान के अगवाड़े-पिछवाड़े घूम-घूमकर देखा। अन्दर जाकर निर्मला के कमरे को गौर से देखा। ऊपर की मुंडेर की जांच की। मुहल्ले के दो-चार आदमियों से चुपके-चुपके कुछ बातें की और तब मुंशीजी से बोले—जनाब, खुदा की कसम, यह किसी बाहर के आदमी का काम नहीं। खुदा की कसम, अगर कोई बाहर का आदमी निकले, तो आज से थानेदारी करना

छोड़ दूं। आपके घर में कोई मुलाजिम ऐसा तो नहीं है, जिस पर आपको शुबहा हो।

मुंशीजी–घर मे तो आजकल सिर्फ एक महरी है।

थानेदार–अजी, वह पगली है। यह किसी बड़े शातिर का काम है, खुदा की कसम।

मुंशीजी–तो घर में और कौन है? मेरे दोनों लड़के हैं, स्त्री है और बहन है। इनमें से किस पर शक करुं?

थानेदार–खुदा की कसम, घर ही के किसी आदमी का काम है, चाहे, वह कोई हो, इन्शाअल्लाह, दो-चार दिन में मैं आपको इसकी खबर दूंगा। यह तो नहीं कह सकता कि माल भी सब मिल जाएगा, पर खुदा की कसम, चोर जरुर पकड़ दिखाऊंगा।

थानेदार चला गया, तो मुंशीजी ने आकर निर्मला से उसकी बातें कहीं। निर्मला सहम उठी–आप थानेदार से कह दीजिए, तफ्तीश न करें, आपके पैरों पड़ती हूं।

मुंशीजी–आखिर क्यों?

निर्मला–अब क्यों बताऊं? वह कह रहा है कि घर ही के किसी का काम है।

मुंशीजी–उसे बकने दो।

जियाराम अपने कमरे में बैठा हुआ भगवान् को याद कर रहा था। उसके मुंह पर हवाइयां उड़ रही थीं। सुन चुका था कि पुलिसवाले चेहरे से भांप जाते हैं। बाहर निकलने की हिम्मत न पड़ती थी। दोनों आदमियों में क्या बातें हो रही हैं, यह जानने के लिए छटपटा रहा था। ज्योंही थानेदार चला गया और भूंगी किसी काम से बाहर निकली, जियाराम ने पूछा–थानेदार क्या कर रहा था भूंगी?

भूंगी ने पास आकर कहा–दाढ़ीजार कहता था, घर ही से किसी आदमी का काम है, बाहर का कोई नहीं है।

जियाराम–बाबूजी ने कुछ नहीं कहा?

भूंगी–कुछ तो नहीं कहा, खड़े 'हूं-हूं' करते रहे। घर मे एक भूंगी ही गैर है न! और तो सब अपने ही हैं।

जियाराम–मैं भी तो गैर हूं, तू ही क्यों?

भूंगी–तुम गैर काहे हो भैया?

जियाराम–बाबूजी ने थानेदार से कहा नहीं, घर में किसी पर उनका शुबहा नहीं है।

भूंगी–कुछ तो कहते नहीं सुना। बेचारे थानेदार ने भले ही कहा–भूंगी तो पगली है, वह क्या चोरी करेगी। बाबूजी तो मुझे फंसाये ही देते थे।

जियाराम–तब तो तू भी निकल गयी। अकेला मैं ही रह गया। तू ही बता, तूने मुझे उस दिन घर में देखा था?

भूंगी–नहीं भैया, तुम तो ठेठर देखने गये थे।

जियाराम–गवाही देगी न?

भूंगी–इसकी जरुरत नहीं पड़ेगी भैया? बहूजी तफ्तीश बन्द करा देंगी।

जियाराम–सच?

भूंगी–हां भैया, बार-बार कहती है कि तफ्तीश न कराओ। गहने गये, जाने दो, पर बाबूजी मानते ही नहीं।

पांच-छः दिन तक जियाराम ने पेट भर भोजन नहीं किया। कभी दो-चार कौर खा लेता, कभी कह देता, भूख नहीं है। उसके चेहरे का रंग उड़ा रहता था। रातें जागते कटतीं, प्रतिक्षण थानेदार की शंका बनी रहती थी। यदि वह जानता कि मामला इतना तूल खींचेंगा, तो कभी ऐसा काम न करता। उसने तो समझा था–किसी चोर पर शुबहा होगा। मेरी तरफ किसी का ध्यान भी न जाएगा, पर अब भण्डा फूटता हुआ मालूम होता था। अभागा थानेदार जिस ढंग से छान-बीन कर रहा था, उससे जियाराम को बड़ी शंका हो रही थी।

सातवें दिन संध्या समय घर लौटा तो बहुत चिन्तित था। आज तक उसे बचने की कुछ-न-कुछ आशा थी। माल अभी तक कहीं बरामद न हुआ था, पर आज उसे माल के बरामद होने की खबर मिल गयी थी। इसी दम थानेदार कांस्टेबिल को लिए आता होगा। बचने का कोई उपाय नहीं। थानेदार को रिश्वत देने से सम्भव है मुकदमे को दबा दे, रुपये हाथ में थे, पर क्या बात छिपी रहेगी? अभी माल बरामद नही हुआ, फिर भी सारे शहर में अफवाह थी कि बेटे ने ही माल उड़ाया है।

माल मिल जाने पर तो गली-गली बात फैल जाएगी। फिर वह किसी को मुंह न दिखा सकेगा।

मुंशीजी कचहरी से लौटे तो बहुत घबराये हुए थे। सिर थामकर चारपाई पर बैठ गये।

निर्मला ने कहा–कपड़े क्यों नहीं उतारते? आज तो और दिनों से देर हो गयी है।

मुंशीजी–क्या कपड़े ऊतारुं? तुमने कुछ सुना?

निर्मला–क्या बात है? मैंने तो कुछ नहीं सुना?

मुंशीजी–माल बरामद हो गया। अब जिया का बचना मुश्किल है।

निर्मला को आश्चर्य नहीं हुआ। उसके चेहरे से ऐसा जान पड़ा, मानो उसे यह बात मालूम थी। बोली–मैं तो पहले ही कर रही थी कि थाने में इत्तला मत कीजिए।

मुंशीजी–तुम्हें जिया पर शक था?

निर्मला–शक क्यों नहीं था, मैंने उन्हें अपने कमरे से निकलते देखा था।

मुंशीजी–फिर तुमने मुझसे क्यों न कह दिया?

निर्मला–यह बात मेरे कहने की न थी। आपके दिल में जरुर खयाल आता कि यह ईर्ष्यावश आक्षेप लगा रही है। कहिए, यह खयाल होता या नहीं? झूठ न बोलिएगा।

मुंशीजी–सम्भव है, मैं इन्कार नहीं कर सकता। फिर भी उस दशा में तुम्हें मुझसे कह देना चाहिए था। रिपोर्ट की नौबत न आती। तुमने अपनी नेकनामी की तो फिक्र की, पर यह न सोचा कि परिणाम क्या होगा? मैं अभी थाने से चला आता हूं। अलायार खां आता ही होगा!

निर्मला ने हताश होकर पूछा–फिर अब?

मुंशीजी ने आकाश की ओर ताकते हुए कहा–फिर जैसी भगवान् की इच्छा। हजार-दो हजार रुपये रिश्वत देने के लिए होते तो शायद मामला दब जाता, पर मेरी हालत तो तुम जानती हो। तकदीर खोटी है और कुछ नहीं। पाप तो मैंने किया है, दण्ड कौन भोगेगा? एक लड़का था, उसकी वह दशा हुई, दूसरे की यह दशा हो रही है। नालायक था,

गुस्ताख था, कामचोर था, पर था ता अपना ही लड़का, कभी-न-कभी चेत ही जाता। यह चोट अब न सही जाएगी।

निर्मला–अगर कुछ दे-दिलाकर जान बच सके, तो मैं रुपये का प्रबन्ध कर दूं।

मुंशीजी–कर सकती हो? कितने रुपये दे सकती हो?

निर्मला–कितना दरकार होगा?

मुंशीजी–एक हजार से कम पर तो शायद बातचीत न हो सके। मैंने एक मुकदमे में उससे एक हजार लिए थे। वह कसर आज निकालेगा।

निर्मला–हो जाएगा। अभी थाने जाइए।

मुंशीजी को थाने में बड़ी देर लगी। एकान्त में बातचीत करने का बहुत देर मे मौका मिला। अलायार खां पुराना घाघ थ। बड़ी मुश्किल से अण्टी पर चढ़ा। पांच सौ रुपये लेकर भी अहसान का बोझा सिर पर लाद ही दिया। काम हो गया। लौटकर निर्मला से बोला-लो भाई, बाजी मार ली, रुपये तुमने दिये, पर काम मेरी जबान ही ने किया। बड़ी-बड़ी मुश्किलों से राजी हो गया। यह भी याद रहेगी। जियाराम भोजन कर चुका है?

निर्मला–कहां, वह तो अभी घूमकर लौटे ही नहीं।

मुंशीजी–बारह तो बज रहे होंगें।

निर्मला–कई दफे जा-जाकर देख आयी। कमरे में अंधेरा पड़ा हुआ है।

गुंशीजी–और सियाराम?

निर्मला–वह तो खा-पीकर सोये हैं।

मुंशीजी–उससे पूछा नहीं, जिया कहां गया?

निर्मला–वह तो कहते हैं, मुझसे कुछ कहकर नहीं गये।

मुंशीजी को कुछ शंका हुई। सियाराम को जगाकर पूछा–तुमसे जियाराम ने कुछ कहा नहीं, कब तक लौटेगा? गया कहां है?

सियाराम ने सिर खुजलाते और आंखों मलते हुए कहा–मुझसे कुछ नहीं कहा।

मुंशीजी–कपड़े सब पहनकर गया है?

सियाराम—जी नहीं, कुर्ता और धोती।

मुंशीजी—जाते वक्त खुश था?

सियाराम—खुश तो नहीं मालूम होते थे। कई बार अन्दर आने का इरादा किया, पर देहरी से ही लौट गये। कई मिनट तक सायबान में खड़े रहे। चलने लगे, तो आंखें पोंछ रहे थे। इधर कई दिन से अक्सर रोया करते थे।

मुंशीजी ने ऐसी ठंडी सांस ली, मानो जीवन में अब कुछ नहीं रहा और निर्मला से बोले—तुमने किया तो अपनी समझ में भले ही के लिए, पर कोई शत्रु भी मुझ पर इससे कठोर आघात न कर सकता था। जियाराम की माता होती, तो क्या वह यह संकोच करती? कदापि नहीं।

निर्मला बोली—जरा डॉक्टर साहब के यहां क्यों नहीं चले जाते? शायद वहां बैठे हों। कई लड़के रोज आते है, उनसे पूछिए, शायद कुछ पता लग जाए। फूंक-फूंककर चलने पर भी अपयश लग ही गया।

मुंशीजी ने मानो खुली हुई खिड़की से कहा—हां, जाता हूं और क्या करुंगा। मुंशीजी बाहर आये तो देखा, डॉक्टर सिन्हा खड़े हैं। चौंककर पूछा—क्या आप देर से खड़े हैं?

डॉक्टर—जी नहीं, अभी आया हूं। आप इस वक्त कहां जा रहे हैं? साढ़े बारह हो गये हैं।

मुंशीजी—आप ही की तरफ आ रहा था। जियाराम अभी तक घूमकर नहीं आया। आपकी तरफ तो नहीं गया था?

डॉक्टर सिन्हा ने मुंशीजी के दोनों हाथ पकड़ लिए और इतना कह पाये थे, 'भाई साहब, अब धैर्य से काम..' कि मुंशीजी गोली खाये हुए मनुष्य की भांति जमीन पर गिर पड़े।

रुक्मिणी ने निर्मला से त्यौरियां बदलकर कहा—क्या नंगे पांव ही मदरसे जाएगा? निर्मला ने बच्ची के बाल गूंथते हुए कहा—मैं क्या करुं? मेरे पास रुपये नहीं हैं।

रुक्मिणी–गहने बनवाने को रुपये जुड़ते हैं, लड़के के जूतों के लिए रुपयों में आग लग जाती है। दो तो चले ही गये, क्या तीसरे को भी रुला-रुलाकर मार डालने का इरादा है?

निर्मला ने एक सांस खींचकर कहा–जिसको जीना है, जियेगा, जिसको मरना है, मरेगा। मैं किसी को मारने-जिलाने नहीं जाती।

आजकल एक-न-एक बात पर निर्मला और रुक्मिणी में रोज ही झड़प हो जाती थी। जब से गहने चोरी गये हैं, निर्मला का स्वभाव बिलकुल बदल गया है। वह एक-एक कौड़ी दांत से पकड़ने लगी है। सियाराम रोते–रोते चहे जान दे दे, मगर उसे मिठाई के लिए पैसे नहीं मिलते और यह बर्ताव कुछ सियाराम ही के साथ नहीं है, निर्मला स्वयं अपनी जरुरतों को टालती रहती है। धोती जब तक फटकर तार-तार न हो जाए, नयी धोती नहीं आती। महीनों सिर का तेल नहीं मंगाया जाता। पान खाने का उसे शौक था, कई-कई दिन तक पानदान खाली पड़ा रहता है, यहां तक कि बच्ची के लिए दूध भी नहीं आता। नन्हे से शिशु का भविष्य विराट् रुप धारण करके उसके विचार-क्षेत्र पर मंडराता रहता।

मुंशीजी ने अपने को सम्पूर्णतया निर्मला के हाथों मे सौंप दिया है। उसके किसी काम में दखल नहीं देते। न जाने क्यों उससे कुछ दबे रहते हैं। वह अब बिना नागा कचहरी जाते हैं। इतनी मेहनत उन्होंने जवानी में भी न की थी। आंखें खराब हो गयी हैं, डॉक्टर सिन्हा ने रात को लिखने-पढ़ने की मुमानियत कर दी है, पाचनशक्ति पहले ही दुर्बल थी, अब और भी खराब हो गयी है, दमें की शिकायत भी पैदा हो चली है, पर बेचारे सबेरे से आधी-आधी रात तक काम करते हैं। काम करने को जी चाहे या न चाहे, तबीयत अच्छी हो या न हो, काम करना ही पड़ता है।

निर्मला को उन पर जरा भी दया नहीं आती। वही भविष्य की भीषण चिन्ता उसके आन्तरिक सद्भावों का सर्वनाश कर रही है। किसी भिक्षुक की आवाज सुनकर झल्ला पड़ती है। वह एक कौड़ी भी खर्च करना नहीं चाहती।

एक दिन निर्मला ने सियाराम को घी लाने के लिए बाजार भेजा। भूंगी पर उनका विश्वास न था, उससे अब कोई सौदा न मंगाती थी। सियाराम में काट-कपट की आदत न थी। औने-पौने करना न जानता था। प्रायः बाजार का सारा काम उसी को करना पड़ता।

निर्मला एक-एक चीज को तोलती, जरा भी कोई चीज तोल में कम पड़ती, तो उसे लौटा देती। सियाराम का बहुत-सा समय इसी लौट-फेरी में बीत जाता था। बाजार वाले उसे जल्दी कोई सौदा न देते। आज भी वही नौबत आयी। सियाराम अपने विचार से बहुत अच्छा घी, कई दूकान से देखकर लाया, लेकिन निर्मला ने उसे सूंघते ही कहा–घी खराब है, लौटा आओ।

सियाराम ने झुंझलाकर कहा–इससे अच्छा घी बाजार में नहीं है, मैं सारी दूकानें देखकर लाया हूं?

निर्मला–तो मैं झूठ कहती हूं?

सियाराम–यह मैं नहीं कहता, लेकिन बनिया अब घी वापिस न लेगा। उसने मुझसे कहा था, जिस तरह देखना चाहो, यहीं देखो, माल तुम्हारे सामने है। बोहिनी-बट्टे के वक्त में सौदा वापस न लूंगा। मैंने सूंघकर, चखकर लिया। अब किस मुंह से लौटने जाऊं?

निर्मला ने दांत पीसकर कहा–घी में साफ चरबी मिली हुई है और तुम कहते हो, घी अच्छा है। मैं इसे रसोई में न ले जाऊंगी, तुम्हारा जी चाहे लौटा दो, चाहे खा जाओ।

घी की हांड़ी वहीं छोड़कर निर्मला घर में चली गयी।

सियाराम क्रोध और क्षोभ से कातर हो उठा। वह कौन मुंह लेकर लौटाने जाए? बनिया साफ कह देगा–मैं नहीं लौटाता। तब वह क्या करेगा? आस-पास के दस-पांच बनिये और सड़क पर चलने वाले आदमी खड़े हो जाएंगे। उन सबों के सामने उसे लज्जित होना पड़ेगा। बाजार में यों ही कोई बनिया उसे जल्दी सौदा नहीं देता, वह किसी दूकान पर खड़ा होने नहीं पाता। चारों ओर से उसी पर लताड़ पड़ेगी। उसने मन-ही-मन झुंझलाकर कहा–पड़ा रहे घी, मैं लौटाने न जाऊंगा।

मातृहीन बालक के समान दुखी, दीन–प्राणी संसार में दूसरा नहीं होता, और सारे दुःख भूल जाते हैं। बालक को माता याद आयी, अम्मां होती, तो क्या आज मुझे यह सब सहना पड़ता? भैया चले गये, मैं ही अकेला यह विपत्ति सहने के लिए क्यों बचा रहा?

सियाराम की आंखों में आंसू की झड़ी लग गयी। उसके शोक कातर कण्ठ से एक गहरे निःश्वास के साथ मिले हुए ये शब्द निकल आये–अम्मां! तुम मुझे भूल क्यों गयीं, क्यों नहीं बुला लेतीं?

सहसा निर्मला फिर कमरे की तरफ आयी। उसने समझा था, सियाराम चला गया होगा। उसे बैठा देखा, तो गुस्से से बोली–तुम अभी तक बैठे ही हो? आखिर खाना कब बनेगा?

सियाराम ने आंखें पोंछ डालीं। बोला–मुझे स्कूल जाने में देर हो जाएगी।

निर्मला–एक दिन देर हो जाएगी तो कौन हरज है? यह भी तो घर ही का काम है?

सियाराम–रोज तो यही धन्धा लगा रहता है। कभी वक्त पर स्कूल नहीं पहुंचता। घर पर भी पढ़ने का वक्त नहीं मिलता। कोई सौदा दो-चार बार लौटाये बिना नहीं जाता। डांट तो मुझ पर पड़ती है, शर्मिंदा तो मुझे होना पड़ता है, आपको क्या?

निर्मला–हां, मुझे क्या? मैं तो तुम्हारी दुश्मन ठहरी! अपना होता, तब तो उसे दुःख होता। मैं तो ईश्वर से मनाया करती हूं कि तुम पढ़-लिख न सको। मुझमें सारी बुराइयां-ही-बुराइयां हैं, तुम्हारा कोई कसूर नहीं। विमाता का नाम ही बुरा होता है। अपनी मां विष भी खिलाये, तो अमृत हैं; मैं अमृत भी पिलाऊं, तो विष हो जाएगा। तुम लोगों के कारण में मिट्टी में मिल गयी, रोते-रोते उम्र काटी जाती है, मालूम ही न हुआ कि भगवान ने किसलिए जन्म दिया था और तुम्हारी समझ में मैं विहार कर रही हूं। तुम्हें सताने में मुझे बड़ा मजा आता है। भगवान् भी नहीं पूछते कि सारी विपत्ति का अन्त हो जाता।

यह कहते-कहते निर्मला की आंखें भर आयी। अन्दर चली गयी। सियाराम उसको रोते देखकर सहम उठा। ग्लानि तो नहीं आयी; पर

शंका हुई कि न जाने कौन-सा दण्ड मिले। चुपके से हांड़ी उठा ली और घी लौटाने चला, इस तरह जैसे कोई कुत्ता किसी नये गांव में जाता है। उसे देखकर साधारण बुद्धि का मनुष्य भी अनुमान कर सकता था कि वह अनाथ है।

सियाराम ज्यों-ज्यों आगे बढ़ता था, आनेवाले संग्राम के भय से उसकी हृदय-गति बढ़ती जाती थी। उसने निश्चय किया—बनिये ने घी न लौटाया, तो वह घी वहीं छोड़कर चला आयेगा। झख मारकर बनिया आप ही बुलायेगा। बनिये को डांटने के लिए भी उसने शब्द सोच लिए। वह कहेगा—क्यों साहूजी, आंखों में धूल झोंकते हो? दिखाते हो चोखा माल और और देते हो रद्दी माल? पर यह निश्चय करने पर भी उसके पैर आगे बहुत धीरे-धीरे उठते थे। वह यह न चाहता था, बनिया उसे आता हुआ देखे, वह अकस्मात् ही उसके सामने पहुंच जाना चाहता था। इसलिए वह चक्कार काटकर दूसरी गली से बनिये की दूकान पर गया।

बनिये ने उसे देखते ही कहा—हमने कह दिया था कि हम सौदा वापस न लेंगे। बोलो, कहा था कि नहीं।

सियाराम ने बिगड़कर कहा—तुमने वह घी कहां दिया, जो दिखाया था? दिखाया एक माल, दिया दूसरा माल, लौटाओगे कैसे नहीं? क्या कुछ राहजनी है?

साह—इससे चोखा घी बाजार में निकल आये तो जरीबाना दूं। उठा लो हांड़ी और दो-चार दूकान देख आओ।

सियाराम—हमें इतनी फुर्सत नहीं है। अपना घी लौटा लो।

साह—घी न लौटेगा।

बनिये की दुकान पर एक जटाधारी साधू बैठा हुआ यह तमाश देख रहा था। उठकर सियाराम के पास आया और हांड़ी का घी सूंघकर बोला—बच्चा, घी तो बहुत अच्छा मालूम होता है।

साह ने शह पाकर कहा—बाबाजी हम लोग तो आप ही इनको घटिया माल नहीं देते। खराब माल क्या जाने-सुने ग्राहकों को दिया जाता है?

साधु—घी ले जाव बच्चा, बहुत अच्छा है।

सियाराम रो पड़ा। घी को बुरा सिद्ध करने के लिए उसके पास अब क्या प्रमाण था? बोला–वही तो कहती हैं, घी अच्छा नहीं है, लौटा आओ। मैं तो कहता था कि घी अच्छा है।

साधु–कौन कहता है?

साह–इसकी अम्मां कहती होंगी। कोई सौदा उनके मन ही नहीं भाता। बेचारे लड़के को बार-बार दौड़ाया करती है। सौतेली मां है न! अपनी मां हो तो कुछ ख्याल भी करे।

साधु ने सियराम को सदय नेत्रों से देखा, मानो उसे त्राण देने के लिए उनका हृदय विकल हो रहा है। तब करुण स्वर से बोले–तुम्हारी माता का स्वर्गवास हुए कितने दिन हुए बच्चा?

सियाराम–छठा साल है।

साधु–तो तुम उस वक्त बहुत ही छोटे रहे होंगे। भगवान् तुम्हारी लीला कितनी विचित्र है। इस दुधमुंहे बालक को तुमने मातृ-प्रेम से वंचित कर दिया। बड़ा अनर्थ करते हो भगवान! छः साल का बालक और राक्षसी विमाता के पाले पड़े! धन्य हो दयानिधि! साहजी, बालक पर दया करो, घी लौटा लो, नहीं तो इसकी माता इसे घर में रहने न देगी। भगवान की इच्छा से तुम्हारा घी जल्द बिक जाएगा। मेरा आशीर्वाद तुम्हारे साथ रहेगा।

साहजी ने रुपये वापस न किये। आखिर लड़के को फिर घी लेने आना ही पड़ेगा। न जाने दिन में कितनी बार चक्कर लगाना पड़े और किस जालिये से पाला पड़े। उसकी दुकान में जो घी सबसे अच्छा था, वह सियाराम को दिया।

सियाराम दिल से सोच रहा था, बाबाजी कितने दयालु हैं? इन्होंने सिफारिश न की होती, तो साहजी क्यों अच्छा घी देते? सियाराम घी लेकर चला, तो बाबाजी भी उसके साथ ही लिये। रास्ते में मीठी-मीठी बातें करने लगे।

'बच्चा, मेरी माता भी मुझे तीन साल का छोड़कर परलोक सिधारी थीं। तभी से मातृ-विहीन बालकों को देखता हूं तो मेरा हृदय फटने लगता हैं।'

सियाराम ने पूछा—आपके पिताजी ने भी तो दूसरा विवाह कर लिया था?

साधु—हां, बच्चा, नहीं तो आज साधु क्यों होता? पहले तो पिताजी विवाह न करते थे। मुझे बहुत प्यार करते थे, फिर न जाने क्यों मन बदल गया, विवाह कर लिया। साधु हूं, कटु वचन मुंह से नहीं निकालना चाहिए, पर मेरी विमाता जितनी ही सुन्दर थीं, उतनी ही कठोर थीं। मुझे दिन-दिन-भर खाने को न देतीं, रोता तो मारतीं। पिताजी की आंखें भी फिर गयीं। उन्हें मेरी सूरत से घृणा होने लगी। मेरा रोना सुनकर मुझे पीटने लगते। अन्त को मैं एक दिन घर से निकल खड़ा हुआ।

सियाराम के मन में भी घर से निकल भागने का विचार कई बार हुआ था। इस समय भी उसके मन में यही विचार उठ रहा था। बड़ी उत्सुकता से बोला—घर से निकलकर आप कहां गये?

बाबाजी ने हंसकर कहा—उसी दिन मेरे सारे कष्टों का अन्त हो गया जिस दिन घर के मोह-बन्धन से छूटा और भय मन से निकला, उसी दिन मानो मेरा उद्धार हो गया। दिन भर मैं एक पुल के नीचे बैठा रहा। संध्या समय मुझे एक महात्मा मिल गये। उनका नाम स्वामी परमानन्दजी था। वे बाल-ब्रह्मचारी थे। मुझ पर उन्होंने दया की और अपने साथ रख लिया। उनके साथ मैं देश-देशान्तरों में घूमने लगा। वह बड़े अच्छे योगी थे। मुझे भी उन्होंने योग-विद्या सिखाई। अब तो मेरे को इतना अभ्यास हो गया है कि जब इच्छा होती है, माताजी के दर्शन कर लेता हूं, उनसे बात कर लेता हूं।

सियाराम ने विस्फारित नेत्रों से देखकर पूछा—आपकी माता का तो देहान्त हो चुका था?

साधु—तो क्या हुआ बच्चा, योग-विद्या में वह शक्ति है कि जिस मृत-आत्मा को चाहे, बुला ले।

सियाराम—मैं योग-विद्या सीख लूं, तो मुझे भी माताजी के दर्शन होंगे?

साधु—अवश्य, अभ्यास से सब कुछ हो सकता है। हां, योग्य गुरु चाहिए। योग से बड़ी-बड़ी सिद्धियां प्राप्त हो सकती हैं। जितना धन

चाहो, पल-मात्र में मंगा सकते हो। कैसी ही बीमारी हो, उसकी औषधि बता सकते हो।

सियाराम–आपका स्थान कहां है?

साधु–बच्चा, मेरा कोई स्थान कहीं नहीं है। देश-देशान्तरों में रमता फिरता हूं। अच्छा, बच्चा अब तुम जाओ, मै जरा स्नान-ध्यान करने जाऊंगा।

सियाराम–चलिए मैं भी उसी तरफ चलता हूं। आपके दर्शन से जी नहीं भरा।

साधु–नहीं बच्चा, तुम्हें पाठशाला जाने की देरी हो रही है।

सियाराम–फिर आपके दर्शन कब होंगे?

साधु–कभी आ जाऊंगा बच्चा, तुम्हारा घर कहां है?

सियाराम प्रसन्न होकर बोला–चलिएगा मेरे घर? बहुत नजदीक है। आपकी बड़ी कृपा होगी।

सियाराम कदम बढ़ाकर आगे-आगे चलने लगा। इतना प्रसन्न था, मानो सोने की गठरी लिए जाता हो। घर के सामने पहुंचकर बोला–आइए, बैठिए कुछ देर।

साधु–नहीं बच्चा, बैठूंगा नहीं। फिर कल-परसों किसी समय आ जाऊंगा। यही तुम्हारा घर है?

सियाराम–कल किस वक्त आइयेगा?

साधु–निश्चय नहीं कह सकता। किसी समय आ जाऊंगा।

साधु आगे बढ़े, तो थोड़ी ही दूर पर उन्हें एक दूसरा साधु मिला। उसका नाम था हरिहरानन्द। परमानन्द से पूछा–कहां-कहां की सैर की? कोई शिकार फंसा?

हरिहरानन्द–इधर चारों तरफ घूम आया, कोई शिकार न मिला, एकाध मिला भी, तो मेरी हंसी उड़ाने लगा।

परमानन्द–मुझे तो एक मिलता हुआ जान पड़ता है! फंस जाए तो जानूं।

हरिहरानन्द–तुम यों ही कहा करते हो। जो आता है, दो-एक दिन के बाद निकल भागता है।

परमानन्द–अबकी न भागेगा, देख लेना। इसकी मां मर गयी है। बाप ने दूसरा विवाह कर लिया है। मां भी सताया करती है। घर से ऊबा हुआ है।

हरिहरानन्द–खूब...अच्छी तरह। यही तरकीब सबसे अच्छी है। पहले इसका पता लगा लेना चाहिए कि मुहल्ले में किन-किन घरों में विमाताएं हैं? उन्हीं घरों में फन्दा डालना चाहिए।

14

निर्मला ने बिगड़कर कहा—इतनी देर कहां लगायी?

सियाराम ने ढिठाई से कहा—रास्ते में एक जगह सो गया था।

निर्मला—यह तो मैं नहीं कहती, पर जानते हो कै बज गये हैं? दस कभी के बज गये। बाजार कुछ दूर भी तो नहीं है।

सियाराम—कुछ दूर नहीं। दरवाजे ही पर तो है।

निर्मला—सीधे से क्यों नहीं बोलते? ऐसा बिगड़ रहे हो, जैसे मेरा ही कोई कामे करने गये हो?

सियाराम—तो आप व्यर्थ की बकवास क्यों करती हैं? लिया सौदा लौटाना क्या आसान काम है? बनिये से घंटों हुज्जत करनी पड़ी यह तो कहो, एक बाबाजी ने कह—सुनकर फेरवा दिया, नहीं तो किसी तरह न फेरता। रास्ते में कहीं एक मिनट भी न रुका, सीधा चला आता हूं।

निर्मला—घी के लिए गये-गये, तो तुम ग्यारह बजे लौटे हो, लकड़ी के लिए जाओगे, तो सांझ ही कर दोगे। तुम्हारे बाबूजी बिना खाये ही चले गये। तुम्हें इतनी देर लगानी था, तो पहले ही क्यों न कह दिया? जाते हो लकड़ी के लिए?

सियाराम अब अपने को संभाल न सका। झल्लाकर बोला—लकड़ी किसी और से मंगाइए। मुझे स्कूल जाने को देर हो रही है।

निर्मला—खाना न खाओगे?

सियाराम—न खाऊंगा।

निर्मला—मैं खाना बनाने को तैयार हूं। हां, लकड़ी लाने नहीं जा सकती।

सियाराम—भूंगी को क्यों नहीं भेजती?

निर्मला—भूंगी का लाया सौदा तुमने कभी देखा नहीं है?

सियाराम—तो मैं इस वक्त न जाऊंगा।

निर्मला—मुझे दोष न देना।

सियाराम कई दिनों से स्कूल नहीं गया था। बाजार-हाट के मारे उसे किताबें देखने का समय ही न मिलता था। स्कूल जाकर झिड़कियां खाने, बेंच पर खड़े होने या ऊंची टोपी देने के सिवा और क्या मिलता? वह घर से किताबें लेकर चलता, पर शहर के बाहर जाकर किसी वृक्ष की छांह में बैठा रहता या पल्टनों की कवायद देखता। तीन बजे से घर लौट आता। आज भी वह घर से चला, लेकिन बैठने में उसका जी न लगा, उस पर आंतें अलग जल रही थीं। हा! अब उसे रोटियों के भी लाले पड़ गये। दस बजे क्या खाना न बन सकता था? माना कि बाबूजी चले गये थे। क्या मेरे लिए घर में दो-चार पैसे भी न थे? अम्मां होतीं, तो इस तरह बिना कुछ खाये-पिये आने देतीं? मेरा अब कोई नहीं रहा।

सियाराम का मन बाबाजी के दर्शन के लिए व्याकुल हो उठा। उसने सोचा—इस वक्त वह कहां मिलेंगे? कहां चलकर देखूं? उनकी मनोहर वाणी, उनकी उत्साहप्रद सान्त्वना, उसके मन को खींचने लगी। उसने आतुर होकर कहा—मैं उनके साथ ही क्यों न चला गया? घर पर मेरे लिए क्या रखा था?

वह आज यहां से चला तो घर न जाकर सीधा घी वाले साहजी की दुकान पर गया। शायद बाबाजी से वहां मुलाकात हो जाए, पर वहां बाबाजी न थे। बड़ी देर तक खड़ा-खड़ा लौट आया।

घर आकर बैठा ही था कि निर्मला ने आकर कहा—आज देर कहां लगाई? सवेरे खाना नहीं बना, क्या इस वक्त भी उपवास होगा? जाकर बाजार से कोई तरकारी लाओ।

सियाराम ने झल्लाकर कहा—दिनभर का भूखा चला आता हूं; कुछ पानी पीने तक को लाई नहीं, ऊपर से बाजार जाने का हुक्म दे दिया। मैं नहीं जाता बाजार, किसी का नौकर नहीं हूं। आखिर रोटियां ही तो खिलाती हो या और कुछ? ऐसी रोटियां जहां मेहनत करुंगा, वहीं मिल जाएंगी। जब मजूरी ही करनी है, तो आपकी न करुंगा, जाइए मेरे लिए खाना मत बनाइएगा।

निर्मला अवाक् रह गयी। लड़के को आज क्या हो गया? और दिन तो चुपके से जाकर काम कर लाता था, आज क्यों त्योरियां बदल रहा है? अब भी उसको यह न सूझी कि सियाराम को दो-चार पैसे कुछ खाने के दे दे। उसका स्वभाव इतना कृपण हो गया था, बोली—घर का काम करना तो मजूरी नहीं कहलाती। इसी तरह मैं भी कह दूं कि मैं खाना नहीं पकाती, तुम्हारे बाबूजी कह दें कि कचहरी नहीं जाता, तो क्या हो बताओ? नहीं जाना चाहते, तो मत जाओ, भूंगी से मंगा लूंगी। मैं क्या जानती थी कि तुम्हें बाजार जाना बुरा लगता है, नहीं तो बला से धेले की चीज पैसे में आती, तुम्हें न भेजती। लो, आज से कान पकड़ती हूं।

सियाराम दिल में कुछ लज्जित तो हुआ, पर बाजार न गया। उसका ध्यान बाबाजी की ओर लगा हुआ था। अपने सारे दुखों का अन्त और जीवन की सारी आशाएं उसे अब बाबाजी के आशीर्वाद में मालूम होती थीं। उन्हीं की शरण जाकर उसका यह आधारहीन जीवन सार्थक होगा। सूर्यास्त के समय वह अधीर हो गया। सारा बाजार छान मारा, लेकिन बाबाजी का कहीं पता न मिला। दिनभर का भूखा-प्यासा, वह अबोध बालक दुखते हुए दिल को हाथों से दबाये, आशा और भय की मूर्ति बना, दुकानों, गलियों और मन्दिरों में उस आश्रय को खोजता फिरता था, जिसके बिना उसे अपना जीवन दुस्सह हो रहा था। एक बार मन्दिर के सामने उसे कोई साधु खड़ा दिखाई दिया। उसने समझा वही हैं। हर्षोल्लास से वह फूल उठा। दौड़ा और साधु के पास खड़ा हो गया। पर यह कोई और ही महात्मा थे। निराश हो कर आगे बढ़ गया।

धीरे-धीरे सड़कों पर सन्नाटा छा गया, घरों के द्वार बन्द होने लगे। सड़क की पटरियों पर और गलियों में बंसखटे या बोरे बिछा-बिछाकर भारत की प्रजा सुख-निद्रा में मग्न होने लगी, लेकिन सियाराम घर न लौटा। उस घर से उसका दिल फट गया था, जहां किसी को उससे प्रेम न था, जहां वह किसी पराश्रित की भांति पड़ा हुआ था, केवल इसीलिए कि उसे और कहीं शरण न थी। इस वक्त भी उसके घर न जाने की किसे चिन्ता होगी?

बाबूजी भोजन करके लेटे होंगे, अम्मांजी भी आराम करने जा रही होंगी। किसी ने मेरे कमरे की ओर झांककर देखा भी न होगा।

हां, बुआजी घबरा रही होंगी, वह अभी तक मेरी राह देखती होंगी। जब तक मैं न जाऊंगा, भोजन न करेंगी।

रुक्मिणी की याद आते ही सियाराम घर की ओर चल दिया। वह अगर और कुछ न कर सकती थी, तो कम-से-कम उसे गोद में चिमटाकर रोती थी? उसके बाहर से आने पर हाथ–मुंह धोने के लिए पानी तो रख देती थीं। संसार में सभी बालक दूध की कुल्लियां नहीं करते, सभी सोने के कौर नहीं खाते। कितनों को पेट भर भोजन भी नहीं मिलता; पर घर से विरक्त वही होते हैं, जो मातृ-स्नेह से वंचित हैं।

सियाराम घर की ओर चला ही कि सहसा बाबा परमानन्द एक गली से आते दिखायी दिये।

सियाराम ने जाकर उनका हाथ पकड़ लिया। परमानन्द ने चौंककर पूछा–बच्चा, तुम यहां कहां?

सियाराम ने बात बनाकर कहा–एक दोस्त से मिलने आया था। आपका स्थान यहां से कितनी दूर है?

परमानन्द–हम लोग तो आज यहां से जा रहे हैं, बच्चा, हरिद्वार की यात्रा है।

सियाराम ने हतोत्साहित होकर कहा–क्या आज ही चले जाइएगा?

परमानन्द–हां बच्चा, अब लौटकर आऊंगा, तो दर्शन दूंगा?

सियाराम ने कातर कंठ से कहा–मैं भी आपके साथ चलूंगा।

परमानन्द–मेरे साथ! तुम्हारे घर के लोग जाने देंगे?

सियाराम–घर के लोगों को मेरी क्या परवाह है? इसके आगे सियाराम और कुछ न कह सका। उसके अश्रु-पूरित नेत्रों ने उसकी करुणगाथा उससे कहीं विस्तार के साथ सुना दी, जितनी उसकी वाणी कर सकती थी।

परमानन्द ने बालक को कंठ से लगाकर कहा–अच्छा बच्चा, तेरी इच्छा हो तो चल। साधु-सन्तों की संगति का आनन्द उठा। भगवान् की इच्छा होगी, तो तेरी इच्छा पूरी होगी।

दाने पर मण्डराता हुआ पक्षी अन्त में दाने पर गिर पड़ा। उसके जीवन का अन्त पिंजरे में होगा या व्याध की छुरी के तले–यह कौन जानता है?

15

मुंशीजी पांच बजे कचहरी से लौटे और अन्दर आकर चारपाई पर गिर पड़े। बुढ़ापे की देह, उस पर आज सारे दिन भोजन न मिला। मुंह सूख गया। निर्मला समझ गयी, आज दिन खाली गया निर्मला ने पूछा–आज कुछ न मिला।

मुंशीजी–सारा दिन दौड़ते गुजरा, पर हाथ कुछ न लगा।

निर्मला–फौजदारी वाले मामले में क्या हुआ?

मुंशीजी–मेरे मुवक्किल को सजा हो गयी।

निर्मला–पंडित वाले मुकदमे में?

मुंशीजी–पंडित पर डिग्री हो गयी।

निर्मला–आप तो कहते थे, दावा खरिज हो जाएगा।

मुंशीजी–कहता तो था, और अब भी कहता हूं कि दावा खारिज हो जाना चाहिए था, मगर उतना सिर मगजन कौन करे?

निर्मला–और सीरवाले दावे में?

मुंशीजी–उसमें भी हार हो गयी।

निर्मला–तो आज आप किसी अभागे का मुंह देखकर उठे थे।

मुंशीजी से अब काम बिलकुल न हो सकता था। एक तो उसके पास मुकदमे आते ही न थे और जो आते भी थे, वह बिगड़ जाते थे। मगर अपनी असफलताओं को वह निर्मला से छिपाते रहते थे। जिस दिन कुछ हाथ न लगता, उस दिन किसी से दो-चार रुपये उधार लाकर निर्मला को देते, प्रायः सभी मित्रों से कुछ-न-कुछ ले चुके थे। आज वह डौल भी न लगा।

निर्मला ने चिन्तापूर्ण स्वर में कहा–आमदनी का यह हाल है, तो ईश्वर ही मालिक है, उस पर बेटे का यह हाल है कि बाजार जाना

मुश्किल है। भूंगी ही से सब काम कराने को जी चाहता है। घी लेकर ग्यारह बजे लौटा। कितना कहकर हार गयी कि लकड़ी लेते आओ, पर सुना ही नहीं।

मुंशीजी–तो खाना नहीं पकाया?

निर्मला–ऐसी ही बातों से तो आप मुकदमे हारते हैं। ईंधन के बिना किसी ने खाना बनाया है कि मैं ही बना लेती?

मुंशीजी–तो बिना कुछ खाये ही चला गया।

निर्मला–घर में और क्या रखा था जो खिला देती?

मुंशीजी ने डरते-डरते कहा–कुछ पैसे-वैसे न दे दिये?

निर्मला ने भौंहे सिकोड़कर कहा–घर में पैसे फलते हैं न?

मुंशीजी ने कुछ जवाब न दिया। जरा देर तक तो प्रतीक्षा करते रहे कि शायद जलपान के लिए कुछ मिलेगा, लेकिन जब निर्मला ने पानी तक न मंगवाया, तो बेचारे निराश होकर चले गये। सियाराम के कष्ट का अनुमान करके उनका चित्त चंचल हो उठा। एक बार भूंगी ही से लकड़ी मंगा ली जाती, तो ऐसा क्या नुकसान हो जाता? ऐसी किफायत भी किस काम की कि घर के आदमी भूखे रह जाएं। अपना संदूकचा खोलकर टटोलने लगे कि शायद दो-चार आने पैसे मिल जाए। उसके अन्दर के सारे कागज निकाल डाले, एक-एक, खाना देखा, नीचे हाथ डालकर देखा पर कुछ न मिला।

अगर निर्मला के सन्दूक में पैसे न फलते थे, तो इस सन्दूकचे में शायद इसके फूल भी न लगते हों, लेकिन संयोग ही कहिए कि कागजों को झाड़ते हुए एक चवन्नी गिर पड़ी। मारे हर्ष के मुंशीजी उछल पड़े। बड़ी-बड़ी रकमें इसके पहले कमा चुके थे, पर यह चवन्नी पाकर इस समय उन्हें जितना आह्लाद हुआ, उतना पहले कभी न हुआ था।

चवन्नी हाथ में लिए हुए सियाराम के कमरे के सामने आकर पुकारा। कोई जवाब न मिला। तब कमरे में जाकर देखा। सियाराम का कहीं पता नहीं–क्या अभी स्कूल से नहीं लौटा? मन में यह प्रश्न उठते ही मुंशीजी ने अन्दर जाकर भूंगी से पूछा। मालूम हुआ स्कूल से लौट आये।

मुंशीजी ने पूछा–कुछ पानी पिया है?

भूंगी ने कुछ जवाब न दिया। नाक सिकोड़कर मुंह फेरे हुए चली गयी।

मुंशीजी आहिस्ता-आहिस्ता आकर अपने कमरे में बैठ गये। आज पहली बार उन्हें निर्मला पर क्रोध आया, लेकिन एक ही क्षण में क्रोध का आघात अपने ऊपर होने लगा। उस अंधेरे कमेरे में फर्श पर लेटे हुए वह अपने पुत्र की ओर से इतना उदासीन हो जाने पर धिक्कारने लगे। दिन भर के थके थे। थोड़ी ही देर में उन्हें नींद आ गयी।

भूंगी ने आकर पुकारा—बाबूजी, रसोई तैयार है।

मुंशीजी चौंककर उठ बैठे। कमरे में लैम्प जल रहा था पूछा—कै बज गये भूंगी? मुझे तो नींद आ गयी थी।

भूंगी ने कहा—कोतवाली के घण्टे में नौ बज गये हैं और हम नाहीं जानत।

मुंशीजी—सिया बाबू आये?

भूंगी—आये होंगे, तो घर ही में न होंगे।

मुंशीजी ने झल्लाकर पूछा—मैं पूछता हूं, आये कि नहीं? और तू न जाने क्या-क्या जवाब देती है? आये कि नहीं?

भूंगी—मैंने तो नहीं देखा, झूठ कैसे कह दूं।

मुंशीजी फिर लेट गये और बोले—उनको आ जाने दे, तब चलता हूं।

आध घंटे द्वार की ओर आंख लगाए मुंशीजी लेटे रहे, तब वह उठकर बाहर आये और दाहिने हाथ कोई दो फर्लांग तक चले। तब लौटकर द्वार पर आये और पूछा—सिया बाबू आ गये?

अन्दर से आवाज आयी—अभी नहीं।

मुंशीजी फिर बायीं ओर चले और गली के नुक्कड़ तक गये। सियाराम कहीं दिखाई न दिया। वहां से फिर घर आये और द्वार पर खड़े होकर पूछा—सिया बाबू आ गये?

अन्दर से जवाब मिला—नहीं।

कोतवाली के घंटे में दस बजने लगे।

मुंशीजी बड़े वेग से कम्पनी बाग की तरफ चले। सोचने लगे, शायद वहां घूमने गया हो और घास पर लेटे-लेटे नींद आ गयी हो। बाग में पहुंचकर उन्होंने हरेक बेंच को देखा, चारों तरफ घूमे, बहुत से

आदमी घास पर पड़े हुए थे, पर सियाराम का निशान न था। उन्होंने सियाराम का नाम लेकर जोर से पुकारा, पर कहीं से आवाज न आयी।

ख्याल आया शायद स्कूल में तमाशा हो रहा हो। स्कूल एक मील से कुछ ज्यादा ही था। स्कूल की तरफ चले, पर आधे रास्ते से ही लौट पड़े। बाजार बन्द हो गया था। स्कूल में इतनी रात तक तमाशा नहीं हो सकता। अब भी उन्हें आशा हो रही थी कि सियाराम लौट आया होगा। द्वार पर आकर उन्होंने पुकारा–सिया बाबू आये? किवाड़ बन्द थे। कोई आवाज न आयी। फिर जोर से पुकारा।

भूंगी किवाड़ खोलकर बोली–अभी तो नहीं आये।

मुंशीजी ने धीरे से भूंगी को अपने पास बुलाया और करुण स्वर में बोले–तू तो घर की सब बातें जानती है, बता आज क्या हुआ था?

भूंगी–बाबूजी, झूठ न बोलूंगी, मालकिन छुड़ा देंगी और क्या? दूसरे का लड़का इस तरह नहीं रखा जाता। जहां कोई काम हुआ, बस बाजार भेज दिया। दिन भर बाजार दौड़ते बीतता था। आज लकड़ी लाने न गये, तो चूल्हा ही नहीं जला। कहो तो मुंह फुलावें। जब आप ही नहीं देखते, तो दूसरा कौन देखेगा? चलिए, भोजन कर लीजिए, बहूजी कब से बैठी हैं।

मुंशीजी–कह दे, इस वक्त नहीं खायेंगे।

मुंशीजी फिर अपने कमरे में चले गये और एक लम्बी सांस ली। वेदना से भरे हुए ये शब्द उनके मुंह से निकल पड़े–ईश्वर, क्या अभी दण्ड पूरा नहीं हुआ? क्या इस अंधे की लकड़ी को हाथ से छीन लोगे?

निर्मला ने आकर कहा–आज सियाराम अभी तक नहीं आये। कहती रही कि खाना बनाये देती हूं, खा लो मगर न जाने कब उठकर चल दिये! न जाने कहां घूम रहे हैं। बात तो सुनते ही नहीं। कब तक उनकी राह देखा करुं! आप चलकर खा लीजिए, उनके लिए खाना उठाकर रख दूंगी।

मुंशीजी ने निर्मला की ओर कठोर नेत्रों से देखकर कहा–अभी कै बजे होंगे?

निर्मला–क्या जाने, दस बजे होंगे।

मुंशीजी–जी नहीं, बारह बजे हैं।

निर्मला—बारह बज गये? इतनी देर तो कभी न करते थे। तो कब तक उनकी राह देखोगे! दोपहर को भी कुछ नहीं खाया था। ऐसा सैलानी लड़का मैंने नहीं देखा।

मुंशीजी—तुम्हें बहुत दिक करता है, क्यों?

निर्मला—देखिये न, इतना रात गयी और घर की सुध ही नहीं।

मुंशीजी—शायद यह आखिरी शरारत हो।

निर्मला—कैसी बातें मुंह से निकालते हैं? जाएंगे कहां? किसी यार-दोस्त के यहां पड़ रहे होंगे।

मुंशीजी—शायद ऐसा ही हो। ईश्वर करे ऐसा ही हो।

निर्मला—सबेरे आवें, तो जरा तम्बीह कीजिएगा।

मुंशीजी—खूब अच्छी तरह करुंगा।

निर्मला—चलिए, खा लीजिए, देर बहुत हुई।

मुंशीजी—सबेरे उसकी तम्बीह करके खाऊंगा, कहीं न आया, तो तुम्हें ऐसा ईमानदार नौकर कहां मिलेगा?

निर्मला ने ऐंठकर कहा—तो क्या मैंने भगा दिया?

मुंशीजी—नहीं, यह कौन कहता है? तुम उसे क्यों भगाने लगीं। तुम्हारा तो काम करता था, शामत आ गयी होगी।

निर्मला ने और कुछ नहीं कहा। बात बढ़ जाने का भय था। भीतर चली आयी। सोने को भी न कहा। जरा देर में भूंगी ने अन्दर से किवाड़ भी बन्द कर दिये।

क्या मुंशीजी को नींद आ सकती थी? तीन लड़कों में केवल एक बच रहा था। वह भी हाथ से निकल गया, तो फिर जीवन में अंधकार के सिवाय और क्या है? कोई नाम लेनेवाला भी नहीं रहेगा।

हा! कैसे-कैसे रत्न हाथ से निकल गये? मुंशीजी की आंखों से अश्रुधारा बह रही थी, तो कोई आश्चर्य है? उस व्यापक पश्चाताप, उस सघन ग्लानि-तिमिर में आशा की एक हल्की-सी रेखा उन्हें संभाले हुए थी। जिस क्षण वह रेखा लुप्त हो जाएगी, कौन कह सकता है, उन पर क्या बीतेगी? उनकी उस वेदना की कल्पना कौन कर सकता है? कई बार मुंशीजी की आंखें झपकीं, लेकिन हर बार सियाराम की आहट के धोखे में चौंक पड़े।

सबेरा होते ही मुंशीजी फिर सियाराम को खोजने निकले। किसी से पूछते शर्म आती थी। किस मुंह से पूछें? उन्हें किसी से सहानुभूति की आशा न थी। प्रकट न कहकर मन में सब यही कहेंगे, जैसा किया, वैसा भोगो! सारे दिन वह स्कूल के मैदानों, बाजारों और बगीचों का चक्कर लगाते रहे, दो दिन निराहार रहने पर भी उन्हें इतनी शक्ति कैसे हुई, यह वही जानें।

रात के बारह बजे मुंशीजी घर लौटे, दरवाजे पर लालटेन जल रही थी, निर्मला द्वार पर खड़ी थी। देखते ही बोली–कहा भी नहीं, न जाने कब चल दिये। कुछ पता चला?

मुंशीजी ने आग्नेय नेत्रों से ताकते हुए कहा–हट जाओ सामने से, नहीं तो बुरा होगा। मैं आपे में नहीं हूं। यह तुम्हारी करनी है। तुम्हारे ही कारण आज मेरी यह दशा हो रही है। आज से छः साल पहले क्या इस घर की यह दशा थी? तुमने मेरा बना-बनाया घर बिगाड़ दिया, तुमने मेरे लहलहाते बाग को उजाड़ डाला। केवल एक ठूंठ रह गया है। उसका निशान मिटाकर तभी तुम्हें संतोष होगा। मैं अपना सर्वनाश करने के लिए तुम्हें घर नहीं लाया था। सुखी जीवन को और भी सुखमय बनाना चाहता था। यह उसी का प्रायश्चित है। जो लड़के पान की तरह फेरे जाते थे, उन्हें मेरे जीते-जी तुमने चाकर समझ लिया और मैं आंखों से सब कुछ देखते हुए भी अंधा बना बैठा रहा। जाओ, मेरे लिए थोड़ा-सा संखिया भेज दो। बस, यही कसर रह गयी है, वह भी पूरी हो जाए।

निर्मला ने रोते हुए कहा–मैं तो अभागिन हूं ही, आप कहेंगे तब जानूंगी? न जाने ईश्वर ने मुझे जन्म क्यों दिया था? मगर यह आपने कैसे समझ लिया कि सियाराम आवेंगे ही नहीं?

मुंशीजी ने अपने कमरे की ओर जाते हुए कहा–जलाओ मत जाकर खुशियां मनाओ। तुम्हारी मनोकामना पूरी हो गयी।

16

निर्मला सारी रात रोती रही। इतना कलंक! उसने जियाराम को गहने ले जाते देखने पर भी मुंह खोलने का साहस नहीं किया। क्यों? इसीलिए तो कि लोग समझेंगे कि यह मिथ्या दोषारोपण करके लड़के से वैर साध रही हैं। आज उसके मौन रहने पर उसे अपराधिनी ठहराया जा रहा है। यदि वह जियाराम को उसी क्षण रोक देती और जियाराम लज्जावश कहीं भाग जाता, तो क्या उसके सिर अपराध न मढ़ा जाता?

सियाराम ही के साथ उसने कौन-सा दुर्व्यवहार किया था। वह कुछ बचत करने के लिए ही विचार से तो सियाराम से सौदा मंगवाया करती थी। क्या वह बचत करके अपने लिए गहने गढ़वाना चाहती थी? जब आमदनी की यह हाल हो रहा था तो पैसे-पैसे पर निगाह रखने के सिवाय कुछ जमा करने का उसके पास और साधान ही क्या था? जवानों की जिन्दगी का तो कोई भरोसा ही नहीं, बूढ़ों की जिन्दगी का क्या ठिकाना? बच्ची के विवाह के लिए वह किसके सामने हाथ फैलाती? बच्ची का भार कुछ उसी पर तो नहीं था। वह केवल पति की सुविधा ही के लिए कुछ बटोरने का प्रयत्न कर रही थी। पति ही की क्यों? सियाराम ही तो पिता के बाद घर का स्वामी होता। बहिन के विवाह करने का भार क्या उसके सिर पर न पड़ता? निर्मला सारी कतर-ब्योंत पति और पुत्र का संकट-मोचन करने ही के लिए कर रही थी। बच्ची का विवाह इस परिस्थिति में संकट के सिवा और क्या था? पर इसके लिए भी उसके भाग्य में अपयश ही बदा था।

दोपहर हो गयी, पर आज भी चूल्हा नहीं जला। खाना भी जीवन का काम है, इसकी किसी को सुध ही न थी। मुंशीजी बाहर बेजान-से पड़े थे और निर्मला भीतर थी। बच्ची कभी भीतर जाती, कभी बाहर। कोई उससे

बोलने वाला न था। बार-बार सियाराम के कमरे के द्वार पर जाकर खड़ी होती और 'बैया-बैया' पुकारती, पर 'बैया' कोई जवाब न देता था।

संध्या समय मुंशीजी आकर निर्मला से बोले–तुम्हारे पास कुछ रुपये हैं?

निर्मला ने चौंककर पूछा–क्या कीजिएगा।

मुंशीजी–मैं जो पूछता हूं, उसका जवाब दो।

निर्मला–क्या आपको नहीं मालूम है? देनेवाले तो आप ही हैं।

मुंशीजी–तुम्हारे पास कुछ रुपये हैं या नहीं अगर हों, तो मुझे दे दो, न हों तो साफ जवाब दो।

निर्मला ने अब भी साफ जवाब न दिया। बोली–होंगे तो घर ही में न होंगे। मैंने कहीं और नहीं भेज दिये।

मुंशीजी बाहर चले गये। वह जानते थे कि निर्मला के पास रुपये हैं, वास्तव में थे भी। निर्मला ने यह भी नहीं कहा कि नही हैं या मैं न दूंगी, पर उसकी बातों से प्रकट हो गया कि वह देना नहीं चाहती।

नौ बजे रात को मुंशीजी ने आकर रुक्मिणी से कहा–बहन, मैं जरा बाहर जा रहा हूं। मेरा बिस्तर भूंगी से बंधवा देना और ट्रंक में कुछ कपड़े रखवाकर बन्द कर देना ।

रुक्मिणी भोजन बना रही थीं। बोलीं–बहू तो कमरे में है, कह क्यों नही देते? कहां जाने का इरादा है?

मुंशीजी–मैं तुमसे कहता हूं, बहू से कहना होता, तो तुमसे क्यों कहता? आज तुम क्यों खाना पका रही हो?

रुक्मिणी–कौन पकावे? बहू के सिर में दर्द हो रहा है। आखिर इस वक्त कहां जा रहे हो? सबेरे न चले जाना।

मुंशीजी–इसी तरह टालते-टालते तो आज तीन दिन हो गये। इधर-उधर घूम-घामकर देखूं, शायद कहीं सियाराम का पता मिल जाए। कुछ लोग कहते हैं कि एक साधु के साथ बातें कर रहा था। शायद वह कहीं बहका ले गया हो।

रुक्मिणी–तो लौटोगे कब तक?

मुंशीजी–कह नहीं सकता। हफ्ता भर लग जाए महीना भर लग जाए। क्या ठिकाना है?

रुक्मिणी–आज कौन दिन है? किसी पंडित से पूछ लिया है कि नहीं?

मुंशीजी भोजन करने बैठे। निर्मला को इस वक्त उन पर बड़ी दया आयी। उसका सारा क्रोध शान्त हो गया। खुद तो न बोली, बच्ची को जगाकर चुमकारती हुई बोली–देख, तेरे बाबूजी कहां जा रहे हैं? पूछ तो?

बच्ची ने द्वार से झांककर पूछा–बाबू दी, तहां दाते हो?

मुंशीजी–बड़ी दूर जाता हूं बेटी, तुम्हारे भैया को खोजने जाता हूं। बच्ची ने वहीं से खड़े-खड़े कहा–अम बी तलेंगे।

मुंशीजी–बड़ी दूर जाते हैं बच्ची, तुम्हारे वास्ते चीजें लायेंगे। यहां क्यों नहीं आती?

बच्ची मुस्कराकर छिप गयी और एक क्षण में फिर किवाड़ से सिर निकालकर बोली–अम बी तलेंगे।

मुंशीजी ने उसी स्वर में कहा–तुमको नहीं ले तलेंगे।

बच्ची–हमको क्यों नई ले तलोगे?

मुंशीजी–तुम तो हमारे पास आती नहीं हो।

लड़की ठुमकती हुई आकर पिता की गोद में बैठ गयी। थोड़ी देर के लिए मुंशीजी उसकी बाल-क्रीड़ा में अपनी अन्तर्वेदना भूल गये।

भोजन करके मुंशीजी बाहर चले गये। निर्मला खड़ी ताकती रही। कहना चाहती थी–व्यर्थ जा रहे हो, पर कह न सकती थी। कुछ रुपये निकाल कर देने का विचार करती थी, पर दे न सकती थी।

अंत को न रहा गया, रुक्मिणी से बोली–दीदीजी जरा समझा दीजिए, कहां जा रहे हैं! मेरी जबान पकड़ी जाएगी, पर बिना बोले रहा नहीं जाता। बिना ठिकाने कहां खोजेंगे? व्यर्थ की हैरानी होगी।

रुक्मिणी ने करुणा-सूचक नेत्रों से देखा और अपने कमरे में चली गईं।

निर्मला बच्ची को गोद में लिए सोच रही थी कि शायद जाने के पहले बच्ची को देखने या मुझसे मिलने के लिए आवें, पर उसकी आशा विफल हो गई? मुंशीजी ने बिस्तर उठाया और तांगे पर जा बैठे।

उसी वक्त निर्मला का कलेजा मसोसने लगा। उसे ऐसा जान पड़ा कि इनसे भेंट न होगी। वह अधीर होकर द्वार पर आई कि मुंशीजी को रोक ले, पर तांगा चल चुका था।

17

दिन गुजरने लगे। एक महीना पूरा निकल गया, लेकिन मुंशीजी न लौटे। कोई खत भी न भेजा। निर्मला को अब नित्य यही चिन्ता बनी रहती कि वह लौटकर न आये तो क्या होगा? उसे इसकी चिन्ता न होती थी कि उन पर क्या बीत रही होगी, वह कहां मारे-मारे फिरते होंगे, स्वास्थ्य कैसा होगा? उसे केवल अपनी और उससे भी बढ़कर बच्ची की चिन्ता थी। गृहस्थी का निर्वाह कैसे होगा? ईश्वर कैसे बेड़ा पार लगायेंगे? बच्ची का क्या हाल होगा? उसने कतर-ब्योंत करके जो रुपये जमा कर रखे थे, उसमें कुछ-न-कुछ रोज ही कमी होती जाती थी। निर्मला को उसमें से एक-एक पैसा निकालते इतनी अखर होती थी, मानो कोई उसकी देह से रक्त निकाल रहा हो। झुंझलाकर मुंशीजी को कोसती। लड़की किसी चीज के लिए रोती, तो उसे अभागिन, कलमुंही कहकर झल्लाती। यही नहीं, रुक्मिणी का घर में रहना उसे ऐसा जान पड़ता था, मानो वह गर्दन पर सवार है। जब हृदय जलता है, तो वाणी भी अग्निमय हो जाती है।

निर्मला बड़ी मधुर-भाषिणी स्त्री थी, पर अब उसकी गणना कर्कशाओं में की जा सकती थी। दिन भर उसके मुख से जली-कटी बातें निकला करती थीं। उसके शब्दों की कोमलता न जाने क्या हो गई! भावों में माधुर्य का कहीं नाम नहीं।

भूंगी बहुत दिनों से इस घर में नौकर थी। स्वभाव की सहनशील थी, पर यह आठों पहर की बकबक उससे भी न सही गई। एक दिन उसने भी घर की राह ली। यहां तक कि जिस बच्ची को प्राणों से भी अधिक प्यार करती थी, उसकी सूरत से भी घृणा हो गई। बात-बात पर

घुड़क पड़ती, कभी-कभी मार बैठती। रुक्मिणी रोती हुई बालिका को गोद में बैठा लेती और चुमकार-दुलार कर चुप करातीं। उस अनाथ के लिए अब यही एक आश्रय रह गया था।

निर्मला को अब अगर कुछ अच्छा लगता था, तो वह सुधा से बात करना था। वह वहां जाने का अवसर खोजती रहती थी। बच्ची को अब वह अपने साथ न ले जाना चाहती थी। पहले जब बच्ची को अपने घर सभी चीजें खाने को मिलती थीं, तो वह वहां जाकर हंसती-खेलती थी। अब वहीं जाकर उसे भूख लगती थी। निर्मला उसे घूर-घूरकर देखती, मुट्ठियां-बांधकर धमकाती, पर लड़की भूख की रट लगाना न छोड़ती थी। इसलिए निर्मला उसे साथ न ले जाती थी। सुधा के पास बैठकर उसे मालूम होता था कि मैं आदमी हूं। उतनी देर के लिए वह चिंताओं से मुक्त हो जाती थी। जैसे शराबी शराब के नशे में सारी चिन्ताएं भूल जाता है, उसी तरह निर्मला सुधा के घर जाकर सारी बातें भूल जाती थी। जिसने उसे उसके घर पर देखा हो, वह उसे यहां देखकर चकित रह जाता। वहीं कर्कशा, कटु-भाषिणी स्त्री यहां आकर हास्यविनोद और माधुर्य की पुतली बन जाती थी। यौवन-काल की स्वाभाविक वृत्तियां अपने घर पर रास्ता बन्द पाकर यहां किलोलें करने लगती थीं। यहां आते वक्त वह मांग-चोटी, कपड़े-लत्ते से लैस होकर आती और यथासाध्य अपनी विपत्ति कथा को मन ही में रखती थी। वह यहां रोने के लिए नहीं, हंसने के लिए आती थी।

पर कदाचित् उसके भाग्य में यह सुख भी नहीं बदा था। निर्मला मामूली तौर से दोपहर को या तीसरे पहर से सुधा के घर जाया करती थी। एक दिन उसका जी इतना ऊबा कि सबेरे ही जा पहुंची। सुधा नदी स्नान करने गई थी, डॉक्टर साहब अस्पताल जाने के लिए कपड़े पहन रहे थे। महरी अपने काम-धंधे में लगी हुई थी। निर्मला अपनी सहेली के कमरे में जाकर निश्चिन्त बैठ गई। उसने समझा सुधा कोई काम कर रही होगी, अभी आती होगी। जब बैठे दो-तीन मिनट गुजर गये, तो उसने अलमारी से तस्वीरों की एक किताब उतार ली और केश खोल पलंग पर लेटकर चित्र देखने लगी। इसी बीच में डॉक्टर साहब

को किसी जरुरत से निर्मला के कमरे में आना पड़ा। अपनी ऐनक ढूंढते फिरते थे। बेधड़क अन्दर चले आये।

निर्मला द्वार की ओर केश खोले लेटी हुई थी। डॉक्टर साहब को देखते ही चौंककर उठ बैठी और सिर ढांकती हुई चारपाई से उतकर खड़ी हो गई। डॉक्टर साहब ने लौटते हुए चिक के पास खड़े होकर कहा-क्षमा करना निर्मला, मुझे मालूम न था कि यहां हो! मेरी ऐनक मेरे कमरे में नहीं मिल रही है, न जाने कहां उतार कर रख दी थी। मैंने समझा शायद यहां हो।

निर्मला ने चारपाई के सिरहाने आले पर निगाह डाली तो ऐनक की डिबिया दिखाई दी। उसने आगे बढ़कर डिबिया उतार ली, और सिर झुकाये, देह समेटे, संकोच से डॉक्टर साहब की ओर हाथ बढ़ाया।

डॉक्टर साहब ने निर्मला को दो-एक बार पहले भी देखा था, पर इस समय के-से भाव कभी उसके मन में न आये थे। जिस ज्वाला को वह बरसों से हृदय में दबाये हुए थे, वह आज पवन का झोंका पाकर दहक उठी। उन्होंने ऐनक लेने के लिए हाथ बढ़ाया, तो हाथ कांप रहा था। ऐनक लेकर भी वह बाहर न गये, वहीं खोए हुए से खड़े रहे। निर्मला ने इस एकान्त से भयभीत होकर पूछा–सुधा कहीं गई है क्या?

डॉक्टर साहब ने सिर झुकाये हुए जवाब दिया–हां, जरा स्नान करने चली गई हैं।

फिर भी डॉक्टर साहब बाहर न गये। वहीं खड़े रहे। निर्मला ने फिर पूछा–कब तक आएगी?

डॉक्टर साहब ने सिर झुकाये हुए कहा–आती होंगी।

फिर भी वह बाहर नहीं आये। उनके मन में घोर द्वन्द्व मचा हुआ था। औचित्य का बंधन नहीं, भीरुता का कच्चा तागा उनकी जबान को रोके हुए था।

निर्मला ने फिर कहा–कहीं घूमने-घामने लगी होंगी। मैं भी इस वक्त जाती हूं।

भीरुता का कच्चा तागा भी टूट गया। नदी के कगार पर पहुंच कर भागती हुई सेना में अद्‌भुत शक्ति आ जाती है। डॉक्टर साहब ने सिर

उठाकर निर्मला को देखा और अनुराग में डूबे हुए स्वर में बोले–नहीं, निर्मला, अब आती ही होंगी। अभी न जाओ। रोज सुधा की खातिर से बैठती हो, आज मेरी खातिर बैठो। बताओ, कब तक इस आग में जला करुं? सत्य कहता हूं निर्मला...।

निर्मला ने कुछ और नहीं सुना। उसे ऐसा जान पड़ा मानो सारी पृथ्वी चक्कर खा रही है। मानो उसके प्राणों पर सहस्रों वज्रों का आघात हो रहा है। उसने जल्दी से अलगनी पर लटकी हुई चादर उतार ली और बिना मुंह से एक शब्द निकाले कमरे से निकल गई। डॉक्टर साहब खिसियाये हुए-से रोना मुंह बनाये खड़े रहे! उसको रोकने की या कुछ कहने की हिम्मत न पड़ी।

निर्मला ज्योंही द्वार पर पहुंची उसने सुधा को तांगे से उतरते देखा। सुधा उसे देखते ही जल्दी से उतरकर उसकी ओर लपकी और कुछ पूछना चाहती थी, मगर निर्मला ने उसे अवसर न दिया, तीर की तरह झपटकर चली गई। सुधा एक क्षण तक विस्मय की दशा में खड़ी रहीं। बात क्या है, उसकी समझ में कुछ न आ सका। वह व्यग्र हो उठी। जल्दी से अन्दर गई महरी से पूछने कि क्या बात हुई है। वह अपराधी का पता लगायेगी और अगर उसे मालूम हुआ कि महरी या और किसी नौकर ने उसे कोई अपमान–सूचक बात कह दी है, तो वह खड़े–खड़े निकाल देगी। लपकी हुई वह अपने कमरे में गई। अन्दर कदम रखते ही डॉक्टर को मुंह लटकाये चारपाई पर बैठे देख। पूछा–निर्मला यहां आई थी?

डॉक्टर साहब ने सिर खुजलाते हुए कहा–हां, आई तो थीं।

सुधा–किसी महरी-अहरी ने उन्हें कुछ कहा तो नहीं? मुझसे बोली तक नहीं, झपटकर निकल गईं।

डॉक्टर साहब की मुख-कान्ति मलिन हो गई, कहा–यहां तो उन्हें किसी ने भी कुछ नहीं कहा।

सुधा–किसी ने कुछ कहा है। देखो, मैं पूछती हूं न, ईश्वर जानता है, पता पा जाऊंगी, तो खड़े-खड़े निकाल दूंगी।

डॉक्टर साहब सिटपिटाते हुए बोले–मैंने तो किसी को कुछ कहते नहीं सुना। तुम्हें उन्होंने देखा न होगा।

सुधा–वाह, देखा ही न होगा! उसके सामने तो मैं तांगे से उतरी हूं। उन्होंने मेरी ओर ताका भी, पर बोलीं कुछ नहीं। इस कमरे में आई थी?

डॉक्टर साहब के प्राण सूखे जा रहे थे। हिचकिचाते हुए बोले–आई क्यों नहीं थी।

सुधा–तुम्हें यहां बैठे देखकर चली गई होंगी। बस, किसी महरी ने कुछ कह दिया होगा। नीच जात हैं न, किसी को बात करने की तमीज तो है नहीं। अरे, ओ सुन्दरिया, जरा यहां तो आ!

डॉक्टर–उसे क्यों बुलाती हो, वह यहां से सीधे दरवाजे की तरफ गईं। महरियों से बात तक नहीं हुई।

सुधा–तो फिर तुम्हीं ने कुछ कह दिया होगा।

डॉक्टर साहब का कलेजा धक्-धक् करने लगा। बोले–मैं भला क्या कह देता क्या ऐसा गंवार हूं?

सुधा–तुमने उन्हें आते देखा, तब भी बैठे रह गये?

डॉक्टर–मैं यहां था ही नहीं। बाहर बैठक में अपनी ऐनक ढूंढ़ता रहा, जब वहां न मिली, तो मैंने सोचा, शायद अन्दर हो। यहां आया तो उन्हें बैठे देखा। मैं बाहर जाना चाहता था कि उन्होंने खुद पूछा–किसी चीज की जरुरत है? मैंने कहा–जरा देखना, यहां मेरी ऐनक तो नहीं है। ऐनक इसी सिरहाने वाले ताक पर थी। उन्होंने उठाकर दे दी। बस इतनी ही बात हुई।

सुधा–बस, तुम्हें ऐनक देते ही वह झल्लाई बाहर चली गई? क्यों?

डॉक्टर–झल्लाई हुई तो नहीं चली गई। जाने लगीं, तो मैंने कहा–बैठिए वह आती होंगी। न बैठीं तो मैं क्या करता?

सुधा ने कुछ सोचकर कहा–बात कुछ समझ में नहीं आती, मैं जरा उसके पास जाती हूं। देखूं, क्या बात है।

डॉक्टर–तो चली जाना ऐसी जल्दी क्या है। सारा दिन तो पड़ा हुआ है।

सुधा ने चादर ओढ़ते हुऐ कहा–मेरे पेट में खलबली मची हुई है, कहते हो जल्दी क्या है? सुधा तेजी से कदम बढ़ती हुई निर्मला के घर की ओर चली और पांच मिनट में जा पहुंची? देखा तो निर्मला अपने

कमरे में चारपाई पर पड़ी रो रही थी और बच्ची उसके पास खड़ी थी–अम्मां, क्यों लोती हो?

सुधा ने लड़की को गोद मे उठा लिया और निर्मला से बोली–बहिन, सच बताओ, क्या बात है? मेरे यहां किसी ने तुम्हें कुछ कहा है? मैं सबसे पूछ चुकी, कोई नहीं बतलाता।

निर्मला आंसू पोंछती हुई बोली–किसी ने कुछ कहा नहीं बहिन, भला वहां मुझे कौन कुछ कहता?

सुधा–तो फिर मुझसे बोली क्यों नहीं और आते-ही-आते रोने लगीं?

निर्मला–अपने नसीबों को रो रही हूं, और क्या।

सुधा–तुम यों न बतलाओगी, तो मैं कसम दूंगी।

निर्मला–कसम-कसम न रखाना भाई, मुझे किसी ने कुछ नहीं कहा, झूठ किसे लगा दूं?

सुधा–खाओ मेरी कसम।

निर्मला–तुम तो नाहक ही जिद करती हो।

सुधा–अगर तुमने न बताया निर्मला, तो मैं समझूंगी, तुम्हें मुझसे जरा भी प्रेम नहीं है। बस, सब जबानी जमा-खर्च है। मैं तुमसे किसी बात का पर्दा नहीं रखती और तुम मुझे गैर समझती हो। तुम्हारे ऊपर मुझे बड़ा भरोसा था। अब जान गई कि कोई किसी का नहीं होता।

सुधा कीं आंखें सजल हो गईं। उसने बच्ची को गोद से उतार लिया और द्वार की ओर चली। निर्मला ने उठकर उसका हाथ पकड़ लिया और रोती हुई बोली–सुधा, मैं तुम्हारे पैर पड़ती हूं, मत पूछो। सुनकर दुख होगा और शायद मैं फिर तुम्हें अपना मुंह न दिखा सकूं। मैं अभगिनी न होती, तो यह दिन ही क्यों देखती? अब तो ईश्वर से यही प्रार्थना है कि संसार से मुझे उठा ले। अभी यह दुर्गति हो रही है, तो आगे न जाने क्या-क्या होगा?

इन शब्दों में जो संकेत था, वह बुद्धिमती सुधा से छिपा न रह सका। वह समझ गई कि डॉक्टर साहब ने कुछ छेड़-छाड़ की है। उनका हिचक-हिचककर बातें करना और उसके प्रश्नों को टालना, उनकी वह ग्लानिमय, कांतिहीन मुद्रा उसे याद आ गई। वह सिर से

पांव तक कांप उठी और बिना कुछ कहे-सुने सिंहनी की भांति क्रोध से भरी हुई द्वार की ओर चली। निर्मला ने उसे रोकना चाहा, पर रोक न सकी। देखते-देखते वह सड़क पर आ गई और घर की ओर चली। तब निर्मला वहीं भूमि पर बैठ गई और फूट-फूटकर रोने लगी।

निर्मला दिन भर चारपाई पर पड़ी रही। मालूम होता है, उसकी देह में प्राण नहीं है। न स्नान किया, न भोजन करने उठी। संध्या समय उसे ज्वर हो आया। रात भर देह तवे की भांति तपती रही। दूसरे दिन ज्वर न उतरा। हां, कुछ-कुछ कम हो गया था। वह चारपाई पर लेटी हुई निश्चल नेत्रों से द्वार की ओर ताक रही थी। चारों ओर शून्य था, अन्दर भी शून्य बाहर भी शून्य कोई चिन्ता न थी, न कोई स्मृति, न कोई दुःख, मस्तिष्क में स्पन्दन की शक्ति ही न रही थी।

सहसा रुक्मिणी बच्ची को गोद में लिये हुए आकर खड़ी हो गई। निर्मला ने पूछा–क्या यह बहुत रोती थी?

रुक्मिणी–नहीं, यह तो सिसकी तक नहीं। रात भर चुपचाप पड़ी रही, सुधा ने थोड़ा-सा दूध भेज दिया था।

निर्मला–अहीरिन दूध न दे गई थी?

रुक्मिणी–कहती थी, पिछले पैसे दे दो, तो दूं। तुम्हारा जी अब कैसा है?

निर्मला–मुझे कुछ नहीं हुआ है? कल देह गरम हो गई थी।

रुक्मिणी–डॉक्टर साहब का बुरा हाल है?

निर्मला ने घबराकर पूछा–क्या, हुआ क्या? कुशल से हैं न?

रुक्मिणी–कुशल से हैं कि लाश उठाने की तैयारी हो रही है! कोई कहता है, जहर खा लिया था, कोई कहता है, दिल का चलना बन्द हो गया था। भगवान् जाने क्या हुआ था।

निर्मला ने एक ठण्डी सांस ली और रुंधे हुए कंठ से बोली–हाय भगवान! सुधा की क्या गति होगी! कैसे जियेगी?

यह कहते-कहते वह रो पड़ी और बड़ी देर तक सिसकती रही। तब बड़ी मुश्किल से उठकर सुधा के पास जाने को तैयार हुई पांव थर-थर कांप रहे थे, दीवार थामे खड़ी थी, पर जी न मानता था। न जाने सुधा ने यहां से जाकर पति से क्या कहा? मैंने तो उससे कुछ कहा भी नहीं, न जाने मेरी बातों का वह क्या मतलब समझी? हाय! ऐसे रुपवान् दयालु, ऐसे सुशील प्राणी का यह अन्त! अगर निर्मला को मालूम होता कि उसके क्रोध का यह भीषण परिणाम होगा, तो वह जहर का घूंट पीकर भी उस बात को हंसी में उड़ा देती।

यह सोचकर कि मेरी ही निष्ठुरता के कारण डॉक्टर साहब का यह हाल हुआ, निर्मला के ह्रदय के टुकड़े होने लगे। ऐसी वेदना होने लगी, मानो ह्रदय में शूल उठ रहा हो। वह डॉक्टर साहब के घर चली।

लाश उठ चुकी थी। बाहर सन्नाटा छाया हुआ था। घर में स्त्रियां जमा थीं। सुधा जमीन पर बैठी रो रही थी। निर्मला को देखते ही वह जोर से चिल्लाकर रो पड़ी और आकर उसकी छाती से लिपट गई। दोनों देर तक रोती रहीं।

जब औरतों की भीड़ कम हुई और एकान्त हो गया, निर्मला ने पूछा–यह क्या हो गया बहिन, तुमने क्या कह दिया?

सुधा अपने मन को इसी प्रश्न का उत्तर कितनी ही बार दे चुकी थी। उसका मन जिस उत्तर से शांत हो गया था, वही उत्तर उसने निर्मला को दिया। बोली–चुप भी तो न रह सकती थी बहिन, क्रोध की बात पर क्रोध आता ही है।

निर्मला–मैंने तो तुमसे कोई ऐसी बात भी न कही थी।

सुधा–तुम कैसे कहती, कह ही नहीं सकती थीं, लेकिन उन्होंने जो बात हुई थी, वह कह दी थी। उस पर मैंने जो कुछ मुंह में आया, कहा। जब एक बात दिल में आ गई, तो उसे हुआ ही समझना चाहिये। अवसर और घात मिले, तो वह अवश्य ही पूरी हो जाती है। यह कहकर कोई नहीं निकल सकता कि मैंने तो हंसी की थी। एकान्त में ऐसा शब्द जबान पर लाना ही कह देता है कि नीयत बुरी थी। मैंने तुमसे कभी कहा नहीं बहिन, लेकिन मैंने उन्हें कई बार तुम्हारी ओर झांकते देखा।

उस वक्त मैंने भी यही समझा कि शायद मुझे धोखा हो रहा हो। अब मालूम हुआ कि उस ताक-झांक का क्या मतलब था! अगर मैंने दुनिया ज्यादा देखी होती, तो तुम्हें अपने घर न आने देती। कम-से-कम तुम पर उनकी निगाह कभी न पड़ने देती, लेकिन यह क्या जानती थी कि पुरुषों के मुंह में कुछ और मन में कुछ और होता है। ईश्वर को जो मंजूर था, वह हुआ। ऐसे सौभाग्य से मैं वैधव्य को बुरा नहीं समझती। दरिद्र प्राणी उस धनी से कहीं सुखी है, जिसे उसका धन सांप बनकर काटने दौड़े। उपवास कर लेना आसान है, विषैला भोजन करना उससे कहीं मुश्किल। इसी वक्त डॉक्टर सिन्हा के छोटे भाई और कृष्णा ने घर में प्रवेश किया। घर में कोहराम मच गया।

एक महीना और गुजर गया। सुधा अपने देवर के साथ तीसरे ही दिन चली गई। अब निर्मला अकेली थी। पहले हंस-बोलकर जी बहला लिया करती थी। अब रोना ही एक काम रह गया। उसका स्वास्थ्य दिन-दिन बिगड़ता गया। पुराने मकान का किराया अधिक था। दूसरा मकान थोड़े किराये का लिया, यह तंग गली में था। अन्दर एक कमरा था और छोटा-सा आंगन। न प्रकाश जाता, न वायु। दुर्गन्ध उड़ा करती थी। भोजन का यह हाल कि पैसे रहते हुये भी कभी-कभी उपवास करना पड़ता था। बाजार से लाए कौन? फिर अपना कोई मर्द नहीं, कोई लड़का नहीं, तो रोज भोजन बनाने का कष्ट कौन उठाये? औरतों के लिये रोज भोजन करने की आवश्यकता ही क्या? अगर एक वक्त खा लिया, तो दो दिन के लिये छुट्टी हो गई। बच्ची के लिए ताजा हलुआ या रोटियां बन जाती थी! ऐसी दशा में स्वास्थ्य क्यों न बिगड़ता? चिन्ता, शोक, दुरवस्था, एक हो तो कोई कहे। यहां तो त्रयताप का धावा था। उस पर निर्मला ने दवा न खाने की कसम खा ली थी। करती ही क्या? उन थोड़े-से रुपयों में दवा की गुंजाइश कहां थी? जहां भोजन का ठिकाना न था, वहां दवा का जिक्र ही क्या? दिन-दिन सूखती चली जाती थी।

एक दिन रुक्मिणी ने कहा—बहू, इस तरह कब तक घुला करोगी, जी ही से तो जहान है। चलो, किसी वैद्य को दिखा लाऊं।

निर्मला ने विरक्त भाव से कहा–जिसे रोने के लिए जीना हो, उसका मर जाना ही अच्छा।

रुक्मिणी–बुलाने से तो मौत नहीं आती?

निर्मला–मौत तो बिन बुलाए आती है, बुलाने से क्यों न आयेगी? उसके आने में बहुत दिन न लगेंगे बहिन, जै दिन चलती हूं, उतने साल समझ लीजिए।

रुक्मिणी–दिल ऐसा छोटा मत करो बहू, अभी संसार का सुख ही क्या देखा है?

निर्मला–अगर संसार का यही सुख है, जो इतने दिनों से देख रही हूं, तो उससे जी भर गया। सच कहती हूं बहिन, इस बच्ची का मोह मुझे बांधे हुए है, नहीं तो अब तक कभी की चली गई होती। न जाने इस बेचारी के भाग्य में क्या लिखा है?

दोनों महिलाएं रोने लगीं। इधर जब से निर्मला ने चारपाई पकड़ ली है, रुक्मिणी के हृदय में दया का सोता-सा खुल गया है। द्वेश का लेश भी नहीं रहा। कोई काम करती हों, निर्मला की आवाज सुनते ही दौड़ती हैं। घण्टों उसके पास कथा-पुराण सुनाया करती हैं। कोई ऐसी चीज पकाना चाहती हैं, जिसे निर्मला रुचि से खाये। निर्मला को कभी हंसते देख लेती हैं, तो निहाल हो जाती है और बच्ची को तो अपने गले का हार बनाये रहती हैं। उसी की नींद सोती हैं, उसी की नींद जागती हैं। वही बालिका अब उसके जीवन का आधार है।

रुक्मिणी ने जरा देर बाद कहा–बहू, तुम इतनी निराश क्यों होती हो? भगवान् चाहेंगे, तो तुम दो-चार दिन में अच्छी हो जाओगी। मेरे साथ आज वैद्यजी के पास चलो। बड़े सज्जन हैं।

निर्मला–दीदीजी, अब मुझे किसी वैद्य, हकीम की दवा फायदा न करेगी। आप मेरी चिन्ता न करें। बच्ची को आपकी गोद में छोड़े जाती हूं। अगर जीती-जागती रहे, तो किसी अच्छे कुल में विवाह कर दीजियेगा। मैं तो इसके लिये अपने जीवन में कुछ न कर सकी, केवल जन्म देने भर की अपराधिनी हूं। चाहे क्वांरी रखियेगा, चाहे विष देकर मार डालिएग, पर कुपात्र के गले न मढ़िएगा, इतनी ही आपसे मेरी

विनय है। मैंनें आपकी कुछ सेवा न की, इसका बड़ा दुःख हो रहा है। मुझ अभागिनी से किसी को सुख नहीं मिला। जिस पर मेरी छाया भी पड़ गई, उसका सर्वनाश हो गया अगर स्वामीजी कभी घर आवें, तो उनसे कहिएगा कि इस करम-जली के अपराध क्षमा कर दें।

रुक्मिणी रोती हुई बोली–बहू, तुम्हारा कोई अपराध नहीं ईश्वर से कहती हूं, तुम्हारी ओर से मेरे मन में जरा भी मैल नहीं है। हां, मैंने सदैव तुम्हारे साथ कपट किया, इसका मुझे मरते दम तक दुःख रहेगा।

निर्मला ने कातर नेत्रों से देखते हुये कहा–दीदीजी, कहने की बात नहीं, पर बिना कहे रहा नहीं जाता। स्वामीजी ने हमेशा मुझे अविश्वास की दृष्टि से देखा, लेकिन मैंने कभी मन मे भी उनकी उपेक्षा नहीं की। जो होना था, वह तो हो ही चुका था। अधर्म करके अपना परलोक क्यों बिगाड़ती? पूर्व जन्म में न जाने कौन-सा पाप किया था, जिसका यह प्रायश्चित करना पड़ा। इस जन्म में कांटे बोती, तो कौन गति होती?

निर्मला की सांस बड़े वेग से चलने लगी, फिर खाट पर लेट गई और बच्ची की ओर एक ऐसी दृष्टि से देखा, जो उसके चरित्र जीवन की संपूर्ण विपत्तिकथा की वृहद् आलोचना थी, वाणी में इतनी सामर्थ्य कहां?

तीन दिनों तक निर्मला की आंखों से आंसुओं की धारा बहती रही। वह न किसी से बोलती थी, न किसी की ओर देखती थी और न किसी का कुछ सुनती थी। बस, रोये चली जाती थी। उस वेदना का कौन अनुमान कर सकता है?

चौथे दिन संध्या समय वह विपत्तिकथा समाप्त हो गई। उसी समय जब पशु-पक्षी अपने-अपने बसेरे को लौट रहे थे, निर्मला का प्राण-पक्षी भी दिन भर शिकारियों के निशानों, शिकारी चिड़ियों के पंजों और वायु के प्रचंड झोंकों से आहत और व्यथित अपने बसेरे की ओर उड़ गया।

मुहल्ले के लोग जमा हो गये। लाश बाहर निकाली गई। कौन दाह करेगा, यह प्रश्न उठा। लोग इसी चिन्ता में थे कि सहसा एक बूढ़ा पथिक एक बकुचा लटकाये आकर खड़ा हो गया। यह मुंशी तोताराम थे।